D1197197

Basic Research Methods for Librarians

Recent Titles in
Library and Information Science Text Series

BROOKHAVEN FREE LIBRARY
273 BEAVER DAM ROAD
BROOKHAVEN, NY 11719

BASIC RESEARCH METHODS FOR LIBRARIANS

Fifth Edition

Lynn Silipigni Connaway and Ronald R. Powell

Library and Information Science Text Series

 LIBRARIES UNLIMITED

AN IMPRINT OF ABC-CLIO, LLC
Santa Barbara, California • Denver, Colorado • Oxford, England

Copyright 2010 by Lynn Silipigni Connaway and Ronald R. Powell

All rights reserved. No part of this publication may be reproduced, stored in a retrieval system, or transmitted, in any form or by any means, electronic, mechanical, photocopying, recording, or otherwise, except for the inclusion of brief quotations in a review, without prior permission in writing from the publisher.

Library of Congress Cataloging-in-Publication Data

Connaway, Lynn Silipigni.
  Basic research methods for librarians / Lynn Silipigni Connaway and Ronald R. Powell. — 5th ed.
    p. cm. — (Library and information science text series)
  Powell's name appears first on the previous edition.
  Includes bibliographical references and indexes.
    ISBN 978–1–59158–863–4 (alk. paper) — ISBN 978–1–59158–865–8 (pbk. : alk. paper) — ISBN 978–1–59158–868–9 (ebook)
  1. Library science—Research—Methodology. I. Powell, Ronald R. II. Title.
  Z669.7.P68   2010
  020'.72—dc22

ISBN: 978–1–59158–863–4 (cloth)
       978–1–59158–865–8 (paper)
EISBN: 978–1–59158–868–9

14 13 12 11 10   1 2 3 4 5

This book is also available on the World Wide Web as an eBook.
Visit www.abc-clio.com for details.

Libraries Unlimited
An Imprint of ABC-CLIO, LLC

ABC-CLIO, LLC
130 Cremona Drive, P.O. Box 1911
Santa Barbara, California 93116-1911

This book is printed on acid-free paper ∞

Manufactured in the United States of America

Excerpts from *Standards for 21st Century Learners* by the American Association of School Librarians, a division of the American Library Association, copyright © 2007 American Library Association. Available for download at www.ala.org/aasl/standards. Used with permission.

Contents

Preface

This text is addressed to the practicing librarian and other information professionals who need to conduct research and publish. It is intended to provide guidance for any librarian who must be able to read and evaluate research reports critically and assist others with their research. It also is designed to be of benefit to the graduate library and information science student.

Although applied and action research methods are included, the book almost exclusively considers basic research methods. Its primary purpose is to help teach the skills necessary for a librarian to conduct rigorous, basic research. Yet many of the methods, techniques, and tenets of basic research are relevant for applied research, and a person conducting applied research should benefit from a solid understanding of basic research methods. The librarian wishing to carry out a cost study, evaluate the performance of his or her library, or survey the library's users will need to be able to apply many of the principles and techniques treated in this book to his or her specific project. The more rigorous the research, the more useful its results, whether it be basic or applied in nature.

The perspective of this work is that library-related research should be as sound as any scientific research, and basic concepts are presented accordingly. A second viewpoint is that the conceptual development of a study is as crucial to its success as are the specific techniques employed in its conduct. That too is reflected in the contents of the text. The methods presented are applicable to most social science research, but the illustrations and applications presented throughout the text are specific to library settings. With the exception of the seventh chapter, quantitative, rather than qualitative, methods are generally emphasized; but a number of the techniques covered are noted as having applications to qualitative research.

The book first addresses the role of research in librarianship and then considers the major steps in the development of a research study. Following that,

it focuses on four major research methodologies—survey, experimental, qualitative, and historical—with extra attention given to sampling procedures.
Chapters on data analysis, research proposals, and research reports conclude
the text.

This text is not intended to be a cookbook for conducting basic research in
library and information science, but it does attempt to introduce the researcher
to the major issues involved in conducting original research and to present the
basic information needed to design effective research. Neither is the text meant
to stand alone. There are a variety of textbooks and other resources which the
reader should consult, and referral to standard texts on statistical analysis is
recommended. This book is an introductory presentation of basic research
methods, and the reader wishing to become an accomplished researcher should
not stop here.

The fifth edition of *Basic Research Methods for Librarians* represents a general revision and some reorganization of the fourth edition. References to other
sources were updated and additional works cited where appropriate. (A number
of Web site URLs were added, but their inherent instability should be kept in
mind.) Additions to the text include: expanded sections on electronic and Web
questionnaires, evaluation research, statistical analysis, and inferential statistics; sections on task-based, evidence-based, and social media research;
usability testing; oral presentations of research; and more consideration of
research into the nature and uses of electronic technology.

The authors would like to thank the many students who have made helpful
comments over the years as well as Lynn Westbrook, Jack Glazier, and Sebastian
Mundt for their contributions to the text. They also are indebted to Catherine
Dishman of Wayne State University and Timothy J. Dickey, Erin Hood, and Larry
Olszewski of OCLC Online Computer Library Center, Inc. for their assistance in
the preparation of the fifth edition.

It is not a simple matter to conduct rigorous research, but it can be interesting, enlightening, and rewarding. Hopefully, this book will help and encourage
librarians and others to become more active, productive researchers.

1

Research and Librarianship

RESEARCH RECORD

The consensus of a number of those individuals who have assessed the previous research of librarians is that the quantity and quality have left something to be desired. For example, "Ennis described library research as 'noncumulative, fragmentary, generally weak and relentlessly oriented to immediate practice.' "[1] Neal stated, "Librarianship is an 'information poor' information profession. Decisions are routinely not supported by the evidence of well-designed investigations. Research in the field is poorly communicated, understood, and applied."[2] But that is not to say that there has not been a substantial amount of good library-related research. In addition, most observers seem to be of the opinion that library-related research of late has shown improvement with regard to its rigorousness, sophistication, and incorporation of multiple methods and statistical analysis. Yet they also seem to agree that there continues to be room for improvement.

This chapter will concern itself only with the relatively recent record of library research. Readers wishing to learn more about the history of library science research may wish to consult Jackson's brief history of research in librarianship in the United States and Canada, or Busha's review of the past status of library science research.[3]

Definition of Research

There is no one definition of research, in part because there is more than one kind. Considering research in the general sense, *Merriam-Webster Online Dictionary* defined it as "studious inquiry or examination; especially: investigation or experimentation aimed at the discovery and interpretation of facts, revision of accepted theories or laws in the light of new facts, or practical applications of such new or revised theories or laws."[4] Hillway, in his introductory text on research methods, defined research as "a method of study by which, through the careful and exhaustive investigation of all the ascertainable evidence bearing upon a definable problem, we reach a solution to that problem."[5] Mouly stated that "Research is best conceived as the process of arriving at dependable solutions to problems through the planned and systematic collection, analysis, and interpretation of data."[6]

These general definitions suggest that there are at least two major types of research, one of which is *basic research*. Basic research, also referred to as pure, theoretical, or scientific research, is primarily interested in deriving new knowledge and is, at most, only indirectly involved with how that knowledge will be applied to specific, practical, or real problems. Or, as Vickery stated, "Scientific research . . . is concerned with elucidating concepts and their relations, hypotheses and theories, and is not necessarily and certainly not directly related to technical and practical problems."[7] It is sometimes labeled as research conducted in order to acquire knowledge for its own sake, but, as will be argued later, that probably is a simplistic viewpoint. Basic research, particularly if quantitative in nature, is usually designed so as to produce new knowledge that is generalizable.

The second major type of research is usually known as *applied research*, and it encompasses a variety of specific research techniques such as systems analysis and operations research. In contrast to pure or basic research, applied research emphasizes the solving of specific problems in real situations. Much of the library-related research has been applied research dealing with everything from evaluating book collections to analyzing automated circulation systems. (See Chapter 3 for additional information on applied and action research.)

But in spite of the fact that basic and applied research have tended to be conducted in isolation from one another, they are not necessarily dichotomous. As Shera noted, "Research is no less 'pure' for leading to useful results, though it most certainly does not have to possess immediate applicability to qualify as research."[8] In other words, basic research often leads to practical applications, while applied research frequently acts as a foundation for subsequent theoretical or basic research. Stokes also dismissed this dichotomous notion of the relationship between basic and applied research. When discussing Pasteur's philosophy of research, Stokes described it as the integration of both basic research in his search for knowledge and applied research in his quest to solve practical problems.[9] According to Mouly, "the distinction between pure and applied research is not very clear. All research findings will be useful and practical—sooner or later—no matter how disinterested in immediate utilitarian goals the pure researcher might be. Both pure and applied research are oriented toward the discovery of scientific truth, and both are practical in the sense that they lead to the solution of man's problems."[10] Perhaps, as Muller argued, the crucial factor is not whether the research is pure or applied but whether it is relevant.[11]

Research also can be dichotomized as quantitative and qualitative. "*Quantitative research* methods involve a problem-solving approach that is highly structured in nature and that relies on the quantification of concepts, where possible, for purposes of measurement and evaluation."[12] *Qualitative research* methods focus on observing events from the perspective of those involved and attempt to understand why individuals behave as they do. They take a more natural approach to the resolution of research problems. Some research projects utilize both quantitative and qualitative research methods to study and report behaviors and events. This book emphasizes quantitative methods; however, Chapter 7 is devoted to qualitative methods, and a number of the procedures covered elsewhere have qualitative applications.

Types of Previous Library Research

According to Shera, Ralph Beals once categorized library literature into the tripartite classification of Glad Tidings, Testimony, and Research, and noted that there was little of the last.[13] Goldhor, in his text on library research, categorized library literature with regard to research as including: one, a relatively small body of published research as defined in the narrow sense; two, a larger amount of published and unpublished services studies, or applied research; three, an even larger number of reports or descriptions of specific situations, or simply opinions; and four, original data.[14] Losee and Worley stated: "There is a tendency among information professionals to write and publish in the 'How I done it good' genre, a genre that is very situation-specific."[15] In short, as was noted earlier, and as Busha and Harter indicated in their textbook, the preponderance of library-related research has been applied in nature.[16]

A 1984 issue of *Library Trends* was devoted to research in librarianship, and it reviewed research as related to the history of library and information science, economics of libraries, political science, sociology, psychology of information use, organization theory, public administration, and operations research. This work thus provided a categorization of library research in terms of both methodology and subject. In the first chapter of this issue of *Library Trends*, Mary Jo Lynch identified her own general categories for describing different research activities as practical research, bibliographical research, scholarly research, and scientific research.[17] She characterized practical research as problem solving with information; bibliographical research as reordering the thoughts of others; scholarly research as systematic collecting, organizing, and analyzing of data; and scientific research as discovering new knowledge.

Mathews described research performed by the U.S. Department of Education from 1977 to 1988.[18] Along with analyzing the products of the research, she also discussed recent research agenda efforts of the Department and implications for future research. McClure and Bishop provided a useful summary of reports published from 1976 to 1988 related to the status of research in librarianship.[19] Several of the reports contained analyses of the types of research methods utilized during various time periods. Powell summarized some methodological studies ranging from an analysis of dissertations dating back to 1925 to an examination of research articles published in 1984.[20] He also characterized more recent trends including qualitative, interdisciplinary, and technology-based research. Buttlar analyzed library and information science (LIS) dissertations to identify the authors' gender, the nature of the most highly cited materials, the most highly cited journals, the literature cited in disciplines other than LIS, the countries of origin of publications cited, and the currency of the cited literature.[21] She did not identify the type of methodologies used, but did report that the literature from the LIS field is cited about 50 percent of the time and identified education, computer science, health and medicine, psychology, communications, and business as disciplines that impact LIS research.

Bao analyzed the articles published in *College & Research Libraries* (*C&RL*) and the *Journal of Academic Librarianship* (*JAL*) between 1990 and 1999.[22] The majority of the refereed articles addressed collections, services, staffing, and the Internet, indicating that some of the research areas identified by the College Library Section of the Association of College & Research Libraries (ACRL) had not been studied by the authors included in the sample. Bao could not identify any research patterns or trends for the journals, except that Internet technology had been a popular research topic since 1994.[23]

Crawford reported research patterns represented by the articles published in *C&RL* and *JAL* for 1996 and 1997.[24] He identified more than 65 percent of the articles published in *C&RL* as quantitative empirical studies while less than 25 percent of the articles published in *JAL* during this same time period were categorized as quantitative empirical studies. How-to, model and issue discussions, project reports, and other nonempirical papers represented 29.6 percent of the articles published in *JAL*, while 14.3 percent of the articles published in *C&RL* were categorized as nonempirical.

Hildreth and Aytac analyzed 206 randomly selected articles in 23 LIS journals published between 2003 and 2005 using 35 factors, such as authorship, topic, type of research, data collection methods, etc. They concluded that "there is little difference in the quality and organization" between the published reports of practitioner and academic research. Not surprisingly, "practitioners conduct more library-specific studies and academics conduct more use and user studies." The authors confirmed that qualitative research methods are being used but have "leveled off" and expressed concern about library practitioners' limited use of qualitative research methods.[25]

In another study focusing on librarians' research productivity, Fennewald identified the factors associated with Penn State librarians' research publication output. The most critical factor was the expectation of the institution. Personal motivation, intellectual curiosity, and education also were identified as important factors influencing the librarians' research productivity.[26]

Hider and Pymm examined librarianship and nonlibrarianship journals published in 2005 to identify the strategies and data collection techniques used in the studies. The survey was the most used strategy (30.5%) for all journals examined, and "the leading technique was questionnaire/interview" (32.5%). Experimental design (20.8%) was the second most used technique, and content analysis was "the only other specific technique with more than 10 percent."[27] Historical research was very low (1.2%) and showed a "marked decline" when compared with the results reported for 1975 and 1985 by Jarvelin and Vakkari and Kumpulainen.[28] Thirty-two percent of all the journals reported no empirical research (these were discussion and theoretical papers), and there was no significant difference between the librarianship and nonlibrarianship journals. In the 1985 analysis 55.9 percent of the articles reported no empirical research, which may indicate that discussion and theoretical papers were less likely to be published in 2005. Hider and Pymm reported that "qualitative approaches including case studies and ethnography are now well established." Bibliometrics are still "valuable tools of investigation" and "the largely quantitative technique of transaction log analysis has grown rapidly to become a major instrument." Approximately 26 percent of the articles in the librarianship journals used both quantitative and qualitative analyses, while 12.2 percent of the articles in the nonlibrarianship journals used both analyses.[29]

Fidel analyzed 465 articles published in four LIS research journals. Five percent (22 articles) used the mixed methods research (MMR) approach, "which integrates qualitative and quantitative methods in one study." Fidel also reported that the use of the MMR name or recognition of MMR "was absent from these articles and from the methodological literature in LIS."[30]

Limitations of Previous Library Research

Unfortunately, the past research record for library and information science is not exemplary. It has been easier to find criticism of library research than praise. Zweizig called for improvements in research methodologies, especially as they related to users of library services.[31] Busha and Harter stated: "a large proportion of librarianship's research has been uneven in quality and demonstrably weak methodologically . . ."[32] Shaughnessy was even more critical in contending that traditionally the field has permitted much of what is not actually research to be called research.[33] Cuadra identified shortcomings in library and information science research so far as purpose is concerned.[34] He noted "a failure to ask the right questions and to establish a proper theoretical foundation for later research or application."

On what else do these writers and others base their rather negative evaluations of much of the previous library research? Martyn and Lancaster pointed out that much of the earlier literature of library science was too heavily based on opinion, as opposed to investigation, to be considered research.[35] Shera noted that because of library research's "excessive dependence upon local observations and limited data, more frequently than not it is provincial and parochial rather than general in applicability."[36] Van House observed that "much of the research in LIS is episodic. Rarely do researchers build a continuing series of projects so that their own work is a coherent whole. Nor do they often build on one another's work."[37]

Garrison, while acknowledging that considerable advances had been made in public library research in the previous decade, went on to itemize several shortcomings of research, including the following:[38]

1. Researchers have not disseminated their results adequately.
2. Practitioners have not kept up with research results that have been reported.
3. The profession has been too content with nonresearch reports.
4. The audiences for research journals have been too limited.
5. Dissertations have seldom had any relationship to previous or subsequent research.
6. The impact of reported research has been weakened due to poor bibliographic control and inadequate availability of copies.

Goodall reported that a variety of topics were being investigated by public librarians in England, yet the methodologies used for the studies were limited.[39]

Survey methodology was employed for the majority of the studies. Although new and varied methodologies are being demonstrated in the library and information science literature, survey methodology continues to dominate.[40]

Gatten criticized library science research for failing to draw upon the research literature and methods of other disciplines and for too often utilizing unsophisticated analytical techniques and limited theoretical frameworks.[41] Trahan stated that library research "is at a relatively primitive stage in its development when compared to the research literature of other disciplines" and that "there has been little, if any, increase in research activity in librarianship."[42] In an editorial, Hernon expressed his concern for the poor quality of research published in library and information science journals.[43] Although Fisher concluded that the professional literature represented in six LIS journals in 1993 validates the results of prior studies in regard to author demographics, he recommended the continued publication of both applied and "rigorous empirical/theoretical research" to meet our professional needs.[44] Dillon was critical of LIS research but stated, "I actually do not share the belief of others that this is a field in crisis . . . I believe this is a wonderful moment of opportunity for us all, but to grasp it, we must be prepared to address the shortcomings in our research operations."[45]

In short, in spite of some progress, there continues to be a need for more and better library-related research. But the limitations of earlier research are not the only reasons for calling for better-conducted research. There are a number of positive justifications that can be made for more rigorous research and, in particular, basic research.

RATIONALE FOR BASIC RESEARCH IN LIBRARY AND INFORMATION SCIENCE

Growth of the Profession

As indicated earlier, one of the major purposes of basic research is to create new knowledge. Or, as stated by Mouly, "it is the purpose of science [scientific research] to go beyond experience and common sense, which frequently are quite limited and inadequate—and often quite incorrect, . . . for advancing knowledge, for promoting progress, and for enabling man to relate more effectively to his environment, to accomplish his purposes, and to resolve his conflicts."[46] "And as Kunge has written: 'Learning to master theoretically and in practical application, the ground rules of research creates the best foundation for continuing growth in a profession.' "[47]

But perhaps even more basic to the advancement of the profession "is the need for the field to test the various myths, assumptions, rules-of-thumb, and other conventions by which it has operated for so long a time, to link concepts which have been proven through testing to be valid, and thereby establish theories indigenous to the field itself."[48] In addition, the profession needs to advance beyond its heavy dependence on descriptive data and establish principles and theories on which libraries and information systems and services can be based.[49] "One of the hallmarks of a profession is the ability of its members to give advice to clientele derived from a body of generalized and systematic knowledge that comprises its theoretical core."[50]

Those concerned about the status of the LIS profession have commented on the need for more and better basic research. Shaughnessy noted: "Of the two primary marks of a profession—a service ideal and a body of theoretical knowledge—it has been suggested that librarianship possesses the first, but not the second. Theoretical knowledge, as distinguished from knowledge based on practice, is generally developed or discovered through the process of research; a process in which librarianship has not had much of a tradition."[51] Busha and Harter argued that "if librarianship is to merit the coveted designation 'science,' a significant number of scholars and research workers must regularly apply scientific method to analyze relationships among the problems which librarians are obligated to explore and which they are qualified to serve."[52] In other words, "A profession that would know itself—that would anticipate or, to use Gabor's phrase, 'invent the future'—must support and engage in productive research."[53]

In 2001, the Special Library Association (SLA) published a research statement, "Putting OUR Knowledge to Work: The Role of Research in Special Libraries," defining library and information science research as not well developed, with fewer peer-reviewed journals and grant-funded research in comparison to other disciplines.[54] The statement identifies ways that special librarians, researchers, and SLA can work together to contribute to the library and information profession and to build a foundation for evidence-based practice.

In short, basic research is crucial if the field of library and information science is "to solve professional problems, develop tools and methods for analysis of organization, services, and behavior, to determine costs and benefits of our services, and most importantly, to establish or develop a body of theory on which to base our practice."[55] It is imperative that academic librarians and higher education libraries (among others) develop and carry out systematic research and development programs. LIS students and professionals must not only be able to " . . . read, understand, and value the LIS research literature," but "they must also be able to locate it within its cultural context . . ." A commitment to understanding and applying research is also essential if the field is to continue to advance."[56] Unfortunately, as Busha and others have noted, the development of new knowledge within the library and information science profession has traditionally received a relatively low priority.[57] In 1994, Riggs argued that the profession seems, in fact, to be reducing the attention that it gives to research.[58]

Management

As has been indicated earlier, basic research has more to offer than the expansion and refinement of the profession's theoretical underpinnings. Much of the knowledge created as the result of basic research is likely to have practical applications for the improvement of practices in actual library operations.[59] Swisher argued that "there is no more important activity than acquiring new information that may now or someday assist in the goal of improving our professional decision making. Assuming the responsibility of practical research is probably the most important role a librarian can accept."[60] The application of research findings should result in "improved decision making, more knowledgeable insights into a wealth of library issues, better and more accountable services and programs, and the continued maturation of LIS as a discipline/profession."[61] "Thus, there is the need for academic librarians to possess an understanding of data-gathering techniques, which are informed by an understanding of the nature of the research methodologies available and an understanding of the nature of the statistical analysis techniques available."[62] Recently there has been much discussion about evidence-based decision making, which requires collecting and analyzing relevant data to make informed decisions for services, policies, etc.[63] Hernon and Schwartz proposed a managerial leadership research agenda that includes evidence-based decision making for assessing, evaluating, and managing.[64] A new open access journal, *Evidence Based Library and Information Science Practice* (http://ejournals .library.ualberta.ca/index.php/EBLIP/index), began publication in 2006. The purpose of the journal is "to provide a forum for librarians and other information professionals to discover research that may contribute to decision making in professional practice" (http://ejournals.library.ualberta.ca/index.php/ EBLIP/about/editorialPolicies#focusAndScope).[65]

The American Library Association (ALA) promotes the need for the dissemination of research findings for support of professional practice and has published "recommendations related to the effective dissemination of research."[66] In addition, ALA initiated the *ALA Research Series* in 2009 "to expand the knowledge base of library research by publishing quantitative and/or qualitative research and analysis that addresses topics important to libraries, librarians, and education in the profession"—"accessible, useful, practical, sustainable research" (http://www.ala.org/ala/professionalresources/publications/ alaresearchseries/alaresearchseries.cfm).[67]

While most research for decision making takes the form of applied research, it typically draws upon the tenets of basic research. McClure observed that "applied research takes the theory and concepts from basic research and by formal methods of inquiry, investigates 'real world' phenomena."[68] In other words, a solid understanding of the basic research process should better enable one to conduct sound applied research. As Goldhor pointed out, "Once one has learned this method [scientific research] he can understand and use any of the less rigorous methods, but learning the latter will not prepare one really to use the former."[69]

ACRL established the Focus on the Future Task Force in the fall of 2001 to identify the issues facing academic librarians, and to assist with developing "... services to further improve learning and research."[70] After extensive interviews and open forum discussions, seven top issues were identified. These issues provide a research agenda that can guide and direct research projects that enable library managers to make intelligent decisions.

Reading Research Reports

Another benefit of having a reasonable mastery of basic research methods is that it should allow one to understand and critically evaluate the research reports of others. According to Swisher "the reader who understands the process of research will question much more about the literature in general, and correctly identify the working limitations of the literature."[71] Some librarians, particularly special librarians, are expected to evaluate or screen research reports (i.e., serve as research intermediaries) for their clientele. Unfortunately, as Sullivan has contended, not only do librarians who are practitioners tend to be too busy and unskilled to conduct their own research, but more seriously, "they are also either uninformed or unwilling to accept or unable to judge critically the research of others in the field of librarianship."[72] Until a majority of the field's practitioners can understand and apply the research results of others, the profession is not likely to realize much benefit from its research efforts. Numerous writers, including Busha and Harter and Grazier have argued for the need to evaluate and apply published research.[73] As Williams and Winston stated, "the research literature in any discipline can serve to further the scholarly discussion, advance the theoretical base of the profession, and inform practice."[74]

A study by Powell, Baker, and Mika provides a more hopeful perspective on the profession's use of research.[75] Members of the American Library Association, the American Society for Information Science and Technology, the Medical Library Association, and the Special Libraries Association were surveyed to identify their involvement in reading, applying, and conducting research. The findings revealed that "almost 90 percent of LIS practitioners in the United States and Canada regularly read at least one research journal, nearly 62 percent regularly read research-based articles, approximately 50 percent occasionally apply research results to professional practices, and 42 percent occasionally or frequently perform research related to their job or to the LIS profession."[76] Only 15 percent of those surveyed indicated that they read more than four research journals, and research activity varied by membership in the professional associations represented in the study. Master's degree courses in research methods were found "to be significantly related to conducting, as well as reading research."[77] A survey of British librarians in academic, health, public, school, and special libraries found that half of the respondents reported that they had been involved in some form of research in the past two years.[78]

Improved Service to Researchers

Yet another advantage to having a basic knowledge of research methods, at least for those librarians who serve researchers, is the greater understanding of the needs of researchers provided by this awareness. Only when the librarian knows the basic process which a researcher utilizes, can the researcher's needs be fully anticipated and met. Or as Engle stated, "A thorough and continuing personal grounding in the experience of learning and research in an academic setting prepares us to join students and faculty in the creative act which bibliographic research can be."[79] In addition, the librarian's status is likely to benefit from being knowledgeable about the researchers' techniques and from being able to discuss them intelligently with his or her clientele. Grover and Hale argued that librarians should assume a proactive role in faculty research and be viewed as key players in the process.[80] Librarians are often recruited to help conduct the literature review for a research proposal and may even help write the proposal and conduct the research.

Personal Benefits

Perhaps most important among the benefits one could expect to realize from a study of research methods is the ability to conduct research. For many librarians, especially in academic settings, research activities are not only desirable but a necessity. A number of academic institutions expect their professional librarians to meet the same requirements for promotion and tenure as do their regular teaching faculty, and these usually include research and publishing. If these librarians, and others, are to conduct the kind of rigorous research that they and their profession need, a thorough understanding of basic research methods is absolutely essential.

An awareness of research methods and design also should prove helpful for those preparing research proposals in order to obtain financial support for their research activities. In addition, it has been pointed out that the study of research methods can improve one's ability to think critically and analytically—competencies associated with leadership. A library's involvement in research can even improve staff morale and enhance the library's status in its community.

THE FUTURE OF LIBRARY RESEARCH

As Busha noted, past weaknesses of library-related research can at least partially be explained by the fact "that research in librarianship is still relatively young. Clear conceptions of the goals, objectives, and methodologies of library science research are only now beginning to be solidly formulated."[81] It does appear clear, however, that it will become more and more "necessary to use the methodology of other disciplines—in particular, those of sociology, psychology, economics, linguistics, history—and to employ more generally applicable methodologies" in order to study the many problems facing librarianship today.[82]

But who is going to be qualified to conduct the kinds of research needed, how will they be trained, and how will practitioners be equipped to read and utilize this research? Shera provided at least one answer to these questions when he wrote: "Research is too important to be left to dilettantes and amateurs, and its pursuit should be reserved for those who are qualified for it by aptitude, education, and motivation."[83] In short, education appears to be one key to solving the problem. Not only can education provide the basic skills needed for conducting research, but it can help to shape attitudes and supply motivations.

Logically, the major responsibility for imparting research skills to librarians must belong to the LIS education programs. As Shera stated, "A specific part of the course of study for a graduate student in librarianship should be the acquiring of a knowledge of the principles and methods of research as applied to the investigation of library problems, together with the ability to evaluate research results, especially research in librarianship ... "[84] As Muller wrote: "Students should learn to appreciate the contribution of research and be urged to rid themselves of the notion that research is something esoteric, remote, or impractical."[85] Yet most students view LIS programs as primarily concerned with providing professional, not academic, training[86] and "too few practitioners have education in the research or knowledge creating process ... "[87] Only

47 percent of the practitioners responding to a survey conducted in 2000 reported that they had taken a course on research methods at the master's degree level, and 59 percent of them reported that their master's degree programs had not adequately prepared them to conduct research.[88]

In other words, the track record of LIS programs regarding the teaching of research skills is not outstanding.[89] O'Connor and Park reported that a research methods course was not required in 38.5 percent of the American Library Association accredited LIS programs and that "only half of the twenty-four top-rated programs required Master of Library Science (MLS) students to take research methods."[90] In 2003, Hernon and Schwartz referred to this as a crisis that should not be allowed to continue,[91] but four years later they still had to conclude that graduates of LIS programs "might emerge with little or no understanding of the research process and how to gather and interpret evidence related to accountability, effectiveness, efficiency, or continuous quality improvement in programs and services."[92] In a study conducted by Dimitroff, she reported that special librarians identified the following as the top barriers to their involvement in research activities: the lack of management support of research, the lack of money/funding for research, the lack of personal interest in research, an insecurity of research skills, and a lack of research ideas.[93]

However, LIS programs do not have the entire responsibility for training competent researchers. It is also the responsibility of professional associations and, in some cases, research organizations, to provide appropriate continuing education opportunities. If libraries and other employers are going to expect librarians to equip themselves to do research, then they must be prepared to provide appropriate incentives, support, and rewards. For example, released time, special leaves, and sabbaticals can be arranged to allow more time for research. Administrative support can be provided through salary raises, in-house training, and financial and clerical support for research projects. Relevant courses such as those in statistical analysis can be taken in departments outside the LIS program when desirable or necessary. And ultimately, of course, it is the responsibility of the would-be researcher to take advantage of continuing education and staff development programs and to commit himself or herself to a substantial program of self-study.

Goldhor's statement made almost four decades ago still rings true: "Librarianship today is particularly in need of the generalized truths which scientific research is designed to uncover."[94] And the research problems will ultimately direct the methodologies employed, which justifies the sustained development of research theories and models as described by Glazier and Grover in their multidisciplinary framework for theory building.[95] In other words, if we are to realize the professional growth needed by the field of library and information science, "Our attention must increasingly be devoted to research which is more basic and less applied . . ."[96] "We must all raise our expectations and challenge the profession to value and use research."[97]

Fortunately, there are promising signs. In an editorial in *Research Strategies*, the authors stated that "a new strain of thought has sprung up in the field of librarianship . . . an interest on the part of practicing librarians in conducting serious research."[98] The professional associations continue to establish more and more units concerned with research. As of 2009–2010, ALA's Research and Statistics Assembly had 23 member units. At the annual conferences of the American Library Association, a considerable number of programs and committee meetings directly deal with research and statistics. ACRL established a Research Mentoring Program to help members with various aspects of the research process. ALA's Committee on Research and Statistics is charged with promoting research to answer questions regarding library services.

SLA's "Research Statement" calls for evidence-based practice, which is decision making " . . . based on the strongest evidence" of what will work best for the libraries' clients.[99] With the expanding role of library and information professionals and the widespread accessibility of information, SLA advocates for the selection, acquisition, organization, and management of information resources to be based on research findings.

The creation and dissemination of research is central to the Vision Statement of the American Society for Information Science & Technology (ASIS&T). The vision of the society includes: " . . . advancing knowledge about information, its creation, properties, and use; providing analysis of ideas, practices, and technologies; valuing theory, research, applications, and service; nurturing new perspectives, interests, and ideas; and increasing public awareness of the information sciences and technologies and their benefits to society."[100]

McClure and Bishop asked 23 leading researchers in library and information science about the status of research in the field.[101] They concluded that it had improved somewhat in the 1980s and expressed "guarded optimism" about the future status of research in library and information science. At least two studies indicated that the number of published research articles is increasing (though there is some evidence that the proportion of research articles in the core journals has declined since 1975).[102] A 1991 book edited by McClure and Hernon was dedicated to the improvement of library and information science research. It provided an overview of LIS research, considered its practical context, and discussed issues and concerns related to research in library and information science.[103]

The annual reports of ALA's Office for Research and Statistics continue to show considerable activity in the research arena. Eisenberg wrote in 1993 that we can take pride in the research that has been conducted in the area of school library media programs.[104] In three editorials, Hernon and Hernon and Schwartz argued that some of the indictments of library research are supported by few references to the LIS literature, LIS researchers have drawn on procedures developed in other disciplines, and LIS researchers have contributed to the development of innovative methods.[105] There have been four national Library Research Seminars since 1996, with a fifth one in the planning stages, and each received numerous proposals for papers representing a wide range of methodologies, including content analysis, historiography, path analysis, discourse analysis, transaction log analysis, protocol analysis, survey, modeling, and meta-analysis. The research topics were equally diverse and often interdisciplinary. These research seminars provided effective forums solely devoted to research ideas and methodologies.

It is always difficult to predict the future, but research in LIS will probably continue to incorporate more multidisciplinary and qualitative methods.[106] Studies addressing the impacts and use of digital resources and technology are currently represented in the literature and will likely continue to pique interest in researchers and practitioners as the resources and technologies evolve and library users become more sophisticated in their demands for and use of these resources. Hernon and Schwartz support this assessment and add, "the problems, research designs, the tool chest of methodologies, and data analysis techniques and software are richer today than ever before."[107]

In conclusion, there is mounting evidence that the quality, if not the quantity, of LIS research is improving. And, hopefully, there is increasing recognition "that the results of research in a broad spectrum of effort extending well beyond librarianship will, in large measure, determine the future directions of library services and the nature of the profession itself" (American Library Association, 1970)—a statement that still resonates after 40 years.[108]

NOTES

1. Laurel Grotzinger, "Methodology of Library Science Inquiry—Past and Present," in *A Library Science Research Reader and Bibliographic Guide*, ed. Charles H. Busha (Littleton, CO: Libraries Unlimited, 1981), 44.

2. James G. Neal, "The Research and Development Imperative in the Academic Library: Path to the Future," *portal: Libraries and the Academy* 6 (2006): 1.

3. Sidney L. Jackson, "Environment: Research," in *A Century of Service: Librarianship in the United States and Canada*, ed. Sidney L. Jackson, Eleanor B. Herling, and E. J. Josey (Chicago: American Library Association, 1976), 341–54. Charles A. Busha, "Library Science Research: The Path to Progress," in *A Library Science Research Reader and Bibliographic Guide*, ed. Charles A. Busha (Littleton, CO: Libraries Unlimited, 1981).

4. "Research," *Merriam-Webster Online Dictionary*, 2010, http://www.merriam-webster.com/dictionary/research.

5. Tyrus Hillway, *Introduction to Research*, 2nd ed. (Boston: Houghton Mifflin, 1964), 5.

6. George J. Mouly, *Educational Research: The Art and Science of Investigation* (Boston: Allyn and Bacon, 1978), 12.

7. B. C. Vickery, "Academic Research in Library and Information Studies," *Journal of Librarianship* 7 (July 1975): 153–60.

8. Jesse H. Shera, "Darwin, Bacon, and Research in Librarianship," *Library Trends* 3 (July 1964): 143.

9. Donald E. Stokes, *Pasteur's Quadrant: Basic Science and Technological Innovation* (Washington, DC: Brookings Institute Press, 1997).

10. Mouly, *Educational Research*, 43.

11. Robert H. Muller, "The Research Mind in Library Education and Practice," *Library Journal* 92 (March 1967): 1129.

12. Jack D. Glazier and Ronald R. Powell, eds., *Qualitative Research in Information Management* (Englewood, CO: Libraries Unlimited, 1992), xi.

13. Shera, "Darwin, Bacon, and Research," 145.

14. Herbert Goldhor, *An Introduction to Scientific Research in Librarianship* (Urbana: University of Illinois, Graduate School of Library Science, 1972).

15. Robert M. Losee, Jr. and Karen A. Worley, *Research and Evaluation for Information Professionals* (San Diego: Academic Press, 1993), ix.

16. Charles A. Busha and Stephen P. Harter, *Research Methods in Librarianship: Techniques and Interpretations* (New York: Academic Press, 1980), 8.

17. Mary Jo Lynch, "Research and Librarianship: An Uneasy Connection," *Library Trends* 32 (Spring 1984): 367.

18. Anne J. Mathews, "An Overview of Issues, Proposals, and Products in Library/Information Research," *Journal of Education for Library and Information Science* 29 (Spring 1989): 251–61.

19. Charles R. McClure and Ann Bishop, "The Status of Research in Library/Information Science: Guarded Optimism," *College & Research Libraries* 50 (March 1989): 127–43.

20. Ronald R. Powell, "Research Competence for Ph.D. Students in Library and Information Science," *Journal of Education for Library and Information Science* 36 (Fall 1995): 319–29.

21. Lois Buttlar, "Information Sources in Library and Information Science Doctoral Research," *Library & Information Science Research* 21 (1999): 227–45.

22. Xue-Ming Bao, "An Analysis of the Research Areas of the Articles Published in *C&RL* and *JAL* between 1990 and 1999," *College & Research Libraries* 66 (2000): 536–44.

23. Ibid., 543.

24. Gregory A. Crawford, "The Research Literature of Academic Librarianship: A Comparison of *College & Research Libraries* and *Journal of Academic Librarianship*," *College & Research Libraries* 60 (May 1999): 224–30.

25. Charles R. Hildreth and Selenay Aytac, "Recent Library Practitioner Research: A Methodological Analysis and Critique," *Journal of Education for Library and Information Science* 48, no. 3 (2007): 254.

26. Joseph Fennewald, "Research Productivity Among Librarians: Factors Leading to Publications at Penn State," *College & Research Libraries* 69 (2008): 104–14.

27. Philip Hider and Bob Pymm, "Empirical Research Methods Reported in High-Profile LIS Journal Literature," *Library & Information Science Research* 30, no. 2 (2008): 111.

28. Kalervo Järvelin and Pertti Vakkari, "Content Analysis of Research Articles in Library and Information Science," *Library & Information Science Research* 12, no. 4 (1990): 395–421. Sisko Kumpulainen, "Library and Information Science Research in 1975: Content Analysis of the Journal Articles," *Libri* 41, no. 1 (1991): 59–76.

29. Hider and Pymm, "Empirical Research Methods," 114.

30. Raya Fidel, "Are We There Yet?: Mixed Methods Research in Library and Information Science," *Library & Information Science Research* 30, no. 4 (2008): 265.

31. Douglas L. Zweizig, "With Our Eye on the User: Needed Research for Information and Referral in the Public Library," *Drexel Library Quarterly* 12 (1976): 48–58.

32. Busha and Harter, *Research Methods in Librarianship*, 7.

33. Thomas W. Shaughnessy, "Library Research in the 70's: Problems and Prospects," *California Librarian* 37 (July 1976): 44–52.

34. W. R. Converse, "Research: What We Need, and What We Get," *Canadian Library Journal* 41 (October 1984): 236.

35. John Martyn and F. Wilfrid Lancaster, *Investigative Methods in Library and Information Science: An Introduction* (Arlington, VA: Information Resources Press, 1981), 193.

36. Shera, "Darwin, Bacon, and Research," 147.

37. Nancy A. Van House, "Assessing the Quantity, Quality, and Impact of LIS Research," in *Library and Information Science Research: Perspectives and Strategies for Improvement*, ed. Charles R. McClure and Peter Hernon (Norwood, NJ: Ablex Publishing, 1991).

38. Guy Garrison, "A Look at Research on Public Library Problems in the 1970's," *Public Libraries* 19 (Spring 1980): 4–8.

39. Deborah Goodall, "It Ain't What You Do, It's the Way That You Do It: A Review of Public Library Research with Special Reference to Methodology," *Public Library Journal* 11 (1996): 69–76.

40. Ronald R. Powell, "Recent Trends in Research: A Methodological Essay," *Library & Information Science Research* 21 (1999): 91–119.

41. Jeffery N. Gatten, "Paradigm Restrictions on Interdisciplinary Research into Librarianship," *College & Research Libraries* 52 (November 1991): 575–84.

42. Eric Trahan, "Applying Meta-Analysis to Library Research and Information Science Research," *Library Quarterly* 63 (January 1993): 73.

43. Peter Hernon, "Editorial: Research in Library and Information Science–Reflections on the Journal Literature," *The Journal of Academic Librarianship* 25 (July 1999): 263–66.

44. William Fisher, "When Write Is Wrong: Is All Our Professional Literature on the Same Page?" *Library Collections, Acquisitions, & Technical Services* 23 (Spring 1999): 61–72.

45. Andrew Dillon, "LIS as a Research Domain: Problems and Prospects," *Information Research* 12, no. 4 supplement (2007), http://informationr.net/ir/12-4/colis/colis03.html.

46. Mouly, *Educational Research*, 12.

47. Busha and Harter, *Research Methods in Librarianship*, 6.

48. Grotzinger, "Methodology of Library Science Inquiry," 45.

49. Vickery, "Academic Research," 155.

50. Carolyn E. Poole, "Guest Editorial: Importance of Research and Publication by Community College Librarians," *College & Research Libraries* 61, no. 6 (2000): 486.

51. Shaughnessy, "Library Research in the 70's," 44.

52. Busha and Harter, *Research Methods in Librarianship*, 4.

53. Shera, "Darwin, Bacon, and Research," 148–49.

54. "Putting OUR Knowledge to Work: A New SLA Research Statement June 2001: The Role of Research in Special Librarianship," *Special Libraries Association*, June 2001, http://www.sla.org/content/resources/research/rsrchstatement.cfm.

55. Shaughnessy, "Library Research in the 70's," 51.

56. Prudence W. Dalrymple, "A Quarter Century of User-Centered Study: The Impact of Zweizig and Dervin on LIS Research," *Library & Information Science Research* 23 (2001): 163.

57. Busha, "Library Science Research," 2.

58. Donald E. Riggs, "Losing the Foundation of Understanding," *American Libraries* 25 (May 1994): 449.

59. Busha and Harter, *Research Methods in Librarianship*.

60. Robert Swisher, "Focus on Research," *Top of the News* 42 (Winter 1986): 176.

61. Peter Hernon and Candy Schwartz, "Can Research Be Assimilated into the Soul of Library and Information Science?" *Library & Information Science Research* 17, no. 2 (Spring 1995): 101.

62. James F. Williams II and Mark D. Winston, "Leadership Competencies and the Importance of Research Methods and Statistical Analysis in Decision Making and Research and Publication: A Study of Citation Patterns," *Library & Information Science Research* 25, no. 4 (2003): 390.

63. Peter Hernon and Candy Schwartz, "Editorial: Research by Default," *Library & Information Science Research* 31, no. 3 (2009): 137.

64. Peter Hernon and Candy Schwartz, "Leadership: Developing a Research Agenda for Academic Libraries," *Library & Information Science Research* 30, no. 4 (2008): 243–49.

65. "Evidence Based Library and Information Practice: Home," *University of Alberta Learning Services*, http://ejournals.library.ualberta.ca/index.php/EBLIP/index. "Editorial Policies: Focus and Scope," *University of Alberta Learning Services*,

http://ejournals.library.ualberta.ca/index.php/EBLIP/about/editorialPolicies#focusAndScope.

66. "Dissemination of Research in LIS: A Statement by the American Library Association Committee on Research and Statistics,"*American Library Association*, June 2001, http://www.ala.org/ala/aboutala/offices/ors/orscommittees/dissemination/dissemination.cfm.

67. "ALA Research Series," *American Library Association*, http://www.ala.org/ala/professionalresources/publications/alaresearchseries/alaresearchseries.cfm.

68. Charles R. McClure, "Management Data for Library Decision Making: The Role of the Researcher," in *Library Lectures*, vol. 56, ed. Robert S. Martin (Baton Rouge: Louisiana State University Libraries, 1988).

69. Goldhor, *Introduction to Scientific Research*, 1–2.

70. W. Lee Hisle, "Top Issues Facing Academic Libraries: A Report of the Focus on the Future Task Force," *College & Research Libraries News* 63 (November 2002): 714.

71. Swisher, "Focus on Research," 175.

72. Peggy A. Sullivan, "Research in Librarianship: Achievements, Needs, and Prospects," *Illinois Libraries* 60 (May 1978): 511.

73. Busha and Harter, *Research Methods in Librarianship*. Margaret H. Grazier, "Critically Reading and Applying Research in School Library Media Centers," *School Library Media Quarterly* 10 (Winter 1982): 135–46.

74. Williams and Winston, "Leadership Competencies," 401.

75. Ronald R. Powell, Lynda M. Baker, and Joseph J. Mika, "Library and Information Science Practitioners and Research," *Library & Information Science Research* 24 (2002): 49–72.

76. Ibid., 55–61.

77. Ibid., 70.

78. Sarah McNicol, "Is Research an Untapped Resource in the Library and Information Profession?" *Journal of Librarianship and Information Science* 36 (September 2004): 119–26.

79. Michael Engle, "Creativity and the Research Process in Academic Libraries," *College & Research Libraries News* 48 (November 1987): 629.

80. Robert Grover and Martha L. Hale, "The Role of the Librarian in Faculty Research," *College & Research Libraries* 49 (January 1988): 9–15.

81. Busha, "Library Science Research," 2.

82. Vickery, "Academic Research," 158.

83. Shera, "Darwin, Bacon, and Research," 149.

84. Grotzinger, "Methodology of Library Science Inquiry," 45–46.

85. Muller, "Research Mind," 1126.

86. Converse, "Research: What We Need," 238.

87. Jane B. Robbins, "Research in Information Service Practice," *Library & Information Science Research* 12 (April 1990): 127.

88. Powell, Baker, and Mika, "Library and Information Science Practitioners," 49–72.

89. Busha and Harter, *Research Methods in Librarianship*, 5, 8.

90. Daniel O. O'Connor and Soyeon Park, "Guest Editorial: Crisis in LIS Research Capacity," *Library & Information Science Research* 23, no. 2 (2001): 105.

91. Peter Hernon and Candy Schwartz, "Editorial: We Will Not Rest on Our Laurels!" *Library & Information Science Research* 25, no. 2 (2003): 125–26.

92. Peter Hernon and Candy Schwartz, "Editorial: A Need for a Greater Commitment in the Profession to Research and Evaluation," *Library & Information Science Research* 29, no. 2 (2007): 161.

93. Alexandra Dimitroff, "Research Knowledge and Activities of Special Librarians: Results of a Survey," *Special Libraries* 87 (Winter 1996): 1–9.

94. Goldhor, *Introduction to Scientific Research*, 2.

95. Jack D. Glazier and Robert Grover, "A Multidisciplinary Framework for Theory Building," *Library Trends* 50 (Winter 2002): 317–29.

96. Shaughnessy, "Library Research in the 70's," 52.

97. Peter Hernon, "Editorial: Components of the Research Process: Where Do We Need to Focus Attention?" *The Journal of Academic Librarianship* 27 (March 2001): 88.

98. Sharon A. Hogan and Mary W. George, "Cropping Up: Librarians' Desire to Conduct Serious Research," *Research Strategies* 4 (Spring 1986): 58.

99. "Putting OUR Knowledge to Work," *Special Libraries Association*.

100. "Mission & Vision," *ASIS&T: The Information Society for the Information Age*, http://www.asis.org/missionvision.html.

101. McClure and Bishop, "Status of Research in Library/Information Science," 127–43.

102. Bluma C. Peritz, "Research in Library Science as Reflected in the Core Journals of the Profession: A Quantitative Analysis (1950–1975)," (Ph.D. diss., University of California at Berkeley, 1977).

103. Charles R. McClure and Peter Hernon, eds., *Library and Information Science Research: Perspectives and Strategies for Improvement* (Norwood, NJ: Ablex Publishing, 1991).

104. Michael B. Eisenberg, "The State of Research Today," *School Library Media Quarterly* 21 (Summer 1993): 241.

105. Peter Hernon, "Library and Information Science Research: Not an Island unto Itself," *Library & Information Science Research* 14 (January–March 1992): 1–3. Peter Hernon, "LIS Extends to the Research Frontier," *College & Research Libraries* 53 (January 1992): 3–5. Peter Hernon and Candy Schwartz, "Library and Information Science Research: Is It Misunderstood?" *Library & Information Science Research* 15 (Summer 1993): 215–17.

106. Powell, "Recent Trends in Research," 91–119.

107. Hernon and Schwartz, "We Will Not Rest on Our Laurels!" 125.

108. *Policy Statement on the Role of Research in the American Library Association* (Chicago: American Library Association, 1970).

Chapter 2

Developing the Research Study

More research effort is wasted by going off half prepared, with only a vague set of ideas and procedures, than in any other way.[1]

PLANNING FOR RESEARCH

The first question that a researcher may well ask is, "Where do I begin?" In other words, where does the planning begin? Leedy and Ormrod state, "... by asking questions, we strike the first spark igniting a chain reaction that leads to the research process. An inquisitive mind is the beginning of research."[2] After all, as we learned earlier, the major purpose of basic research is to discover new knowledge.

Historically, new knowledge has been sought either by means of deductive logic or through the use of inductive reasoning. Deductive or systematic logic, which was developed by Aristotle, is characterized by use of the syllogism. A syllogism starts with a basic premise, which is then logically applied to a particular case; for example: "All men are mortal; John Doe is a man; therefore John Doe is mortal." The truth of the conclusion obviously depends upon the truth of the basic premise, which in this example was "All men are mortal."

In contrast to the deductive method, inductive reasoning proceeds from particular instances to general principles, or from facts to theories. Using inductive logic, one might note that John Doe is mortal and then observe a number of other men as well. One might next decide that all of the *observed* men were mortals and arrive at the conclusion that *all* men are mortal. The obvious limitation to this method is that it is virtually impossible to observe all of the instances supporting the inductive generalization.

Let us consider one more example which may help to illustrate the distinction between deductive and inductive logic. Suppose we are interested in the possible relationship between the amount of library instruction received by certain college students and their subsequent academic performance. Using the deductive method, we could hypothesize that library instruction improves academic performance. We could then specify that library instruction would be represented by the number of hours spent receiving library instruction in an English literature course, and that academic performance would be represented by the final grade for the course. If we were to observe that, as the hours of instruction increase, grades improve, we could then conclude that our hypothesis describes the relationship that exists.

Using inductive reasoning, we could start with an observation that the students in a particular English literature class who had received library instruction seemed to do quite well in the course. We might then wonder if most library instruction methods have a positive effect on the academic performance of college students. We could proceed to make a variety of observations related to both library instruction and academic performance. Next, we would look for a pattern that best represents or summarizes our observations. In other words, we would attempt to generalize that, based on our observations, library instruction of all types tends to improve academic performance. As Babbie has pointed out, with the deductive method we would have reasoned *toward* observations; with the inductive method we would have reasoned *from* observations.[3]

THE SCIENTIFIC METHOD OF INQUIRY

Inductive reasoning contributed to the development of what is known as the scientific method or the scientific method of inquiry (SMI). This approach to the discovery of knowledge, which arose during the Renaissance, gained major support in the sixteenth century. Many scholars still consider the scientific method of inquiry to be the most valid method for resolving unanswered questions and solving problems. There are other viewpoints, however. Budd, for example, argues that the SMI is too positivist in nature, and that LIS needs more research that is based on a different epistemological foundation—one that is less concerned with universal laws and invariant relationships.[4]

There is a general consensus among researchers regarding the basic pattern of the scientific method of inquiry, but specific elements do sometimes vary. Leedy describes the scientific method of inquiry as a means by which insight into an undiscovered truth is sought by (a) identifying the problem that will provide the goal of the research, (b) gathering the data needed to resolve the problem, (c) developing a tentative hypothesis, and (d) empirically testing the hypothesis by analyzing the data.[5]

Babbie, who sees the scientific method of inquiry as a combination of the inductive and deductive methods, depending upon the research phase, summarizes the basic steps of the scientific method as (a) identification of an idea or interest, (b) theory construction, (c) derivation of theoretical hypotheses/ expectations, (d) operationalization of concepts, and (e) testing of hypotheses.[6] Frankfort-Nachmias and Nachmias state that the research process consists of seven principal stages: problem, hypothesis, research design, measurement, data collection, data analysis, and generalization. They point out that "Each stage influences the development of *theory* and is influenced by it in turn."[7]

Some believe that LIS has little formal theory of its own;[8] others call for more LIS research to advance practice and theory.[9] Budd reminds us that "general progress only occurs when there has been deep critical investigation into the workings of our field."[10] This means that we must study the intellectual foundations of the LIS field. This type of reflection will influence not only our research but also the development of systems and services for the practice of LIS. Glazier (see his section below) argues that, before we begin the research process, we should consider our basic epistemological and ontological assumptions and presuppositions. They influence how we approach and carry out research in the social and behavioral sciences.

A General Outline for Research

Given differences in subject disciplines and/or the types of data to be collected, researchers find it necessary to employ a variety of specific methodologies, but most true research does follow the same general outline and exhibits similar characteristics. In developing a research study, the investigator typically begins with a question about something of interest. For example, a college librarian may wonder why the use of his or her library seems to be declining or, better yet, increasing. As early as this point, and throughout the development of the research study, the investigator is likely to benefit from a thorough review of the literature (see Chapter 10 for tips on reviewing the related research).

The next important, logical step would be for the librarian to identify the problem that this question represents. He or she may have a hunch that library use is low because the majority of the students do not have adequate library skills. In other words, the actual problem facing the librarian may be poor library skills, which ultimately tend to be evidenced by low library use. The librarian may also conclude that he or she is actually confronted with several problems, or at least subproblems of the main problem. For example, the librarian turned researcher may need to consider specific types of library skills or different class levels.

Having identified the specific research problem, the researcher should then attempt to place the problem in its broader theoretical framework. An adequate theory might have been articulated already, or it may be necessary to develop one.

Keeping in mind the main problem, subproblems if any, and the relevant theory, the librarian should consider developing one or more hypotheses to guide the future investigation or study. In this case, the librarian may wish to hypothesize that library skills have a positive effect on library use. This hypothesis may be based on obvious assumptions, such as "library instruction will in fact be reasonably effective at teaching certain library skills," or "students will be able to transfer skills learned as a result of an instructional program to actual use of a library."

Throughout this process, but perhaps particularly at this point, the librarian will need to develop a plan for attempting to resolve the problem. In other words, it will be necessary to decide what methodology and data collection techniques, among other procedures, to utilize in the investigation. The librarian could elect to conduct an experiment during which a particular type of library instruction would be given, and after which the students' library skills would be posttested. Or a survey could be conducted in which students would, for example, be asked about their library use and/or skills.

Another characteristic of research inherent to most of the process is the necessity to deal with facts and their meanings. This activity is particularly crucial during the data collection and analysis stages. It is here that the researcher must attempt to gather information needed to solve the problem, organize it in meaningful categories, and analyze its significance. Data collected during the library instruction study could include scores on tests, attitudes toward the library, and self-perceptions of library skills.

And last, but not least, the librarian should keep in mind that this process is almost always circular in nature. The researcher's analysis and interpretation of the results of his or her study may well lead to new questions, or fail to answer the original question, thereby starting the research process again. Leedy and Ormrod developed a diagram, reproduced below as Figure 2.1, which helps to illustrate the circular nature of research.[11] As they state, "Every researcher soon learns that genuine research yields as many problems as it resolves. Such is the nature of the discovery of knowledge."[12]

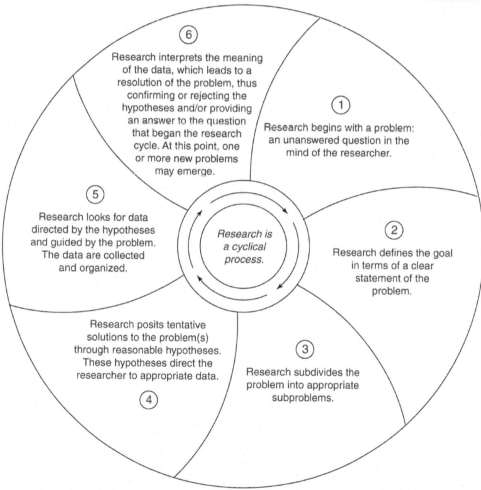

Figure 2.1 The Research Process Is Cyclical. From Leedy, Paul D. & Jeanne E. Ormrod, *Practical Research; Planning and Design,* 8th edition. Published by Allyn and Bacon/Merrill Education, Boston, MA. Copyright © 2005 by Pearson Education. Reprinted by permission of the publisher.

General Criteria for Basic Research

In addition to adhering to a general outline, basic research studies generally should meet certain criteria to qualify as basic or pure research:

1. Universality, which means that the study should be researchable by any other qualified investigator. In other words, another researcher should be able to conduct the study as designed and get essentially the same results as the original researcher would have obtained and also to generalize the results to a comparable situation.

2. Replication, which is related to the criterion of universality. It means that the research study is repeatable. Not only should another competent researcher be able to conduct the study and get essentially the same results, but also should be able to do so time and time again.

3. Control, which relates to the parameters of the research study. This criterion is important for isolating the critical factors and for facilitating replication. As will be emphasized later, control is relatively easy to realize in experimental research and much more difficult, if not impossible, to realize in survey and historical research.

4. Measurement, which constitutes the observation and recording of phenomena. This activity requires, of course, that the data be susceptible to measurement. Measurement (and control) generally is easier to accomplish in physical science research than in the humanities and social science research. The latter typically require more comparative and subjective judgments. Consequently, measurement in the humanities and social sciences is seldom as precise as in the physical and natural sciences.

Hernon categorizes the criteria for basic research into the following five components:

1. Reflective inquiry, which includes a problem statement, a literature review, a theoretical framework, a logical structure, objectives, research questions, and hypotheses (if appropriate);

2. Procedures or research design and data collection methods;

3. Data gathering, processing, and analysis;

4. Reliability and validity, for quantitative studies, and credibility, trustworthiness, transferability, dependability, and confirmability for qualitative studies;

5. Presentation of the research findings.[13]

More specific criteria for basic research are contained in the checklist reproduced on p. 24 as Table 2.1. This checklist refers specifically to research in educational psychology, but most of the criteria can be applied to any basic research in the social sciences. As can be seen, some of the criteria presented here also relate to the feasibility of a research study. For example, the third question asks, "Have you sufficiently limited your problem?" Leedy and Ormrod, in their textbook on research, provide the reader with an Estimation Sheet to

TABLE 2.1   A Checklist for Planning a Research Study*

A. Scope and Definition of Study

1. Is your study related to an educational problem?

2. Is your problem being considered broadly enough?

3. Have you sufficiently limited your problem?

4. Have you made the educational implications of the study clear?

5. Have your decisions benefited by the experiences of investigators who have preceded you?

6. Have you consulted the *Encyclopedia of Educational Research*, the *Handbook of Research on Teaching*, the *Review of Educational Research*, and other background sources?

B. Hypotheses or Questions to Be Answered

1. Are the hypotheses clearly and precisely stated?

2. Are the hypotheses stated in a form that permits them to be tested?

C. Definitions

1. Are concepts adequately and accurately defined?

2. Are your sample and experimental procedures sufficiently described so that another investigator would be able to replicate the study?

3. Do the measurements of variables in the study have validity and reliability?

D. Method of Study

1. Is there a direct relation between the question which the study is trying to answer and the data to be collected?

2. Do you have a plan for securing the data necessary for your study?

3. When more than one investigational approach is available, is it worthwhile to compare the results using different criteria?

4. Can you draw conclusions as to cause and effect from evidence as to relationships from the design employed?

5. How do you propose to select your subjects for study?

E. Design

1. Have you conferred with the persons and/or agencies involved?

2. Is the design of your study clearly formulated?

3. Do you have a PERT chart or a systematic schedule of procedures for the study?

4. Is it feasible to assign subjects randomly to treatment groups?

5. Have you considered the possibility of statistically equating groups on relevant factors?

6. Have you included the most relevant variables in a factorial design so that you can detect interaction among variables?

7. Is your choice of statistical methods the most efficient for the intended purposes?

8. Have you consulted statistics, measurements, and research specialists in the design and analysis of your study?

TABLE 2.1 (Continued)

9. Are there standard library computer programs available for your purposes?

10. Have you determined limitations of time, cost, materials, manpower, instrumentation, and other facilities and extraneous conditions?

11. Have you given consideration to the human and personal relations "side effects?"

F. Sampling

1. Is your sample representative of the group to which you wish to generalize your findings?

2. What factors may be biasing the selection of subjects?

3. Are you taking into account the subgroups in your total sample?

G. Criteria Factors

1. How do you propose to measure achievement, intelligence, attitudes, and interests you plan to investigate?

2. Have you purchased or developed the tests, instruments, and materials needed?

3. Are you going to attempt to ensure that your subjects or judges express their true feelings and attitudes?

4. Have you given sufficient study to determine the best criteria for your study?

5. Have you taken into account the difficulty level and readability of your test for your subjects?

6. If you are using a nonstandardized test, how are you determining its reliability and validity?

7. Have you consulted Buros's *Mental Measurements Yearbook* for critical reviews of standardized measures to be employed in your study?

8. If you plan to use judgments, have you specified the basis on which your judgments would be made?

9. If you plan to use judgments, are you sure your judges have the necessary intelligence, information, background, and other qualifications to permit them to make the judgments?

10. To what extent will bias enter into judgments that you propose to make (or use), and how can these be avoided?

H. Interpretation of Results

1. Have you confined your conclusions to the evidence at hand?

2. Have you tempered your conclusions with the practical meaning of the results as well as with their statistical significance?

3. Have you pointed out implications of the findings for application and for further study?

4. Have you accounted for any inconsistencies and limitations imposed by the methods used?

5. Have you interpreted findings in light of *operational* definitions of variables investigated?

(continued)

TABLE 2.1 (Continued)

I. Preparing the Report

1. Have you described your work clearly in order that, if necessary, it could be replicated by a later investigator?

2. Have you used tabular and graphic methods for presenting the results where possible?

3. Have you supplied sufficient information to permit the reader to verify results and draw his or her own conclusions?

4. Have you plans for publishing your study?

*Adapted from P. M. Symonds, "A Research Checklist in Educational Psychology," *Journal of Educational Psychology* 47 (1959): 101–09; Charles A. Bieking, "Some Uses of Statistics in the Planning of Experiments," *Industrial Quantity Control*, 10 (1954): 23.

Determine the Feasibility of the Research Project (see Figure 2.2 on p. 27).[14] Feasibility is one of the most important questions that the researcher can raise before initiating a study. Consequently, the estimation sheet is reproduced below.

This estimation inventory represents a useful exercise, and it is highly recommended that the would-be researcher work through this, or a similar exercise, before undertaking a research study of any magnitude. Some particularly important practical concerns raised by the feasibility exercise are represented by the questions asking about the aptitudes of the researcher, the availability of data, and the data collection techniques to be used. No matter how potentially worthwhile a research study is, if it cannot be managed, it is not likely to be of any value.

IDENTIFICATION OF THE PROBLEM

The research problem is essentially the topic to be investigated or what needs to be known. It is assumed that one plans a research study because he or she has identified some problem worthy of investigation. In fact, Einstein and Infield have been quoted as saying, "The formulation of a problem is often more essential than its solution."[15] Or as Leedy and Ormrod stated, "The heart of every research project is the problem. It is paramount in importance to the success of the research effort. To see the problem with unwavering clarity and to state it in precise and unmistakable terms is the first requirement in the research process."[16]

But given the primary importance of identifying a problem before conducting research, where and how are problems found? The answer to the first part of this question is that problems are all around us. In response to the second part of the question, we can take a variety of approaches. For example, one important, if not essential, approach toward identifying problems for research in a given field is to develop a thorough knowledge and understanding of that field. More specifically, the would-be researcher should be fully familiar with the known facts and accepted ideas in the field, be knowledgeable of previous, related research in the area, and be aware of gaps in knowledge in the field or unresearched areas.

Figure 2.2. Estimation Sheet to Determine the Feasibility of the Research Project*

The Problem

1. With what area(s) will the problem deal?

   ____ People ____ Things ____ Records ____ Thoughts and ideas ____ Dynamics and Energy

2. Are data that relate directly to the problem available for each of the categories you have just checked?

   Yes ____ No ____.

3. What academic discipline is primarily concerned with the problem?
   _____

4. What other academic disciplines are possibly also related to the problem?
   _____

5. What special aptitude do you have as a researcher for this problem? ____ Interest in the problem ____ Education and/or training ____ Experience in the problem area ____ Other: Specify _____

The Data

6. How available are the data to you? ____ Readily available ____ Available, with permission ____ Available with great difficulty or rarely available ____ Unavailable

7. How often are you personally in contact with the source of the data? ____ Once a day ____ Once a week ____ Once a month ____ Once a year ____ Never

8. Will the data arise directly out of the problem situation? Yes ____ No ____ If your answer is no, where or how will you secure the data?

9. How do you plan to gather the data? ____ Observation ____ Questionnaire ____ Tests or inventories ____ Photocopying of records ____ Interview and tape recording ____ Other (Please Explain): _____

10. Is special equipment or are special conditions necessary for gathering or processing the data? Yes ____ No ____ If your answer is "yes" specify:
    _____

11. If you will need special equipment, do you have access to such equipment and the skill to use it? Yes ____ No ____ If the answer is "no" how do you intend to overcome this difficulty? _____

12. What is the estimated cost in time and money to gather the data?
    _____

13. What evidence do you have that the data you gather will be valid and reliable indicators of the phenomena you wish to study? _____

Criterion-Based Evaluation

14. Does your research project meet the four criteria applicable to all research?

    Universality   ___ Yes___No

    Replication   ___ Yes___No

    Control   ___ Yes___No

    Measurement ___ Yes___No

15. As you review your responses to this checklist, might any of the factors you have just considered, or perhaps any other factors, hinder a successful completion of your research project? Yes ____ No ____

    If your answer is "yes," list those factors. _____

*From Leedy, Paul D. & Jeanne E. Ormrod, *Practical Research; Planning and Design*, 8th edition. Published by Allyn and Bacon/Merrill Education, Boston, MA. Copyright ©2005 by Pearson Education. Reprinted by permission of the publisher.

These objectives can be met, at least in part, by reading published research, which often identifies needed research in the field. Doctoral dissertations are particularly good sources of suggestions for further research. Another potentially useful activity can be the checking of new bibliographies and other lists of related materials. Specific titles can suggest new topics for research.

Domain Assumptions of Research

By Jack D. Glazier

BASIC DOMAIN QUESTIONS

While there are many elements and aspects of the research process that are important to the production of valid and reliable research results, there is one general aspect that tends to be overlooked. That aspect has to do with the domain assumptions that individuals carry into any research project. Domain assumptions are those assumptions that are the most basic and serve to structure individuals' belief systems as well as their lives in general. In structuring belief systems and lives, domain assumptions and the modern concept of research intersect.

Research is a complex undertaking because, whether basic or applied, it is the pursuit of knowledge. The ancient Greeks classified knowledge in two forms—"doxa" or opinion and "episteme" or knowledge or truth. The early Greek philosophers and historians, for the most part, generated "doxa" or opinion. They did so because they relied on speculation and myth as opposed to sensation or experience for their knowledge. This did not mean that they accepted "doxa" as the only legitimate means for knowing the world around them as evidenced by the fact that the Greeks had a separate word, "episteme," that they used for "knowledge or truth." This means that two problems that existed for the ancient Greeks are still relevant for modern researchers. The first problem has to do with the epistemological and ontological assumptions that all researchers carry into their work. The second one is concerned with the meta-theoretical organization, dynamics, and linkages among theories, paradigms, and disciplines.

Before researchers can begin designing research projects, deciding on the methods and methodologies to be employed, and making decisions relative to sample size or strategies, they must first reflect upon their basic epistemological and ontological assumptions. These are the personal assumptions that all researchers and most individuals encounter in the process of figuring out who one really is, what is accepted as knowledge or "episteme," what is opinion or "doxa," and how persons come to know what they think they know. What one believes comprises both how reality is ascertained and the content of such a reality.

These philosophical questions are fundamental to learning and discovery. They are as old as learning itself. But they are also questions to which mankind has been unable to find a single correct answer. They are part of each individual's worldview ("weltanschauung") or belief system that is taken for granted as one goes about his or her daily activities.

However, when it comes to research, one's belief system takes on greater significance because it provides the domain assumptions upon which the work and knowledge of research are based.

Before one examines the nature of epistemology and ontology, consideration must be given to how individuals acquire their belief systems and knowledge. This has implications for researchers in terms of what Camic refers to as the predecessor-selection processes.[1] It also has implications for the formulation of what Mullins calls theory groups and the ultimate emergence of new disciplines.[2]

Individuals acquire knowledge and belief systems from parents, teachers, experiences, and other sources too numerous to list here. Some of this knowledge and the basis for one's value and belief system appear early in life as a result of conditioning and role imitation of parents and siblings and link all phases of one's upbringing.[3] Most of this early knowledge and training is formative and not gained by the choice of the receiver. However, as people grow older they are able to select, within limits, what to learn and from whom.

This selection process is a topic considered in the works of Mullins[4] and Camic.[5] Mullins documents how individuals choose the theories they adopt and how they carry and transmit these to others who in turn carry on the traditions of their predecessors.[6] Camic articulates with more specificity the processes by which scholarly knowledge is transmitted.[7] This transmission, he argues, is driven by rational linkages between concepts and cumulative growth. It is contingent on a "content-fit" that brings together, according to Maines, Bridger, and Ulmer, "scholars [who] purposely select predecessors whose work fits their own intellectual purposes."[8] This relates directly to the development and transmission of theories, paradigms, and disciplines discussed later in this section.

UNDERSTANDING THEORIES OF KNOWLEDGE

Etymology, Nature, and Role of Epistemology and Ontology

The study of knowledge has been referred to since the time of the ancient Greeks as epistemology. The Greek root word for this term is, "episteme," the word used earlier, meaning "knowledge or truth." The suffix "ology" comes from the Greek "logos" meaning "the principle of reason or theory." These elements come together to form the concept of epistemology as "theory of knowledge." Runes formally defines epistemology as, "[t]he origin, structure, methods, and validity of knowledge."[9] However, understanding the etymology and formal definition of the term conveys only limited information about the role of epistemology, the historical and modern range of theories of knowledge, and their impact on research.

Grounding our epistemological perspective is our ontological perspective. The term ontology comes from the Greek words "ontos" meaning "being" and "logos" meaning "theory." "Being" is the extended term with the concept of existence subsumed under it. Together, the word ontology is formed to mean "theory of being or existence." Aristotle argued that this was the First Philosophy—the study of the nature of things. Runes defines ontology as "The science of fundamental principles."[10]

The role of ontology is to serve as the basis for all things including the nature of knowledge. The role of epistemology is to serve as the foundation upon which to build one's knowledge of the world. An individual's ontological perspective must come first, followed by her or his epistemological position. However, as is frequently the case, articulating one requires simultaneously considering the other. In this case, as epistemology is discussed, by necessity so is ontology. This is especially true when the subjective/objective continuum is examined. Ontology not only encompasses the fundamentals of knowledge but also has implications for our understanding of being.

However, it is epistemology that is the foundation of the assumptions that ground the research methodologies that we employ to gather data and that supplies the basis for the means of analysis from which we interpret our data and draw our conclusions. These assumptions are not universals. They can and frequently do differ from individual to individual. As a result, there may be as many interpretations of the meaning of data as there are individuals doing the analysis and interpretation. As sociologist Scott McNall observes, "Just because someone has grown up in society, he is not a qualified interpreter of human experience."[11] And so it is in libraries and library and information science. The very fact that one has been socialized in, or is intimately familiar with, libraries and their ways brings with it certain assumptions and biases that can impede rather than facilitate research related to libraries and matters associated with them.

Subjective/Objective Continuum

The subjective/objective continuum encompasses a broad range of ontological perspectives on knowledge. At one end of the continuum there is pure or radical subjectivism. A radical subjectivist, if there is such a person, believes in a world that is entirely phenomenal (see Figure 1 on page 30). That is, a person understands that a world of objects is a mere projection of the mind and there is no truly external or objective world. The world of reality exists in the mind of the individual. This position is often referred to as "idealism." It is the position of radical subjectivists who pose problems in terms of empirical data gathering for several reasons. First, in an entirely subjective world, how do minds communicate since there is no independent existence? If all a person can know is what is in her or his own mind and everything else is an extension of individual minds, are individuals not truly "islands unto [ourselves]?" Such isolation, according to Runes, is solipsistic to the extent that the individual self is viewed as the whole of reality while others and the external world are only representations of the self with no independent existence.[12] What this implies is that there can be no independent, external sense data to gather and analyze. This is a problem with which philosophers historically have

Figure 1. The Subjective/Objective Continuum.

struggled—the question of a mind/matter duality. In fact, the question becomes, how do we even know that we as individuals exist? This was the question that provoked the famous aphorism by the seventeenth-century philosopher Rene Descartes: "Cogito ergo sum," (I think, therefore I am).

Second, at the other end of the spectrum, is the view of pure or radical objectivism. An individual who would be labeled a radical objectivist believes in a world that is entirely nominal and empirically accessible. This position is often referred to as "materialism." This is a world in which individuals are able to perceive sense data directly and objectively without the interference of personal values or opinions.

However, most modern researchers fall somewhere between the two poles of radical subjectivism and radical objectivism. Most individuals recognize the existence of an external world that can be perceived in the form of sense data. Sense data are data that can be empirically gathered and analyzed, and from which conclusions can be drawn. Still, most also recognize that when a researcher gathers data and begins the process of analysis, that researcher must be aware that he or she carries within himself or herself sets of values and beliefs that influence perception. In other words, what we perceive is filtered through our systems of values and beliefs and to that extent loses some degree of objectivity.

It is this filtering system of which the researcher must first be aware. By understanding personal dynamics and being reflexive (aware of one's self and what is going on in the general proximity and broader contexts which might influence perception), the researcher attempts to limit the extent to which sense data are colored by these personal and proximal influences. Hence, the degree of objectivity that the researcher is able to achieve depends largely on his/her skill at recognizing and limiting subjective or outside influences. As the renowned social psychologist/philosopher Campbell notes, ". . . the goal of objectivity in science is a noble one, and dearly to be cherished. It is in true worship of this goal that we remind our selves that our current views of reality are partial and imperfect."[13]

The second point that must concern the researcher is the transition from sense data to words and concepts. This has to do with what Maines and Chen call "human symbolization."[14] In essence the process begins with the assignment of a symbol or set of symbols to perceived sense data.[15] The symbols become a representation in communication of the elements in sense data. Representations are interpretations by the observer calling for, once again, care in their application. Such representations are a form of communicative action within the context of the social process in what has been described as "structuration."[16] These are first-order symbols that later are translated into second-order symbols in the form of printed or electronic words and concepts; thereby they become critical elements in Habermas's "theory of communicative action."[17] In other words, the assignment of symbols (first-order) to sense data and the late transfer of those symbols to word and concepts (second-order symbols) becomes an important link in the process of social action, an important end for research and society.

However, research by itself is of little value until it is communicated by means of print or other media. Understanding the communication processes is, therefore, an important part of understanding the research process. The application of symbols to sense data supports Maines and Chen's contention that consciousness is a result of social interaction.[18] The assignment of symbols is an important part of the communication process, for without symbols mankind has nothing with which to communicate. Accordingly, Couch argues that "referential symbols designate objects, events, qualities, and sequences."[19] While not limited to vocalizations, referential symbols begin at that point but are further extended to print and other forms of communication relative to research results and processes. It is the pursuit of this goal that is the point of our meticulous efforts to design good research and select appropriate methods and methodologies. It is to this end that the sciences, natural and social, must be committed.

METHODS AND METHODOLOGIES

Etymology and Role of Methods and Methodologies

Understanding what is meant by methods and methodology and the difference between the two is found again in the examination of each term. Method comes from the Greek words "meta" meaning "from or after" and "hodos" meaning "journey." These terms can be understood to mean the "journey or pursuit after or of" some end. Runes defines method as, "Any procedure employed to attain a certain end."[20] In this case, the end is the data to be gathered and the method is the means. However, the habit of referring to research methods and methodologies as interchangeable is misleading.

The term methodology originates with the same Greek terms as the word method. This enables individuals to use the term method as the root word in understanding the intricacies of the broader term methodology. Adding the now familiar Greek suffix "logos" meaning "study, theory, or principle of reason" to the root word "method" leaves the word methodology meaning "a study of the plans which are used to obtain knowledge" as defined by Polkinghorne.[21] Thus, while the term method refers to specific means of collecting data, methodology refers to the strategies surrounding the use of multiple methods of data collection as required by different types of data attempts to achieve higher degrees of reliability and validity. The topics of triangulation and the various types of validity and reliability are covered in more detail elsewhere in this book.

Methods, Methodologies and Theories of Knowledge

The methodological selection of particular data collection methods relies on various criteria. At this juncture, the concern is with the epistemological bases for selection. Earlier, the discussion centered around the extremes of the subjective/objective continuum. However, these only represent theoretical polar extremes and have few operational implications for day-to-day research design and implementation. Now consideration will be extended to both the actual role, historical and present, of epistemological perspectives and the research process.

Historically, arguments concerning what constituted acceptable research centered around the degree of empiricism required. Some ancient Greeks chose to speculate hypothetically on objects of interest to scholars of the time. The subjective aspect of the speculative arts became suspect, tainted by an individual's values and beliefs. Others, particularly Aristotle, attempted to forge links between the more objective empiricism of science and the more subjective speculation of philosophy through the process of systematizing the knowledge of their predecessors. Aristotle accomplished this by utilizing empirical observation, conceptual categorization, and analysis through the development and use of categorical logic.

Many philosophers relied upon what Francis Bacon later formalized as the inductive method for the means of studying nature. It was a method grounded in empiricism and in search of increased objectivity, through empirical data gathering and generalization or extrapolation. Extrapolation, then, became a key element in the reemergence of a predictive natural science that relies upon strict objectivity. This was the deductive method. Many natural and social scientists now rely on the scientific method, (i.e., deductive research as discussed in more detail in this book).

The pursuit of objectivity became reified as the scientific method became widely used, leaving its proponents little tolerance for other, more subjective methods of gathering data. This was the position of the positivists who sought to rely on the most objective methods available and the logic that converted language into a mathematical form, abandoning emotion as subjective, noninformative, and purely emotive.

Positivism with its formal origins in the works of Comte in the mid-nineteenth century emerged in the twentieth century as modernism. It is characterized as structured, rigid, and highly rational. It revered the natural sciences for their certainty and rationality. However, the modernist tradition was marked by the emergence of multiple, rival paradigms to challenge the hegemony of positivism. Out of this came a theoretical, multidisciplinary synthesis that became known as postmodernism. It is characterized by its theoretical flexibility and pluralistic paradigms.

The differences among the belief systems and methodological debates involving positivism, modernism, and the postmodern movement occur within the framework of the distinction between the Greek terms "episteme" and "doxa." The term "episteme" comes from two terms: "epi" meaning "upon" and "(hi)stanai" meaning "to stand, or something on which we can stand, certainty and knowledge." The second term, "doxa," means "opinion or belief." In other words, "doxa" is "what we believe is true" and "episteme" is "what we know is true." "Episteme" is representative of positivism just as "doxa" is representative of postmodernism. In addition, the change in emphasis from a more positivist orientation to a more postmodern orientation involves a return to more inductive approaches to research.

Objectivity preoccupied the positivists, while more subjective perspectives were increasingly prevalent during the modern and postmodern periods from which many of the newer methodological approaches have emerged. First, keep in mind that when trends regarding the legitimacy of various types of knowledge (objective/ subjective) are considered, it is not the continuum's extremes that are being discussed. The methodological implications being considered here are to be viewed from a more generalist perspective. Second, if a theoretical exemplar of postmodernism were to be held up, constructionism might be a key. Constructionism is consistent with more subjective paradigms and methodological approaches. And, as in the case of symbolic interactionism, both qualitative (i.e., more subjective) and more quantitative (i.e., more objective or less subjective) approaches emphasize that the same theoretical paradigm can spawn multiple methodologies. Both quantitative (e.g., surveys, experiments) and qualitative (e.g., participant observation, interviews) methods are discussed in detail in this text.

DISCIPLINES, PARADIGMS, AND THEORIES

History and Context of Paradigmatic Change

Disciplines, paradigms, and theories are social constructions. They are not epiphenomenal in their origins. They are creations of scholars and theorists. They are not independent beings with lives separate from their creators. It is the reification of these concepts and the processes by which they are created and perpetuated that capture our attention here.

Numerous historians and sociologists of science have addressed these issues. Among the better known have been Thomas Kuhn, Nicholas Mullins, Charles Camic, and Stephen J. Gould. It is, however, Thomas Kuhn's formulation that has been more widely discussed, and he is best known for his views on paradigmatic revolution.[22] While Kuhn's position is not consistent with the one proposed here, he makes some important observations and is a good example of the dialectical process that occurs through intellectual exchanges.

Kuhn argues that paradigmatic revolutions are episodes, "in which a scientific community abandons one time-honored way of regarding the world . . . in favor of another, usually incompatible approach to its discipline."[23] He suggests that it is these "revolutionary episodes" that advance science. The process, he argues, is a competition for domination of a particular discipline. His argument begins with the acknowledgement that scholars tend to congregate in ideological communities or as Mullins noted, "theory groups." These are communities/groups in which members define themselves and are defined by others as being uniquely responsible for a specific set of shared goals, values, methods, and means of socialization.[24] The socialization processes include training their successors by passing on the rituals, myths, heroes, and traditions of the community. Thus, Kuhn's view that "[p]aradigms are something shared by members of such groups" becomes significant.[25]

In essence, Kuhn argues that paradigms are ways of collecting and understanding the nature of sense data. This is a process composed of the collection, understanding, and translation of sense data into theories and theories into paradigms that become a structuring device for understanding future data. This process is what he called the maturation of a paradigm. For Kuhn, "What changes with the transition to maturity is not the presence of a paradigm but rather its nature."[26]

When change comes for a mature paradigm, it does not come incrementally but in the form of a radical change—a revolution. Kuhn defines a revolution as "a special sort of change involving a certain sort of reconstructing of group commitments."[27] For example, Kuhn would argue that Einstein's theory of relativity was a revolutionary paradigmatic change within physics. This type of change is defined as revolutionary because it involves a sudden, unexpected change in the basic assumptions and theories grounding what was then Newtonian physics. While it was an extraordinary situation, Einstein's discovery was preceded by various theories regarding quantum mechanics and other foundational work in the general area of relativity that prepared the scientific community for Einstein's formulation. Hence, the ensuing reconstruction was less radical than we tend to recognize.

The processes associated with innovation tend to be dialectical in nature. Innovation builds on existing knowledge. New ideas are combined with existing belief systems, resulting in a synthetic concept. This is an incremental process with new ideas being introduced in cloistered intellectual environments until a new paradigm and the public are ready for its introduction.

In actuality, the dynamics of innovation tend to be incremental for utilitarian reasons. The process itself is gradual in nature. Discoveries often are limited in scope because researchers work in narrow environments. Next is the dialectical stage in which the new discoveries are interpreted in light of existing facts and circumstances, producing innovation. Finally, if people are not prepared for an innovation, if they cannot imagine it as possible, they will not intellectually invest in it. It will be simply viewed as an anomaly. Acceptance comes much more readily if people are prepared for change.

A familiar example of change that was slow to be accepted was the introduction of the online public access catalog (OPAC). The technology was available long before it was introduced in libraries on a large scale. In those communities that were gradually prepared for the move from the card catalog to the OPAC, the introduction was more easily accepted. It also helped that most communities operated both systems until patrons became familiar with using the new technology and that the International Standard Bibliographic Description (ISBD) record structure was familiar to patrons. Those who moved too fast with the introduction of the technology encountered much more resistance from patrons and others than those who were more deliberate.

Other examples of change introduced through technology are self check service for patrons and in some libraries the removal of the reference desk in favor of a more flexible and fluid staffing model, identified here as the "roving librarian" model. Libraries that planned for the implementation of these new models using lessons learned from earlier technological implementations found library staff members more accepting of the new services. In other words, the lessons learned from the adoption of earlier technologies pave the way for later innovations.

While innovation is viewed here as dialectical and incremental, it may appear to the public as revolutionary at first. It is also defined by most as progress. This is a value judgment that Gould argues is a bias of our species.[28] His argument begins with a criticism of the view that Darwinism is evolutionary in an upward cycle with Homo sapiens at the top of the hierarchy. This, he argues rightly, is an egocentric tendency that allows our bias to influence the interpretation of sense data. The data indicate that there are numerous species that change at their own rate and according to their needs without an innate natural order that favors mankind. Change is change for its own sake and out of necessity for survival based on its environment. This is the case with disciplines, paradigms, and theories. They change in response to their environments, which are socially constructed. The idea that the dynamic of change is progress implies an egocentric social construction. Change is the response to environmental variables and whether it betters our situation is a value judgment.

Another Perspective on the Emergence of New Paradigms and Disciplines

One way of looking at disciplinary development and change that is less value laden is to understand it as an incremental social process that can be analyzed and understood in terms of social theory. The following formulation has emerged out of the works of Kuhn, Mullins, Grover and Glazier; Powell and DiMaggio; Glazier and Hall and Glazier and Grover.[29] However, Mullins's seminal work on theory and theory groups as well as Powell and DiMaggio's work on the new institutionalism were central in formulating the general thesis presented here.

To begin, theories, paradigms, and disciplines, though reified, are merely labels we place on individuals so we can categorize their interests and beliefs.[30] Theories are no more than the people who develop them and believe in them. As with theories, paradigms are no more than the individuals who construct and subscribe to them. They are each comprised of people interacting with others. The unit of analysis is people and their social relationships. They are not ethereal phenomena that can be studied and understood as abstract entities. This having been said, we will now begin what will at the outset appear to be an abstract analysis of the dynamics of disciplines, paradigms, and theories. However, we should again remember that what we will actually be talking about are people, their relationships, and social constructions that structure their relationships.

The process of structuring the social constructions which enable research is referred to as "structuration" by Giddens.[31] This process of structuring phenomena in the form of the self and society; social and individual knowledge; and, discovered and undiscovered knowledge produces the context for the work of individuals as they endeavor to explain the conceptualization of the sense data they encounter as they go about both their daily activities and their specialized activities in the form of research. Glazier and Grover further argue that theories, paradigms, and, eventually, disciplines emanate from a context of these socially constructed arenas of knowledge discovery and production.[32]

As these dynamics work themselves out, often in the form of scholarly research which results in the theories that scholars come to represent, they are drawn together into what Mullins calls theory groups.[33] It is these theories which are the seeds of new divergent paradigms. Divergent paradigms are the products of initial research which is sporadic and yields loosely coupled, disorganized, and often inconsistent theories.[34] This is referred to as internal divergence. (See Figure 2 on page 37.)

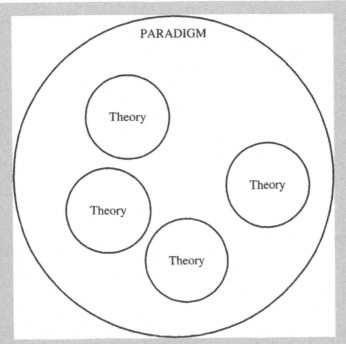

Figure 2. Paradigm Internal Divergence.

As research proceeds, the theories that make up each paradigm become more consistent, more organized, and more tightly coupled. This is referred to as internal convergence. (See Figure 3 below.)

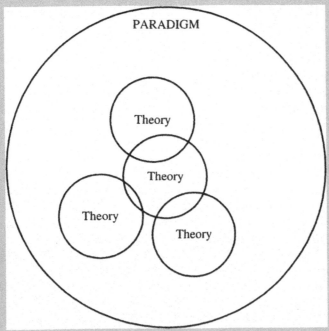

Figure 3. Paradigm Internal Convergence.

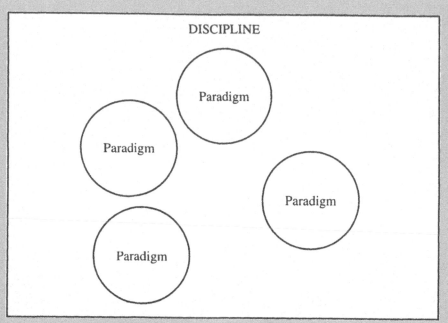

Figure 4. Discipline Internal Divergence.

Convergence yields planned research agendas and broader ranges of theorizing, resulting in the emergence of new paradigms. The more theories converge, the more consistent the paradigms. Again, initially these paradigms are externally divergent. The relations between divergent paradigms can be characterized as loosely coupled, accompanied by a high degree of environmental ambiguity, and generally lacking external consistency (see Figure 4 above). These relations also reflect the internal structure of divergent paradigms relative to their constituent theories discussed above.

It is important to keep in mind at this point that a paradigm is "a framework of basic assumptions with which perceptions are evaluated and relationships are delineated and applied to a discipline or profession."[35] The danger of studying paradigms is that they tend to become reified and treated as though they had a life of their own. They have a life only in the sense that their proponents use them to orient and direct their work.

Internal and external divergence and convergence of theories and paradigms are not the result of "natural law" or mystical force. Theoretical and paradigmatic change and organization are the result of the work of individual researchers and teachers working collectively or privately. Organizations are created between these loosely knit individuals and groups through both formal and informal communication. As a result, many of the same principles that we apply to the study of organizations and collectives are applicable here. In this case, the organizations and collectives are identified by the paradigms they employ. Dynamics such as power, resource allocation and dependency, socialization, environmental ambiguity, values, negotiated order, and dialectical relations are useful in understanding the political and social aspects of paradigms as organizational entities.

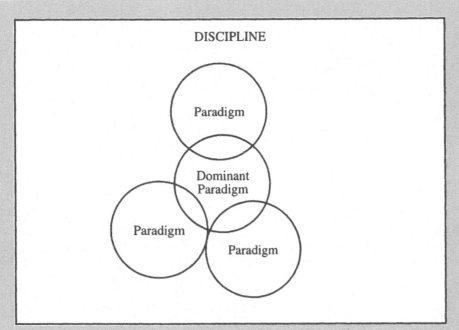

DISCIPLINE

Paradigm

Dominant
Paradigm

Paradigm

Paradigm

Figure 5. Discipline Internal Convergence.

The internal convergence of a paradigm is characterized by increased political and intellectual influence in the discipline in question (see Figure 5 above). Fully internally and externally convergent paradigms are what Kuhn refers to as mature paradigms.[36]

This convergence is based on the perceived degree of higher internal consistency and its increased ability to gain agreement to explain a given state of affairs or set of variables. The increase in influence of a paradigm means an increase in the power of the proponents of the paradigm to control vital resources, disciplinary norms, and definition of disciplinary and paradigmatic boundaries. When this level of influence is achieved and a paradigm has achieved its maximum degree of maturity, it is said to be the dominant paradigm in a discipline.

At this point in the development of a discipline, the emergence of a dominant paradigm tends to coincide with a general external convergence of other paradigms such as the information transfer paradigm in the discipline around that dominant paradigm. Such a state of general convergence can be methodological, ideological or both. While, in this case, the dominant paradigm tends to be more quantitatively oriented, emphasizing a systems perspective, subordinate paradigms tend to be more qualitatively oriented (though not exclusively) emphasizing the individual needs of the patrons. Most paradigms within the discipline do not give up their own identities. Subordinate paradigms continue to work out their theoretical inconsistencies through increased research while acknowledging the superordinate position of the dominant paradigm in the discipline. These processes relative to subordinate paradigms are characteristic of a state of internal divergence, until they are able to achieve internal convergence.

Disciplinary Dynamics Components

The tendency of external convergence can be best explained by viewing the discipline in social organizational terms. The discipline can be viewed as analogous to an organizational field and the various paradigms in the discipline would be viewed as one might view the organizations in an organizational field.

Organizational behavior under situations of stress that tend to be present when environmental ambiguity is present cause some notable patterns of organizational field structuration. In other words, divergent paradigms in a discipline behave in a fashion similar to organizations in an organizational field in which there is little leadership to assure needed resources. As convergence takes place over time, a dominant paradigm will frequently emerge that promotes disciplinary stability by bringing other paradigms in the discipline into conformity with the dominant paradigm.

Conformity is facilitated by resource dependency of subordinate paradigms to the dominant paradigm (in some cases multiple dominant paradigms). Resource dependency stems from dominant paradigms having proponents serving as editors and referees of important disciplinary journals, having proponents in control of key departmental positions at universities, and having proponents in positions in foundations that supply grant monies for research. All of these are resources that lend legitimacy and power to the dominant paradigm.

When applied to a discipline, the result is that proponents of alternative paradigms in the discipline are forced into conformity with the dominant paradigm. This is based on a perceived asymmetry of power favoring the proponents of the dominant paradigm. This power differentiation can be the result of inequities in the distribution and control of resources as well as other perceived power structures favoring proponents of the dominant paradigm. Hence, if one wants to get articles published in mainstream journals, or gain faculty and research positions at top universities and foundations, or get the grants that are the lifeblood of research, he or she must conform by acknowledging the gatekeeper role of proponents of the dominant paradigm.

Conformity is usually voluntary and frequently unconscious since most of those in the discipline have been socialized in light of the ideologies of the dominant paradigm. To resist conforming yields environmental ambiguity and uncertainty within the discipline. Conformity occurs when other paradigms echo the dominant paradigm by adopting similar methodologies and ideologies in order to receive favorable treatment in resource allocations or institutional appointments and so forth.

The final component of conformity to be discussed here is socialization of discipline members. Socialization occurs when the values, norms, and standards of the other paradigms are brought into conformity with the perceived definitions of values, norms, and standards of the dominant paradigm. This is evidenced in the control of the processes of socialization through education of a majority of the members of a discipline. These are the dynamics and processes in which member paradigms in a discipline conform to the dominant paradigm's definitions of the appropriate values, ideologies, and individual boundaries.

Conformity is viewed as the external convergence of the various paradigms in a discipline. However, the dominance of any individual paradigm is not necessarily assured for an indefinite length of time. This is because other variables besides internal convergence affect the dominance of any given paradigm. Those variables can include the perceived dominance of one discipline over another, the amount of ambiguity and environmental turbulence between disciplines, and the values acknowledged by disciplines. When definitions cease to be shared, external convergence is likely to dissolve into external divergence among member paradigms.

Divergence will tend to remain until another paradigm asserts its dominance. Theoretically, all paradigms in a discipline could be convergent to such a degree that zero growth is being experienced by the paradigm or the discipline as a whole. Zero growth, however, seems highly unlikely because of the number of variables involved. It is conceivable that when a dominant paradigm is experiencing zero growth, it is in such a strong position of dominance that the discipline as a whole may experience paradigmatic divergence yet not be able to gain dominance. If multiple, highly divergent paradigms continue to vie for disciplinary dominance, structural conditions develop that require one to give way to the other, or more likely, one will split from the existing discipline to establish a new discipline (for example, the separation of the natural sciences from philosophy).

SUMMARY

In our efforts to gain increasingly higher levels of objectivity, we must remain vigilant relative to our own inner subjective selves. We accomplish this by being as aware and reflexive as possible. We cannot deny our own belief and value systems, but we can control for them. We are aware of the role epistemology and ontology play in helping to locate ourselves ideologically with respect to the selection of research methodologies and specific methods as ways of controlling outside variables. This process is supplemented by sampling and other strategies for methodological selection discussed elsewhere in this book.

Finally, we began by locating the role of research in the process of theorizing. The role of theorizing also is dealt with in other sections of this text. However, research is a part of the context of paradigms and disciplines which tend to be self-structuring and self-reproducing. And as paradigms change so, too, do disciplines. These changes frequently come in the form of observable behaviors that can be studied using social science technologies. Theories, paradigms, and disciplines present observable behaviors because they are represented by individuals and groups which interact socially and, hence, have observable behaviors. These behaviors can be studied using social science methods and frequently understood using social science concepts and theories.

This approach to research is about change and innovation, which are the basis and reason for research in general. However, it is important to remember that change does not necessarily mean progress but only that some degree of difference is discernible. To make judgments beyond the fact that change has taken place is, as Gould reminds us, "egregiously biased."[37]

NOTES

1. Charles Camic, "Reputation and Predecessor Selection: Parsons and the Institutionalists," *American Sociological Review* 57 (1992): 421–45.

2. Nicholas Mullins, *Theories and Theory Groups in Contemporary American Sociology* (New York: Harper and Row, 1973).

3. Charles H. Cooley, *Human Nature and the Social Order* (New York: Schocken, 1964).
James M. Baldwin, *The Mental Development in the Child and the Race* (New York: Macmillan, 1906).
James M. Baldwin, *Social and Ethical Interpretations in Mental Development* (New York: Macmillan, 1907).
Sigmund Freud, *The Future of an Illusion* (Garden City, NY: Doubleday Anchor, 1961).
George H. Mead, *Mind, Self and Society* (Chicago: University of Chicago Press, 1962).

4. Mullins, *Theories and Theory Groups.*

5. Camic, "Reputation and Predecessor Selection."

6. Mullins, *Theories and Theory Groups.*

7. Camic, "Reputation and Predecessor Selection."

8. David R. Maines, Jeffery C. Bridger, and Jeffery T. Ulmer, "Mythic Facts and Park's Pragmatism: On Predecessor-Selection and Theorizing in Human Ecology," *Sociological Quarterly* 37 (Summer 1969): 521.

9. Dagobert D. Runes, ed., *The Dictionary of Philosophy* (New York: Citadel Press, 2001), 167.

10. Ibid., 388.

11. Scott G. McNall, *The Sociological Experience* (Boston: Little, Brown and Company, 1969), 3.

12. Dagobert D. Runes, ed., *Dictionary of Philosophy* (Totowa, NY: Little field, Adams and Company, 1962).

13. Donald T. Campbell, "Evolutionary Epistemology," in *The Philosophy of Popper*, ed. P. A. Schilpp (LaSalle, IL: Open Court, 1974), 447.

14. David R. Maines and Shing-Ling Chen, "Information and Action: An Introduction to Carl Couch's Analysis of Information Technologies," in *Information Technologies and Social Orders*, ed. Carl J. Couch (New York: Aldine de Gruyter, 1996).

15. Jack D. Glazier and Robert Grover, "A Multidisciplinary Framework for Theory Building," *Library Trends* 50 (Winter 2002): 317–29.

16. Anthony Giddens, *The Constitution of Society: Outline of the Theory of Structuration* (Cambridge, England: Polity, 1984).

17. Jurgen Habermas, *The Theory of Communicative Action*, vol. 1, *Reason and the Rationalization of Society* (Boston: Beacon, 1984).

18. Maines and Chen, "Information and Action."

19. Carl J. Couch, *Information Technologies and Social Orders* (New York: Aldine de Gruyter, 1996), 3.

20. Runes, *The Dictionary of Philosophy*, 346.

21. Donald Polkinghorne, *Methodology for the Human Sciences: Systems of Inquiry* (Albany: State University of New York Press, 1983), 5.

22. Thomas S. Kuhn, *The Structure of Scientific Revolutions* (Chicago: University of Chicago Press, 1970).

23. Thomas S. Kuhn, *The Essential Tension: Selected Studies in Scientific Tradition and Change* (Chicago: University of Chicago Press, 1977), 226.

24. Mullins, *Theories and Theory Groups.*

25. Kuhn, *The Structure of Scientific Revolutions*, 178.

26. Ibid., 179.

27. Ibid., 180–81.

28. Stephen J. Gould, *Full House: The Spread of Excellence from Plato to Darwin* (New York: Harmony Books, 1996).

29. Kuhn, *The Structure of Scientific Revolutions*, 180–81.

Kuhn, *The Essential Tension*, 226.

Mullins, *Theories and Theory Groups.*

Robert J. Grover and Jack D. Glazier, "A Conceptual Framework for Theory Building in Library and Information Science," *Library & Information Science Research* 8 (1986): 237–42.

Walter W. Powell and Paul J. DiMaggio, *The New Institutionalism in Organizational Analysis* (Chicago: University of Chicago Press, 1991).

Jack D. Glazier and Peter M. Hall, "Constructing Isomorphism in an Interorganizational Network" *Humboldt Journal of Social Relations* 22 (1996): 47–62.

Glazier and Grover, "A Multidisciplinary Framework for Theory Building," 317–29.

30. Ibid.

31. Giddens, *The Constitution of Society,* 376.

32. Grover and Glazier, "A Proposed Taxonomy of Theory," 234.

33. Mullins, *Theories and Theory Groups.*

34. Glazier and Grover, "A Multidisciplinary Framework for Theory Building," 317–29.

35. Grover and Glazier, "A Proposed Taxonomy of Theory," 234.

36. Kuhn, *The Structure of Scientific Revolutions.*

37. Gould, *Full House,* 14.

Other "techniques" which can be used to identify research topics or problems include disagreeing with some previous research and developing a study to test its findings, becoming involved in the design and development of research tools and techniques relevant to some area of interest, and attempting to deal with actual problems in real work situations (this last approach is more likely to lead to applied research, however). Networking, or sharing ideas and information, with colleagues can be a very productive activity as well.

But perhaps the two best methods for identifying research topics or problems simply involve being curious about items of interest and being a clear and critical reader and thinker. For again, research problems abound and one simply needs to recognize them. And only by being a curious, critical observer is one likely to do so with any regularity.

Characteristics of a Problem Suitable for Basic Research

In order to be suitable for basic research, a problem should exhibit several characteristics. First, the problem should represent conceptual thinking, inquiry, and insight—not merely activity. For example, simply collecting data and making comparisons are not activities representative of true research problems. Activities such as studying a subject field and reading earlier research are more likely to be indicative of a conceptually developed research problem.

Second, the variables related to the problem should represent some sort of meaningful relationship. The study of miscellaneous, unrelated facts is not likely to be true research, though it may lead to true research. For example, a tabulation of library circulation statistics is nothing more than a series of calculations, which at best may provide the basis for a thorough categorization of such statistics. On the other hand, if the circulation librarian wonders about the nature of the relationship between certain circulation statistics and certain user characteristics, he or she may in effect be conducting exploratory research and be well on the way to identifying a problem for more formal research.

Inherent in a problem representing some kind of relationship between two or more variables is consideration of the cause of the relationship. If evidence suggests, for example, a relationship between the level of college library use and the class level of student users, why does such a relationship exist? Why does a higher class level seem to "cause" greater use of the library? Again, what is the nature of the relationship, and does the research problem incorporate this concern? Or, if there is not a causal relationship between the variables, how are they related, if at all? To answer this, the problem must reflect some interpretation of the relationship. For example, perhaps the variables are not related directly but indirectly, through the influence of yet another variable or variables. Only a problem represented by a conceptual, insightful development and statement will be able to lead to this kind of understanding.

There are also several more practical considerations that the researcher should make before settling on a specific problem. Among these is the researcher's interest in the problem. Does it represent a topic that he or she is likely to enjoy researching after several months, if not years, of study? This is a question that is particularly important for doctoral students to ask of themselves.

Does the problem represent an area of research that is reasonably new? Does anyone have a prior claim to the area? Again, this is of particular concern to doctoral students. However, a problem does not have to be entirely new and unresearched in order to be worthy of investigation. Some of the most important research builds on and improves or refines previous research. The degree of uniqueness desired will depend, in part, on the purpose of the research.

More important is the question of whether the research will contribute to the knowledge of the field and ultimately have some impact, or does the problem represent a trivial question of no real importance? Again, whether the research should make a significant contribution to the field is determined in part by the purpose of the research. For example, if it is intended solely to meet the requirements for a doctoral dissertation, perhaps some justification can be made for emphasizing the design and conduct of the research over its likely contribution to knowledge of the field.

Last, but not least, the problem should point to research that is manageable. In short, is the problem researchable? Due to real constraints, such as time and money, perfectly designed research is not always possible. The researcher typically is in the position of having to compromise what is ideal and what is practicable. This is particularly true of research which is relatively applied in nature. As Martyn and Lancaster stated, "In any investigation within a library or information center, some compromises may be necessary between what is most desirable from the investigator's viewpoint and what appears feasible to the manager of the service."[17]

Statement of the Problem

Having identified a suitable problem for research, the next logical step is to write a statement of it for future reference. Perhaps it goes without saying, but the problem should be written in complete, grammatical sentences, not in mere phrases. For example, the problem statement, "library instruction and library use," would be better expressed as "The problem to be resolved is whether providing college students with library instruction will have some effect on their use of the library." The problem should be written as clearly as possible, and it should be stated in straightforward, unambiguous terms; vague terms and clichés are to be avoided.

In addition, the problem should be stated as precisely as possible. There should be no discrepancy between what the researcher writes and what he or she actually means. The problem statement should be both specific and explicit. Since this statement should guide all of the research that follows, it is essential that it be well developed and clearly expressed. In order to achieve an appropriately stated problem, it is a good idea to edit the problem statement as initially written, at least once, in order to eliminate needless or ambiguous words and to increase its precision and clarity.

As suggested by the characteristics of a researchable problem, it is also important that it be stated responsibly. It should not be so broad in scope that it will be unmanageable. For example, the problem statement just given was, "whether providing college students with library instruction will have some effect on their use of the library." While this was seen as an improvement on the preceding phrase, in light of our criteria for a suitable statement, it still needs work. Though it seems reasonably clear, it should be more precise or specific and thereby more manageable. An improved problem statement might be: The problem to be resolved by this study is whether the frequency of library use of first-year college students given course-integrated library instruction is different from the frequency of library use of first-year college students not given course-integrated library instruction.

Some research methods textbooks indicate that the research problem may be written as a question and/or as a purpose statement.[18] The view of this textbook is that a research question is typically more precise and specific than a problem statement and that the purpose and problem for a research study are not interchangeable. As Hernon stated, "Many studies published in LIS do not contain a problem statement or confuse such a statement with a statement of purpose."[19] The issue of absent or incomplete problem statements was mentioned again by Hernon and Schwartz in 2007. Based on lectures by David Clark, they suggest writing three, short sentences: "(1) the lead-in, (2) a statement about originality, and (3) a justification."[20] The *problem* is what the research is about and the *purpose* is why the research is conducted. The problem is in effect "the first proposition."[21] For example, one might conduct research on the relationship between certain teaching methods and the effectiveness of bibliographic instruction (the problem) in order to increase the success of future bibliographic instruction programs (the purpose).

Identifying Subproblems

Virtually all problems contain components or subproblems, which should be appropriate for study, if not solution. Subproblems can facilitate resolving a large problem piecemeal, as they are often more manageable or researchable than the general problem and can be investigated separately. They should be amenable to some realistic research method and suggest adequate data with which to resolve the problem. The interpretation of the data within each subproblem must be apparent. It should not be necessary to go outside the parameters of the study as dictated by the focus of the subproblem in order to relate data to the subproblem.

In addition, the subproblems should, when combined, equal the whole of the main problem. On the other hand, the subproblems should not add up to more than the totality of the main problem. If they do, it is likely that the main problem actually represents more than one problem. While rules of thumb should be used with caution, most well-defined research problems can be broken down into between two to six subproblems. More than that may suggest that the main problem was too broadly or vaguely conceived.

Another possible explanation for an excess of subproblems may be that some of the subproblems are in fact what Leedy and Ormrod have labeled "pseudo-subproblems."[22] While related to the study, pseudosubproblems are more procedural in nature and do not actually relate to the conceptual matters raised by the problem. They often arise from such questions as how to select the sample or how to observe certain phenomena. For example, the question of how to *measure* library use as included in the earlier example of a problem would be more of a pseudo- than a true subproblem. It is more methodological than conceptual, though the distinction is sometimes fine, as is the case here.

Actually, identifying subproblems is generally a relatively straightforward process involving two basic, related steps: (1) the researcher should break the main problem down into its components, and (2) he or she should identify the words that indicate a need for the collection and interpretation of data. In order to illustrate this process, let us return to the last formulation of the problem. It was as follows:

> The problem to be resolved by this study is whether the frequency of library use of first-year college students given course-integrated library instruction is different from the frequency of library use of first-year college students not given course-integrated library instruction.

In analyzing this problem statement, one can see that there are three components that will require investigation before the main problem can be resolved. These three subproblems can be written as follows:

1. What is the frequency of library use of the first-year college students who did receive course-integrated library instruction?
2. What is the frequency of library use of the first-year college students who did *not* receive course-integrated library instruction?
3. What is the difference in the frequency of library use between the two groups of students?

As is commonly done, these subproblems have been posed as questions. Again, they are questions that must be answered before the main, more complex problem can be resolved. In many studies, the researcher will attempt to do no more than answer one or two subproblems or research questions; additional studies may be necessary to deal with the entire problem.

Having identified and stated what hopefully is a satisfactory research problem, the investigator must next turn his or her attention to providing further guidance for the study. For example, the researcher should indicate precisely the limitations of the problem, which in turn help to limit the goals of the study. Limitations implicit in the problem statement given above include the fact that it is concerned with the frequency of library use, not quality. It is concerned with course-integrated library instruction as opposed to the many other types that could have been considered.

The researcher should also consider providing both conceptual and operational definitions for important terms related to the study, particularly if they are used in an unusual sense or can be interpreted in more than one way. This procedure will be covered in more detail later, but, generally speaking, this step is necessary in order to indicate how certain terms are to be used by the researcher in relation to his or her study.

Further delineation of the problem can be achieved by stating assumptions, or what the researcher takes for granted. Returning to our problem on library instruction, the researcher appears to be assuming, for example, that those persons teaching the library instruction can in fact teach. The quality of their teaching is not something that will be tested in the study.

Finally, when feasible, the researcher should develop one or more hypotheses to further limit the problem and project. Development of the hypothesis, as well as identification of the basic assumptions, will be treated in greater depth later in the text.

THE ROLE OF THEORY IN THE DESIGN OF RESEARCH

Before taking up assumptions and hypotheses, we should consider the role of theory in the design of a research study. But before discussing theory, the term, metatheory, should be considered briefly although it does not appear much in LIS literature. "Metatheory can be seen as the philosophy behind the theory, the fundamental set of ideas about how phenomena of interest in a particular field should be thought about and researched."[23] Paradigm, as presented by Kuhn in the field of science, is closely related to metatheory.[24] Theory or theory construction, however, is the first major component of the scientific method of inquiry. It tends to be the base from which the subsequent stages of the scientific method flow. But exactly how does theory fit into or affect this process? An understanding of how a field of knowledge develops should help to explain the role of theory in the design of research.

As Goldhor and others have explained, a field of knowledge usually develops in a logical sequence of three stages.[25] The first stage typically involves the accumulation of specific facts regarding a variety of isolated phenomena. These facts are derived from actual experience or the observation of certain activities. The specific facts are usually historical or descriptive in nature and are unlikely to be quantitative. Bates refers to this and subsequent stages as "description, prediction, explanation."[26]

The second main stage typically involves the definition, review, and classification of these existing facts or data into a meaningful set of categories, a procedure that will be covered in more detail later. In this stage Bates believes "it should be possible to predict relationships, processes, or sequences associated with the phenomenon."[27] It is also worth noting that it is essential that the observations which produce the data be categorized as accurately as possible. The categorization can be improved or made more precise by quantifying the data to the greatest extent possible. For example, data relating to library use are difficult to classify if subjective in nature, but once they have been quantified in terms of frequency of use, number of books checked out, number of reference questions asked, and so on, it is a relatively simple, straightforward process to classify them.

Related to the simplification of complex phenomena, classification of the data can help to point out gaps in the existing knowledge. In attempting to observe and categorize all of the various activities that constitute library use, it is conceivable that the researcher may identify certain activities that represent heretofore unrecognized types of library use, or at least variants of already identified library use activities. For example, in studying the use of an academic library, the researcher may discover that part-time students use the library somewhat differently than do full-time students. Such knowledge could have important ramifications for the library's services and policies.

The classification of existing data can also help to identify relationships between various categories within the classification scheme. The formulation and testing of these groupings of data, or variables, make up the third main stage in the development of a field of knowledge. At this stage one should be able to develop a theory,[28] which can be considered the formal research stage of a discipline. Years ago Goldhor stated that this is probably the stage at which library and information science exists.[29] Goldhor's statement is still supported by Kim and Jeong, who conducted "a content analysis of 1661 articles in four LIS journals from 1984–2003" to identify the number and quality of articles that have contributed to the development or use of theory.[30] Forty-one percent of the articles were identified as contributing to or using theory. (The majority of these articles addressed the topics of information seeking, use, and retrieval.)

But to return to the original question, how does theory fit into the scheme of things? In fact, theory plays a crucial role in the just-mentioned research stage, which in turn often utilizes the scientific method of inquiry. Theory helps to make research more productive in that it organizes a number of "unassorted facts, laws, concepts, constructs, and principles into a meaningful and manageable form."[31] Or, as Goldhor observed, theory can explain a group of phenomena, suggest relationships between facts, structure concepts, organize facts into a meaningful pattern, and provide logical explanations for facts.[32] If certain facts or variables appear to be causally related, theory can help to explain the nature of the relationship.

Theory also can act as a guide to discovering facts. It identifies gaps to be investigated, crucial aspects on which to focus, and major questions to be answered. In short, theory can stimulate research in areas that warrant study.[33] The research can, in turn, develop new theories or improve existing ones. Theory also can help to connect studies and facilitate the interpretation of the larger meaning of research findings.

In addition, theory helps to produce an economy of research effort. It can be used to identify the most important and/or manageable propositions for testing, define and limit the area of research, and relate the research to other relevant studies. Theory can provide an economical or simple summary of actual or anticipated research results.[34] In short, the main value of theory in research derives from its ability to "summarize existing knowledge, to provide an explanation for observed events and relationships, and to predict the occurrence of as yet unobserved events and relationships on the basis of the explanatory principles embodied in the theory."[35]

Definition of Theory

Having determined the role and value of theory in research, it should be relatively easy to define. Babbie defines theory as "a systematic explanation for the observations that relate to a particular aspect of life."[36] It also has been defined as something which interrelates a set or sets of variables on the basis of the rules of logic. In a workshop for health science librarians, Marshall described a theory as "A set of related propositions that suggest why events occur in the manner that they do. The propositions that make up theories are of the same form as hypotheses; they consist of concepts and the linkages or relationships between them."[37] McGrath defines theory as "an explanation for a quantifiable phenomenon."[38] It can also be thought of as a unified explanation for discrete observations. Goldhor defines theory as "a deductively connected set of laws, in the logical form of an explanation and with all statements as generalizations."[39]

Goldhor goes on to point out that those laws (hypotheses whose validity is relatively established) that do the explaining are axioms, and those laws that are explained by, deduced from, or based on the axioms are theorems.[40] He also notes that the theorems usually are known first, and axioms must be identified in order to explain the theorems. On the other hand, axioms can be used to predict new laws not yet identified. If any axioms are found to be false, then the theory itself must be considered false.

The Formation of Theories

Suitable theories do not always exist for the researcher in need of one. In many cases they must be developed or "built." Goldhor defines theory building as the accumulation of empirical findings and the development of a system of intermeshing hypotheses concerning their relationships.[41] He notes that this process requires the identification of the variables that are appropriate for a theoretical system and represent the relevant concepts. Theory construction also requires that the person developing the theory have a thorough understanding of the already accepted facts and theories of the field in question, as well as of related fields.

Grover and Glazier propose a model for theory building, which displays relationships among phenomena and various levels of theory and research. Their taxonomy ranges from phenomena, or individual objects and events, through hypotheses, to a "world view" or general orientation.[42]

Mouly states that a good theory should meet the following criteria:

1. A theory, or theoretical system, should permit deductions that can be tested empirically; in other words, it should provide the means for its own testing.

2. A theory should be compatible with both observation and previously verified theories. It must be well grounded and should be able to explain the phenomena under study.

3. A theory should be stated as simply as possible. It should explain adequately the existing knowledge but should not be any more complex than necessary. This characteristic represents the so-called law of parsimony.[43]

At this point, based on previous research and recent observations, one could construct a theory related to the earlier stated problem involving the effect of library instruction on library use. Such a theory, even in an abbreviated version, might include the following:

It has been observed, and previous research has indicated, that certain facts are related to student use of college libraries. Among these facts are (a) some students use their college library more than others, (b) some students have better library skills than others, and (c) appropriate library instruction is capable of teaching students how to use the college library. Based on these and other facts, one could formulate a theorem stating that some students use their college library more than others do because they have the necessary library skills (or at least more than the nonusers). At least one axiom which could help to explain the theorem might claim that students who know how to use the college library are more inclined to do so than those with fewer or no library skills because they are more aware of the library's resources, have more confidence in their abilities, and so on.

At this point, the theory already identified several facts, laws, and variables (library instruction, library skills, library use, confidence, etc.). It also has identified possible relationships among some of the variables and has suggested how and why they are related. In short, it is helping to bring some order to what would otherwise be a less meaningful group of facts and concepts.

Published examples of theory building include works by Mellon and Poole. Based on data gathered from diaries and essays, Mellon constructed a grounded theory (a unique theory based on the event or situation studied) of library anxiety.[44] Poole, after analyzing 97 studies published in the *Annual Review of Information Science and Technology*, constructed three theoretical statements on the behavior of scientists and engineers in formal information systems.[45] McKechnie and Pettigrew did a content analysis of 1,160 LIS articles published between 1993 and 1998 and found that 34.2 percent of the articles incorporated theory in the title, abstract, or text.[46]

Testing the Theory

Having developed, or at least identified, a suitable theory, the next requisite step is to test it. Much of the rest of this text will directly or indirectly concern itself with testing procedures, but a brief indication of some of the implications of theory testing is in order here. For example, it should be kept in mind that, in order to test a theory, one must determine how well each of its theorems and related propositions agrees with the observed facts in one or more test situations.[47]

Second, it should be noted that a well-constructed, informative theory would provide specific hypotheses or statements of certain relationships by which the theory can be tested. In fact, a theory can be thought of as a large hypothesis comprising a number of more specific, more testable subhypotheses, though a theory typically rests on a more sophisticated basis than does an individual hypothesis. Consequently, the entire theory can be tested by testing each of the hypotheses individually.

FORMULATING HYPOTHESES

Definitions of Hypotheses

The second major step in the standard scientific method of inquiry is the formulation of one or more theoretical hypotheses. A variety of definitions of hypotheses found in the literature reflect slightly different perspectives or emphases. Babbie defines the hypothesis as "a specified testable expectation about empirical reality that follows from a more general proposition."[48] Leedy and Ormrod view hypotheses as "tentative propositions set forth to assist in guiding the investigation of a problem or to provide possible explanations for the observations made."[49] Mouly considers a hypothesis to be "a tentative generalization concerning the relationship between two or more variables of critical interest in the solution of a problem under investigation."[50] Finally, Selltiz, quoting Webster, defines a hypothesis as "a proposition, condition, or principle, which is assumed, perhaps without belief, in order to draw out its logical consequences and by this method to test its accord with facts which are known or may be determined."[51]

To complicate the picture a bit more, there are several types of hypotheses, including the following:

1. Working or research hypothesis—the hypothesis with which a research study begins. It should help to delimit and guide the study.

2. Final hypothesis—the hypothesis that reflects the findings of the research study. It often is synonymous with the study's final conclusion.

3. Particular hypothesis—a hypothesis which merely explains a specific fact or situation; for example, "not all college students are skilled library users."

4. Causal hypothesis—a hypothesis which states that there is a causal relationship between two or more variables (i.e., that a particular factor or condition determines or affects another factor or condition).

5. Alternative hypothesis—a rival hypothesis which provides another possible and plausible solution to the problem (i.e., a different explanation of the same facts). This is sometimes used interchangeably with a "minor" or "secondary" hypothesis, though the latter, which has less well-accepted concepts, seems to suggest something quite different.

6. Null hypothesis—a hypothesis which asserts that there is no real relationship between or among the variables in question. It involves the supposition that chance, rather than an identifiable cause, has produced some observed result. It is used primarily for purposes of statistical testing.

7. Inductive hypothesis—a hypothesis which moves from the particular to the general, or a generalization based on observation.

8. Deductive hypothesis—a hypothesis which shifts from the general to the particular, or a hypothesis derived from a theory.

9. Nondirectional hypothesis—a hypothesis which merely indicates that a relationship or difference exists. It says nothing about the nature or direction of the relationship. For example, one might hypothesize that a student's grade point average and use of libraries are related without going so far as to argue that either factor causes the other.

10. Directional hypothesis—a hypothesis which indicates the nature of the relationship between or among variables. For example, it could logically be hypothesized that the assignment of term papers results in more library use by certain students.

11. Multivariate hypothesis—a hypothesis proposing a relationship among more than two phenomena or variables.

12. Bivariate hypothesis—a hypothesis proposing a relationship between two phenomena or variables.

13. Univariate hypothesis—a hypothesis concerned with only one phenomenon or variable. In that no relationship is involved, one could argue that this kind of statement does not meet the minimal criteria for a hypothesis. It might better be termed a research question.

Not all of these hypotheses are mutually exclusive. For example, one might begin a study with a research hypothesis that proposes a causal relationship between two variables and indicates which variable affects the other.

To complicate the picture yet again, Hillway states that "the terms hypothesis, theory, law, generalization, and conclusion all mean much the same thing in relation to a study."[52] He argues that what differences do exist are slight and relative. Other writers would disagree, however. It also may be worth noting here that the term "model" is often used interchangeably with hypothesis, as well as with theory, but in fact it has a slightly different meaning. Mouly defines a model as "a descriptive analogy designed to help visualize a complex phenomenon."[53]

Sources of Hypotheses

As was suggested earlier, one of the most convenient and logical sources of hypotheses is a theory, since it can be considered to be a broad hypothesis or a set of subhypotheses. However, theories seldom, if ever, simply appear when needed. They are a result of one's being thoroughly knowledgeable about a field, staying abreast of the literature, and so on. Indeed, the findings of other studies reported in the literature are excellent sources of hypotheses. Existing and assumed relationships reported in research results often provide the basis for formulating hypotheses. Similarly, certain relationships often can be observed in a work setting; such observations or hunches frequently lead to more formal hypotheses.

Pilot or exploratory studies also are good sources of hypotheses. In fact, Mouly states that some amount of data gathering, such as the recall of past experience, the review of related literature, or a pilot study, must precede the formulation and refinement of the hypothesis.[54]

Mouly also argues that "reasoning by analogy" is an excellent source of hypotheses.[55] In other words, if two situations agree with one another in one or more respects relevant to the problem in question, they will probably agree in yet other respects. Such an assumption may then be restated as one or more hypotheses.

Developing the Hypothesis

Again, the formulation of a hypothesis ideally begins with consideration of a theory, and more specifically, one or more components of a theory. But at the very least, this process starts with a set of specific facts or observations, which the researcher is attempting to explain. Generally, this explanation, or hypothesis, will be written as a statement of a possible relationship between two or more variables.

The basis for the hypothesis almost always rests on one or more assumptions. The most closely related assumption and the hypothesis are considered to constitute the premises from which the facts to be explained must logically be implied. In some research only the most basic assumption is referred to as the premise. Basic assumptions are assumed, for the purposes of a particular research study, to be true and therefore are not tested during the research.

Basic assumptions should not be confused with methodological assumptions. The former help to support or explain the hypothesis. For example, a hypothesis which predicts that older people are less likely to use information technology than are younger people might be partially explained by the assumption that older people have more anxiety regarding the use of technology. In conducting a study on the use of information technology by different age groups, one might make the methodological assumption that adequate numbers of people of different ages will be willing to participate in the study.

Goldhor points out that, having identified the hypothesis and basic assumptions, it should then be possible to develop additional explanations of relationships between or among the variables in specific situations.[56] These additional explanations constitute, in effect, alternative hypotheses.

The most viable hypothesis must then be identified by evaluating the various alternative hypotheses and eliminating the less effective ones. As was noted earlier, one guiding principle is the law of parsimony, which dictates selecting the simplest explanation or hypothesis and the one requiring the fewest assumptions. The hypothesis selected should nevertheless explain the most facts. Other characteristics of good hypotheses will be identified later, but next let us consider the major components of the hypothesis—the variables.

Variables

A *variable* may be thought of as "any property of a person, thing, event, setting, and so on that is not fixed."[57] Variables, or factors, can be perceived or labeled in a variety of ways depending on the nature of the relationship between or among them. For example, in a causal relationship the factor (or factors) typically identified first in the hypothesis is referred to as the *independent variable*. Other labels used for the independent variable include the predictor variable and the experimental variable. This is the variable that determines, influences, or produces the change in the other main factor.

The second main factor (or factors) in the causal hypothesis is usually referred to as the *dependent variable* or the subject variable. This variable is dependent on or influenced by the independent variable(s). The statement of the hypothesis should at least imply the nature of the relationship between the independent and dependent variables. For example, "the *more* library instruction a college student receives, the *more* he or she will use the college library."

However, hypotheses often take the form of conjectural statements. For example, "librarians are as assertive as other professional groups" or "the information needs of researchers are different from those of practitioners."[58] Thus, the independent and dependent variables are not always as easily identified as perhaps they should be. Given below are the titles of ten studies. Identify the independent and dependent variables within each title. For example, "assertiveness training" would appear to be the independent variable and "job satisfaction" the dependent variable in the title, "A note on the contribution of assertiveness training to job satisfaction of professional librarians."

1. A study of the relationship of role conflict, the need for role clarity, and job satisfaction for professional librarians.
2. Library design influences on user behavior and satisfaction.
3. An investigation of the relationships between quantifiable reference service variables and reference performance in public libraries.
4. The impact of differing orientations of librarians on the process of children's book selection: a case study of library tensions.
5. Book selection and book collection usage in academic libraries.
6. The effect of prime display location on public library circulation of selected adult titles.
7. Implications of title diversity and collection overlap for interlibrary loan among secondary schools.
8. The attitudes of adults toward the public library and their relationships to library use.
9. Early libraries in Louisiana: a study of the Creole influence.
10. The Great Depression: its impact on 46 large American public libraries; an inquiry based on a content analysis of published writings of their directors.*

*__Title number 1:__ independent variable—role conflict, dependent variables—need for role clarity and job satisfaction; *title number 2:* independent variable—library design, dependent variables—user behavior and satisfaction; *title number 3:* independent variable—quantifiable reference service variables, dependent variable—reference performance; *title number 4:* independent variable—differing orientations of librarians, dependent variable—process of children's book selection; *title number 5:* independent variable—book selection, dependent variable—book collection usage; *title number 6:* independent variable—prime display location, dependent variable—circulation of selected adult titles, *title number 7:* independent variables—title diversity and collection overlap, dependent variable—interlibrary loan among secondary schools; *title number 8:* independent variable—attitudes of adults toward the public library, dependent variable—library use; *title number 9:* independent variable—Creole influence, dependent variable—early libraries in Louisiana; *title number 10:* independent variable—Great Depression, dependent variable—large American public libraries.

As can be seen from these examples, relationships between variables often are indicated by the use of such terms as "influence," "impact," and "effect." But such clues are not always present, and they do not always convey the specific nature of the relationship nor distinguish between independent and dependent variables. In fact, a hypothesized relationship may not even include independent and dependent variables as such. The researcher may not be knowledgeable enough to predict that one variable causes another. For example, does an increase in grade point average cause an increase in library use or vice versa? In a given study, a variable might logically be viewed as either an independent or a dependent variable, or neither. Other types of variables include the following:

1. Intervening variable—any variable which occurs in the causal chain between some independent variable and its dependent variable. It also serves as an independent variable for the dependent variable. For example, we might hypothesize that library instruction (the independent variable) causes more library use (the dependent variable) when in actuality, library instruction produces greater confidence (the intervening variable), which in turn, causes more library use.

2. Antecedent variable—a variable which occurs prior to some already identified or hypothesized independent variable. In the previous example, had confidence been initially identified as the independent variable, then library instruction could have been thought of as the antecedent variable.

3. Extraneous variable—a variable at first perceived as the real cause of some effect when, in fact, it was only a coincidental correlate of that effect. It can also be defined as a variable that influences both the independent and the dependent variables so as to create a spurious association between them that disappears when the extraneous variable is controlled. (Extraneous variables are discussed in more detail in the section on experimental research methods.)

4. Component variables—two or more variables which represent the same variable. For example, reference questions and book loans are components of a variable called library use.

5. Conditioning or moderating variable—a variable which represents the conditions under which a hypothesized relationship between other variables holds true. For example, more library instruction might cause

more library use *only if* the instruction is relevant to the interests or needs of the learner.

6. Confounding or interfering variable—another influence that may affect the dependent variable but one in which the researcher is not interested.

Concepts

A researcher, in order to organize his or her data so as to perceive relationships among variables, must first make use of concepts. A *concept* may be defined as an abstraction from observed events or a shorthand representation of a variety of facts. Its purpose is to simplify thinking by subsuming a number of events under one general heading.[59] Library use is a concept representing or abstracting the many characteristics and types of library use. As indicated in the earlier example, there are a variety of specific kinds of library use such as reading, browsing, and borrowing books.

Not only can concepts be broken down into more concrete elements, they can be elevated to more abstract levels. These higher level concepts, often referred to as *constructs*, generally represent such phenomena as attitudes, perceptions, roles, and so on. For a specific phenomenon, the conceptual hierarchy would thus range from the construct, at the most abstract level, to the concept, and finally to the variable at the most concrete level.

It should be noted at this point that the greater the distance between the concepts or constructs and the facts to which they are supposed to refer, the greater the possibility of their being misunderstood or carelessly used. In addition, constructs, due to their greater abstractness, are more difficult to relate to the phenomena they are intended to represent. Therefore, it is important to define carefully the concepts and constructs, both in abstract terms and in terms of the operations by which they will be represented in the study. The former may be considered formal or *conceptual definitions*; the latter are referred to as working or *operational definitions*.

In providing a conceptual definition of a phenomenon such as "library use," the researcher would no doubt rely heavily on the already established definition as reflected in other studies. If a conceptual definition did not already exist, the researcher would need to develop his or her own, keeping it consistent, where possible, with current thought and attempting to link it to the existing body of knowledge using similar concepts or constructs.

In order to carry out the planned research, the investigator must translate the formal definitions of the concepts into observable or measurable events (i.e., variables) via working definitions. Most concepts cannot be directly observed, so they must be broken down into more concrete phenomena which can be measured.

Some argue that working definitions should state the means by which the concept will be measured and provide the appropriate categories. While this may not be a necessary part of the actual definition, at some point this step will be necessary, and the working definition should at least imply how the concept will be measured.

Returning to the example of library use, one could formally define library use, as did Zweizig, as "the output of libraries, the point at which the potential

for service becomes kinetic."[60] While this may be a suitable conceptual definition, it does little to suggest how one would actually measure library use.
Consequently, the researcher would need to develop one or more working
definitions in order to operationalize "library use."

In fact, more than one working definition for a concept is generally considered to be desirable, if not necessary. A given concept may be too complex to
be reduced to a single measurable phenomenon. In addition, having more than
one working definition for a concept helps to increase the reliability of the
findings, as the different measurements tend to serve as cross-checks for one
another. For example, if a person were found to own a library card, which could
be one definition of library use, but were found never to use the library, then one
would question the validity of using card ownership to represent library use.
The researcher would be better advised to utilize a variety of working definitions, including borrowing books, asking reference questions, requesting interlibrary loans, and so on.

Again, at some point, the researcher would need to specify exactly how the
activities specified by the working definitions would be measured. For example,
will only substantive, as opposed to directional, reference questions be counted?
What categories, such as research, bibliographic, and so on, will be used to organize the questions? It should be kept in mind that working definitions are usually
considered adequate only to the extent that the instruments or procedures based
on them gather data that constitute satisfactory indicators of the concepts they
are intended to represent. So, if the asking of reference questions does not
represent the kind of library use that the researcher had in mind, then obviously
it should not be used.

One other note of caution—in developing both conceptual and working
definitions, one should avoid so-called *spurious definitions*. These are circular
definitions, which tend to define terms using those same terms. If one defined
"library use" as "using the library," then one would be providing a circular
definition of no real value to the researcher or reader.

Desirable Characteristics of Hypotheses

In addition to representing the simplest possible explanation of a specific
phenomenon or relationship, an ideal hypothesis should possess several other
characteristics, including the following:

1. Generalizability, or universality—a hypothesis with this trait should
   hold up in more than one situation. On the other hand, valid hypotheses can be formulated legitimately for specific situations.
2. Compatibility with existing knowledge—a hypothesis is more likely to be
   generalizable if it has been based on the findings of other studies. The
   hypothesis should not be isolated from the larger body of knowledge.
3. Testability—the suitability of the hypothesis for empirical testing may
   be its most important characteristic. Regardless of its other traits, if it
   cannot be tested adequately, it is of little or no value. It even can be
   argued that the hypothesis should imply how it can be tested.

4. Invariability—simply put, the relationship stated in the hypothesis should not vary over a reasonable period of time.

5. Causality—the ideal hypothesis states a relationship that is causal in nature (i.e., that the independent variable(s) actually causes or determines one or more dependent variables). Many researchers also argue that the hypothesis should be predictive. Hillway states that "the success of a theory [of which the hypothesis is a part] for predictive purposes constitutes one of the most useful criteria by which it may be judged."[61]

Unfortunately, it often is not possible in the social sciences to formulate hypotheses that are causal or predictive in nature. Social science researchers frequently have to settle for associative type hypotheses, or hypotheses which state a correlational but not causal relationship between two or more variables. For example, one may argue that, as a student's library use increases, his or her grades improve, without being prepared to contend that greater library use actually causes the improvement in grades. It could be that some other factor, such as an interest in reading, is causing both the library use and the high grades. The concept of causality will be discussed in greater detail in the section on experimental research.

Goldhor, among others, argues that a good hypothesis should contain a "causal element" that explains why it is thought that the hypothesized relationship holds true. An example of a causal element is provided by Goldhor in the following hypothesis (the causal element follows the word "because"):

The more a person is interested in a hobby, the more he will read books about that hobby, because the intensive development of a hobby calls for knowledge and skills usually available only in print.[62]

It may well be that the causal element is synonymous with the most basic assumption, or premise of the hypothesis. Regardless of the terminology used, however, the process of identifying why the relationship exists is an important one, producing several benefits. For example, the researcher cannot hope to explain why a certain relationship exists without acquiring a thorough understanding of the phenomenon under study. Explaining why a relationship holds true forces the investigator to go beyond mere description of it. Consideration of causality also forces the researcher to distinguish between the independent and dependent variables. Otherwise, one cannot state which factor causes which. Finally, after specifying why a relationship exists, the researcher is more likely to be able to predict what the hypothesized relationship will produce.

Testing the Hypothesis

In testing the validity of a hypothesis, the researcher typically employs the deductive method in that he or she begins with a theoretical framework, formulates a hypothesis, and logically deduces what the results of the test should be if the hypothesis is correct. This is usually accomplished in two stages.

First, the researcher deductively develops certain logical implications (also known as logical consequences and criteria) which, when stated in operational terms, can help to reject or support the hypothesis. These logical implications should indicate evidence which must be collected and which must be valid for an adequate test. Considering our hypothesis regarding library instruction and library use, several criteria could logically represent library use or provide evidence of use. Operationally defined, such criteria could include the number of visits to the library, the number of books borrowed, and so on.

The second basic step in testing a hypothesis involves actually subjecting it to a trial by collecting and analyzing relevant data. For example, one would, at this point, collect data on the subjects' actual library use, as evidenced by criteria already established. This stage requires the use of one or more criterion measures in order to evaluate the evidence that has been collected. "The choice of the criterion measure is crucial: not only must it be reliable and valid, it must also be sufficiently sensitive to detect changes as they occur."[63] If one were using the number of visits to the library as evidence of library use, it would be important to detect all library visits, not just some of them. It might also be necessary to determine types of library visits—their purpose and duration, for example.

As was indicated earlier, in order to measure library use adequately, it probably would be necessary to measure it in more than one way (i. e., employ more than one operational definition). If more than one operational definition is considered, then it follows that more than one logical consequence can be expected and that more than one criterion measure must be employed. In fact, establishment of "the truth of an hypothesis in the absolute sense is not accomplished until all possible logical consequences have been tested and the hypothesis becomes a law."[64] Until a hypothesis is tested in every appropriate situation, the researcher is at best building support for the hypothesis, not proving it. In effect, each logical consequence can provide several different bases for testing the same hypothesis or relationship.

Causality also plays an important role in the testing of hypotheses. As Goldhor has noted, "The testing or verification of an hypothesis is strengthened or augmented by analysis of available relevant data so as to show (1) that they agree with predictions drawn logically from the one hypothesis, (2) that they do not also confirm the consequences of alternative hypotheses, and (3) that they involve points in a logical chain of cause and effect."[65] Consideration of the causal relationship (when it exists) forces the investigator to employ or measure consequences that will provide evidence of the nature of the hypothetical relationship. This usually can be accomplished by utilizing data collection procedures and criterion measures that have the ability to support or reject the hypothetical cause of the relationship. For example, if college students who had high grades and who were heavy users of the library were found to be using the library strictly for recreational reading, we probably would have to reject the hypothesis and consider some phenomenon other than library use to be the cause of high grades. Such a finding might well suggest other possible relationships, however.

At this point, two reminders appear to be in order. One, it should not be forgotten that the hypothesis should be related to existing knowledge as closely as possible. This caveat also applies to the findings resulting from the testing of the hypothesis. This process is crucial if research is to build on previous studies and not merely produce fragmentary, unrelated bits of data.

Two, it is important to remember that scientific research should produce a circular movement from facts to hypotheses, to laws, to theories, and back to facts as the basis for the testing and refinement of more adequate hypotheses.

In other words, the research process should never end; it should merely continue to build on previous research, and to shape and reshape its findings.

An appropriate question to ask at this point is whether a hypothesis is always possible and/or helpful. In fact, it is not always possible, desirable, or justifiable to develop a formal hypothesis for a research study. This is particularly the case for exploratory research in areas too undeveloped to provide the basis for formally stated hypotheses and for most qualitative research. A formal research hypothesis can even be a hindrance to exploratory research, and the investigator may have more to gain by entering into an exploratory study with few preconceived ideas. It may not be possible, or at least not advisable, to predict relationships and outcomes of exploratory research because doing so may bias the researcher and encourage neglect of potentially important information.

Also, when fact-finding alone is the purpose of the study, which is often the case with descriptive surveys, there may be little use for a hypothesis. At the very least, however, the researcher should have some "research questions" which he or she is attempting to answer and which will help, in lieu of a hypothesis, to guide the research. Some researchers distinguish between "descriptive research questions," which ask what is the amount or extent of a given variable, and "explanatory research questions," which ask how or whether certain variables are related. The following are examples of the former: How many students use their college library during specific time periods? What are the subject majors of the users of a college library? The following are examples of the latter: Is there a relationship between the subject majors of students and how often they use their college library? Is there a relationship between the subject majors of students and the types of reference questions that they ask? It is probably safe to say, however, that most major studies, particularly those involving some interpretation of facts, should incorporate a research hypothesis. "Not the facts alone, but the conclusions that we can draw from them must be regarded as the chief objective of research."[66] Without the rigorous testing of a valid hypothesis, fully generalizable conclusions are not possible.

VALIDITY AND RELIABILITY

As one develops, and conducts, a research study, one should always be concerned with its validity and reliability. Generally speaking, research is considered to be valid when the conclusions are true, and reliable when the findings are repeatable. But validity and reliability are actually requirements for both the design and the measurement of research. Regarding the design, the researcher should ask whether the conclusions are true (valid) and repeatable (reliable).[67] Measurement, of course, is the process of ascertaining the dimensions, quantity, or capacity of something, and it is closely related to the notion of operational definitions discussed earlier. "More specifically, *measurement* is a procedure where a researcher assigns numerals—either numbers or other symbols—to empirical properties (variables) according to a prescribed set of rules."[68] Research design is the plan and structure of the research framework. It is influenced by the nature of the hypothesis, the variables, the constraints of the real world, and so on. Research design must occur at the beginning of a research project, but it involves all of the steps that follow.

Validity of Research Design

"Validity is a multi-faceted word or concept,"[69] and there are at least three types of validity as it relates to the design of research. One is referred to as *internal validity*. Briefly stated, a research design is internally valid if it accurately identifies causal relationships, if any, and rules out rival explanations of the relationships. Internal validity is particularly crucial to experimental research design.

Research design is considered to have *construct validity* if the variables being investigated can be identified and labeled properly. The design should permit the specification of the actual cause and effect and the identification of the concepts or constructs involved. (A somewhat different view of construct validity will be considered later in the discussion of validity as it relates to the measurement process.)

The third kind of validity critical to the design of research is external validity. Research has *external validity* or generalizability when its conclusions are true or hold up beyond the confines of a particular study. In other words, the findings should be generally true for studies conducted under a variety of circumstances or conditions (e.g., other times, people, places). The quality of external validity can best be determined by replicating a study or retesting to see if the results will be repeated in another setting. (This aspect of validity is similar to the concept of reliability.)

Validity in Measurement

In brief, the extent to which an instrument measures what it is designed to measure indicates the level of validity of that measure. Data collection instruments may be high in reliability and low in validity, or vice versa. For example, a test intended to measure the effect of library skills on library use might actually be measuring the influence of instructors on library use, and it would therefore be low in validity. On the other hand, repeated applications of the test, in comparable circumstances, may produce essentially the same results, indicating high reliability. Ideally, the instrument would be high in both validity and reliability.

As is the case for reliability, correlation coefficients can be calculated for the validity of an instrument. Reliability coefficients are correlations between identical or similar methods, while validity coefficients are correlations between dissimilar methods based on dissimilar operational definitions but measuring the same concepts. In other words, the validity coefficient indicates the extent to which independent instruments or observations measure the same thing.

One example of a method for calculating the validity of an instrument involves the multitrait-multimethod matrix, which is a table of correlations for two or more traits measured by two or more methods. The matrix should produce relatively high correlations between scores that reflect the same trait measured by different methods, while the correlations obtained from measuring two different traits with different instruments or measuring traits with the same instrument should be low. If two separate tests, measuring two different concepts, are highly correlated, then the two concepts are probably not truly separate and distinct.

For some standardized tests, such as IQ and personality tests, reliability and validity scores have been calculated based on past applications and validation studies and are available in the literature. For many tests or instruments, and obviously for newly developed ones, however, scores are not available. Reliability scores can be calculated by correlating the scores for repeated tests. The method used to evaluate the validity of an instrument is determined by the type of validity with which one is concerned.

The standard texts on research methods do not evidence unanimity on their categorization of validity. A careful reading of several works, however, suggests that the terminology and classification schemes vary more than the types of validity themselves. What follows is hopefully at least a consensual overview of the basic types of validity as they relate to measurement.

Logical Validity

Logical validity is a type of validity generally based on expert judgment. It includes content validity and face validity. *Content* validity represents the degree to which an instrument measures a specific content area. For example, a test designed to measure a student's mastery of library skills must measure what the student was supposed to learn.

In order to be adequate, content validity must contain both item validity and sampling validity. *Item* validity reflects whether the items of the instrument or test actually represent measurement in the intended content area. Does a question about the Library of Congress classification scheme in fact measure a student's understanding of how materials are arranged in a library's collection? *Sampling* validity is concerned with how well the instrument samples the total content area. A test on library skills should not be limited to measuring library users' ability to check out books. The test should cover catalog use, search strategy, and so on.

Face validity is similar to content validity, and the terms are sometimes used interchangeably. Face validity is a sort of catchall term often used rather loosely. It has been defined as "the degree to which a test appears to measure what it claims to measure."[70] Face validity is usually based on the opinion of subject experts who have been asked to evaluate an instrument. (This method of determining validity is quite subjective, but sometimes it is the only feasible one available.)

Empirical Validity

The second basic type of validity regarding measurement has been referred to as empirical and criterion-related validity. In contrast to logical validity, empirical validity is based on external, objective criteria. It includes concurrent validity and predictive validity.

Concurrent validity indicates the degree to which the scores on a test or other data collection instrument are related to the scores on another, already validated, test administered at the same time, or to some other valid criterion (e.g., grade point average) available at the same time. Concurrent validity also represents the ability of an instrument to discriminate among people (or whatever) who are known to differ. For instance, in developing an instrument to measure *how* people use a university library, one would expect it to distinguish between undergraduates and graduate students, as we already have evidence indicating that their library use differs. If members of these two groups "scored" the same on the test, then there would be a good chance that the test was actually measuring something other than types of library use—perhaps simply frequency.

Predictive validity has to do with the degree to which an instrument can identify differences that will evidence themselves in the future. If one were predicting that frequent library users were more likely to go on to graduate school than were infrequent or nonusers, then subsequent observations should support that prediction. A greater proportion of the people who scored relatively high on an initial library use questionnaire should be found enrolled in graduate school at a later date.

Construct Validity

It is possible for validity of measurement to be based on both logical judgment and external criteria. Such validity is usually known as construct validity. The definition for construct validity sounds like the definition for face validity in that construct validity represents the extent to which an instrument measures the concept or construct that it is intended to measure. As is the case with face validity, when selecting a test or instrument to employ in a research study, one must take care to choose one that accurately measures the construct of interest. This selection process should be based on the judgment of subject experts. Unlike face validity, however, construct validity requires more than expert opinion for determination. In order to ensure construct validity, it must be demonstrated that an instrument measures the construct in question and no other. In operational terms, construct validity requires that two or more measures of different constructs, using similar instruments, produce low correlations (i.e., *discriminant* validity) and that two or more measures of the same construct result in high correlations, even though different instruments are used (i.e., *convergent* validity). In other words, an instrument should be capable of measuring the construct (as represented by appropriate variables) it is supposed to measure, of distinguishing the construct from others, and of measuring other constructs simultaneously. (The multitrait-multimethod matrix discussed earlier represents one method for determining the convergent and discriminant validity of an instrument and thereby measuring its construct validity.)

Reliability of Research Design

If the design of a research study is reliable, then its findings should be repeatable or replicable and generalizable beyond the one study. Exact replications of the study, including specific procedures, can be made to assess the reliability of the design. (Conceptual replications of only the ideas or concepts can be used to evaluate the external validity of the design.)

Reliability in Measurement

As was stated earlier, research requires that one be able to measure concepts and constructs as represented by variables which often are translated into, or operationally defined as, a set of categories or a scale. Unfortunately, however, virtually all measurement is imperfect. Consequently, a measurement, or observed score, comprises the true score (which may never be known) and the error of measurement, or the discrepancy between the observed and the true scores. A measurement is generally considered to be reliable when the error component is reasonably small and does not fluctuate greatly from one observation to another. Thus reliability can be defined as the degree to which an instrument accurately *and* consistently measures whatever it measures. In short, a reliable data collection instrument is one that is relatively free from measurement error.

There are methods for assessing the reliability or *stability* of measurement techniques. One of the most commonly used methods results in what is known as a test-retest correlation. When the researcher employs this technique, he or she uses the same data collection instrument to observe or collect scores twice for the same group of subjects. (The instrument should be administered at different times but under equivalent conditions.) The two sets of scores are then correlated to see how consistent or reliable the instrument was in measuring the variables. The smaller the error of measurement, the more likely the correlation will be high.

If it is not feasible to repeat the measurement process, or if the *internal consistency* or homogeneity of the test is of concern, other methods can be used to determine the reliability of the instrument. For example, in utilizing the split-half method, the researcher splits the measuring instrument into two sets of questions or items after it is administered. The scores on the two halves are then correlated to provide an estimate of reliability. (The instrument should be split in equivalent halves, each of which is representative of the total. This can be done by assigning the odd-numbered items to one set and the even-numbered items to the other, or by using some random assignment technique. Keep in mind, however, that a data collection instrument may have been designed to measure one variable or several variables.)

Other methods for assessing the reliability of measurement include the average item-total correlation, in which each item's score is correlated with the total score, and the coefficients are averaged. With a technique called the average interitem correlation, each item is correlated with every other item, and the average of the coefficients represents a measure of internal consistency and indicates how well the items all measure the same construct. (If these conditions do exist, then the test-retest correlation of the total score will be higher than the test-retest correlation of the individual items.) When data are gathered by observers, it is important that their observations agree if they observed the same phenomena. *Interrater reliability* (also known as *intercoder reliability*) refers to the extent to which two or more observers agree.

Reliability also can be expressed in terms of the *standard error of measurement*, which is an estimate of how often one can expect errors of a given size. It is calculated with the following formula:

$$SE_m = SD\sqrt{1 - r}$$

where

SE$_m$ = standard error of measurement

SD = standard deviation of scores

r = reliability coefficient.

A small standard error of measurement indicates high reliability and vice versa.

In considering the reliability of the data collection tool, one must, as has been stated, be concerned with the amount of measurement error. It is also essential that the instrument measure only the constructs of interest, not a variety of others. Otherwise it is difficult, if not impossible, to know which construct, or variable, to credit for the magnitude of the score.

A reasonable question to ask at this point would be, what is a satisfactory reliability coefficient? Ideally, every score or observation should have a reasonably high correlation with the construct or variable measured, but the determination of what constitutes a "high" correlation must be somewhat subjective. This question is comparable to asking what constitutes a high correlation between two variables. Both answers depend on a variety of factors. Regarding measurement, it should be noted that the reliability is always contingent on the degree of uniformity of the given characteristics in the population. The more homogeneous the population with regard to the variable in question, the more reliable the instrument is likely to be. For example, if an instrument has been designed to measure library use, and library use varies little among the subjects being studied, the instrument should be able to measure use consistently.

The level of reliability needed by a researcher also will vary according to the desired degree of distinction among cases. High reliability is more important, or at least more difficult to achieve, when making fine discriminations among cases than when merely identifying extremes. If the latter is all that is desired, a relatively crude measurement device should suffice. If a librarian merely wished to know what proportion of the library's patrons were children, young adults, and adults, then users could be observed and assigned to one of the three broad categories. If it were important to know exact ages, then patrons would have to be asked for that information on a questionnaire or during an interview. The resultant set of categories or the measurement scale would contain the number of ages reported and would require a more reliable data collection instrument.

Scales

The level of discrimination is in large part a function of the measurement scale used by the research instrument. The *American Heritage Dictionary* defines scale as "a progressive classification, as of size, amount, importance, or rank; a relative level or degree."[71] There are generally considered to be four types of measurement scales:

1. Nominal scale—The nominal or categorical scale consists of two or more named categories into which objects, individuals, or responses are classified. For example, a survey of academic library users could employ a nominal scale for the purpose of categorizing users by subject major. The simplest nominal scale is the dichotomous scale, which has only two values, such as male-female, yes-no, and so on. The important characteristic of the nominal scale is that the categories are qualitative, not quantitative.

2. Ordinal scale—An ordinal scale defines the relative position of objects or individuals with respect to a characteristic, with no implication as to the distance between positions. This type of scale is also referred to as a "rank order." Attitude or Likert-type scales are examples of ordinal

scales. (It should be noted, however, that some researchers do consider Likert-type scales to be interval level scales.) For example, one could rank order patrons' level of satisfaction on a scale such as the following:

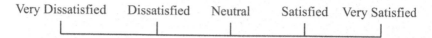

Very Dissatisfied   Dissatisfied   Neutral   Satisfied   Very Satisfied

But one could not assume that the distance from "Very Dissatisfied" to "Dissatisfied" is the same as the distance from "Neutral" to "Satisfied." In other words, the second range might represent a greater change than the first range.

3. Interval scale—The interval scale provides a ranking of positions, as does the ordinal scale, but the intervals of measurement are equal. In addition, the interval scale has a zero point below which scores are given a negative value if they occur. A temperature scale is an example of an interval scale. Interval level data are less common than ordinal in the social sciences.

4. Ratio scale—The ratio scale is comparable to the interval scale except that it has an absolute zero, below which values cannot occur. The ratio scale allows one to compare the magnitude of responses or measurements. Frequency of library use could be considered to be ratio level data; in analyzing such information, one would be able to correctly state, for example, that one person has used the library twice as often as another. Ratio level data are relatively rare in the social sciences because few scales actually have true zero points.

In considering the issue of measurement, it should be kept in mind that measurement presupposes theory. In order for any measurement to have meaning, one must have a solid understanding of the relationship between the variable and the underlying construct that it represents. Kidder refers to this relationship as "epistemic correlation."[72] To some extent, epistemic correlation can be established by developing an intuitive theory regarding the relationship and identifying a second variable that also stands for the construct. If a significant epistemic correlation exists, then there should be a correlation between each variable and the construct, and between the two variables.

SUMMARY

As was stated earlier, a research project that adheres to the basic scientific method of inquiry consists of certain stages; this chapter has considered four of these stages: identification or development of the theory; identification of the problem; formulation of the hypothesis; and measurement as related to validity, reliability, and level. A research project is not likely to succeed unless careful attention has been paid to these steps. Yet it is tempting for the researcher to slight, if not ignore, these steps in order to get involved in the design of the study and the collection and analysis of data. Unfortunately, such research is generally inefficient and less productive and meaningful than it could be. Would-be researchers should realize that the time that goes into the conceptual development and planning of a research study is time well spent, and it will result in fewer problems in the later stages of the research. As has been written elsewhere, "A question well-stated is a question half answered."[73]

NOTES

1. Paul D. Leedy and Jeanne Ellis Ormrod, *Practical Research: Planning and Design*, 8th ed. (Upper Saddle River, NJ: Pearson Merrill Prentice Hall, 2005), 85.

2. Ibid., 3.

3. Earl R. Babbie, *The Practice of Social Research*, 12th ed. (Belmont, CA: Wadsworth/Cengage Learning, 2010), 22–23.

4. John M. Budd, "An Epistemological Foundation for Library and Information Science," *Library Quarterly* 65, no. 3 (1995): 295–318.

5. Leedy, *Practical Research.*

6. Babbie, *The Practice of Social Research*, 48.

7. Chava Frankfort-Nachmias and David Nachmias, *Research Methods in the Social Sciences*, 7th ed. (New York: Worth Publishers, 2008), 18.

8. Karen E. Pettigrew and Lynne (E. F.) McKechnie, "The Use of Theory in Information Science Research," *Journal of the American Society for Information Science and Technology* 52 (2001): 62–73. William E. McGrath, "Current Theory in Library and Information Science," *Library Trends* 50, no. 3 (2002): 309–569.

9. Donald E. Riggs, "Losing the Foundation of Understanding," *American Libraries* 25 (May 1994): 449. Peter Hernon, "Editorial: Publishing Research," *The Journal of Academic Librarianship* 22 (January 1996): 1–2.

10. John M. Budd, *Knowledge and Knowing in Library and Information Science: A Philosophical Framework* (Lanham, MD: Scarecrow Press, 2001).

11. Leedy and Ormrod, *Practical Research*, 7.

12. Ibid., 8.

13. Peter Hernon, "Editorial: Components of the Research Process: Where Do We Need to Focus Attention?" *The Journal of Academic Librarianship* 27 (March 2001): 81–89.

14. Leedy and Ormrod, *Practical Research*, 107–10.

15. Claire Selltiz, Lawrence S. Wrightsman, and Stuart W. Cook, *Research Methods in Social Relations*, rev. ed. (New York: Holt, Rinehart and Winston, 1959), 26.

16. Leedy and Ormrod, *Practical Research*, 43.

17. John Martyn and F. Wilfrid Lancaster, *Investigative Methods in Library and Information Science: An Introduction* (Arlington, VA: Information Resources Press, 1981), 3.

18. Peter Hernon and Cheryl Metoyer-Duran, "Problem Statements: An Exploratory Study of their Function, Significance, and Form," *Library & Information Science Research* 15 (Winter 1993): 71–92.

19. Hernon, "Components of the Research Process," 87.

20. Peter Hernon and Candy Schwartz, "Editorial: What is a Problem Statement?" *Library & Information Science Research* 29, no. 3 (2007): 308.

21. Ibid., 309.

22. Leedy and Ormrod, *Practical Research*, 57.

23. Marcia J. Bates, "An Introduction to Metatheories, Theories, and Models," in *Theories of Information Behavior*, ed. Karen E. Fisher, Sandra Erdelez, and Lynne (E. F.) McKechnie (Medford, NJ: Information Today, Inc., 2005), 2.

24. Thomas S. Kuhn, *The Structure of Scientific Revolutions*, 3rd ed. (Chicago: University of Chicago Press, 1996).

25. Herbert Goldhor, *An Introduction to Scientific Research in Librarianship* (Urbana: University of Illinois, Graduate School of Library Science, 1972).

26. Bates, "An Introduction to Metatheories, Theories, and Models," 3.

27. Ibid.

28. Ibid.

29. Goldhor, *An Introduction to Scientific Research*, 42.

30. Sung-Jin Kim and Dong Y. Jeong, "An Analysis of the Development and Use of Theory in Library and Information Science Research Articles," *Library & Information Science Research* 28, no. 4 (2006): 548.

31. George J. Mouly, *Educational Research: The Art and Science of Investigation* (Boston: Allyn and Bacon, 1978), 35.

32. Goldhor, *An Introduction to Scientific Research*, 42.

33. Mouly, *Educational Research*, 35.

34. Goldhor, *An Introduction to Scientific Research*, 49.

35. Selltiz, Wrightsman, and Cook, *Research Methods in Social Relations*, 481.

36. Babbie, *The Practice of Social Research*, G12.

37. Joanne G. Marshall, *An Introduction to Research Methods for Health Sciences Librarians* (Chicago: Medical Library Association, Courses for Continuing Education, 1989), 16.

38. McGrath, "Current Theory," 310.

39. Goldhor, *An Introduction to Scientific Research*, 43.

40. Ibid.

41. Ibid., 42.

42. Robert J. Grover and Jack D. Glazier, "A Conceptual Framework for Theory Building in Library and Information Science," *Library & Information Science Research* 8 (1986): 227–42.

43. Mouly, *Educational Research*, 35–36.

44. Constance A. Mellon, "Library Anxiety: A Grounded Theory and Its Development," *College & Research Libraries* 47 (March 1986): 160–65.

45. Herbert L. Poole, *Theories of the Middle Range* (Norwood, NJ: Ablex Publishing, 1985).

46. Lynne (E. F.) McKechnie and Karen E. Pettigrew, "Surveying the Use of Theory in Library and Information Science Research: A Disciplinary Perspective," *Library Trends* 50, no. 3 (2002): 406–17.

47. Goldhor, *An Introduction to Scientific Research*, 45.

48. Babbie, *The Practice of Social Research*, 46.

49. Leedy and Ormrod, *Practical Research*, 60.

50. Mouly, *Educational Research*, 62.

51. Selltiz, Wrightsman, and Cook, *Research Methods in Social Relations*, 35.

52. Tyrus Hillway, *Introduction to Research*, 2nd ed. (Boston: Houghton Mifflin, 1964), 132.

53. Mouly, *Educational Research*, 38.

54. Ibid., 64.

55. Ibid., 50.

56. Goldhor, *An Introduction to Scientific Research*, 55.

57. Marshall, *An Introduction to Research Methods*, 17.

58. Ibid., 15.

59. Selltiz, Wrightsman and Cook, *Research Methods in Social Relations*, 41.

60. Douglas L. Zweizig, "Measuring Library Use," *Drexel Library Quarterly* 13 (July 1977): 3.

61. Hillway, *Introduction to Research*, 128.

62. Goldhor, *An Introduction to Scientific Research*, 59.

63. Mouly, *Educational Research*, 69.

64. Goldhor, *An Introduction to Scientific Research*, 81.

65. Ibid., 86.

66. Hillway, *Introduction to Research*, 131.

67. Charles M. Judd, Eliot R. Smith, and Louise H. Kidder, *Research Methods in Social Relations*, 6th ed. (Fort Worth, TX: Harcourt Brace Jovanovich College Publishers, 1991), 49.

68. Frankfort-Nachmias and Nachmias, *Research Methods in the Social Sciences*, 139.

69. Peter Hernon and Candy Schwartz, "Reliability and Validity," *Library & Information Science Research* 31, no. 2 (2009): 73.

70. L. R. Gay, Geoffrey E. Mills, and Peter Airasian, *Educational Research: Competencies for Analysis and Applications*, 8th ed. (Upper Saddle River, NJ: Pearson Merrill Prentice Hall, 2006), 135.

71. *American Heritage Dictionary: Second College Edition* (Boston: Houghton Mifflin Co., 1982), 1095.

72. Louise H. Kidder, *Research Methods in Social Relations*, 4th ed. (New York: Holt, Rinehart and Winston, 1981), 139.

73. Stephen Isaac and William B. Michael, *Handbook in Research and Evaluation: A Collection of Principles, Methods and Strategies Useful in Planning, Design, and Evaluation of Studies in Education and the Behavioral Sciences*, 3rd ed. (San Diego: EdITS Publishers, 1995), 36.

Chapter 3

Selecting the Research Method

Having identified the research problem, identified or built a theory, and formulated a hypothesis (where appropriate), the researcher is ready to select a methodology for his or her study. The researcher must first decide whether the proposed research will be primarily applied or basic, and quantitative or qualitative in nature. As was previously indicated, the emphases of this book are basic and quantitative approaches to research. The methods that fall into those categories will be given minimal attention in this section as they are treated more fully later in the text.

APPLIED RESEARCH

As was noted in Chapter 1, there is a distinction to be made between basic and applied research. Basic research tends to be theoretical in nature and concerns itself primarily with theory construction, hypothesis testing, and production of new, generalizable knowledge. Applied research tends to be more pragmatic and emphasizes providing information that is immediately usable in the resolution of actual problems, which may or may not have application beyond the immediate study.

On the other hand, both types of research ultimately should add to the existing body of knowledge within a field, and in doing so, they may utilize similar methods and techniques. Such utilization is nicely illustrated by the discussion of the evaluation of information storage and retrieval systems in *Guide to Information Science* by Davis and Rush.[1] Davis points out that "the interplay between academics [basic researchers] and practitioners [applied researchers] can be extremely valuable," and it should be encouraged.[2] There is no good reason to assume that basic and applied research are mutually exclusive. In fact, basic and applied research can be considered as two parts of a continuum. Furthermore,

> Although the criteria for merit vary somewhat along the continuum, there is more overlap than typically realized. For example, basic research is judged by its clarity of purpose and interpretation, by its ability to support

or refute particular hypotheses, by the incisiveness of the new hypotheses it generates, by the generalizability of the results, and by its technical accuracy, but in addition by the degree to which the results can be utilized in developing a product, a process, or a policy, to mention just a few types of application.[3]

Applied research, on the other hand, can validate theories and lead to the revision of theories. It "takes the theory and concepts from basic research and, by formal methods of inquiry, investigates 'real world' phenomena."[4]

Action Research

A major type of applied research, and one sometimes treated interchangeably with applied research, is action research. According to Wilson, "action research in the original sense is participative organizational research, focused on problem definition and resolution, which involves (usually) an external researcher who works with organizational members to arrive at workable solutions to their problems, within the framework of some theoretical perspective."[5] Action research differs from applied research in that "it has direct application to the immediate workplace of the researcher, whereas applied research may have the broader purpose of improving the profession at large."[6] Isaac and Michael, for example, state that the purpose of action research is "to develop new skills or new approaches and to solve problems with direct application to the classroom or working world setting."[7] They characterize action research as practical, orderly, flexible and adaptive, and empirical to a degree, but weak in internal and external validity.

Isaac and Michael identify the following basic steps in action research:

1. Defining the problem or setting the goal
2. Reviewing the literature
3. Formulating testable hypotheses
4. Arranging the research setting
5. Establishing measurement techniques and evaluation criteria
6. Analyzing the data and evaluating the results.[8]

As can be seen, these steps do not differ significantly from those typically followed in a basic research study. It is likely, however, that they would be carried out somewhat less rigorously than for basic research, and hypotheses, if any, would be treated in a more flexible manner. Typically, the data are provided to library decision makers who in turn take some action; for example, they may improve a service, develop a new one, or discontinue a service.

Kristiansson makes a case for the use of scenario planning as "an accompanying tool in the context of action research."[9] The purpose for building scenarios is to address critical events and uncertain conditions, and to create action plans. The technique provides opportunities for generating new ideas, which can be used for library strategic planning.

As an action research technique, scenario planning involves workshops or dialogue sessions "where participants discuss library development with focus on strategies, practices and knowledge about the library's surroundings."[10] Scenario planning provides an opportunity for library staff to gather information in a structured environment to create plans of action.

Evidence-Based Research

Evidence-based research for decision making could be considered a type of applied or action research and has become very popular within the library and information science domain during the past five years. This interest may have been spurred by the twentieth-century movement in healthcare and policy that calls for healthcare professionals to make decisions for medical practice based on the current best evidence provided by medical research and data. In an economic environment of decreasing library budgets for staff, materials, and services and increasing library usage, there is a demand for library and information professionals to make decisions based on current, valid data.

The quarterly, open access journal, *Evidence Based Library and Information Practice*, was first published in 2006 "to provide a forum for librarians and other information professionals to discover research that may contribute to decision making in professional practice."[11] Evidence-based research "reflects both the efforts of practitioners, who 'consume' the results of research in making those decisions, and the efforts of applied researchers, who strive to 'produce' the research evidence intended for use by practitioners."[12] Evidence-based research has been addressed by professional organizations, practitioners, and researchers.

School Library Journal's 2008 Leadership Summit was titled, "Where's the Evidence? Understanding the Impact of School Libraries."[13] OCLC Online Computer Library Center, Inc., created a data mining research area to utilize the data that are created by library services and systems to provide intelligence to librarians to make informed decisions.[14] OCLC Research scientists also have published numerous papers and presentations using library-generated data, including WorldCat data,[15] to make collection decisions for preservation, digitization, and deaccessioning; to compare collections; to identify the characteristics of collections; and to determine whether to provide resources in electronic or paper format. The prevalence of the literature addressing evidence-based research exemplifies the interest and importance this method has gained in the library and information professions in the past several years.

Evaluative Research

Evaluative or evaluation research, as a type of applied research, has as its primary goal, not the discovery of knowledge, but rather a testing of the application of knowledge within a specific program or project. Thus it is usually practical or utilitarian in nature, and it is generally less useful than basic research for developing theoretical generalizations. In most evaluative studies there is an implicit, if not explicit, hypothesis in which the dependent variable is a desired value, goal, or effect such as better library skills and higher circulation statistics; the independent variable is often a program or service.

Evaluative research studies typically have a rather large number of uncontrolled variables, as they are carried out in real settings. They are usually limited in terms of time and space, and if the evaluative researcher has a vested interest in the project being evaluated, he or she is highly susceptible to bias.

Two *general types* of evaluative research are summative evaluation and formative evaluation. *Summative*, or outcome, research is concerned with the effects of a program. It tends to be quantitative in nature and often is used as the basis for deciding whether a program will be continued. *Formative*, or process, evaluation, which is done during a program, not following its completion, examines how well the program is working. It is often more qualitative and frequently is used for revising and improving programs. In both types, feedback from program participants is usually considered important. Other broad categories that can encompass a variety of methods include: quantitative, qualitative, subjective, and objective evaluation; and macroevaluation and microevaluation.

More *specific types* of evaluative research include the use of standards and cost analysis. "When applied to libraries . . . *standards* refer to a set of guidelines or recommended practices, developed by a group of experts, that serve as a model for good library service."[16] Simple *cost analysis* is basically a descriptive breakdown of the costs incurred in operating an organization. Cost related techniques more concerned with the assessment of whether monies are being spent in an optimal fashion usually fall into one of two groups—cost-effectiveness studies and cost-benefit analysis. "The term 'cost-effectiveness' implies a relationship between the cost of providing some service and the level of effectiveness of that service . . . Cost-effective analyses can be thought of as studies of the costs associated with alternative strategies for achieving a particular level of effectiveness."[17] Some examples of cost-effectiveness measures include: the cost per relevant informational resource retrieved, cost per use of a resource, cost per user, cost per capita, and cost by satisfaction level.[18]

Cost-effectiveness analysis can be seen as "a truncated form of cost-benefit analysis that stops short of putting an economic value on . . . outcomes [benefits] of programs."[19] "'Cost-benefit,' clearly, refers to a relationship between the cost of some activity and the benefits derived from it . . . In effect, a cost-benefit study is one that tries to justify the existence of the activity by demonstrating that the benefits outweigh the costs."[20] A typical cost-benefit analysis involves determining who benefits from and pays for a service, identifying the costs for each group of beneficiaries, identifying the benefits for each group, and comparing costs and benefits for each group to determine if groups have net benefits or net costs and whether the total benefits exceed the total costs.

Types of cost-benefit analysis described by Lancaster[21] are

1. Net value approach—the maximum amount the user of an information service is willing to pay minus the actual cost.

2. Value of reducing uncertainty in decision-making.

3. Cost of buying service elsewhere.

4. Librarian time replaces user time (i.e., the librarian saves the user time by performing his or her task).

5. Service improves organization's performance or saves it money.

Other kinds of cost analysis discussed by Weiss[22] and Matthews[23] include:

1. Cost-minimization analysis—seeks to determine the least expensive way to accomplish some outcome.
2. Cost-utility analysis—considers the value or worth of a specific outcome for an individual or society.
3. Willingness-to-pay approach—asks how much individuals are willing to pay to have something they currently do not have.
4. Willingness-to-accept approach—asks individuals how much they would be willing to accept to give up something they already have.
5. Cost of time.

Performance measurement is another specific type of evaluative research. Performance or *output* measures are made in order to determine what was accomplished as a result of specific programs, services, and resources being available. Performance measures focus on indicators of library output and effectiveness, rather than merely on input such as monetary support, number of books, and number of staff. They are clearly related to the impact of the library on the community, are often concerned with user satisfaction, and can be used with longitudinal as well as current data. Other examples of performance measures have included service area penetration, level of use of facilities and equipment, circulation statistics, availability of materials and staff, and reference service use. Lately, the LIS profession has been concerned with using performance measures to evaluate electronic resources and services, including networked services (see Bertot, McClure, and Ryan, for example).[24]

A variety of techniques can be used for measuring performance; they have included the collection of statistics, questionnaires, interviews, observations, unobtrusive reference questions, diaries, consumer panels, and document delivery tests. One of the more recent approaches to measuring the performance of libraries and other organizations is benchmarking. Benchmarking "represents a structured, proactive change effort designed to help achieve high performance through comparative assessment. It is a process that establishes an external standard to which intended operations can be compared."[25] "Benchmarking not only allows for the establishment of a systematic process to indicate the quality of outputs, but also allows for an organization to create its own definition of quality for any process or output."[26] It is critical to keep in mind, however, that whatever technique(s) is used to assess performance, it should be related to the organization's goals and objectives.

Other relatively recent attempts to evaluate the effectiveness of libraries have focused on their *outcomes* or actual *impact*. In other words, rather than stop with the measurement of output or performance, an increasing number of researchers are attempting to determine how the lives of individuals are actually affected by their use of libraries and other information resources and services. For example, an impact assessment of a university library would go beyond measures of reference activity and circulation statistics and attempt to determine how the borrowing of books and procurement of answers to reference questions ultimately affect a student's test scores, papers, course grades, and so on. Impact or effect may well be the most important indicator of a library's effectiveness and represents its most meaningful approach to accountability, but, unfortunately, impact is elusive and no doubt more difficult to measure than input and performance. Steffen, Lance, and Logan measured the impact of public library services on the lives of library users.[27] Lance has also completed studies for individual states to measure the impact of school libraries on student achievement.[28]

In the past several years there has been much discussion of assessing library *service quality* based on customer feedback.[29] Hernon and Dugan argue that outcomes assessment must be linked to accountability, which can be measured by user satisfaction and service quality.[30] The economic environment, the convenience of the Internet, and the availability of mega-book stores with online presences have encouraged librarians to view library users as customers and to develop library services accordingly. This approach, derived from the business world, "cannot adequately be conveyed by output and performance measures."[31] In an attempt to assess university library users' perceptions of services, the Association of Research Libraries has undertaken a research and development project now called *LibQUAL+*. The project attempts "to define and measure library service quality across institutions and to create useful quality-assessment tools for local planning, such as the evaluation of a library's collections-related services from the user's point of view."[32] "Impact" and "outcomes" are often used interchangeably in the literature.

With regard to *methods and techniques*, evaluative research is much like basic research. Verification of the explicit or implicit hypothesis requires a design that will show that the desired effect was more likely to occur in the presence of the program than in its absence. Evaluative researchers must be concerned with threats to validity, such as intervening variables, measurement techniques, and faulty operational definitions. Evaluation research conceivably can employ most of the same methods that are used in basic research. Such methods are often labeled according to their primary design (survey, experiment, and the like). Another approach to categorizing evaluation methods used in library and information science is according to the program, service, or resource to be evaluated. A book by Wallace and Van Fleet,[33] for example, has chapters devoted to the evaluation of reference and information services and to library collections (see also an article by Whitlatch, on the evaluation of electronic reference services).[34] Bawden[35] presents a user-oriented approach for the evaluation of information systems and services. An issue of *Library Trends*[36] has chapters on the evaluation of administrative services, collections, processing services, adult reference service, public services for adults, public library services for children, and school library media services. Lancaster's text[37] includes the evaluation of collections, collection use, in-house library use, periodicals, library space, catalog use, document delivery, reference services, and resource sharing.

In order to conduct an evaluative study, the researcher must collect data or measure what needs to be measured. *Measurement* by itself is not true evaluation, but it is one of the building blocks for quantitative evaluation. Common types of measures for library evaluation studies include number and types of users, number and duration of transactions, user and staff activities, user satisfaction levels, and costs of resources and services. They can be related to input, output, effectiveness, costs, and so on.

It is critical that the measurement process and the measures be reasonably high in reliability and validity. The validity and/or reliability of measures can be affected by such factors as inconsistent data collection techniques, biases of the observer, the data collection setting, instrumentation, behavior of human subjects, and sampling. The use of multiple measures can help to increase the validity and reliability of the data. They are also worth using because no single technique is up to measuring a complex concept, multiple measures tend to complement one another, and separate measures can be combined to create one or more composite measures.[38] (See Chapter 2 for further consideration of validity and reliability.)

Many measures are in the form of *statistics*, which, in some cases, can be drawn from already existing sources of data. Types of statistics include administrative data, financial statistics, collections and other resources or inputs, use and other output/performance measures, outcomes, and staff and salary information. Sources of statistics include governmental agencies, professional associations, and other organizations such as state library agencies. Among the noteworthy sources of library-related statistics are the National Center for Education Statistics (NCES), American Library Association and its divisions (such as the Public Library Association's Public Library Data Service and the Association of College and Research Libraries' Trends and Statistics series), Association of Research Libraries, and federal programs such as the Federal State Cooperative System and the Integrated Postsecondary Education Data System. (See Chapter 10 for additional information about sources of statistical data.) The collection of data, must, of course, be followed by an *analysis* of data, as is the case for any other kind of research.

Readers wanting to consider evaluation research further may wish to consult a 2006 overview in *Library Trends*[39] and a recent book titled *The Evaluation and Measurement of Library Services*.[40] The latter work devotes considerable attention to evaluation process and models, methodological concerns, issues related to the evaluation of specific types of libraries and library services, and how to communicate the results of an evaluative study.

QUALITATIVE RESEARCH

In addition to having to decide whether one's research will be primarily basic or applied, the researcher must determine whether it will be quantitative or qualitative in nature. Quantitative research, which is emphasized in this book, "is appropriate where quantifiable measures of variables of interest are possible, where hypotheses can be formulated and tested, and inferences drawn from samples to populations. Qualitative methods, on the other hand, are appropriate when the phenomena under study are complex, are social in nature, and do not lend themselves to quantification."[41] Qualitative research (field studies and ethnographic techniques are related terms) focuses on attempting to understand why participants react as they do.[42] Qualitative research tends to apply a more holistic and natural approach to the resolution of a problem than does quantitative research. It also tends to give more attention to the subjective aspects of human experience and behavior. Small samples are often acceptable in qualitative studies.

Qualitative researchers have used a variety of methods and techniques, many drawn from anthropology and sociology. They have ranged from ones traditionally used in quantitative research, such as observation and the interview, to less common ones, such as mechanical recording and photography. Gorman and Clayton have written an excellent guide to qualitative research methods, with a practical, how-to approach for information professionals.[43]

While the bulk of basic research in library science has taken the form of quantitative research, which tends to adhere relatively closely to the scientific method of inquiry, qualitative methods have been employed to a greater degree in more recent years. In the report of a study utilizing structured observation, Grover and Glazier argue that qualitative research methods can be useful for gathering data about information users' behavior and information needs.[44] Qualitative methods can be especially useful in exploratory research. Chapter 7 of this book is devoted to qualitative research methods.

SPECIFIC RESEARCH METHODS

Having decided on the general approach to be taken in the research study, the researcher must next identify one, or more, specific methods that he or she wishes to employ to gather the necessary data. As was indicated at the beginning of this chapter, what follows is a brief introduction to a number of research methods. Several of the methods are treated in some detail; others are merely identified with an indication that more information is to be provided elsewhere in the text. A number of additional related readings are provided near the end of the chapter.

Survey Research

Survey research has been defined as "the research strategy where one collects data from all or part of a population to assess the relative incidence, distribution, and interrelations of naturally occurring variables."[45] This methodology, which is most commonly used in descriptive studies, is dealt with in Chapters 4 and 5.

Experimental Research

"In experimental research the researcher manipulates at least one independent variable, controls other relevant variables, and observes the effect on one or more dependent variables."[46] This method is considered to be the best method for testing causal relationships and is treated more fully in Chapter 6.

Historical Research

Isaac and Michael describe the purpose of historical research as one of "reconstruct[ing] the past systematically and objectively by collecting, evaluating, verifying, and synthesizing evidence to establish facts and reach defensible conclusions, often in relation to particular hypotheses."[47] Gay defines it as "the systematic collection and objective evaluation of data related to past occurrences in order to test hypotheses concerning causes, effects, or trends of those events which may help to explain present events and anticipate future events."[48] These are useful definitions, but they both raise issues related to the role of hypotheses in historical research, the feasibility of determining cause and effect, and so on. Such issues, and others, are addressed in Chapter 8.

Operations Research

Operations research (OR) is the application of scientific method to management operations in an effort to aid managerial decision making. It is used to identify optimal solutions to real problems, utilizing analytical mathematical techniques. Some general types of operations research are resource allocation, sequencing, inventory, replacement, queuing theory, and competitive strategies.

According to O'Neill, the standard approach to applying operations research includes the following steps:

1. Formulating the problem
2. Constructing a mathematical model to represent the system under study
3. Deriving a solution from the model
4. Testing the model and the solution derived from it
5. Establishing controls over the solution
6. Putting the solution to work: implementation.[49]

Modeling

Modeling, which is sometimes used synonymously with simulation, is "at the heart of the operations research methodology . . . A model is an abstraction, a mental framework for analysis of a system."[50] Modeling involves the use of simplified representations of real-world phenomena. Modeling is typically used to determine the performance of a real system (e.g., interlibrary loan) by observing the behavior of a representational or analogous system. Computers are often used in simulating complex problems. Modeling can also be part of the process used in the development of a theory.[51]

Systems Analysis

Systems analysis is another process that might better be thought of as a management technique than a research method; it actually has characteristics of both. It is similar in concept to operations research but tends to place greater emphasis on the total system and how the various components of the system interact. Systems analysis often utilizes operations research type techniques, and typically takes into consideration the objectives and performance, the environment, the resources, the components, and the management of the entire system. Libraries sometimes conduct systems analyses before adding a new service or revising an existing one, such as an online catalog.

Case Study

The case study is a specific field or qualitative research method and thus is an investigation "of phenomena as they occur without any significant intervention of the investigators."[52] It seems to be appropriate for investigating phenomena when "(1) a large variety of factors and relationships are included, (2) no basic laws exist to determine which factors and relationships are important, and (3) when the factors and relationships can be directly observed."[53]

Yin defines a case study as "an empirical inquiry that 1) investigates a contemporary phenomenon within its real-life context, especially when 2) the boundaries between phenomenon and context are not clearly evident . . . in which 3) there will be many more variables of interest than data points, and as one result 4) relies on multiple sources of evidence . . . with data needing to converge in a triangulating fashion, and as another result 5) benefits from the prior development of theoretical propositions to guide data collection and analysis."[54]

Leedy and Ormrod define case study research as "a type of qualitative research in which in-depth data are gathered relative to a single individual, program, or event, for the purpose of learning more about an unknown or poorly understood situation."[55]

The case study is often useful as an exploratory technique and can be used for investigating organizational structure and functions or organizational performance. In contrast to most survey research, case studies involve intensive analyses of a small number of subjects rather than gathering data from a large sample or population. A number of data collection techniques are usually employed in case studies. For example, an investigation of staff burnout in a reference department might utilize questionnaires, interviews, observation, and the analysis of documents.

If several phenomena exist, a multiple case design may be desirable. Leedy and Ormrod state that "many separate pieces of information must all point to the same conclusion"[56] for convergence or triangulation of the data. Yin also stresses replication logic, rather than sampling logic, for multiple case studies. "Each case must be carefully selected so that it either a) predicts similar results (a literal replication) or b) predicts contrasting results but for anticipatable reasons (a theoretical replication)."[57] Multiple case studies were conducted, in conjunction with individual interviews and task log analyses, in dissertation research by Connaway to investigate academic technical services librarians' levels of decisions and involvement in decision making.[58]

Most researchers consider the case study to be relatively low in internal and external validity (see Paris[59] for an alternative view), but it certainly has the potential to be a valuable research tool. As Paris points out, the nature of the problem is the major determinant of the most appropriate research methodology, and the case study is well suited to collecting descriptive data.

"The detailed observations that case studies provide are especially useful in documenting phenomena occurring over a period of time or whose implications are complex."[60]

Delphi Study

The Delphi study or technique "is a procedure using sequential questionnaires by which the opinions of experts can be brought to bear on issues that are essentially non-factual."[61] It can be employed for issues that are quantitative and non-quantitative in nature and helps to support informed decision making. The Delphi study is designed to generate consensus by systematically refining prior responses of study participants. "This form of data gathering is effective when policy level decision making is necessary."[62] For example, a library administrator might be faced with creating a collection development policy for electronic resources. After reviewing the professional literature, networking with colleagues at conferences, and so on, the administrator would develop a list of experts on the acquisition of electronic resources and a list of relevant issues. The latter list would then be distributed to the experts for their reactions, which could be suggestions for revision of the list and/or possible resolutions of the issues. The administrator would revise the list based on the responses. The list would be sent back to the experts for further suggestions, if any. This process would continue for more rounds of polling until a consensus among the experts had been reached. This methodology is also useful when the participants are hostile toward one another, argumentative, or unable to meet easily in person.[63]

Content Analysis

The *ALA Glossary of Library and Information Science* defines content analysis as "analysis of the manifest and latent content of a body of communicated material (as a book or film) through a classification, tabulation, and evaluation of its key symbols and themes in order to ascertain its meaning and probable effect."[64] Content analysis is essentially a systematic analysis of the occurrence of words, phrases, concepts, and so on in books, films, and other kinds of materials. Content analysis has been used, for example, to determine how frequently racist and sexist terms appear in certain books. Kracker and Peiling used content analysis to study students' research anxiety and their perceptions of research.[65] See Chapter 7 on qualitative research for more information about content analysis.

Bibliometrics

Bibliometrics is a special type of documentary research or inquiry into the tools of library and information science. It has been defined as "the application of mathematics and statistical methods to books and other media of communication."[66] It also has been referred to as "a series of techniques that seek to quantify the process of written communication"[67] and as "the quantification of bibliographical data."[68] Related terms are scientometrics, informetrics, and librametrics.

The early bibliometric studies produced three basic laws: 1) Bradford's Law of Scatter, which describes how the literature of a subject area is distributed in its journals and which forms the basis for calculating how many journals contain a certain percentage of the published articles; 2) Lotka's Law, a formula for measuring/predicting the productivity of scientific researchers; and 3) Zipf's Law, which describes the frequency of the appearance of certain words or, more specifically, suggests that people are more likely to select and use familiar, rather than unfamiliar, words. (See Wallace[69] and Osareh[70] for useful overviews of the origins of bibliometrics.)

Following early research, bibliometrics branched into quantitative analyses, qualitative studies, and most recently, studies combining quantitative and qualitative methods. Bibliometric research, especially if quantitative, involves the application of mathematical formulas and considerable counting and statistical analysis. Bibliometric analyses have greatly benefited from the availability of computerized bibliographic databases, citation indexes, and statistical programs.

Perhaps the most common type of bibliometric research is concerned with citations. Citation analysis is essentially concerned with "who cites whom."[71] The three basic concepts of citation analysis are 1) "direct citation, which establishes the relationship between documents and the researchers who use them;"[72] 2) bibliographic coupling, where the reference lists of two documents share one or more of the same cited documents;[73] and 3) co-citation, which occurs when two citations are cited together.[74]

Applications of bibliometric research identified by White,[75] von Ungern-Sternberg,[76] Wallace,[77] Osareh,[78] and others include:

1. Improving the bibliographic control of a literature
2. Identifying a core literature, especially journals
3. Classifying a literature
4. Tracing the spread of ideas and growth of a literature
5. Designing more economic information systems and networks
6. Improving the efficiency of information handling services
7. Predicting publishing trends
8. Describing patterns of book use by patrons
9. Developing and evaluating library collections
10. Evaluating journal performance (e.g., citation impact).

Bibliometric and informetric methods are being applied to Internet-based research. "Informetrics investigates characteristics and measurements of persons, groups, institutions, countries; publications and information sources; disciplines and fields; and information retrieval processes."[79] These methods are used to study Web documents, sites, information retrieval tools (such as search engines), and user studies. Webometrics, which focuses on the quantitative study of Web phenomena, encompasses a variety of types of research. Bertot, McClure, Moen, and Rubin, for example, considered the use of Web server-generated log files to evaluate the use of the Web.[80] Shachaf and Shaw analyzed email and chat reference transactions from public and academic libraries to identify core reference sources.[81] *The Journal of the American Society for Information Science and Technology* (*JASIST*) published a special issue on webometrics in December 2004, and covered such topics as structures, patterns, and topologies of hyperlinks on the Web; methodological issues related to the use of search engines; social, cultural, and linguistic factors in Web use; and Web impact measurements.[82]

There continues to be an interest in bibliometric research. A cursory examination of *JASIST* from 2004 through 2010 identified hundreds of published papers addressing the topics of bibliometrics and informetrics. The bimonthly newsletter, *Research Trends*, provides "objective, up-to-the minute insights into scientific trends based on bibliometric analysis."[83] Recognizing that "bibliometrics emerged as a field in its own right" almost 40 years ago, *Research Trends* interviewed Wolfgang Glänzel, of the Expertisecentrum O&O Monitoring in Leuven, Belgium. Glänzel stated that "the quantity and quality of bibliometric tools have increased and improved considerably during the last three decades."[84] However, he identifies three major challenges of bibliometrics: 1) the need for a different approach to bibliometric research to accommodate the different publication and citation practices of humanities and social science researchers; 2) "the development of web-based tools"[85] to document and reproduce results of scholarly communication has not kept pace with the changes in electronic communication made available by the Internet and open-access publishing; and 3) the capability to model and measure the social impacts of communication outside research communities. In other words, bibliometric and citation analysis are not without their limitations and potential problems. The three basic laws identified above have not held up in every situation where they have been applied. A number of people have concerns about using citation counts to evaluate the scholarship of researchers because of issues such as self-citation and incomplete citation databases. Sound bibliometric analysis can be followed by faulty interpretation, and quantity and quality of citations are not necessarily related. Treating Web links as citations begs questions about validity because of variability in the search engines, the lack of quality control, the automatic replication of links, and so on.

Task-Based Research

Task-based research is research that focuses on the scrutiny of specific tasks; it is not a research methodology per se. Task-based research has been designed to utilize multiple research methods within the linguistics, teaching and learning, and Human Computer Interface communities. Tasks play an important role in functional software and system and user interface design as well as understanding users' needs.

This is normally done through observations, user studies, and interviews and from working experience with systems and people. The majority of today's systems use an interactive and event-driven paradigm. Events are messages the user, or the system, sends to the program. A keystroke is an event. So is a mouse-click. Interactive task based design systems place more emphasis on people and their needs to achieve a specific task.

Identifying the user's tasks enables the designer to construct user interfaces reflecting the tasks' properties, including efficient usage patterns, easy-to-use interaction sequences, and powerful assistance features.[86]

Within the past decade task-based information-seeking theory[87] and modeling[88] has developed, enabling researchers to work within the user's task domain instead of within the technology domain. The emphasis is on the users and their tasks in order to identify their workflows for the development of embedded systems and user-centered interface designs. Task-based research design also recognizes that users' tasks can change with the integration of new technologies and systems and new designs may affect the way in which users perform tasks.

Comparative Librarianship

Interestingly, there is a long-standing debate over whether comparative librarianship is a research method or a subject matter. As a subject, it deals with phenomena in librarianship that can be compared. As a research method, it provides the framework for conducting an appropriate comparative analysis. In either case, comparative librarianship often has an international element. A definition that nicely incorporates all of these aspects, found in the *Encyclopedia of Library and Information Science*, reads as follows:

> The systematic analysis of library development, practices, or problems as they occur under different circumstances (most usually in different countries), considered in the context of the relevant historical, geographical, political, economic, social, cultural, and other determinant background factors found in the situations under study. Essentially it constitutes an important approach to the search for cause and effect in library development, and to the understanding of library problems.[89]

"It is commonly stressed in defining the term that (1) comparative librarianship involves two or more national, cultural, or societal environments; (2) the study includes a comparable comparison; and (3) it induces philosophical or theoretical concepts of librarianship through the analysis of similarities and differences of phenomena in various environments."[90] Danton and others have argued that the scientific method of inquiry is the most satisfactory method for comparative studies in librarianship while recognizing that history and comparison are essential elements of this process.[91] The four basic steps for research in comparative librarianship have been identified as description, interpretation, juxtaposition, and comparison. Specific data collection techniques have included case histories, personal interviews, observation, and documentary analysis.

Technology-Based Research Methods

As libraries and other information agencies embrace more and ever-changing technology, including social networking, and employ personnel with technological backgrounds, the profession must facilitate and encourage technology-based research. "One of the difficulties in doing so has to do with reconciling the scientific method with activities that are more similar to product development than to basic research."[92] A perusal of some of the information-related sections of *Dissertation Abstracts International* identifies turns up titles such as "Mining Help Desk Emails for Problem Domain Identification and Email Feature Engineering for Routing Incoming Emails," "Rewriting the 'Rules' of Online Networked Community Information Services: A Case Study of the mycommunityinfo.ca Model," "Using Social Network Analysis to Investigate Potential Bias in Editorial Peer Review in Core Journals of Comparative/International Education," and "Modeling the Role of Blogging in Librarianship." The inclusion of the technology-based research methods in the literature affirms the importance of developing new techniques for utilizing the data made available through new discovery and access technologies. As more libraries become involved in "Web 2.0" technologies and other social media, both qualitative and quantitative research into these technologies have slowly begun.[93]

"Geographic information system (GIS) technology is a rapidly growing and powerful method for managing and analyzing spatial data and information for libraries. . . . A GIS is designed for the collection, storage, and analysis of objects and phenomena where geographic location is an important characteristic or critical to the analysis."[94] While not a basic research method itself, GIS technology certainly has the potential to be a data collection and analysis tool for research, especially applied research. However, there has been little research published using GIS data, which is surprising given the growing popularity of Google Earth and MapQuest. Libraries have been using geographic information for decision making for the development of services and marketing.[95] "The basic operations for GIS spatial analysis are: retrieval, map generalization, map abstractions, map sheet manipulation, buffer generation, polygon overlay and dissolve, measurements, digital terrain analyses, and network analyses."[96] Ottensmann discusses how geographic information systems can be employed to analyze patterns of library utilization in public libraries with multiple branches.[97]

Libraries are particularly interested in utilizing appropriate methods to evaluate their new information technologies. Online catalog use, for example, has been evaluated with traditional research methods and techniques such as questionnaires, interviews, focus group interviews, observation, and experiments. A less common method, protocol analysis, has been found useful for studying the use of online catalogs. Protocol analysis has been called "the thinking aloud technique" because it represents an analysis of subject searchers' thoughts as they perform their subject searches at the catalog.[98] During a protocol analysis, the user verbalizes the decisions and behaviors that he or she is performing in order to search the catalog. A video camera may be used to record the activity being analyzed.[99] As a type of obtrusive observation, the process itself can affect the behavior being analyzed, but using a camera is likely to be less intrusive than direct human observation.

It is often difficult to recruit subjects for protocol analysis research projects; therefore, only two or three subjects may be included for each user group. Researchers may have assumptions about user behaviors or preferences skewing their observations and reporting of the protocols. It also is difficult to interpret and use the data generated by protocols unless behaviors are identified and defined, and quantitative metrics are developed prior to the initiation of the protocols.[100]

In contrast, transaction log analysis, transaction monitoring, search log analysis, or query log analysis has become more popular in the past several years and is not only unobtrusive but also takes advantage of the technology that is being evaluated. Online public access catalogs (OPACs) and Web search engines are able to record and monitor use of the catalog and site; transaction log analysis is the examination of those records. Transaction log analysis can take the form of macroanalysis and microanalysis. The former is concerned with aggregate use data and patterns, the latter with the dynamics of individual search patterns. The transaction log analysis methodology is used to study scholarly communication and productivity in bibliometric studies by analyzing the logs of online journals and data bases and to help researchers understand the behaviors of users of online information retrieval systems. The rationale of the analyses is for the development of information retrieval systems that will better fulfill the needs of users, based on their actual search behaviors. Peters, however, believes that log analysis has been underutilized in practice where it can provide data for library managers to develop systems and services for library users.[101] Banks suggests that practicing library managers could use OPAC usage transaction log data to schedule reference service staff based on the high and low usage patterns during a specified time period.[102]

One of the most important early online catalog use studies, begun in 1980, was sponsored by the Council on Library Resources (CLR) (now the Council on Library and Information Resources). This study utilized questionnaires, focus group interviews, and transaction log analysis as means to study use and users. Five organizations were involved in this research: 1) J. Matthews & Associates, 2) the Library of Congress, 3) Online Computer Library Center (OCLC), 4) Research Libraries Group, and 5) the University of California, Division of Library Automation and Library Research and Analysis Group.[103] A total of 29 academic, public, state, and federal libraries participated in the catalog study, represented by 16 online catalogs.[104] A questionnaire was developed and used by all five of the organizations involved in the CLR-funded research to examine patron and staff experiences with online public access catalogs. In addition to the questionnaire, OCLC conducted focus group interviews, and transaction logs were analyzed to study the use of online public access catalogs.

Since transaction logs provide a record of the search strategy employed by users without interfering with the searcher, an analysis of transaction logs can reflect users' actual online search experiences. This methodology clearly demonstrates how users really employ search strategies rather than how users describe their search strategies. There is also no chance of the interference of interviewer bias in the data collection.

Among other studies of transaction logs, Norden and Lawrence,[105] Tolle,[106] Dickson,[107] Nielsen,[108] Peters,[109] Hunter,[110] Zink,[111] Kalin,[112] Nelson,[113] Cherry,[114] Wallace,[115] Lucas,[116] and Millsap and Ferl,[117] examined transaction logs to study the search methods used by OPAC users. These studies report failures and successes of online searches in regard to the improvement of OPAC capabilities and screen presentation and of OPAC user instruction. Kalin, Lucas, and Millsap and Ferl studied the search methods of remote users.[118] Ciliberti, Radford, and Radford studied the transaction logs of library users of the OPAC and CD-ROM journal indexes to verify the accuracy of user self-reports on the availability of the resources.[119] Mudrock described how the University of Washington libraries used server usage statistics and email reference queries to create a user-oriented ready reference Web site.[120] Simpson has provided an exhaustive review of the literature on transaction log analysis.[121]

In addition to the report of search type and failure and success rates and search method types, errors and problems are also calculated for most of the studies. Unfortunately, the search types, failure or success rates, and errors or problems are not defined or calculated consistently throughout the published literature, and the data provided from each system are not standardized.[122] In addition to these disadvantages, the actual users are not identifiable from the transaction logs, and it is often difficult or impossible to determine when one searcher ends a search session and another begins a session. It is also impossible to discern from the transaction logs who is doing the search and why.

For these reasons, it is often useful to incorporate the transaction log analysis method with other data collection methods. Nielsen linked transaction log analysis data with user demographic data,[123] as did Millsap and Ferl, and Connaway, Budd, and Kochtanek.[124] Connaway, Budd, and Kochtanek interviewed subjects, using a questionnaire, after the subjects completed their online searches.[125] This enabled the researchers to link the transaction logs (subjects' search behaviors) with demographic data. Structuring a study in this way allows for the search behaviors to be analyzed in relation to the searchers' experience with online systems, educational background, reason for the search, and so on, thus requiring the researcher to infer less about the nature of the search and maintaining the validity of the study.

With the popularity and high visibility of the Internet, many researchers have used transaction or Web log analysis to investigate information retrieval on the Web. Zhang, Wolfram, and Wang "investigated eleven sports-related query keywords extracted from a public search engine query log to better understand sports-related information seeking on the Internet."[126] Keily and Moukdad and Large analyzed queries from the search engine WebCrawler.[127] Silverstein, Henzinger, Marais, and Moricz analyzed approximately one billion queries from Alta Vista during a 43-day period.[128] Smith, Ruocco and Jansen,[129] Xu,[130] Jansen, Spink and Saracevic,[131] Spink and Xu,[132] and Spink, Wolfram Jansen, and Saracevic[133] used queries from the search engine Excite to study information retrieval patterns on the Web. These studies have identified query characteristics submitted to several Internet search engines. Jansen and Pooch give an overview of the findings of several Web user studies.[134] The *Handbook of Research on Web Log Analysis* offers an overview of research-based approaches to log analysis, including methodological and ethical issues and limitations of the method.[135]

Covey provides an extensive overview of transaction log analysis.[136] Her study of the methods used by 24 libraries "to assess the use and usability of their online collections and services" includes why and how these libraries used the transaction log analysis approach. The problems and challenges associated with this methodology and information on the analysis, interpretation, and presentation of the data collected from transaction log analysis are outlined and discussed by Covey. The book also includes an excellent bibliography on the topic.

A special issue of *Library Hi Tech* provided a useful overview of transaction log analysis. Kaske's article in the issue addressed a number of issues and questions relevant to using transaction log analysis as a research method, including:

1. Basic constraints
2. Proposed general model
3. Research or management
4. Quantitative or qualitative methods
5. Micro or macro evaluation
6. Sample or population
7. Controlled or uncontrolled experiments
8. Ethics and transaction logs.[137]

The next-to-last item in the list above reinforces that transaction log analysis may be used in conjunction with other research methods; for example, transaction logs can be matched with questionnaire data, as discussed above. The last item serves as a reminder that any research method that is unobtrusive, or does not inform the subjects they are being observed, raises ethical questions related to the invasion of privacy.

ETHICS OF RESEARCH

Ethics are in fact of importance to all kinds of social and behavioral research, especially when the research involves human subjects. Unfortunately, unethical practices seem to have become more common in recent years, and a growing percentage of unethical practices are relatively difficult to detect. An increasing number of research studies are conducted by large groups of researchers, making it harder to observe misconduct and attribute it to the appropriate person(s). Experimental replication, a traditional safeguard against unethical conduct, is more problematic given the size, cost, and complexity of many contemporary studies. The proliferation of journals has resulted in less stringent editing, and more of what is published is going unchallenged. At the same time, the rate at which scientific journal articles are being retracted has increased significantly over the last several years. Finally, what is ethical practice and what is not is not always clear-cut.

General Guidelines

A book by Sieber provides a reasonably comprehensive, but succinct, guide to planning ethical research. In her opening chapter, she commented:

the ethics of social research is not about etiquette; nor is it about considering the poor hapless subject at the expense of science or society. Rather, we study ethics to learn how to make social research 'work' for all concerned. The ethical researcher creates a mutually respectful, win-win relationship with the research population; this is a relationship in which subjects are pleased to participate candidly, and the community at large regards the conclusions as constructive.[138]

Or, as Hoyle, Harris, and Judd noted, the issue of ethics often comes down to balancing the costs of questionable practices against the potential benefits of the research.[139]

Sieber's first chapter also includes a discussion of IRBs, or Institutional Review Boards (also known as Human Subjects Committees, Human Investigation Committees, and Human Subjects Review Boards). The U.S. government requires that all universities and other organizations that conduct research involving human subjects and that receive federal funding for research involving human subjects (virtually all universities granting doctoral degrees) must have an IRB. "The purpose of the IRB is to review all proposals for human research before the research is conducted to ascertain whether the research plan has adequately included the ethical dimensions of the project."[140] They are to help ensure that no harm will come to human subjects, that they are informed of and consent to the protocol of the research study, and that their confidentiality or anonymity will be provided. Miller's textbook on research design includes facsimiles of the IRB documents used by the University of Kansas.[141] Those documents address submission criteria, application forms, audio and video recording of subjects, payment to subjects, subject selection considerations, implied consent, inclusion of research instruments, deception of subjects, the review process, and so on. Readers wishing to know more about IRBs may wish to consult *The IRB Reference Book*.[142]

Many professional associations have guidelines for ethical research. Miller and Salkind's book provides a reprint of the *Code of Ethics* published by the American Sociological Association.[143] That code covers issues such as professional competence, integrity, respect for people's rights, dignity and diversity, social responsibility, ethical standards, harassment, conflicts of interest, disclosure of financial support and relevant relationships, confidentiality, and the publication process.[144]

The other chapters in the book by Sieber cover the research protocol (proposal), general ethical principles, voluntary informed consent and debriefing (interaction with subjects immediately following their participation in the research), privacy, confidentiality, deception, elements of risk, benefits, research on children and adolescents, and community-based research on vulnerable urban populations and AIDS. Sieber's appendix includes sample consent and assent forms for use with older children.[145]

A number of other standard textbooks on research methods in the social and behavioral sciences devote space to ethics in research. Hoyle, Harris, and Judd, for example, give considerable attention to the ethical implications of research.[146] Johanson stated, "It is impossible for any research to avoid ethics. They are inextricably entwined."[147] He then proceeds to take a rather philosophical approach to ethics in research in discussing social ideals and research and principles and ethical codes, but he also addresses some of the more pragmatic concerns such as ethics committees and the publishing of research results. Johanson provides several useful examples or case studies relating to the links among practice, ethics, and research. Chapter 7 of this book discusses ethics in the context of qualitative research.

Schutt deals with ethical issues in experimental research and in survey research separately. He notes, "[subject] deception is an essential part of many experimental designs. As a result, contentious debate continues about the interpretation"[148] of research ethics. He then discusses the issue of deception in more detail and next considers the question of how much subjects may be harmed by the way benefits are distributed as part of a field experiment.

In his section on ethics in survey research, Schutt points out that "special care must be taken when . . . sensitive personal questions are to be asked."[149] He notes that many surveys employ questions that might prove damaging to the subjects if their answers were disclosed, and in such cases it is critical to preserve subject confidentiality, if not anonymity. Schutt stresses that the "cover letter or introductory statement that identifies the sponsors of, and motivations for, the survey"[150] must "point out that the respondent's participation is completely voluntary."[151] The cover letter or opening statement should also disclose the researcher's affiliation and the project's sponsors and identify any possible harm or benefits for subjects.

Kimmel focuses on ethics in applied social research.[152] He covers many of the same topics treated by other textbooks, but there is a particularly useful chapter on special problems in applied settings. One section of that chapter discusses some of the ethical issues in organizational research, which often deals with issues such as personnel evaluation, program evaluation, and the implementation of interventions designed to improve employee performance and relations. Such activities are quite susceptible to ethical abuse. He also addresses some of the unanticipated consequences of prevention research. For example, a preventive intervention designed to increase worker productivity might cause psychological harm. Kimmel concludes the chapter with a consideration of ethical issues that may arise after the research is completed related to possible consequences of applying the results, misuse of the new knowledge, and responsibilities of the applied social researcher.

A brief consideration of ethical issues regarding the use of and reporting of the results of statistical analysis is provided by Losee and Worley.[153] Some of those issues relate to the biased use and/or interpretation of statistical techniques and data. Others have to do with "the level of effort researchers should make to ensure that no errors in their research or in the writing up of their results will appear in print or in distributed electronic form."[154] Krathwohl raises two possible ethical issues related to ownership of the data: availability of the data to others for secondary analysis and apportionment of credit on publication.[155]

Goetz makes a case for making dark data (the data that did not support the researchers' hypotheses) openly accessible for further analysis. He premises his discussion on the idea of publication bias, "where science gets skewed because only positive correlations see the light of day."[156]

Guidelines for LIS Professionals

"Although LIS has imported [methodologies] from other disciplines, it has not turned its attention to 'research ethics' to the extent of the fields it borrows from."[157] However, a few books and articles have been concerned, at least in part, with ethical issues somewhat specific to LIS practitioners and researchers. Westbrook, for example, in her book on the analysis of community information needs, incorporates guidelines for ethical practices as appropriate. These guidelines stress that anonymity, or confidentiality, of everyone involved must be maintained; that library services should never appear to depend on patron participation in the study; and that no harm should come to any subject.[158] She reminds the reader that, upon completion of the study, all confidential data should be destroyed, including interview transcripts, lists of subject names, and observation notes, and that both electronic and paper files should be weeded as much as possible. Westbrook also stresses the importance of emphasizing ethical practices when training staff to conduct information needs analyses.

In his article on the ethical considerations of information professionals, Froehlich discusses the ethical issues that can arise when decisions are being made about who should publish research results and take the credit. Other issues related to the publication process can include plagiarism, falsification or fabrication of data, dual submissions of manuscripts to journals, and duplicate publication of identical or largely identical manuscripts without permission from the editors.[159] Losee and Worley, in their book about research for information professionals, also provide brief, but useful, information about ethics in the dissemination of research results.[160] They, too, deal with plagiarism and the submission of results to more than one journal or conference at the same time. Hauptman's book includes a discussion of ethical issues related to research and publication by academic librarians.[161]

Smith focuses on the ethics of research about the uses of information provided by librarians. In other words, to what extent are librarians justified in investigating the information use activities of patrons in order to improve information services provided to them? What are the ethics of user studies? Smith noted that there is a need for guidelines for research on user needs and information use, but one concludes that such guidelines should not scare practitioners away from "the serious evaluation and research that needs to be conducted if librarians are to serve the public and to preserve the profession."[162]

Carlin, while pointing out the need for more consideration of the place of ethics in LIS research, presents several cases and debates from other disciplines so as to raise the visibility of research ethics for researchers in LIS.[163] He also discusses the possibility of an "ethics of interdisciplinarity" and stresses the importance of being accountable for the presentation of research strategies and accurately distinguishing between primary and secondary sources.

Ethics for Research on the Internet

As Case indicated, a relatively new ethical issue has to do with the uses of the Internet for research:

> The ubiquity of information exchange on the Internet, for example, has led to discussion among researchers regarding the ethics of collecting public submissions to mailing lists, discussion boards, and Web sites. Although chat rooms and individual e-mail exchanges are considered to be "private,"

some researchers maintain that postings to public channels like Usenet and open mailing lists are fair game for analysis and reporting. Yet the increasingly common practice of collecting electronic discussions, particularly on controversial topics, raises the issue of whether the contributors are "fully informed" that they are subjects of study. Whatever individual investigators think about the ethicality of studying public discussions, institutional review boards typically ask for evidence that research subjects are informed of possible observation and its consequences. If the investigator is taking an active role in the discussion—posing questions to the list, for example—the issue becomes even more complex.

As computer and biomedical technology provide increased monitoring capability of overt behavior and physical responses, we can expect more challenges to the boundaries of acceptable research. Witness the increased awareness of privacy brought about by use of the Internet. Many users gradually became aware that commercial entities were not only tracking the most obvious data—their demographic background (such as they were willing to supply voluntarily) and electronic purchases—but were even recording their visits to Web sites in which transactions were not conducted. The pervasive use of tracking cookies and of online forms and questionnaires, coupled with the ability to aggregate and cross-reference data by individual computer user, has led to massive collections of data on electronic information seeking. That much of this has been collected without the full consent and understanding of Internet users is an example of how far things can go if ethical data-collection principles are not observed.[164]

Most existing guidelines for ethical research were not developed with such information technologies in mind. Jones pointed out, for example, that issues such as public versus private information and informed consent in an electronic environment are not adequately addressed by the guidelines provided by the typical research university. He cautioned researchers to recognize the limitations of existing guidelines and to take steps to ensure that research on the Internet is just as ethical as any other research.[165] To help meet the need for more information on these issues a new journal, *International Journal of Internet Research Ethics*, was founded in 2008.

Scientific and Research Misconduct

As Krathwohl stated, ethical standards are, in effect, a constraint on research; and they can be divided "into two aspects: (1) the legal and institutional constraints designed to protect the people from whom data are gathered and (2) the responsibility of the individual researcher for proper conduct above and beyond legalities. The former, covered by U.S. federal regulations, ensures that the researcher's institution provides adequate safeguards for the protection of human subjects in all federally funded research."[166] Hence the Institutional Review Boards discussed earlier.

In addition to IRBs, many universities have policies and procedures regarding scientific misconduct. Wayne State University, in Detroit, Michigan, for example, has a four-page policy that provides necessary definitions and procedures for handling allegations of scientific misconduct, initial inquiries, formal investigations, possible resolutions, and appeals. Other mechanisms for minimizing scientific misconduct have included 1) the mentor-apprentice relationship, in which the senior researcher imparts the importance of intellectual honesty; 2) the communal review of research results via scholarly communication; 3) the replication of research results; and 4) the review of proposals before the research is conducted.[167]

In spite of the guidelines and codes of ethics for research, scientific/research misconduct can and does still occur. In fact, "the Commission on Research Integrity, which was created as part of the National Institutes of Health Revitalization Act of 1993, proposed new procedures for addressing scientific misconduct"[168] "because, beyond the high-profile cases, widespread problems in the conduct of research remain."[169] "The lay public presumes that professions are self-regulating. ... However, the effectiveness of self-regulation in the academic profession is currently being challenged."[170]

There is at least a perception that research misconduct in library and information science is less of a problem than it is in other fields, "principally because the stakes are not terribly high in LIS, as compared with fields such as biology, physics, medicine, and the like."[171] Or as Wiberley stated, "there is less of it than in other fields that have greater funding or greater prestige. The greater the stakes, the more incentive there is to cheat."[172]

But what is scientific or research misconduct; how is it defined? According to Wayne State University's policy, "scientific misconduct includes fabrication, falsification, plagiarism, or other practices that seriously deviate from commonly accepted practices within the scientific community for proposing, conducting, or reporting research. Misconduct does not include honest error or honest differences of interpretation in judgments of data. Nor does it include the innocent failure to comply with the terms of research grants."[173] Altman noted an agreement among professional organizations, governmental agencies, and scientists "that fabrication, falsification, or plagiarism in proposing, performing, or reporting research constitute scientific misconduct."[174]

Library and information professionals desiring more information about scientific and research misconduct are encouraged to consult a book edited by Altman and Hernon.[175] Chapters in that work address such issues as misconduct and the scholarly literature, implications of misconduct for bibliographic instruction, and implications of research misconduct for libraries and librarians. Also included are appendices with references to codes of ethics from professional societies, guidelines for instructions to authors, and sources for information about cases of research misconduct.

Another useful resource is a special issue of the *Journal of Information Ethics* (1996) devoted to research misconduct.[176] Articles treat, among other topics, information ethics in the workplace, the lure of scientific misconduct, the influence of academic departments/disciplines on misconduct, federal actions against plagiarism, misconduct involving digital imaging, and the legal aspects of scientific misconduct. Finally, readers interested in electronic guides to research ethics can consult the bibliography on Tom Wilson's Web site: *InformationR.net*[177] (see the section Electronic Resources for Information Research Methods); and Sharon Stoerger's *Research Ethics Webliographies*,[178] which include resources on research ethics in general, plagiarism, and research ethics in specific subject fields.

SUMMARY

This chapter pertains to the fifth stage of the basic scientific method of inquiry—the methodology. The reader is reminded that the researcher must first decide if his or her research will be quantitative and/or qualitative in nature, applied or basic. Then a number of specific research methods are introduced. The list and discussion of various methods and their uses in LIS is not, however, exhaustive. Nor are the descriptions detailed enough to provide adequate instruction in how to use the methods. Readers wishing to employ one or more of these methods should refer to the relevant sections of this work, other standard texts on research methods, and appropriate readings listed below. The last section addresses the important issue of ethics in research.

ADDITIONAL READINGS

Abdullahi, Ismail. *Global Library and Information Science: A Textbook for Students and Educators, with contributions from Africa, Asia, Australia, New Zealand, Europe, Latin America and the Caribbean, the Middle East, and North America.* München: Saur, 2009. (a textbook on comparative librarianship)

Adeyami, Nat M. "Library Operations Research—Purpose, Tools, Utility, and Implications for Developing Libraries." *Libri* 27 (March 1977): 22–30.

Allen, G. G. "Management and the Conduct of In-House Library Research." *Library & Information Science Research* 8, no. 1 (1986): 155–62.

Baker, Lynda M., ed. "Research Methods." *Library Trends* 55, no. 1 (Summer 2006).

Baker, Sharon, and F. Wilfrid Lancaster. *The Measurement and Evaluation of Library Services.* 2nd ed. Arlington VA: Information Resources Press, 1991.

Beck, Susan E., and Kate Manuel. *Practical Research Methods for Librarians and Information Professionals.* New York: Neal-Schuman Publishers, 2008.

Bethlehem, Jelke. *Applied Survey Methods: A Statistical Perspective.* Hoboken: Wiley, 2009.

Bogdan, Robert C., and Sari Knopp Biklen. *Qualitative Research for Education: An Introduction to Theory and Methods.* 5th ed. Boston: Allyn and Bacon, 2007.

Borbinha, José, ed. *Research and Advanced Technology for Digital Libraries: 4th European Conference ECDL 2000 Proceedings.* New York: Springer, 2000. (examples of several technology-based research methods in use, including transaction log analysis)

Boyce, Bert R., Charles T. Meadow, and Donald H. Kraft. *Measurement in Information Science.* San Diego: Academic Press, 1994.

Budd, Richard, Robert K. Thorp, and Lewis Donohew. *Content Analysis of Communication.* New York: Macmillan, 1967.

Burgess, Robert G. *Field Research: A Sourcebook and Field Manual.* London: George Allen & Unwin, 1982.

———. *In the Field: An Introduction to Field Research.* Contemporary Social Research Series 8. London: George Allen and Unwin, 1984.

Busha, Charles H., and Stephen P. Harter. *Research Methods in Librarianship: Techniques and Interpretation.* New York: Academic Press, 1980.

Chen, Ching-Chih, ed. *Quantitative Measurement and Dynamic Library Service.* Phoenix, AZ: Oryx Press, 1978.

Childers, Thomas A., and Nancy A. Van House. *What's Good? Describing Your Public Library's Effectiveness.* Chicago: American Library Association, 1993.

Covey, Denise Troll. *Usage and Usability Assessment: Library Practices and Concerns.* Washington, DC: Digital Library Federation and Council on Library and Information Resources, 2002.

De Bellis, Nicola. *Bibliometrics and Citation Analysis: From the Science Citation Index to Cybermetrics.* Lanham, MD: Scarecrow, 2009.

deMarrais, Kathleen, and Stephen D. Lapan. *Foundations for Research: Methods of Inquiry in Education and the Social Sciences.* Mahwah, NJ: Erlbaum, 2004. (Full chapters on historical research, critical incident technique, focus groups, surveys, and case studies.)

Denzin, Norman K., and Yvonna S. Lincoln, eds. *The Landscape of Qualitative Research.* 3rd ed. Thousand Oaks, CA: Sage, 2008.

———. *The SAGE Handbook of Qualitative Research.* 3rd ed. Thousand Oaks, CA: Sage, 2005.

———. *Strategies of Qualitative Inquiry.* 3rd ed. Thousand Oaks, CA: Sage, 2008.

DeProspo, Ernest R., Ellen Altman, and Kenneth Beasley. *Performance Measures for Public Libraries.* Chicago: Public Library Association, 1973.

Diodato, Virgil. *Dictionary of Bibliometrics.* New York: Haworth Press, 1994.

Dougherty, Richard M., and Fred J. Heinritz. *Scientific Management of Library Operations.* 2nd ed. Metuchen, NJ: Scarecrow Press, 1982.

Dugan, Robert E., and Peter Hernon. "Outcomes Assessment: Not Synonymous with Inputs and Outputs." *Journal of Academic Librarianship* 38 (November 2002): 376–80.

Dyer, Esther R. "The Delphi Technique in Library Research." *Library Research* 1 (Spring 1979): 41–52.

Franzozi, Roberto, ed. *Content Analysis.* Thousand Oaks, CA: Sage, 2008.

Gass, Saul I., and Carl M. Harris, eds. *Encyclopedia of Operations Research.* Boston: Kluwer, 1996.

Hart, Chris. *Doing a Literature Review: Releasing the Social Science Research Imagination.* London: Sage, 2009.

Hernon, Peter, and Charles McClure. *Evaluation and Library Decision Making.* Norwood, NJ: Ablex Publishing, 1990.

Hesse-Biber, Sharlene Nagy, and Patricia Leavy. *Emergent Methods in Social Research.* Thousand Oaks, CA: Sage, 2006.

Hoadley, Irene Braden, and Alice S. Clark, eds. *Quantitative Methods in Librarianship: Standards, Research, Management.* Westport, CT: Greenwood Press, 1972.

Kantor, Paul B. *Objective Performance Measures for Academic and Research Libraries.* Washington, DC: Association of Research Libraries, 1984.

Krippendorff, Klaus, and Mary Angela Bock, eds. *The Content Analysis Reader.* Thousand Oaks, CA: Sage, 2009.

Lancaster, F. Wilfrid. *If You Want to Evaluate Your Library . . .* Champaign, IL: University of Illinois, Graduate School of Library and Information Science, 1988.

Leimkuhler, Ferdinand F. "Operations Research." In *Encyclopedia of Library and Information Science*, vol. 20, edited by Allen Kent, Harold Lancour, and J. E. Daily, 412–39. New York: Dekker, 1977.

Lofland, John, David A. Snow, Leon Anderson, and Lyn H. Lofland. *Analyzing Social Settings: A Guide to Qualitative Observation and Analysis.* 4th ed. Belmont, CA: Wadsworth/Thomson Learning, 2006.

MacKee, Monique. *A Handbook of Comparative Librarianship.* 3rd ed. London: Clive Bingley, 1983.

Mertens, Donna M., and Pauline E. Ginsberg, eds. *The Handbook of Social Research Ethics.* Los Angeles: Sage, 2009.

Neuendorf, Kimberly. *The Content Analysis Guidebook.* Thousand Oaks, CA: Sage, 2002.

Nicholas, David, and Maureen Ritchie. *Literature and Bibliometrics*. London: Clive Bingley, 1984.

Orr, R. H. "Measuring the Goodness of Library Services: A General Framework for Considering Quantitative Measures." *Journal of Documentation* 29 (September 1973): 315–32.

Partnership: The Canadian Journal of Library and Information Practice and Research. http://www.criticalimprov.com/index.php/perj/.

Peritz, Bluma C. "On the Objectives of Citation Analysis: Problems of Theory and Method." *Journal of the American Society for Information Science* 43, no. 6 (July 1992): 448–51.

Powell, Ronald R. "Impact Assessment of University Libraries." In *Encyclopedia of Library and Information Science*, vol. 55, edited by Allen Kent, 151–64. New York: Marcel Dekker, 1994.

Rao, I. K. Ravichandra. *Quantitative Methods for Library and Information Science*. New York: John Wiley and Sons, 1983. (See the chapter on bibliometrics.)

Reilly, Kevin D. "The Delphi Technique: Fundamentals and Applications." In *Targets for Research in Library Education*, edited by Harold Borko. Chicago: American Library Association, 1973.

Shi, Xi. "A Theory-Guided Approach to Library Services Assessment." *College & Research Libraries* 66 (May 2005): 266–77.

Simpson, Ian S. *Basic Statistics for Librarians*. 3rd rev. ed. London: Library Association, 1989. (See the chapter on bibliometrics.)

Simsova, Sylva. *A Primer of Comparative Librarianship*. London: Clive Bingley, 1982.

Strauss, Anselm L. *Qualitative Analysis for Social Scientists*. New York: Cambridge University Press, 1987.

Suchman, Edward A. *Evaluative Research*. New York: Russell Sage Foundation, 1967.

Swisher, Robert, and Charles R. McClure. *Research for Decision Making: Methods for Librarians*. Chicago: American Library Association, 1984.

Taylor, Steven J., and Robert Bogdan. *Introduction to Qualitative Research Methods: A Guidebook and Resource*. 3rd ed. New York: John Wiley & Sons, 1998.

Trochim, William M. K., and James P. Donnelly. *The Research Methods Knowledge Base*. 3rd ed. Mason, OH: Thomson, 2007.

Van House, Nancy, Beth Weil, and Charles McClure. *Measuring Academic Library Performance: A Practical Approach*. Chicago: American Library Association, 1990.

Van House, Nancy A., and others. *Output Measures for Public Libraries: A Manual of Standardized Procedures*. 2nd ed. Chicago: American Library Association, 1987.

Weiss, Carol H. *Evaluation Research: Methods for Assessing Program Effectiveness*. Englewood Cliffs, NJ: Prentice-Hall, 1972.

Wildemuth, Barbara M. *Applications of Social Research Methods to Questions in Information and Library Science*. Westport, CT: Libraries Unlimited, 2009.

Wilson, Concepcion S. "Informetrics." In *Annual Review of Information Science and Technology*, vol. 34, edited by Martha E. Williams. Medford, NJ: American Society for Information Science, 1999.

Wolfram, Dietmar. *Applied Informetrics for Information Retrieval Research*. Westport, CT: Libraries Unlimited, 2003.

Zhang, Yin, and Athena Salaba. "What is Next for Functional Requirements for Bibliographic Records? A Delphi Study." *Library Quarterly* 79/2 (April 2009): 233–55.

Zweizig, Douglas L. "Measuring Library Use." *Drexel Library Quarterly* 13 (July 1977): 3–15.

Zweizig, Douglas, and Eleanor Jo Rodger. *Output Measures for Public Libraries: A Manual of Standardized Procedures.* Chicago: American Library Association, 1982.

Zweizig, Douglas, Debra Wilcox Johnson, and Jane Robbins, with Michele Besant. *The Tell It! Manual: The Complete Program for Evaluating Library Performance.* Chicago: American Library Association, 1996.

NOTES

1. Charles H. Davis, and James E. Rush, *Guide to Information Science* (Westport, CT: Greenwood Press, 1980), 101–39.

2. Charles H. Davis, "Information Science and Libraries: A Note on the Contribution of Information Science to Librarianship," *The Bookmark* 51 (1982): 96.

3. Judson D. Sheridan, "Perspectives from 202 Jesse Hall: The Research Continuum," *Graduate School and Research Notes* 14, no. 6 (February 1988): 1.

4. Charles R. McClure, "Increasing the Usefulness of Research for Library Managers: Propositions, Issues, and Strategies," *Library Trends* 38 (Fall 1989): 282.

5. Tom D. Wilson, "Electronic Resources for Research Methods: Research Methods," *InformationR.net,* http://informationr.net/rm/RMeth6.html.

6. Anna H. Perrault and Ron Blazek, "Transforming Library Services Through Action Research," *Florida Libraries* 40, no. 3 (1997): 60.

7. Stephen Isaac and William B. Michael, *Handbook in Research and Evaluation: A Collection of Principles, Methods and Strategies Useful in Planning, Design, and Evaluation of Studies in Education and the Behavioral Sciences,* 3rd ed. (San Diego: EdITS Publishers, 1995), 59.

8. Ibid.

9. Michael René Kristiansson, "Strategic Reflexive Conversation–A New Theoretical-Practice Field within LIS," Information Research 12, no. 4 (2007), http://InformationR.net/ir/12-4/colis/colis18.html.

10. Ibid.

11. University of Alberta Learning Services, "Evidence Based Library and Information Practice: Home," http://ejournals.library.ualberta.ca/index.php/EBLIP/index.

12. Jonathan Eldredge, "Evidence-Based Librarianship: The EBL Process," *Library Hi Tech* 24, no. 3 (2006): 342.

13. Ross Todd, "The Evidence-Based Manifesto for School Librarians," *School Library Journal* 4 (2008), http://www.schoollibraryjournal.com/article/CA6545434.html.

14. OCLC Research "Data Mining Research Area," 2009, http://www.oclc.org/research/activities/past/orprojects/mining/default.htm.

15. Lynn Silipigni Connaway, "Capturing Untapped Descriptive Data: Creating Value for Librarians and Users" (paper presented at the ASIS&T 2006 Annual Conference, Austin, TX, November 8, 2006), http://www.oclc.org/research/presentations/connaway/20061108-asist-untappeddata.ppt.

Lynn Silipigni Connaway, "Making Data Work Harder," *OCLC Newsletter* (April/May/June 2005): 268. http://www.oclc.org/news/publications/newsletters/oclc/2005/268/downloads/research.pdf.

Lynn Silipigni Connaway and Timothy J. Dickey, "Beyond Data Mining: Delivering the Next Generation of Service from Library Data" (paper presented at the ASIS&T 2008 Annual Meeting, Columbus, OH, October 24–29, 2008), http://www.oclc.org/research/presentations/connaway/asist2008.ppt.

Lynn Silipigni Connaway and Timothy J. Dickey, "Beyond Data Mining: Delivering the Next Generation of Service from Library Data," in *ASIS&T 2008: Proceedings of the 71st Annual Meeting, Vol. 45, 2008: People Transforming Information—Information Transforming People*, ed. Andrew Grove and Abebe Rorissa (Silver Springs, MD: American Society for Information Science and Technology, 2008).

Lynn Silipigni Connaway and Timothy J. Dickey, "Data Mining, Advanced Collection Analysis, and Publisher Profiles: An Update on the OCLC Publisher Name Authority File" (paper presented at the XXVIII Annual Charleston Conference, Charleston, SC, November 7, 2008). http://www.oclc.org/research/presentations/connaway/charleston2008.ppt.

Lynn Silipigni Connaway, Brian Lavoie, and Lorcan Dempsey, "Anatomy of Aggregate Collections: The Example of Google Print for Libraries," *D-Lib Magazine* 11, no. 9 (2005). http://www.dlib.org/dlib/september05/lavoie/09lavoie.html.

Lynn Silipigni Connaway, Brian Lavoie, and Edward T. O'Neill, "Mining for Digital Resources: Identification and Characterizing Digital Materials in WorldCat," in *Currents and Convergence: Navigating the Rivers of Change: Proceedings of the Twelfth National Conference of the Association of College and Research Libraries, April 7–10, 2005, Minneapolis, Minnesota*, ed. Hugh A. Thompson (Chicago: Association of College and Research Libraries, 2005).

Lynn Silipigni Connaway and Larry Olszewski, "A Geographical Representation of WorldCat Resources: A Decision Making Tool for Acquisitions and Collection Management" (paper presented at the XXVI Annual Charleston Conference, Charleston, SC, November 10, 2006). http://www.oclc.org/research/presentations/connaway/20061110-charleston-worldmap.pdf.

Lynn Silipigni Connaway and Larry Olszewski, "OCLC WorldMap: Visualizing Information about Collections and Libraries Worldwide" (paper presented at the OCLC Inclusion Council, Dublin, OH, January 31, 2008), http://www.oclc.org/research/presentations/connaway/worldmapfinal2008-01-31.ppt.

Lynn Silipigni Connaway and Lawrence Olszewski, "Visualizing the Globalization of WorldCat," *NextSpace* 9 (2008), http://www.oclc.org/nextspace/009/research.htm.

Lynn Silipigni Connaway, Edward T. O'Neill, and Eudora Loh, *Changing Global Book Collection Patterns in ARL Libraries* (Washington, DC: Association of Research Libraries, 2006), http://www.crl.edu/sites/default/files/attachments/pages/grn_global_book.pdf.

Lynn Silipigni Connaway, Clifton Snyder, and Lawrence Olszewski, "Geographical Representation of Library Collections in WorldCat: A Prototype," in *Sparking Synergies: Bringing Research and Practice Together at ASIS&T '05, October 28-November 2, Charlotte, NC*, ed. Andrew Grove (Medford, NJ: Information Today, 2005).

Lynn Silipigni Connaway, Clifton Snyder, and Lawrence Olszewski, "What in the World: Leveraging Corporate Assets for Internal and External Use" (paper presented at the SLA Annual Conference, Toronto, Canada, June 5–8, 2005), http://www.sla.org/Documents/conf/toronto/Olszewski.doc.

Mary E. Jackson, Lynn Silipigni Connaway, Edward T. O'Neill, and Eudora Loh, *Changing Global Book Collection Patterns in ARL Libraries* (report prepared for the Global Resources Network, http://www.arl.org/resources/pubs/grn_global_book.shtml or http://www.crl.edu/sites/default/files/attachments/pages/grn_global_book.pdf).

Jennifer Knievel, Heather Wicht, and Lynn Silipigni Connaway, "Collection Analysis Using Circulation, ILL, and Collection Data," *Against the Grain* 16, no. 6 (December 2004-January 2005): 25–26.

Jennifer Knievel, Heather Wicht, and Lynn Silipigni Connaway, "Use of Circulation Statistics and Interlibrary Loan Data in Collection Management," *College & Research Libraries* 67, no. 1 (2006): 35–49, http://www.ala.org/ala/mgrps/divs/acrl/publications/crljournal/2006/jan/knieval-06.pdf.

Brian Lavoie, "Mining for Copyright Evidence" (paper presented at the ASIS&T 2008 Annual Meeting, Columbus, OH, October 28, 2008).

Brian Lavoie, Lorcan Dempsey, and Lynn Silipigni Connaway, "Making Data Work Harder," *Library Journal* 131, no. 1 (2006): 40–42. http://www.libraryjournal.com/article/CA6298444.html.

Brian Lavoie, "On Lemons and Bibliographic Data . . . Creating Value through WorldCat Data-Mining" (paper presented at the OCLC Members Council Digital Libraries Research Interest Group meeting, Dublin, OH, May 16, 2005).

Brian Lavoie, Lynn Silipigni Connaway, and Edward T. O'Neill, "Mapping World-Cat's Digital Landscape," *Library Resources and Technical Services (LRTS)* 51, no. 2 (April 2007): 106–15.

Brian Lavoie, Lynn Silipigni Connaway, and Edward O'Neill, "Mining for Digital Resources: Identifying and Characterizing Digital Materials in WorldCat" (paper presented at the ACRL 12th National Conference: Currents and Convergence: Navigating the Rivers of Change, Minneapolis, MN, April 7–10, 2005).

Brian Lavoie and Roger C. Schonfeld, "A Systemwide View of Library Collections" (paper presented at the CNI Spring 2005 Task Force Meeting, Washington DC, April 4–5, 2005).

Justin Littman and Lynn Silipigni Connaway, "A Circulation Analysis of Print Books and e-Books in an Academic Research Library,"*Library Resources & Technical Services* 48, no. 4 (2004): 256–62. http://www.oclc.org/research/publications/archive/2004/littman-connaway-duke.pdf.

Scott Nicholson, Lynn Silipigni Connaway, and Bob Molyneux, "Capturing Untapped Descriptive Data: Creating Value for Librarians and Users," in *Information Realities Shaping the Digital Future for All: Proceedings of the ASIS&T Annual Meeting, Vol. 43, 2006*, ed. Andrew Grove (2006). Silver Springs, MD: American Society for Information Science and Technology, 2006.

Edward T. O'Neill, "OhioLINK Collection Analysis Project: Preliminary Analysis" (paper presented at the ASIS&T 2008 Annual Meeting, Columbus, OH, October 28, 2008).

Edward T. O'Neill, Lynn Silipigni Connaway, and Timothy J. Dickey, "Estimating the Audience Level for Library Resources,"*Journal of the American Society for Information Science and Technology* 59, no. 13 (2008): 2042–50.

Heather Wicht and Lynn Silipigni Connaway, "Using Circulation, ILL, and Collection Characteristics for the Development of Policies for Collections and ILL Services," in *Charleston Conference Proceedings, 2003*, ed. Katina P. Strauch, Rosann Bazirjian, and Vicky H. Speck (Westport, CT: Libraries Unlimited, 2004).

16. Sharon L. Baker and F. Wilfrid Lancaster, *The Measurement and Evaluation of Library Services*, 2nd ed. (Arlington, VA: Information Resources Press, 1991), 321.

17. F. Wilfrid Lancaster, *If You Want to Evaluate Your Library . . .*, 2nd ed. (Champaign, IL: University of Illinois, Graduate School of Library and Information Science, 1993), 267.

18. Ibid.

Joseph R. Matthews, *Measuring for Results: The Dimensions of Public Library Effectiveness* (Westport, CT: Libraries Unlimited, 2004).

19. Herbert E. Klarman, "The Road to Cost-Effectiveness Analysis," *Health and Society* 60 (Autumn 1982): 586.

20. Lancaster, *If You Want to Evaluate Your Library . . .*, 294.

21. Ibid.

22. Carol H. Weiss, *Evaluation Methods for Studying Programs and Policies*, 2nd ed. (Upper Saddle River, NJ: Prentice Hall, 1998).

23. Matthews, *Measuring for Results*.

24. John Carlo Bertot, Charles R. McClure and Joe Ryan, *Statistics and Performance Measures for Public Library Networked Services* (Chicago: American Library Association, 2001).

25. Susan R. Jurow, "Tools for Measuring and Improving Performance," in *Integrating Total Quality Management in a Library Setting*, ed. Susan R. Jurow and Susan B. Bernard (New York: Haworth, 1993), 120.

26. Thomas M. Peischl, "Benchmarking: A Process for Improvement," *Library Administration & Management* 9, no. 2 (Spring 1995): 100.

27. Nicolle O. Steffen, Keith Curry Lance, and Rochelle Logan, "Time to Tell the Who Story: Outcome-Based Evaluation and the Counting on Results Project," *Public Libraries* 41 (July-August 2002): 222–28.

28. Keith Curry Lance, "What Research Tells Us About the Importance of School Libraries," *Knowledge Quest* 31 Supplement (September-October 2002): 17–22.

29. Peter Hernon and Ellen Altman, *Assessing Service Quality: Satisfying the Expectations of Library Customers* (Chicago: American Library Association, 1998); Peter Hernon and John R. Whitman, *Delivering Satisfaction and Service Quality: A Customer-Based Approach for Librarians* (Chicago: American Library Association, 2001).

30. Peter Hernon and Robert E. Dugan, *An Action Plan for Outcomes Assessment in Your Library* (Chicago: American Library Association, 2002).

31. Peter Hernon and Ellen Altman, *Service Quality in Academic Libraries* (Norwood, NJ: Ablex Publishing, 1996), xv.

32. Julia C. Blixrud, "The Association of Research Libraries Statistics and Measurement Program: From Descriptive Data to Performance Measures," *67th IFLA Council and General Conference: Conference Programme and Proceedings*, 2001, http://archive.ifla.org/IV/ifla67/papers/034-135e.pdf.

33. Danny P. Wallace and Connie Jean Van Fleet, *Library Evaluation: A Casebook and Can-Do Guide* (Englewood, CO: Libraries Unlimited, 2001).

34. Jo Bell Whitlatch, "Evaluating Reference Services in the Electronic Age." *Library Trends* 50, no. 2 (2001): 207–17.

35. David Bawden, *User-Oriented Evaluation of Information Systems and Services* (Brookfield, VT: Gower, 1990).

36. Sarah R. Reed, ed. "Evaluation of Library Service," *Library Trends* 22, no. 3 (1974).

37. Lancaster, *If You Want to Evaluate Your Library . . .*

38. Weiss, *Evaluation Methods for Studying Programs and Policies*, 136.

39. Ronald R. Powell, "Evaluation Research: An Overview," *Library Trends* 55 (Summer 2006): 102–20.

40. Joseph R. Matthews, *The Evaluation and Measurement of Library Services* (Westport, CT: Libraries Unlimited, 2007).

41. Peter Liebscher, "Quantity with Quality? Teaching Quantitative and Qualitative Methods in an LIS Master's Program," *Library Trends* 46, no. 4 (1998): 669.

42. Constance A. Mellon, "Library Anxiety: A Grounded Theory and Its Development," *College & Research Libraries* 47 (March 1986): 160.

43. G. E. Gorman and Peter Clayton, *Qualitative Research for the Information Professional: A Practical Handbook*, 2nd ed., with contributions by Sydney J. Shep and Adela Clayton (London: Facet Publishing, 2005).

44. Robert J. Grover and Jack D. Glazier, "Implications for Application of Qualitative Methods to Library and Information Science Research," *Library & Information Science Research* 7 (July 1985): 247–60.

45. Louise H. Kidder and Charles M. Judd, *Research Methods in Social Relations*, 5th ed. (New York: Holt, Rinehart and Winston, 1986), 519.

46. L. R. Gay, Geoffrey E. Mills, and Peter Airasian, *Educational Research: Competencies for Analysis and Application*, 8th ed. (Upper Saddle River, NJ: Pearson Merrill Prentice Hall, 2006), 233.

47. Isaac and Michael, *Handbook in Research and Evaluation*, 48.

48. L. R. Gay, *Educational Research: Competencies for Analysis and Application*, 2nd ed. (Columbus, OH: Charles E. Merrill, 1981), 432.

49. Edward T. O'Neill, "Operations Research," *Library Trends* 32 (Spring 1984): 512.

50. Donald H. Kraft and Bert R. Boyce, *Operations Research for Libraries and Information Agencies: Techniques for the Evaluation of Management Decision Alternatives* (San Diego: Academic Press, 1991), 12.

51. Marcia J. Bates, "An Introduction to Metatheories, Theories, and Models," in *Theories of Information Behavior*, ed. Karen E. Fisher, Sandra Erdelez, and Lynne (E. F.) McKechnie (Medford, NJ: Information Today, Inc., 2005), 3.

52. Raya Fidel, "The Case Study Method: A Case Study," *Library & Information Science Research* 6 (July 1984): 274.

53. Ibid., 273.

54. Robert K. Yin, *Case Study Research: Design and Methods*, 4th ed. (Thousand Oaks, CA: Sage, 2008), 18.

55. Paul D. Leedy and Jeanne E. Ormrod, *Practical Research: Planning and Design*, 8th ed. (Upper Saddle River, NJ: Pearson Merrill Prentice Hall, 2005), 108.

56. Ibid., 136.

57. Yin, *Case Study Research*, 53.

58. Lynn Silipigni Connaway, "The Levels of Decisions and Involvement in Decision-Making: Effectiveness and Job Satisfaction in Academic Library Technical Services" (Ph.D. diss., University of Wisconsin—Madison, 1992).

59. Marion Paris, "Thoughts on the Case Study," *Journal of Education for Library and Information Science* 29 (Fall 1988): 138.

60. Ibid.

61. Robert M. Hayes, *Use of the Delphi Technique in Policy Formulation: A Case Study of the "Public Sector/Private Sector" Task Force* (Los Angeles: University of California, Graduate School of Library and Information Science, 1982), 1.

62. Robert M. Losee, Jr. and Karen A. Worley, *Research and Evaluation for Information Professionals* (San Diego: Academic Press, 1993), 158.

63. Delbert C. Miller and Neil J. Salkind, *Handbook of Research Design & Social Measurement*, 6th ed. (Thousand Oaks, CA: Sage, 2002).

64. Heartsill Young, ed., *The ALA Glossary of Library and Information Science* (Chicago: American Library Association, 1983), 57.

65. Jacqueline Kracker and Wang Peiling, "Research Anxiety and Students' Perceptions of Research: An Experiment. Part II. Content Analysis of Their Writings on Two Experiences Using Kuhlthau's Information Search Process at a Large Southeastern University," *Journal of the American Society for Information Science and Technology* 53 (February 2002): 295–307.

66. Barbara Kopelock Ferrante, "Bibliometrics: Access in Library Literature," *Collection Management* 2 (Fall 1987): 201.

67. Linus Ikpaahindi, "An Overview of Bibliometrics: Its Measurements, Laws, and Their Implications," *Libri* 35 (June 1985): 163.

68. Emilie C. White, "Bibliometrics: From Curiosity to Convention," *Special Libraries* 76 (Winter 1985): 35.

69. Danny P. Wallace, "Bibliometrics and Citation Analysis," in *Principles and Applications of Information Science for Library Professionals*, ed. John N. Olsgaard (Chicago: American Library Association, 1989), 10–26.

70. Farideh Osareh, "Bibliometrics, Citation Analysis and Co-Citation Analysis: A Review of Literature I," *Libri* 46 (1996): 149–58.

71. John Martyn and F. Wilfrid Lancaster, *Investigative Methods in Library and Information Science: An Introduction* (Arlington, VA: Information Resources Press, 1981): 52.

72. White, "Bibliometrics," 35–42.

73. Linda C. Smith, "Citation Analysis," *Library Trends* 30 (Summer 1981): 85.

74. White, "Bibliometrics," 39.

75. Ibid.

76. Sara von Ungern-Sternberg, "Teaching Bibliometrics," *Journal of Education for Library and Information Science* 39, no. 1 (1989): 76–80.

77. Wallace, "Bibliometrics and Citation Analysis."

78. Osareh, "Bibliometrics," 149–58.

79. Judit Bar-Ilan and Bluma C. Peritz, "Informetric Theories and Methods for Exploring the Internet: An Analytical Survey of Recent Research Literature," *Library Trends* 50 (Winter 2002): 371.

80. John Carlo Bertot, Charles R. McClure, William E. Moen, and Jeffrey Rubin, "Web Usage Statistics: Measurement Issues and Analytical Techniques," *Government Information Quarterly* 14, no. 4 (1997): 373–95.

81. Pnina Shachaf and Debora Shaw, "Bibliometric Analysis to Identify Core Reference Sources of Virtual Reference Transactions,"*Library & Information Science Research* 30 (2008): 291–97.

82. *Journal of the American Society for Information Science and Technology* 55, no. 14 (2004): 1213–1306.

83. Research Trends' Editorial Board, "What is Research Trends?" *Research Trends*, http://info.scopus.com/researchtrends/whatis.html.

84. Gert-Jan Geraeds and Judtih Kamalski, "Bibliometrics Come of Age," *Research Trends*, http://www.info.scopus.com/researchtrends/archive/RT15/re_tre_15.html.

85. Ibid.

86. Narayanan Meyyappan, Suliman Al-Hawamdeh, and Schubert Foo, "Task Based Design of a Digital Work Environment (DWE) for an Academic Community," *Information Research* 7, no. 2 (2002), http://InformationR.net/ir/7-2/paper125.html.

87. Katriina Byström and Kalervo Järvelin, "Task Complexity Affects Information Seeking and Use," *Information Processing & Management* 31, no. 2 (1995): 191–213.

Pertti Vakkari, "Growth of Theories on Information Seeking. An Analysis of Growth of a Theoretical Research Program on Relation between Task Complexity and Information Seeking," *Information Processing & Management* 34, no. 3/4 (1998): 361–82.

Pertti Vakkari, "Task Complexity, Problem Structure and Information Actions: Integrating Studies on Information Seeking and Retrieval," *Information Processing & Management* 35, no. 6 (1999): 819–37.

Pertti Vakkari and Martti Kuokkanen, "Theory Growth in Information Science: Applications of the Theory of Science to a Theory of Information Seeking," *Journal of Documentation* 53, no. 5 (1997): 497–519.

88. Katriina Byström, "Task Complexity, Information Types and Information Sources: Examination of Relationships," (Ph.D. diss., University of Tampere, 1999).

Kalervo Järvelin and T. D. Wilson, "On Conceptual Models for Information Seeking and Retrieval Research," *Information Research* 9, no. 1 (2003), http://InformationR.net/ir/9-1/paper163.html.

89. Dorothy G. Collings, "Comparative Librarianship," in *Encyclopedia of Library and Information Science*, vol. 5 (New York: Marcel Dekker, 1971), 492.

90. Chih Wang, "A Brief Introduction to Comparative Librarianship," *International Library Review* 17 (1985): 109.

91. J. Periam Danton, *The Dimensions of Comparative Librarianship* (Chicago: American Library Association, 1973).

92. Ronald R. Powell, "Research Competence for Ph.D. Students in Library and Information Science," *Journal of Education for Library and Information Science* 36 (Fall 1995): 327.

93. See, for example, Matthew M. Bejune, "Wikis in Libraries," *Information Technology & Libraries* 26, no. 3 (Sept. 2007): 26–38; Lani Draper and Marthea Turnage, "Blogmania: Blog Use in Academic Libraries," *Internet Reference Services Quarterly* 31, no. 1 (2008): 15–55; Martin R. Kalfatovic, Effie Kapsalis, Katherine P. Spiess, Anne Van Camp, and Michael Edson, "Smithsonian Team Flikr: A Library, Archives, and Museums Collaboration in Web 2.0 Space," *Arch Sci* 8 (2008): 267–77; Michael Stevens, "The Pragmatic Biblioblogger: Examining the Motivations and Observations of Early Adopter Librarian Bloggers,"*Internet Reference Services Quarterly* 13, no. 4 (2008): 311–45; Chen Xu, Fenfei Ouyang, and Heting Chu, "The Academic Library meets Web 2.0: Applications and Implications," *Journal of Academic Librarianship* 35, no. 4 (2009): 324–31.

94. Allan B. Cox and Fred Gifford, "An Overview to Geographic Information Systems," *Journal of Academic Librarianship* 23, no. 6 (1997): 449.

95. The Florida State University College of Information, "About GeoLib," http://www.geolib.org/about.cfm.

96. Cox and Gifford, "Geographic Information Systems," 454.

97. John R. Ottensmann, "Using Geographic Information Systems to Analyze Library Utilization," *Library Quarterly* 67 (1997): 24–49.

98. Thomas A. Peters, *The Online Catalog: A Critical Examination of Public Use* (Jefferson, NC: McFarland, 1991), 151.

99. Susan Wiedenbeck, Robin Lampert, and Jean Scholtz, "Using Protocol Analysis to Study the User Interface," *Bulletin of the American Society for Information Science* 15 (1989): 25–26.

100. Denise Troll Covey, *Usage and Usability Assessment: Library Practices and Concerns* (Washington, DC: Digital Library Federation and Council on Library and Information Resources, 2002), 25.

101. Thomas Peters, "Using Transaction Log Analysis for Library Management Information," *Library Administration & Management* 10 (Winter 1996): 20–25.

102. Julie Banks, "Are Transaction Logs Useful? A Ten-Year Study," *Journal of Southern Academic and Special Librarianship* 1, no. 3 (2000), http://southernlibrarianship.icaap.org/content/v01n03/banks_j01.html.

Julie Banks, "Can Transaction Logs Be Used for Resource Scheduling? An Analysis," *Reference Librarian* 63 (Special Report, 1999): 95–108.

103. Neal K. Kaske, "Studies of Online Catalogs," in *Online Catalogs/Online Reference*, ed. Brian Aveney and Brett Butler (Chicago: American Library Association, 1984).

104. Joseph R. Matthews, Gary S. Lawrence, and Douglas K. Ferguson, *Using Online Catalogs: A Nationwide Survey, A Report of a Study Sponsored by the Council on Library Resources* (New York: Neal-Schuman, 1983).

105. David J. Norden and Gail Herndon Lawrence, "Public Terminal Use in an Online Catalog: Some Preliminary Results," *College & Research Libraries* 42 (1981): 308–16.

106. John E. Tolle, *Current Utilization of Online Catalogs: A Transaction Log Analysis*, vol. 1 (Dublin, OH: OCLC Office of Research, 1983).

107. Jean Dickson, "An Analysis of User Errors in Searching an Online Catalog," *Cataloging & Classification Quarterly* 4, no. 3 (1984): 19–38.

108. Brian Nielsen, "What They Say They Do and What They Do: Assessing Online Catalog Use Instruction Through Transaction Log Monitoring," *Information Technology and Libraries* 5 (1986): 28–33.

109. Thomas Peters, "When Smart People Fail: An Analysis of the Transaction Logs of an Online Public Catalog," *Journal of Academic Librarianship* 15 (1989): 267–73.

110. Rhonda N. Hunter, "Successes and Failures of Patrons Searching the Online Catalog at a Large Academic Library: A Transaction Log Analysis," *RQ* 30 (1991): 395–402.

111. Steven D. Zink, "Monitoring User Search Success Through Transaction Log Analysis: The Wolf-PAC Example," *Reference Services Review* 19, no. 1 (1991): 49–56.

112. Sally W. Kalin, "The Searching Behavior of Remote Users: A Study of One Online Public Access Catalog (OPAC)," in *Proceedings of the 54th Annual Meeting of the American Society for Information Science*, ed. Jose-Marie Griffiths (Medford, NJ: Learned Information Inc, 1991), 175–85.

113. Janet L. Nelson, "An Analysis of Transaction Logs to Evaluate the Educational Needs of End Users," *Medical Reference Services Quarterly* 11, no. 4 (1992): 11–21.

114. Joan M. Cherry, "Improving Subject Access in OPACs: An Exploratory Study of Conversion of Users' Queries," *Journal of Academic Librarianship* 18 (1992): 95–99.

115. Patricia M. Wallace, "How Do Patrons Search the Online Catalog When No One's Looking? Transaction Log Analysis and Implications for Bibliographic Instruction and System Design," *RQ* 33 (1993): 239–352.

116. Thomas A. Lucas, "Time Patterns in Remote OPAC Use," *College & Research Libraries* 54 (1993): 439–45.

117. Larry Millsap and Terry Ellen Ferl, "Research Patterns of Remote Users: An Analysis of OPAC Transaction Logs," *Information Technology and Libraries* 12 (1993): 321–43.

118. Kalin, "Searching Behavior," 175–85.

Lucas, "Time Patterns," 439–45.

Millsap and Ferl, "Research Patterns," 321–43.

119. Anne C. Ciliberti, Marie L. Radford, and Gary P. Radford, "Empty Handed? A Material Availability Study and Transaction Log Analysis Verification," *Journal of Academic Librarianship* 24 (July 1998): 282–99.

120. Theresa Mudrock, "Revising Ready Reference Sites: Listening to Users Through Server Statistics and Query Logs," *Reference and User Services Quarterly* 42 (Winter 2002): 155–63.

121. Charles W. Simpson, "OPAC Transaction Log Analysis: The First Decade," in *Advances in Library Automation and Networking*, ed. Joe Hewitt (Greenwich, CT: JAI Press, 1989), 35–67.

122. Tolle, *Current Utilization of Online Catalogs*.

123. Nielsen, "What They Say They Do," 28–33.

124. Millsap and Ferl, "Research Patterns," 321–43.

Lynn Silipigni Connaway, John M. Budd, and Thomas R. Kochtanek, "An Investigation of the Use of an Online Catalog: User Characteristics and Transaction Log Analysis," *Library Resources and Technical Services* 39, no. 2 (April 1995): 142–52.

125. Ibid.

126. Jin Zhang, Dietmar Wolfram, and Peiling Wang, "Analysis of Query Keywords of Sports-Related Queries Using Visualization and Clustering," *Journal of the American Society for Information Science and Technology* 60, no. 8 (2009): 1550.

127. Lyn Keily, "Improving Resource Discovery on the Internet: The User Perspective," in *Proceedings of the 21st International Online Information Meeting* (Oxford: Learned Information, 1997), 205–12.

Haidar Moukdad and Andrew Large, "Users' Perceptions of the Web as Revealed by Transaction Log Analysis," *Online Information Review* 25, no. 6 (2001): 349–59.

128. Craig Silverstein, Hannes Marais, Monika Henzinger, and Michael Moricz, "Analysis of a Very Large Web Search Engine Query Log," *SIGIR Forum* 33, no. 1 (1999): 6–12.

129. Todd Smith, Anthony Ruocco, and Bernard J. Jansen, "Digital Video in Education," in *Proceedings of the 30th ACM SIGCSE Technical Symposium on Computer Science Education*, ed. Daniel T. Joyce (New York: Association of Computing Machinery, 1999): 122–36.

130. Jack L. Xu, "Internet Search Engines: Real World IR Issues and Challenges" (paper presented, Conference on Information and Knowledge Management, CIKM99, Kansas City, MO: 1999).

131. Bernard J. Jansen, Amanda Spink, and Tefko Saracevic, "Real life, Real Users, and Real Needs: A Study and Analysis of User Queries on the Web," *Information Processing and Management* 36 (2000): 207–77.

132. Amanda Spink and Jack L. Xu, "Selected Results from a Large Study of Web Searching: The Excite Study," *Information Research* 6, no.1 (2000).

133. Amanda Spink, Dietmar Wolfram, Bernard J. Jansen, and Tefko Saracevic, "Searching the Web: The Public and Their Queries,"*Journal of the American Society for Information Science and Technology* 52, no. 3 (2001): 226–34.

134. Bernard J. Jansen and Udo Pooch, "A Review of Web Searching Studies and a Framework for Future Research," *Journal of the American Society for Information Science* 52, no. 3 (2001): 235–46.

135. Bernard J. Jansen, Amanda Spink, and Isak Taksa, *Handbook of Research on Web Log Analysis* (Hershey, PA: Information Science Reference, 2008).

136. Covey, *Usage and Usability Assessment*, v.

137. Neal K. Kaske, "Research Methodologies and Transaction Log Analysis: Issues, Questions, and a Proposed Model," *Library Hi Tech* 11 (1993): 79–86.

138. Joan Sieber, *Planning Ethically Responsible Research: A Guide for Students and Internal Review Boards* (Newbury Park, CA: Sage, 1992), 5.

139. Rick H. Hoyle, Monica J. Harris, and Charles M. Judd, *Research Methods in Social Relations*, 7th ed. (Fort Worth, TX: Wadsworth/Thomson Learning, 2002).

140. Sieber, *Planning Ethically Responsible Research*, 5.

141. Miller and Salkind, *Handbook of Research Design*.

142. Michele K. Russell-Einhorn, and Thomas Puglisi, *Institutional Review Board (IRB) Reference Book: Protecting the People Who Volunteer to Participate in Research* ([Washington, DC]: PricewaterhouseCoopers, 2001).

143. Delbert C. Miller, and Neil J. Salkind, *Handbook of Research Design & Social Measurement*, 6th ed. (Thousand Oaks, CA: Sage, 2002), 100–117.

144. Miller and Salkind, *Handbook of Research Design*.

145. Sieber, *Planning Ethically Responsible Research*.

146. Hoyle, Harris, and Judd, *Research Methods in Social Relations*.

147. Graeme Johanson, "Ethics in Research," in *Research Methods for Students, Academics and Professionals: Information Management and Systems*, 2nd ed., ed. Kirsty Williamson (Wagga Wagga, Australia: Charles Sturt University, Centre for Information Studies, 2002), 67.

148. Russell K. Schutt, *Investigating the Social World: The Process and Practice of Research*, 5th ed. (Thousand Oaks, CA: Sage, 2006), 225.

149. Ibid., 281.

150. Ibid., 278.

151. Ibid., 259.

152. Allan J. Kimmel, "Ethics and Values in Applied Social Research," in *Applied Social Research Methods*, vol. 12 (Newbury Park, CA: Sage, 1988).

153. Losee and Worley, *Research and Evaluation for Information Professionals*.

154. Ibid., 200.

155. David R. Krathwohl, *Methods of Educational & Social Science Research: An Integrated Approach*, 2nd ed. (Long Grove, IL: Waveland Press, Inc, 2004): 217.

156. Thomas Goetz, "Freeing the Dark Data of Failed Scientific Experiments," *Wired* 15, no. 10 (2007), http://www.wired.com/science/discoveries/magazine/15-10/st_essay.

157. Andrew P. Carlin, "Disciplinary Debates and Bases of Interdisciplinary Studies: The Place of Research Ethics in Library and Information Science," *Library & Information Science Research* 25, no. 1 (Spring 2003): 3.

158. Lynn Westbrook, *Identifying and Analyzing User Needs* (New York: Neal-Schuman Publishers, 2001), 47.

159. Thomas J. Froehlich, "Ethical Considerations of Information Professionals," in *Annual Review of Information Science and Technology*, vol. 27, ed. Martha E. Williams, vol. 27 (Medford, NJ: Learned Information Inc, 1992), 309.

160. Losee and Worley, *Research and Evaluation for Information Professionals*.

161. Robert Hauptman, *Ethics and Librarianship* (Jefferson, NC: McFarland, 2002).

162. Martha M. Smith, "Survival and Service: The Ethics of Research on the Uses of Information Provided by Librarians," *North Carolina Libraries* 65 (1994): 64–67.

163. Carlin, "Disciplinary Debates," 14.

164. Donald O. Case, *Looking for Information: A Survey of Research on Information Seeking, Needs, and Behavior*, 2nd ed. (Amsterdam: Elsevier/Academic Press, 2007), 187–88.

165. Robert A. Jones, "The Ethics of Research in Cyberspace," *Internet Research: Electronic Networking Applications and Policy* 4 (1994): 30–35.

166. Krathwohl, *Methods of Educational & Social Science Research*, 204.

167. "Wayne State University Policy and Procedures Regarding Scientific Misconduct, Executive Order 89–4," *Wayne State University: University Policy*, 1995, http://wayne.edu/fisops/universitypolicy.pdf.

168. Mary Burke, Min-min Chang, Charles Davis, Peter Hernon, Paul Nicholls, Candy Schwartz, Debora Shaw, Alastair Smith, and Stephen Wiberley, "Editorial: Fraud and Misconduct in Library and Information Science Research," *Library & Information Science Research* 18 (1996): 199.

169. Kenneth J. Ryan, "Scientific Misconduct in Perspective: The Need to Improve Accountability," *Chronicle of Higher Education* B1 (1996).

170. John M. Braxton and Alan E. Bayer, "Perceptions of Research Misconduct and an Analysis of Their Correlates," *Journal of Higher Education* 65 (1994): 351.

171. Burke et al., "Fraud and Misconduct," 200.

172. Ibid.

173. "Wayne State University Policy and Procedures," 89.

174. Ellen Altman and Peter Hernon, eds., *Research Misconduct: Issues, Implications, and Strategies* (Greenwich, CT: Ablex Publishing, 1997), 2.

175. Ibid.

176. Robert Hauptman, ed., *Journal of Information Ethics* 5, no. 1 (Spring 1996).

177. Tom D. Wilson, "InformationR.net: The Quality Source for Research on Information Management, Information Science and Information Systems," http://informationr.net.

178. Sharon Stoerger, "Research Ethics," http://www.web-miner.com/researchethics.htm.

Chapter 4

Survey Research and Sampling

The survey is a group of research methods commonly used to determine the present status of a given phenomenon. The basic assumption of most survey research is that, by carefully following certain scientific procedures, one can make inferences about a large group of elements by studying a relatively small number selected from the larger group. For example, if one wanted to learn the opinions of all academic librarians in the United States regarding information literacy, one could study a sample of several hundred librarians and use their responses as the basis for estimating the opinion of all of them. For a discussion of sampling in-library use, see the section written by Mundt after the Nonsampling Error section of this chapter.

SURVEY RESEARCH

The word *survey* literally means to look at or to see over or beyond or, in other words, to observe. *Observations* made during the course of a survey are not limited to those of the physical type, however, and techniques commonly used for collecting survey data will be considered later.

As was just indicated, a key strength of survey research is that, if properly done, it allows one to generalize from a smaller group to a larger group from which the subgroup has been selected. The subgroup is referred to as the *sample*, and techniques for drawing samples will be treated in considerable detail later. The larger group is known as the *population;* it must be clearly defined, specifically delimited, and carefully chosen.

The observations or measurements made during survey research, or any other kind of research, generate *data* or information. These data are particularly susceptible to *bias* introduced as a result of the research design (and at other stages in the research process), so that problem will be considered here and other places throughout this work.

MAJOR DIFFERENCES BETWEEN SURVEY RESEARCH AND OTHER METHODS

As has been noted, survey research has characteristics common to most other research methods, but at the same time, it exhibits certain important differences. For example, survey research is used to gather contemporary data, while historical research is, of course, primarily concerned with past data. Some argue that historical research, at least at present, is less bound to the scientific method of inquiry.

In contrast to experimental research, survey research does not enable the researcher to manipulate the independent variable, provides less control of the research environment, and therefore is not considered capable of definitely establishing causal relationships. In other words, survey research is considered to be less rigorous than experimental research.

On the other hand, survey research is better suited than experimental research to studying a large number of cases, including those that are geographically dispersed. Also, survey research is generally considered to be more appropriate for studying personal factors and for exploratory analysis of relationships.

TYPES OF SURVEY STUDIES

In selecting a research method, and a type of survey research in particular, the researcher must keep in mind the research problem, the sources of the desired information, the nature of the data to be collected, and the major purpose of the research. For example, if the purpose of the study is to formulate a problem for a more precise investigation or to develop more formal hypotheses, then a formative or exploratory type of survey may well be in order.

Exploratory Surveys

An exploratory survey, often conducted as qualitative research, can increase the researcher's familiarity with the phenomenon in question; it can help to clarify concepts, it can be used to establish priorities for future research, it can identify new problems, and it can be used to gather information with practical applications, although such results cannot always be anticipated. Specific kinds of exploratory research surveys include:

1. *Literature surveys.* Literature surveys or reviews are in some respects exploratory in nature in that they often focus on developing hypotheses, based on previous research, that may suggest further research. Literature surveys may stand alone, but more often they are a part of a larger study. In the latter case, they are considered to be supportive of the research that follows rather than as research studies themselves.

2. *Experience surveys.* Experience surveys, as the name suggests, are surveys that gather and synthesize the experiences of specialists and/or practitioners in a particular field. They too are exploratory in that their

aim is to obtain "insight into the relationships between variables rather than to get an accurate picture of current practices or a simple consensus as to best practices."[1] The researcher's primary interest is in gaining provocative ideas and useful insights (i.e., suggestions for future research, rather than specific statistics). Experience surveys, as well as suggesting hypotheses, can provide information on the feasibility of doing other research. For example, they can provide information on where the facilities for research can be obtained, which factors can and cannot be controlled, how readily available the necessary data are, and so on. Experience surveys also may help to establish priorities for research in the area and to summarize the knowledge of practitioners regarding the effectiveness of various methods and procedures, or best practices in a particular field.

3. *Analysis of "insight-stimulating" examples.* Where there is little experience to serve as a guide, researchers have found the intensive study of selected examples to be a useful method of stimulating insights and suggesting hypotheses for future research. This method differs from the case study approach in that it tends to be more intensive and narrow in scope. The types of examples or cases likely to be of most value depend on the problem under study, but, in general, cases that provide sharp contrasts or have striking features tend to be the most useful.

Speaking of exploratory surveys in general, it is important to remember that exploratory studies merely suggest insights or hypotheses; they cannot test them. By selecting examples that have special characteristics, one no longer has cases that are typical, but a biased sample instead. In addition, exploratory studies do not provide enough control of extraneous variables, nor should they, to permit the testing of a specific relationship. "An exploratory study must always be regarded as simply a first step; more carefully controlled studies are needed to test whether the hypotheses that emerge have general applicability."[2]

Analytical and Descriptive Surveys

A second general type of survey, but one that is seldom labeled as such in the literature, is the analytical survey. Leedy describes the analytical survey method as "appropriate for data that are quantitative in nature and that need statistical assistance to extract their meaning."[3] In practice, however, most researchers seem to consider an analytical survey essentially as a kind of descriptive survey, and they do not distinguish between the two. In fact, descriptive surveys are the most common type of survey, and many researchers use "survey research methods" and "descriptive surveys" synonymously.

Other Types of Surveys

In a workbook developed for an ACRL workshop, Golden listed nine different types of surveys, some of which could no doubt be subsumed under the broader types of surveys just discussed. These nine types are the following:

1. Cross-sectional study—a typical survey, such as a Gallup poll, designed to measure one or more phenomena across a sample representative of the population or whole.

2. Trend study—a survey conducted over a period of time so as to measure trends, patterns, or changes.

3. Cohort study—a survey conducted in order to collect data from the same population more than once. The same people are not surveyed, but the subjects are selected from the same population.

4. Panel study—a survey designed to collect data from the same sample of subjects, often over time. In fact, the trend study and the panel study may be treated as *longitudinal* studies.

5. Approximation of a longitudinal study—an attempt to simulate a true longitudinal study by asking people to recall past behavior and activities.

6. Parallel samples study—a survey of separate samples regarding the same research problem. For example, a study of university library use might necessitate surveying both students and faculty.

7. Contextual study—a survey of a person's environment, conducted so as to learn more about the person. For example, a study of a person's information use might benefit from a consideration of the information resources available to that person.

8. Sociometric study—a comprehensive survey of more than one group, including the interrelationships among the groups. For example, a thorough study of children's literature might well entail surveying authors, critics, publishers, librarians, parents, and children.

9. Critical incident study—an in-depth examination of a specific event or activity rather than a broad survey of many occurrences; similar to the "analysis of insight-stimulating examples" described above.[4] The critical incident technique (CIT) was used by John C. Flanagan as part of his behavior studies in the United States Army Air Forces during World War II.[5]

Readers wishing to know more about these specific types of studies should consult some of the standard texts on survey research.

BASIC PURPOSES OF DESCRIPTIVE SURVEYS

The basic purposes of descriptive surveys usually are to describe characteristics of the population of interest, estimate proportions in the population, make specific predictions, and test associational relationships. (They can be used to *explore* causal relationships.) Looking first at describing the population, it should be kept in mind that a description of characteristics of the population is often based on a description of the characteristics of a (hopefully) representative sample—hence the importance of the sampling technique.

Having identified characteristics of the population, it then becomes important to estimate (if using a sample) their proportions in the population. Without such data, one can say little about the significance of the traits. For example, it may be interesting to learn that some academic librarians hold subject master's degrees, but little can be done to interpret the possible impact of this phenomenon without knowing what percentage of all academic librarians hold subject master's degrees.

Information regarding characteristics or proportions is also necessary in order to make predictions about specific relationships. In the course of the study just alluded to, one may find that a high percentage of libraries with an acquisitions budget of a certain size employs librarians with subject master's degrees. On the basis of such data, the researcher may be prepared to predict that, in most cases, libraries having an acquisitions budget over a certain amount will indeed have librarians with subject master's degrees.

In fact, the researcher may wish to go a step further and "test" the relationship between budget size and librarians' credentials. The testing of a relationship between two or more variables will be described in greater detail later, but it should be noted that some tests are more rigorous than others. The consensus is that descriptive survey research can consider but not test causal relationships, but that it can test associational relationships. In other words, by using a survey, the researcher may find that libraries with large acquisitions budgets do tend to have more librarians with subject master's degrees, but such a study legitimately could conclude only that there seemed to be a correlation between budget size and librarians' credentials, not that budget size caused librarians with subject master's degrees to be hired. There are other factors or variables, such as degree of departmentalization, faculty role in book selection, and so on, that could have had as much or more influence than budget size on the criteria for hiring certain librarians. As the survey research study could not control these other variables, it could not test a causal relationship. (As was discussed earlier, the relationship must make sense conceptually as well, regardless of the methodology or technique used.)

Yet descriptive survey research, while usually less rigorous than experimental research, is stronger than exploratory research for testing relationships between variables. In gaining rigorousness, however, it tends to lose flexibility. In short, it tends to provide a compromise method for studying specific phenomena.

BASIC STEPS OF SURVEY RESEARCH: AN OVERVIEW

Formulating Objectives

As is true of any research, in selecting the method (and in designing the techniques to be employed) one must consider the objectives of the study, or how the data will be used. In turn, the objectives should be based on the problem to be investigated or the questions to be answered. The important concern here is that the method selected be precise enough to ensure that the data collected will be relevant to the question or problem under study.

Selecting Data Collection Techniques

Having selected the method (e.g., survey, historical, experimental), the next basic step is to select or design the specific technique or techniques to be used to collect the necessary data. Such techniques as observation, interviews, and questionnaires often are used, but if no suitable technique already exists, then a new one must be devised.

This stage is a critical point at which safeguards against bias and unreliability should be introduced. As Leedy and Ormrod warn, "bias can creep into a research project in a variety of subtle and undetected ways. It can be easily overlooked by even the most careful and conscientious researcher;"[6] therefore, the researcher should safeguard the data from the influence of bias. Leedy and Ormrod define bias as "any influence, condition, or set of conditions that singly or together distort the data."[7] Bias can creep into a study at several points, including during sampling and data collection activities. Bias is difficult, if not impossible, to avoid completely, but at the very least it should be minimized. When bias does appear to exist, the researcher should acknowledge its presence and indicate how it affects the results of the study. Examples of such occurrences will be given later when these topics are discussed.

It is important to pretest the data collection tool at this time. This step will be covered in the section on questionnaires, but the desirability of pretesting applies to all data collection techniques.

Selecting the Sample

Another activity to be treated at some length later is the selection of the sample, a necessary step for all surveys based on portions of a population. It is worth reemphasizing at this time, however, that findings based on a sample should provide a reasonably accurate representation of the state of affairs in the total group, and consequently considerable attention must be given to the sampling technique.

Also, it is worth noting that, in deciding how representative of the total group the sample is, the researcher should consider both statistical and practical differences between the sample and total group. For example, in comparing libraries of a sample with their total group on collection size, one may find that a difference of a few thousand volumes in collection size indicates a statistically significant difference. If one were looking at small, or possibly even medium-sized libraries, this statistical difference might be noteworthy. But if one were studying large university library collections of two million volumes or more, a difference of a few thousand volumes would probably have no real significance, regardless of what the statistics indicated. In other words, the average size of the sample library collections might differ from the average collection size of the population being sampled, but one could still have a reasonably accurate or representative sample for most purposes.

Collecting the Data

Having selected an appropriate data collection tool and the sample to which it will be applied, the next basic step is to collect the data. If one is conducting a relatively large survey, there is a good chance that it will be necessary to employ one or more field workers—persons charged with actually gathering the data. It goes without saying that such field workers should be well trained in the techniques of data collection and should be familiar with the specific tool being used in the researcher's study.

Throughout the survey, the collectors should be supervised closely, and checks should be established to help ensure that they are accurate and that their data are unbiased. As soon as possible after collection, the data should be checked for completeness, comprehensibility, consistency, and reliability. This step is often referred to as "cleaning" the data, and a thorough cleaning of possibly "dirty" data can avoid numerous problems in subsequent statistical analysis. Cleaning the data can involve everything from simply reading the results, looking for surprising responses and unexpected patterns, to verifying or checking the coding of the data.

Analyzing and Interpreting the Results

The process of analyzing the data gathered basically involves coding the responses, or placing each item in the appropriate category (more on this later); tabulating the data; and performing appropriate statistical computations. It is advisable to improve the economy of the study by planning these steps well in advance and in considerable detail. As was indicated earlier, it is also important to provide safeguards against error. This can be accomplished, in part, by checking the reliability of the coders and by checking the accuracy of the tabulations and statistical analysis.

Looking ahead to the interpretation phase, it is useful to be systematic in describing the treatment of the data. The researcher should state clearly and specifically what data are needed to resolve the problem, where they are located, and how they were obtained. The researcher also should describe fully the different steps that will be taken to interpret the data. In addition, he or she should try to ensure that the statistics calculated have a rational base (i.e., explain why they were chosen; their limitations, if any; and how they will be used). Finally, the researcher should distinguish between the mere presentation of the data and the interpretation of the data. The former is basically descriptive in nature; the latter involves analysis and explanation.

Survey Research Designs

The most straightforward type of survey research is descriptive, and it is designed to ensure that the sample is reasonably representative of the population to which the researcher wishes to generalize, and that the relevant characteristics have been accurately measured.

Where more than mere description and simple tabulations are desired, for example in an analytical survey, it may be necessary to develop a more sophisticated design. A common design for survey research, and one that facilitates the analysis of relationships, is known as the "static-group comparison." It is quite similar to a so-called preexperimental design and can be diagrammed as follows:

$$\frac{X \quad O}{O}$$

With more than one level of X, the design becomes

$$\frac{X_1 \quad O_1}{X_2 \quad O_2}$$

This design depicts two groups, as indicated by the two lines or rows, with two levels of X. The "independent" variable X could represent age, and X_1 retired adults and X_2 middle-aged adults. The "dependent" variable O could represent library use, with O_1 representing library use for the retired adults and O_2 representing library use for the middle-aged adults. In other words, the Os represent observations or measurements of the dependent variable—library use.

The line between the two groups means that they are naturally occurring groups, or that X is a naturally occurring condition, in this case, age. This is in contrast to the manipulated independent variables to be discussed in the section on experimental research.

In analyzing the results of a survey employing the latter example of a static-group comparison design, the researcher would compare the O scores of the comparison groups to determine whether there is a relationship between X and O. In other words, does one age group seem to use the library more than the other?

The difficulty in interpreting the results of a static-group comparison is that there is a real possibility that other differences between the two groups may also be affecting library use. For example, retired adults may have more leisure time than middle-aged adults and therefore may be more inclined to use libraries. Or, had the middle-aged adults been found to be heavier library users, it might have been because they tended to have higher incomes and that something about higher income encourages library use.

As has been stated, the best that survey research can demonstrate is correlational or associational relationships, and correlation does not demonstrate causation. On the other hand, correlation is necessary for causation, so evidence of a strong correlation between two variables would strengthen the case for causation.

A second, relatively common example of a survey research design is known as the "panel design." The panel design is a slightly stronger design than the static-group comparison because it takes into account the time sequence and changes over time by collecting data on the Xs and Os at two or more times. The panel design is diagrammed as follows:

$$\frac{X_{1_1} \quad X_{1_2} \quad X_{1_3} \quad O \ldots X_{1_2} \quad X_{1_3} \quad O \ldots X_{1_2} \quad O}{X_{2_1} \quad X_{2_2} \quad X_{2_3} \quad O \ldots X_{2_2} \quad X_{2_3} \quad O \ldots X_{2_2} \quad O}$$

The first of the two subscripts on the Xs indicates the level of the "independent" variable, for example, for gender—male and female. The second subscript represents the variable identification. For example, X_{1_1} could represent males with a certain level of income, X_{1_2} males with a certain educational background. The Os represent the "dependent" variable or, in this example, frequency of library use. The line continues to indicate naturally occurring groups. The fact that the Xs and Os occur more than once in each group indicates that the data are collected and observations are made more than once for at least some of the variables.

In analyzing the results of survey research employing this design, the researcher may conclude that females, in conjunction with certain levels of income, education, and age, are more likely to use libraries than males with comparable values on those variables. But the researcher should draw such conclusions cautiously, as the time intervals may not be adequate to allow the Xs to effect changes in library use and, once again, there may be other important group differences affecting library use that have not been taken into account. Such designs do, however, help the researcher to understand and analyze relationships between variables and to generalize from natural processes that have occurred. While they cannot establish causation, they can help to build a case for it.

Survey research has been applied in library-related research for a variety of purposes. It has been proven to be particularly useful for use and user studies, state-of-the-art surveys, and library performance evaluations. Busha and Harter review in some detail a selection of projects that were based on survey methods and that they consider to be successful.[8] Library surveys are indexed in *Library Literature & Information Science*. A book by Fink provides a useful step-by-step guide to conducting surveys in any discipline.[9]

Survey Research Costs

Survey research tends to be relatively inexpensive, at least if the sample or population being surveyed is not large, but it is still often desirable to reduce the costs. Recommended guidelines for reducing survey costs include the following:

1. Shorten the length of data collection
2. Reduce the number of follow-ups
3. Limit pilot or pretesting to a small number of participants
4. Shorten time spent developing data collection instruments by adapting already existing instruments
5. Make the instrument as short as possible
6. Use nonmonetary incentives to encourage respondents
7. Minimize staff costs
8. Shop around for least expensive supplies and equipment
9. Reduce the number of survey activities
10. Minimize the amount of time each activity takes.[10]

SAMPLING

As was indicated earlier, sampling is often one of the most crucial steps in survey research. In fact, rigorous sampling methods have been developed and used primarily within the context of survey research. However, "the basic logic and many of the specific techniques of sampling are equally applicable to other research methods such as content analysis, experimentation, and even field research."[11]

Basic Terms and Concepts

Before considering some standard techniques of sampling, it is important to have an understanding of the following basic terms and concepts related to sampling.

1. Universe—the theoretical aggregation of all units or elements that apply to a particular survey. For example, if one were surveying librarians, the study universe would include all librarians, regardless of type, location, and so on. Universe is not frequently used today; it is often used synonymously with "population" and is essentially a useless term.

2. Population—the total of all cases that conform to a prespecified criterion or set of criteria. It is more specific or better defined than a universe and is in effect a designated part of a universe. For example, American academic librarians would be part of the universe of librarians and could represent the population for a survey study. The population is the aggregation of units to which one wishes to generalize the results of a research study.

   Selection of the population must precede the selection of the sample, assuming a sample is to be drawn, and is crucial to the success of the sampling stage. Selection of the population must be done carefully with regard to the selection criteria, desired size, and the parameters of the survey population. It is also important to consider costs, in terms of time and money, when selecting a population. If the population is too large or expensive to manage, then the study is handicapped from the start. Obviously, the members of the population must be readily accessible to the researcher; otherwise, it will be difficult, if not impossible, to collect the necessary data.

3. Population stratum—a subdivision of a population based on one or more specifications or characteristics. A stratum of the population of all U.S. academic librarians could be U.S. academic librarians of libraries with a collection of at least one million volumes or with a budget of a certain size.

4. Element—an individual member or unit of a population. Each academic librarian would be an element of the population of academic librarians. The total number of elements of a population is usually designated by N.

5. Census—a count or survey of all the elements of a population, and the determination of the distribution of their characteristics. A complete census is usually not possible, or at least is impractical and unnecessary, so typically a sample of the population rather than the entire population is surveyed

6. Sample—a selection of units from the total population to be studied. It is usually drawn because it is less costly and time consuming to survey

than is the population, or it may be impossible to survey the population. However, one can never be absolutely certain how representative a sample is of its population, unless a census is also made, which would obviate using the sample. The concept of representativeness is crucial to sampling and will be treated in greater depth later.

7. Case—an individual member of the sample. The total number of cases in a sample is usually designated by lower-case n.

8. Sampling frame—the actual list of units from which the sample, or some part of the sample, is selected. It is often used interchangeably with "population list." One problem with email surveys is the acquiring of email address lists, but the Web has made it possible to select samples without having to know respondents' email addresses.[12]

TYPES OF SAMPLING METHODS

It is useful to distinguish between two basic types of sampling methods— probability sampling and nonprobability sampling. Probability sampling is the more scientific and useful of the two methods, and the bulk of this section will be devoted to that technique. Nonprobability sampling will be considered first.

Nonprobability Sampling

With a nonprobability sample, the researcher cannot state the probability of a specific element of the population being included in the sample. In fact, one cannot be assured that a specific element has any probability of being included in the sample. Therefore, nonprobability samples suffer from important weaknesses. When selection probabilities are unknown, one cannot make legitimate use of statistical inference. That is, a nonprobability sample does not permit generalizing from the sample to the population because the researcher has no assurance that the sample is representative of the population. Nor can the researcher, relying on a nonprobability sample, evaluate the risks of error involved in making inferences about the sample.

On the other hand, nonprobability samples are usually easier and cheaper to obtain than are probability samples, and for some purposes, such as where the focus is on the sample itself, may be quite adequate. "Samples of several" are commonly used for pretests. In some cases nonprobability samples may be the only feasible samples. There are measures one can take to try to improve the representativeness of nonprobability samples; these techniques will be referred to when discussing some of the different kinds of nonprobability samples that follow.

Accidental Sample

In utilizing an accidental sampling technique, the researcher simply selects the cases that are at hand until the sample reaches a desired, designated size. If one wished to conduct an academic library user study, one might elect to survey library patrons as they entered or exited the library, on a "first-come, first-served" basis. There would be little or no preferential selection of respondents.

Obviously, there would be relatively little if any assurance that the sample was reasonably representative of the library's users. One could not assume that the accidental sample was not atypical. The researcher might query users during some other time period and end up with quite different responses. Accidental sampling is seldom adequate for any kind of survey. Synonyms include convenience and availability samples.

Quota Sample

A type of nonprobability sample that improves somewhat on the simple accidental sample is the quota sample. Quota sampling is the same as accidental sampling except that it takes steps to ensure that the significant, diverse elements of the population are included. The quota sample method also attempts to ensure that the different elements are included in the sample in the proportions in which they occur in the population.

Returning to the researcher who wishes to survey the users of an academic library, he or she, in selecting a quota sample, would take measures to ensure that the sample includes the same percentages of faculty, graduate students, and so on as exist in the entire academic community. Or the researcher may choose to sample the same number of persons representing each element of the population, and then to assign them a weight according to their portion of the total population. The latter technique obviously requires knowledge of the proportions of the population according to each element.

Among the problems inherent in quota sampling is the difficulty in determining that the proportions for each element are accurate. Second, biases may exist in the selection of cases representing the various elements, even though their proportion of the population might have been accurately estimated. For example, the researcher sampling academic library users may survey the correct proportions of seniors, graduate students, and so on, but for whatever reason may tend to query those inclined to be more competent library users. If one were investigating library skills, such a bias would be damaging to the validity of the study.

Yet quota samples, while they should be used cautiously, are useful for exploratory studies, as are other nonprobability sampling techniques. Quota sampling is often used for public opinion surveys.

Snowball Sample

Some refer to this type of sampling as accidental sampling. It is an appropriate method to use when members of the population are difficult to identify and locate, such as migrants and homeless individuals. The researcher contacts members of the population who can be identified and located and then asks these individuals to provide information to identify and locate other members of the population to participate in the research. This type of sampling is cumulative, hence the name, snowball sampling.[13] This type of nonprobability sampling is used in exploratory research since the technique can result in "samples with questionable representativeness."[14] It is commonly used in qualitative research and is described in Chapter 7 of this book.

Purposive Sample

At times, it may seem preferable to select a sample based entirely on one's knowledge of the population and the objectives of the research. In designing a survey of the directors of large university libraries that are in the process of developing electronic reference services, one may decide that the easiest way of obtaining a sample of such libraries would be to select libraries known to the researcher to be engaged in such activities.

The researcher would be making the assumption that such a sample would be reasonably typical of all university libraries involved in developing electronic reference services. Unfortunately, such an assumption may not be justified. There is no assurance that a purposive sample is actually representative of the total population. Any sampling method not utilizing random selection is overly susceptible to bias.

Self-Selected Sample

As the label suggests, a self-selected sample is a group of cases, usually people, who have essentially selected themselves for inclusion in a study. A researcher might, for example, publish a notice in a professional journal asking individuals to volunteer to submit certain information or to participate in some other way. Again, there would be a strong possibility that these volunteers would not be representative of the entire population to which they belong.

Incomplete Sample

An incomplete sample, while not originally intended to be a nonprobability sample, in effect becomes one. For example, if a large percentage of the cases selected do not respond or participate in a study, then assurance that the sample is representative of the population is quite possibly lost, even though the sample may have been selected randomly. Another example of an incomplete sample is one drawn from an incomplete population list. Again, the sample may have been drawn randomly, but as the faulty list was in effect biased or not fully representative of the population, the sample must be considered unrepresentative and in effect a nonprobability sample.

Probability Sampling

As was indicated earlier, the primary purpose of sampling is to select elements that accurately represent the total population from which the elements were drawn. Probability sampling enhances the likelihood of accomplishing this objective and also provides methods for estimating the degree of probable success; that is, it incorporates probability theory, which provides the basis for estimating population parameters and error.[15] The crucial requirement of probability sampling is that every element in the population has a known probability of being included in the sample. A discussion of major types of probability sampling follows.

Simple Random Sample (SRS)

Simple random sampling is the basic sampling method of survey research. The technique of simple random sampling gives each element in the population an equal chance of being included in the sample. It also makes the selection of every possible combination of elements equally likely. In other words, if one had a population or sampling frame of 500 elements, in drawing a simple random sample of that population one should be as likely to include elements 1 and 3 as 2 and 4, or 1 and 2, and so on.

In order for the probabilities of including each element and each combination of elements to be equal, it is necessary that there be independence from one draw to the next. This means that the selection of an element should have no effect on the chances of remaining elements being selected. But this condition cannot be met fully unless the sampling is done with replacement. In sampling with replacement, the researcher would place every element back in the population list after being selected for the sample so that it is again available for selection. If replacement is not done, then the remaining elements would not have the same likelihood of being drawn as did the elements already selected. The remaining population would decrease in number as elements were selected, and the elements still in the population would have an increasingly greater chance of being selected. Similarly, the likelihood of every combination being selected would not remain constant, because, as some elements were removed from the population and not replaced, certain combinations would no longer be possible.

However, if the elements selected for the sample are subsequently put back in the population list (after making note that they are now a part of the sample), then there is the possibility that some of them may be selected for the sample again. This obviously presents practical problems, so sampling with replacement is not often done. This normally does not invalidate the sample, however, as the sample usually represents a relatively small percentage of the population, and the chances of any element being selected two or more times is slight. But if the sample is as much as one-fifth the size of the population, technically one should introduce correction factors if possible. However, samples drawn without replacement do tend to be more representative.

There are mathematical formulas that can be used to correct for sampling without replacement, but if the sample represents a relatively small proportion of the population, use of a formula is unnecessary. In addition, exact correction factors are seldom known. Yet, if correction does seem to be warranted, using such formulas is generally preferable to sampling with replacement and taking a chance of drawing some elements more than once. Those readers interested in correction formulas should refer to a standard text on sampling.

Selecting the Simple Random Sample

There are several techniques available for selecting a simple random sample. Traditional methods include the roulette wheel or lottery type approach. Such methods have been criticized as being at least potentially biased, or not fully random, however, because of physical or logistical imperfections. For example, if one were drawing ping pong balls from a large bowl or revolving drum, there is the possibility that the balls might not have been adequately mixed to begin with and that those placed in the container early, or late, have a greater chance of being selected. Consequently, it is advisable to consider other, more reliable techniques.

One recommended method commonly used for drawing a simple random sample involves the use of a table of random numbers. A well-known example is the Rand Corporation's *A Million Random Digits* (see Table 4.1 for an illustrative page). A table of random numbers is simply that—a listing of randomly arranged numbers. The basic steps involved in using such a table are as follows:

1. The first step would be to number sequentially the elements of the population. Let us assume that we have a population of elements numbered from 1 to 500. (Obviously, each element now has a unique number.)

2. The next step is to determine how many of the elements are to be selected for the sample. Techniques for determining a desirable sample size will be discussed later, so for now let us assume that we have decided on a sample of 50.

3. As there are three-digit numbers in the population, it will be necessary to select three-digit numbers from the table in order to give every element a chance of being selected.

4. The next step is to choose the starting point in the table and the pattern for moving through the table. Pure chance must determine the starting point. A simple way of selecting the starting point is to close one's eyes and place a pencil point on the table. The number under or nearest the pencil point then becomes the starting point.

5. For ease of illustration, let us assume that the pencil came down at the head of the fifth column of the table. As we must select three-digit numbers, we could then consider, along with the seven, the next two digits, and 732 becomes the first number to be considered for our sample. (It would be possible to move down the column from seven and consider 722 as the first three-digit number.) Regarding the pattern of movement, we could proceed from there across to the right, or left, down, or diagonally through the table. All that matters is that we be consistent.

6. As stated, we will first consider 732 for our sample. But as it is larger than any number in our population (the largest is 500), we will have to reject or ignore it and move to the next number. Assuming we have decided to move down the three-digit column to the bottom and then back up to the top of the next three-digit column, the next number to be considered would be 204. The number 204 does fall within the population, so the element represented by 204 would be included in the sample. This process would continue until 50 elements had been selected. If sampling without replacement, we would skip numbers that have already been included in the sample.

TABLE 4.1   Random Numbers[a]

10 09 73 25 33	76 52 01 35 86	34 67 35 48 76	80 95 90 91 17	39 29 27 49 45
37 54 20 48 05	64 89 47 42 96	24 80 52 40 37	20 63 61 04 02	00 82 29 16 65
08 42 26 89 53	19 64 50 93 03	23 20 90 25 60	15 95 33 47 64	35 08 03 36 06
99 01 90 25 29	09 37 67 07 15	38 31 13 11 65	88 67 67 43 97	04 43 62 76 59
12 80 79 99 70	80 15 73 61 47	64 03 23 66 53	98 95 11 68 77	12 17 17 68 33
66 06 57 47 17	34 07 27 68 50	36 69 73 61 70	65 81 33 98 85	11 19 92 91 70
31 06 01 08 05	45 57 18 24 06	35 30 34 26 14	86 79 90 74 39	23 40 30 97 32
85 26 97 76 02	02 05 16 56 92	68 66 57 48 18	73 05 38 52 47	18 62 38 85 79
63 57 33 21 35	05 32 54 70 48	90 55 35 75 48	28 46 82 87 09	83 49 15 56 24
73 79 64 57 53	03 52 96 47 78	35 80 83 42 82	60 93 52 03 44	35 27 38 84 35
98 52 01 77 67	14 90 56 86 07	22 10 94 05 58	60 97 09 34 33	50 50 07 39 98
11 80 50 54 31	39 80 82 77 32	50 72 56 82 49	29 40 52 41 01	52 77 56 78 51
83 45 29 96 34	06 28 89 80 83	13 74 67 00 78	18 47 54 06 10	68 71 17 78 17
88 68 54 02 00	86 50 75 84 01	36 76 66 79 51	90 36 47 64 93	29 60 91 10 62
99 59 46 73 48	87 51 76 49 69	91 82 60 89 28	93 78 56 13 68	23 47 83 41 13
65 48 11 76 74	17 46 85 09 50	58 04 77 69 74	73 03 95 71 86	40 21 81 65 44
80 12 43 56 35	17 72 70 80 15	43 31 82 23 74	21 11 57 82 53	14 38 55 37 63
74 35 09 98 17	77 40 27 72 14	43 23 60 02 10	45 52 16 42 37	96 28 60 26 55
69 91 62 68 03	66 25 22 91 48	36 93 68 72 03	76 62 11 39 90	94 40 05 64 18
09 89 32 05 05	14 22 56 85 14	46 42 72 67 88	96 29 77 88 22	54 38 21 45 98
91 49 91 45 23	68 47 92 76 86	46 16 28 35 54	94 75 08 99 23	37 08 92 00 48
80 33 69 45 98	26 94 03 68 58	70 29 73 41 35	53 14 03 33 40	42 05 08 23 41
44 10 48 19 49	85 15 74 79 54	32 97 92 65 75	57 60 04 08 81	22 22 20 64 13
12 55 07 37 42	11 10 00 20 40	12 86 07 46 97	96 64 48 94 39	28 70 72 58 15
63 60 64 93 29	16 50 53 44 84	40 21 95 25 63	43 65 17 70 82	07 20 73 17 90
61 19 69 04 46	26 45 74 77 74	51 92 43 37 29	65 39 45 95 93	42 58 26 05 27
15 47 44 52 66	95 27 07 99 53	59 36 78 38 48	82 39 61 01 18	33 21 15 94 66
94 55 72 85 73	67 89 75 43 87	54 62 24 44 31	91 19 04 25 92	92 92 74 59 73
42 48 11 62 13	97 34 40 87 21	16 86 84 87 67	03 07 11 20 59	25 70 14 66 70
23 52 37 83 17	73 20 88 98 37	68 93 59 14 16	26 25 22 96 63	05 52 28 25 62
04 49 35 24 94	75 24 63 38 24	45 86 25 10 25	61 96 27 93 35	65 33 71 24 72
00 54 99 76 54	64 05 18 81 59	96 11 96 38 96	54 69 28 23 91	23 28 72 95 29
35 96 31 53 07	26 89 80 93 54	33 35 13 54 62	77 97 45 00 24	90 10 33 93 33
59 80 80 83 91	45 42 72 68 42	83 60 94 97 00	13 02 12 48 92	78 56 52 01 06
46 05 88 52 36	01 39 09 22 86	77 28 14 40 77	93 91 08 36 47	70 61 74 29 41
32 17 90 05 97	87 37 92 52 41	05 56 70 70 07	86 74 31 71 57	85 39 41 18 38
69 23 46 14 06	20 11 74 52 04	15 95 66 00 00	18 74 39 24 23	97 11 89 63 38
19 56 54 14 30	01 75 87 53 79	40 41 92 15 85	66 67 43 68 06	84 96 28 52 07
45 15 51 49 38	19 47 60 72 46	43 66 79 45 43	59 04 79 00 33	20 82 66 95 41
94 86 43 19 94	36 16 81 08 51	34 88 88 15 53	01 54 03 54 56	05 01 45 11 76

[a]*Source*: The RAND Corporation. *A Million Random Digits* (Glencoe, Il.: Free Press, 1955).

If the population list or sampling frame is in an electronic file, a random sample can be selected by a computer. In effect, the computer numbers the elements in the population, generates its own series of random numbers, and prints the list of elements selected. Computer generation of samples is particularly useful when drawing very large samples or working with large populations.

Systematic Sample

A method of selecting a random sample that is considered by most to be as reliable and accurate as simple random sampling is systematic sampling. This technique involves taking every nth element from a list until the total list has been sampled. For example, the researcher may have a population list of 1,000 elements and decide to select every tenth element for the sample. This would be a sampling interval of 10, and would result in a sampling ratio of 1:10 and a sample of 100. The list should be considered to be circular in that the researcher would select every nth name, beginning with a randomly chosen starting point and ending with the first name of the interval immediately preceding the starting point.

Systematic sampling is easier and faster than simple random sampling for long lists. If one wished to draw a random sample from a telephone directory, for example, it would be considerably faster to take every nth name than to use a table of random numbers.

However, with systematic sampling not every combination of elements has an equal chance of being drawn. So, if the list is not randomly arranged, such as is the case with an alphabetical listing, the sample would not be random. (For some variables or problems, however, an alphabetical arrangement would have no relevance and could be treated as a randomly arranged list.) For example, ranked lists such as lists of personnel, and hierarchically arranged, or cyclical lists, such as lists of houses, can easily produce biased samples. To elaborate on the first example, if one were selecting every 10th individual from an organization's personnel list arranged by department and rank within the department, and if the departments had approximately the same number of employees, then the sample might tend to include people of the same rank. If these individuals tended to have certain characteristics in common, then the sample would be biased. In short, systematic sampling is generally as satisfactory as simple random sampling, but only if the population list exhibits no trends or patterns.

Stratified Random Sample

In selecting a stratified random sample, one must first divide all of the population elements into groups or categories and then draw independent random samples from each group or stratum. This technique represents a modification of simple and systematic random sampling in that it reduces the number of cases needed to achieve a given degree of accuracy or representativeness. The strata should be defined in such a way that each element appears in only one stratum. Different sampling methods may be used for different strata. For example, a simple random sample may be drawn from one stratum and a systematic sample from another.

There are two basic types of stratified random samples—proportional and disproportional. In drawing a proportional stratified sample, one would draw the same percentage from each stratum. If there were 1,000 elements in a population, divided into ten strata of 100 each, and if one desired a total sample of 100, then ten elements, or 10 percent, would be drawn from each stratum. (It is more likely, however, that the strata would not all have the same number of elements. In that case, the same percentage would still be taken from each stratum, but the resulting numbers would vary.)

If a researcher were to stratify all public libraries in a state according to budget size, it is probable that there would be different numbers of libraries in each group. But if the groups were roughly equal in their number of libraries, and if the categories tended to be internally homogeneous, then it would be reasonable to select the same percentage of libraries from each stratum or to use a constant sampling rate. Doing so would produce a *proportional stratified sample* with libraries of certain budget sizes being included in the sample in the same proportions in which they occur in the population.

On the other hand, if there were considerable variations within individual strata, or if some strata were so small as to be in danger of barely being represented in the total sample, if at all, the researcher would be well advised to draw a *disproportional stratified sample*, sometimes referred to as optimum allocation. In doing so, one would draw approximately the same number of elements from each stratum regardless of its size. In order to do so, it would be necessary to use different sampling fractions or to select different percentages of cases from the strata. Consequently, some cases would represent a greater percentage of the sample than of the population. "Optimum precision is attained if sampling fractions in the different strata are made proportional to the standard deviations in the strata."[16]

This method would provide enough cases per category to allow meaningful comparisons among categories. As is true for proportional stratified sampling, it would help to assure a more representative total sample than might be expected with simple or systematic random sampling. Unlike proportional sampling, it could do so even when the groups are lacking in internal homogeneity. Disproportional stratified random sampling also can be used to take a relatively large sample from the stratum from which it is cheapest to gather data. In an interview survey of libraries, for example, this may be the group of libraries closest to the researcher. However, the increase in precision over proportional stratified sampling tends to be small, and optimizing the sample for group comparisons means the sample is no longer optimal for estimating the total population.

The choice of stratification variables typically depends on which ones are available and which ones are presumably related to the variables that one wants to represent accurately. Returning to the survey of public libraries within a state, it may well be that the researcher would decide to stratify public libraries by known budget size on the assumption that budget size would correlate with collection size—the actual variable to be studied, but yet to be determined. In other words, stratifying on budget size would help to ensure that there would be proper representation of collection sizes, and other variables, related to budget size. In general, the stratified sample would be more representative of a number of variables than would a simple random sample taken for the same purpose.

Table 4.2 presents stratification figures for a hypothetical population of 1,000 public libraries. As can be seen in the first row, 100 libraries have budgets of

TABLE 4.2   Proportional and Disproportional Stratified Sampling

| Strata/Samples | Library Budget in Thousands of Dollars | | | |
	0–100	101–250	251–500	501
Strata	100	300	400	200 (N = 1000)
Proportional sample	10	30	40	20 (n = 100)
	10%	10%	10%	10%
Disproportional sample	25	24	24	24 (n = 97)
	25%	8%	6%	12%

$100,000 or less, 300 libraries have budgets of $101,000–$250,000, and so on. If one were to draw a proportional stratified sample using a uniform sampling ratio of 10 percent, then the sample would contain 10 libraries with budgets of $100,000 or less, and so on. The researcher might conclude, however, that a sample of 10 is too small to be very reliable and that comparisons of samples of such disparate size might be chancy. Therefore, he or she might decide to vary the sampling ratio across strata in order to end up with samples of about the same size (see the bottom line where sampling ratios vary from 6% to 25%). With either sampling technique, the total sample contains about 100 cases.

One statistical note—when computing estimates of means and estimating standard errors for disproportional stratified samples, one should compute values separately for each of the strata and then weight them according to the relative size of the stratum in the population. (This is not necessary for proportional stratification, as it is in effect "self-weighting.") In addition, it should be recognized that, in theory, one cannot make legitimate use of various nonparametric statistical tests, tests for the significance of correlation, analysis of covariance, and so on, without substantial modifications. Unfortunately, statistical textbooks seldom address this issue.

Cluster Sample

In social science research, it is not unusual to encounter situations where the populations cannot be listed easily for sampling purposes. Examples include the populations of countries and states, all college students within the United States, and so on. When it is impossible or impractical to compile an exhaustive list of the elements of a total population, cluster sampling may be used effectively.

Essentially, the technique of cluster sampling involves dividing a population into clusters or groups and then drawing a sample of those clusters. In fact, the population might already be grouped into subpopulations, and cluster sampling becomes merely a matter of compiling a list of the subpopulations, or clusters, and selecting a random sample from them. For example, while a list of a city's residents may not exist, people do live on discrete blocks. Therefore, one could draw a sample of city blocks, compile lists of persons residing on those blocks, and then sample the people living on each block.

In using cluster sampling, it is desirable that each cluster's units be as heterogeneous as possible, but that characteristics of the clusters themselves be similar. This is particularly important if all members of each selected cluster are to be included in the final sample. Yet, typically, the elements constituting a given natural cluster within a population are more homogeneous than are all the elements of the total population. Therefore, relatively few elements may be needed to represent a natural cluster, while a relatively large number of clusters will be required to represent the diversity of the total population. The more heterogeneous the clusters, the fewer will be needed. "With a given total sample size, however, if the number of clusters is increased, the number of elements within a cluster must be decreased,"[17] unless the clusters are known to be especially heterogeneous.

Cluster sampling may be either single-stage or multistage sampling. Single-stage cluster sampling occurs only once. In the earlier example involving the selection of city blocks, all elements or persons residing on each block would be included in a single-stage design. In a two-stage design, the simple random sampling of city blocks would be followed by a random sampling of the persons living on the blocks. Or, in a more complex design, a sampling of census tracts could be followed by a random sampling of smaller clusters of blocks, followed by a sampling of individual houses, and conclude with a sampling of persons living in those houses. A combination of probability and nonprobability sampling may be used in multistage sampling, but the researcher should keep in mind the likely loss of accuracy with nonrandom sampling.

The sampling procedure illustrated in Figure 4.1 is a combination of cluster, stratified, and simple random sampling that has been employed by the Institute for Social Research at the University of Michigan. The procedure involves the following steps:

1. The entire geographical area of the 48 contiguous states is divided into small areas called *primary sampling units* (PSU). The PSUs are usually counties, metropolitan areas, or telephone exchange areas. A stratified random sample of about 75 PSUs are selected from the total list.

2. Each PSU is stratified into large cities, smaller cities and towns, and/or rural areas. Each unit within a stratum is referred to as a *sample place*, and one or more sample places is selected from each stratum.

3. Each sample place is divided into *chunks*, which are distinct areas such as blocks. A number of chunks are randomly selected from each sample place.

4. The chunks are broken down into *segments*—areas containing from 4 to 12 dwelling units. Segments are then randomly drawn from each chunk.

5. *Dwelling units*, selected from each segment, constitute the final sample. A city directory can be used to obtain telephone numbers for the dwelling units so chosen.

As was noted earlier, cluster sampling may be the only feasible or practical design where no population list exists. It also tends to be a cheaper sampling method for large surveys. But multistage cluster sampling does sacrifice accuracy, because sampling error can occur at each stage. In a two-stage sampling

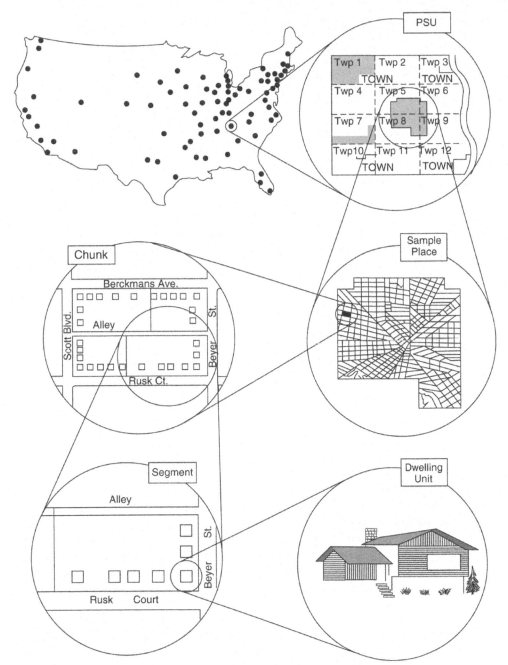

Figure 4.1 Cluster Sampling Method. From Survey Research Center, *Interviewer's Manual*, rev. ed. Ann Arbor: Institute for Social Research, University of Michigan, 1976, p. 8–2.

design, the initial selection of clusters is subject to sampling error, and the sampling of elements within each cluster is subject to error. The researcher must decide if the greater efficiency gained from cluster sampling is worth the greater risk of sampling error, and must attempt to minimize the error by optimizing the number of clusters and elements selected. Theoretically, cluster sampling

TABLE 4.3   Population Characteristics and Appropriate Random Sampling Techniques

Population Characteristics	Example of Population Type	Appropriate Sampling Technique
A general homogeneous mass of individual units	First-year students of a private university	Simple random sampling (systematic sampling if the population list is long)
Definite strata, each as internally homogeneous as possible and of approximately the same size.	All undergraduate students of a private university; each level represents a stratum	Proportional stratified sampling
Definite strata, some of which are quite small and/or internally heterogeneous	All public libraries in a state, stratified by budget size, resulting in an upper budget category containing only a few libraries	Disproportional stratified sampling
Clusters whose group characteristics are similar, but whose elements or internal characteristics are quite heterogeneous	A population consisting of the users of the major urban public libraries in the nation; the libraries tend to be similar, but their users vary widely in characteristics	Cluster sampling

necessitates using special statistical formulas, especially when the clusters are of greatly differing sizes. Again, a text on sampling should be consulted if more information about this issue is desired.

With the availability of Web 2.0 social media, "such as blogs, forums, and instant polls, researchers are building communities to freely discuss issues."[18] These communities provide opportunities for researchers with individuals who may not respond to other types of data collection methods. However, these individuals only represent a small percentage of the population who are comfortable using this medium to communicate; therefore, researchers should use social media as sample frames only when they represent the intended target groups.

In summarizing the characteristics of some major random sampling techniques, the somewhat simplified outline presented in Table 4.3 may be helpful.

DETERMINING THE SAMPLE SIZE

The general rule of thumb for the size of the sample is, quite simply, the larger the better. Babbie states that probability samples of less than 100 are not likely to be very representative of the population.[19] Yet there is no point in utilizing a sample that is larger than necessary; doing so unnecessarily increases the time and money needed for a study. There are at least four general criteria that can help to determine the necessary sample size. One is the degree of precision required between the sample and the population. The less accuracy needed, the smaller the necessary sample. Two, the variability of the population influences the sample size needed to achieve a given level of accuracy or representativeness. In general, the greater the variability, the larger the sample needed. (Statistics commonly used to estimate the variability of a population will be noted in the chapter on data analysis.) Three, the method of sampling to be used can affect the size of the appropriate sample. As was noted in the discussion of random sampling, stratified sampling requires fewer cases to achieve a specified degree of accuracy than does simple or systematic random sampling. Four, the way in which the results are to be analyzed influences decisions on sample size. Samples that are quite small place significant limitations on the types of statistical analyses that can be employed.

Use of Formulas

Statistical formulas have been developed for calculating appropriate sample sizes. They typically take into account the confidence level, which relates to the probability of the findings, or differences between samples, being due to chance rather than representing a real difference. The confidence level is equal to 1 minus the level of significance, or 1 minus the probability of rejecting a true hypothesis. Formulas also consider the degree of accuracy with which one wishes to estimate a certain characteristic of the population and the variability of the population, usually as represented by its estimated standard deviation—a standard measure of dispersion. (The greater the spread of scores about the mean, the larger the standard deviation.)

One such formula is stated as follows:

$$n = \frac{S^2}{[S_1 E_1(\bar{x})]^2}$$

where

n = sample size,

S = standard deviation of the variable or characteristic of the population (estimated), and

$S_1 E_1(\bar{x})$ = standard error of the mean or sampling error.

The difficulty in using formulas is that S, the population's standard deviation, must be estimated. It is known only if the total population is analyzed, therein eliminating the need for taking a sample. In addition, if the sample represents a large proportion of the population, a finite population correction has to be included. "Usually, sampling units have numerous attributes, one or more of which are relevant to the research problem."[20] Therefore, if more than one variable is to be studied, a sample that is adequate for one variable may not be satisfactory for another. One should consider the variability of all of the variables; the sample size tends to increase as the number of variables increases.

A proportional allocation formula, based on the assumption that a characteristic occurred 50 percent of the time, was used by Krejcie and Morgan to develop

TABLE 4.4   Table for Determining Sample Size from a Given Population

N	S	N	S	N	S
10	10	220	140	1200	291
15	14	230	144	1300	297
20	19	240	148	1400	302
25	24	250	152	1500	306
30	28	260	155	1600	310
35	32	270	159	1700	313
40	36	280	162	1800	317
45	40	290	165	1900	320
50	44	300	169	2000	322
55	48	320	175	2200	327
60	52	340	181	2400	331
65	56	360	186	2600	335
70	59	380	191	2800	338
75	63	400	196	3000	341
80	66	420	201	3500	346
85	70	440	205	4000	351
90	73	460	210	4500	354
95	76	480	214	5000	357
100	80	500	217	6000	361
110	86	550	228	7000	364
120	92	600	234	8000	367
130	97	650	242	9000	368
140	103	700	248	10000	370
150	108	750	254	15000	375
160	113	800	260	20000	377
170	118	850	265	30000	379
180	123	900	269	40000	380
190	127	950	274	50000	381
200	132	1000	278	75000	382
210	136	1100	285	1000000	384

Note: N is population size, S is sample size. The degree of accuracy = 0.05.
From Krejcie, Robert V., and Daryle W. Morgan, "Determining Sample Size for Research Activities," *Educational and Psychological Measurement* 30 (Autumn 1970): 608.

a table of sample sizes for given population sizes. This table is presented here (see Table 4.4) but, as was noted earlier, a variety of factors can influence desirable sample size. A table of sample sizes may represent a rather simplistic, and quite possibly conservative, method for ascertaining a sample size.

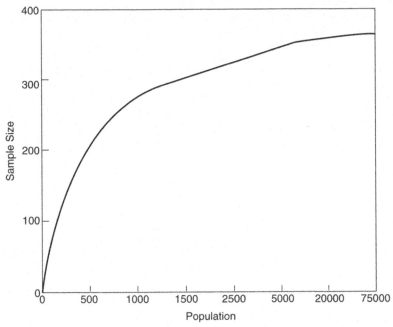

Figure 4.2 Relationship between Sample Size and Total Population. Adapted from Krejcie, Robert V., and Daryle W. Morgan, "Determining Sample Size for Research Activities," *Educational and Psychological Measurement* 30 (Autumn 1970): 609.

Again, there is seldom much justification for using a sample that is larger than necessary.

Table 4.4 does not require any calculations. To obtain the required sample size, one need only enter the table at the given population size (e.g., 9,000) and note the adjacent sample size (368). Figure 4.2 illustrates the relationship between sample size and total population. It, as well as the table, indicates that, as the population size increases, the rate of requisite increase in sample size decreases.

To calculate the optimal sample size when dealing with a continuous variable such as age, one could use the following formula:

$$n = \frac{z^2 s^2}{E^2}$$

where

n = sample size

z = z score for desired confidence level (see the chapter on analysis of data for a discussion of z scores)

s = standard deviation of the population

E = allowable error.

Readers wanting to know more about determining sample size may wish to refer to works by Kraemer and Thiemann, Hernon, and Cohen.[21] The last work provides several tables of sample sizes as functions of the type and power (the probability that a statistical test will yield statistically significant results) of the statistical test being used.

Sample size calculators also are freely available on the Web. Both Creative Research Systems http://www.surveysystem.com/sscalc.htm and DSS Research http://www.dssresearch.com/toolkit/sscalc/size.asp provide sample size calculators that will determine the sample size and the confidence level.

SAMPLING ERROR

Formulas are also available for estimating the "sampling error" or, as it is often referred to, the "standard error of the mean." The standard error of the mean represents how much the average of the means of an infinite number of samples drawn from a population deviates from the actual mean of that same population. For example, if a population consisted of 50 libraries with collections averaging 500,000 volumes, one should be able to draw all possible sample combinations of 10 libraries, average the means of all the samples, and end up with 500,000 volumes as the mean of the sampling distribution. If the mean of the sampling distribution were based on a limited number of samples, it is possible that it would deviate somewhat from the actual population mean, thus indicating some sampling error.

If the population is large relative to the sample, the formula for calculating the standard error of the mean, or in fact the standard deviation of the sampling distribution of means, is as follows:

$$S_1 E_1(\bar{x}) = \frac{S}{\sqrt{n}}$$

where

S = the standard deviation of the population

n = the number of cases in the sample.

If the sample represents a relatively small proportion of the population, or if the population standard deviation is not known and must be estimated, as is usually the case, then modified versions of the formula must be used. The formula for the first situation is as follows:

$$S_1 E_1(\bar{x}) = \sqrt{\frac{S^2}{n} \cdot \frac{N - n}{N - 1}}$$

where

S = the standard deviation of the population

N = the number of elements in the population

n = the number of cases in the sample.

The formula for the standard error of the mean, where the population standard deviation is not known, requires substituting an unbiased estimate (s), or the standard deviation of the sample, for the standard deviation of the population (S). "The term *unbiased estimate* refers to the fact that as one draws more and more samples from the same population and finds the mean of all these unbiased estimates, the mean of these unbiased estimates approaches the population value."[22]

The formula for the standard deviation of the sample is as follows:

$$s = \sqrt{\frac{\sum_{i-1}^{n}(x_i - \bar{x})^2}{n-1}}$$

where

x_i = sample score,

$\bar{x}$ = sample mean, and

n = the number of cases in the sample.

Dividing by $n–1$ instead of n is done in order to reduce bias or, according to some texts, to help compensate for a small sample. The value for s can then be substituted for S in the first formula given for calculating the standard error of the mean:

$$S_1E_1(\bar{x}) = \frac{s}{\sqrt{n}}$$

As was indicated earlier, there is a point of diminishing returns with regard to the sample size and sampling error. Starting with a sample of one person and then increasing the sample size, the accuracy of the sample will improve rapidly up to about 500 cases. Beyond 500, a relatively large increase in the number of cases is needed in order to increase significantly the accuracy of the sample. For example, if 600 cases are drawn for the sample, the amount of sampling error involved is about 4 percent. To decrease this to 3 percent, it would be necessary to increase the sample size to 1,067; to reduce error to 2 percent requires an increase to 2,401 cases. In other words, after a certain point is reached, increasing the sample size will increase the researcher's workload without appreciably improving the accuracy of the sample. Thus, the researcher is well advised to base his or her decision regarding sample size on desired precision and confidence levels, and not to decide arbitrarily that some percentage of the population represents an optimal sample size. (See Figure 4.3 for an illustration of the relationship between sample size and error in this example.)

Again, one of the main purposes for selecting and analyzing samples is to obtain information about the population from which the sample has been drawn. "If an unbiased sample were taken from the population, it would be hoped that the sample mean would be a reasonable estimate of the population

Figure 4.3 Relationship between Sample Size and Percent Error. From Benson, Dennis K., and Jonathan L. Benson, A *Benchmark Handbook: Guide to Survey Research Terms*, Columbus, OH: Academy for Contemporary Problems, 1975. 2.

mean. Such an estimate is known as a *point estimate* but it is unlikely that the mean of a sample will be identical to the mean of the population."[23] Statisticians often content themselves with calculating *interval estimates* or the ranges within which the actual population means are likely to fall.

Other Causes of Sampling Error

The size of a sample, or, more specifically, having too few cases, is not the only cause of sampling error. A variety of factors can contribute to a sample's being less representative of its population than is satisfactory. If not guarded against, bias of one sort or another can easily contaminate a research study. Bias is particularly a problem with nonrandom samples, as there is less of a safeguard against personal attitudes, preferences, and so on affecting the researcher's selection of cases. For example, if a researcher were selecting library users for an interview on library services, he or she might be inclined, if even unconsciously, to slight persons who appeared to be unskilled library users or were sloppily dressed.

Even utilizing probability or random sampling techniques, the unwary researcher can end up with a biased or inaccurate sample. Bookstein, in a *Library Quarterly* article, discussed several faulty selection procedures that can result in inadequate samples.[24] The first of these he referred to as "faulty use of random-number tables." This problem includes any techniques used by the researcher resulting in each element in the list not having an equal chance of being included.

The second general category of faulty selection procedures is labeled by Bookstein as "frame problems." In this case, he is referring to problems related to faulty listing of the population. For instance, if one desired to draw a random sample of a library's holdings, and did so by selecting a random sample of catalog records, a certain amount of bias would be unavoidable. This is so because there is not a one-to-one correspondence between books and catalog records, and the more records representing a title in the catalog, the greater the probability that that book will be selected. Books tending to be represented by a large number of catalog records probably tend to have certain characteristics in common, hence a biased sample.

The third general category of "bad" sampling discussed by Bookstein is referred to as "unintentional modification of population." This category represents more subtle problems than does "frame problems," and it is even more difficult to deal with. Bookstein includes an illustration of this type of problem in which he considers how one might attempt to randomly sample a library's holdings without using a list or catalog. In one simple example, he points out that if one sampled the collection by randomly sampling locations on the shelves, fat books would have a greater chance of being selected than would thin books. In another example, if a researcher were attempting to survey catalog use by randomly selecting times and then randomly selecting users during those times, this technique would be biased toward users tending to spend more time using the catalog. Users of subject headings, for example, might be more likely than some others to be included in the sample.

As Bookstein notes in his conclusions, some of these problems can be corrected by such methods as using weighted averages to compensate for biased sampling techniques. Regardless, it is important for the researcher to be careful to avoid faulty selection techniques. It is critical that random samples be drawn correctly if one is to have "some insurance against the impact of extraneous factors that can distort our results, but whose existence we may not be aware of at the time the sample is taken."[25]

NONSAMPLING ERROR

The information gathered from a sample can be inaccurate not only as a result of the inaccuracy or the lack of representativeness of the sample but also errors of measurement. For example, in responding to a questionnaire or interview, persons may lie about their age or report figures inaccurately for a variety of reasons. Nonsampling error is difficult to estimate but, generally, as sample size goes up, so does nonsampling error. Another way of stating this relationship is that as sampling error decreases, nonsampling error tends to increase. Since sampling error generally decreases as sample size increases, one is faced with some conflict between sampling and nonsampling error. Some sort of balance is usually desirable, and the largest sample size possible is not necessarily the best.

Sampling In-Library Use

by Sebastian Mundt

Whenever a full count or census is practically impossible, too time-consuming or costly and/or too monotonous, libraries traditionally apply sampling procedures to study specifics of the collection and to revise their card catalogues.[1] More recent applications focus on sampling for user surveys and on collecting data for performance indicators.[2]

In general, sampling has been used to reduce complexity by selecting and analyzing a subset of the population in question. It can be "selective" as regards

1. time (e.g., reporting period)
2. location (e.g., branches or service points)
3. objects of library use (e.g., collection)
4. subjects of library use (e.g., users).

Literature on sampling in libraries regularly provides thorough information and guidance on estimating *percentages;* examples mostly focus on user surveys. Statistics of library use, however, usually aim at *total numbers.* Selecting over time is the most widely applied form of sampling totals and will be the focus of this section. Other perspectives of "selecting" a sample have been described in the literature: Cullen and Gray have sampled branches and service points of a public library system;[3] Fussler and Simon,[4] Line and Sandison,[5] and Baker and Lancaster[6] have gone into detail about the methodology and issues of sampling collections. For the basics of sampling, especially for random and nonrandom sampling methods, sampling and measurement error and the calculation of sample sizes, the reader should refer to the relevant sections of this chapter.

NONRANDOM SAMPLING

To achieve the highest possible accuracy, "official" library statistics have usually required that all statistical reporting should be based on a full count: "Data referring to a period should cover the specified period in question, not the interval between two successive surveys."[7] In most countries, important activities of use were therefore not reported on a national level.

The revised International Standard ISO 2789:2003 "Information and documentation—International library statistics" now allows for the use of sampling procedures to estimate annual totals of library visits, in-house use and information requests. It denotes that "the annual total is to be established from a sample count" and "the sample should be taken in one or more normal weeks and grossed up."[8] This principle was regarded as the "highest common factor" for statistical reporting on the international level. It takes into consideration that this kind of purposive (judgement) sampling only requires basic statistical knowledge. Expanding upon this definition, the ANSI/NISO Z39.7 details in its Data Dictionary a *typical week* as "*time that is neither unusually busy nor unusually slow*" and "*in which the library is open its regular hours.*"[9] Holidays, vacation periods, days when unusual events are taking place in the community or in the library should be avoided.

In the following example, gate count data from Münster University Library are used to discuss the potentials and pitfalls of (1) weekly sampling and (2) sampling by judgement. Figure 1 displays the average number of gate counts per weekday between 1998 and 2000. Although the number of visits per weekday was not found to be normally distributed, visits to the library seem to follow a weekly pattern with relatively low standard deviation. Note that the average number of visits (gate counts) starts to decline on Tuesday, and due to the academic week Fridays and Saturdays (and Sundays if applicable) are generally less busy. Weeks can therefore be regarded as *clusters* which represent various activity levels in recurrent order. Depending on the level of detail required, other (e.g., daily) sampling units may be preferable. Cullen and Gray[10] and Maxstadt,[11] for example, chose to sample service hours as they had to consider different opening hours across several service points in a public library system. Clearly, one week of sampling requires less organizational input than an equivalent number of separate days or hours, and many libraries therefore prefer to count in weekly intervals.

In contrast to a random selection of the sample, the deliberate preselection of *normal* or *typical* weeks implies detailed knowledge about the variable in question. It is well known that, for example, daily use of academic libraries' services is being influenced by general factors like the "academic year," events inside the library, and the availability of "competitive" library services on the campus. It can be argued furthermore that a number of

Figure 1 Average Gate Counts per Weekday (Münster University Library, 1998–2000).

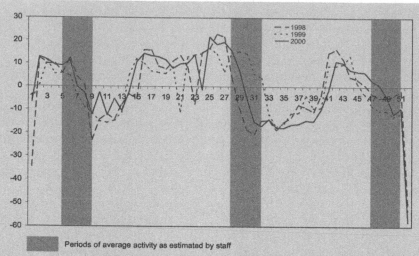

Figure 2 Weekly Gate Counts in Percent of Deviation from Yearly Mean (Münster University Library, 1998–2000).

randomized factors like technical readiness of buildings and systems, local daily weather conditions, or important cultural or other events in the vicinity will blur any set of in-library use data.

Even if it is difficult, if not impossible, to take these fuzzy elements into consideration, the selection of "normal" weeks implies that data of previous years provide sufficiently reliable information on weeks representing an average level of activity, and that library staff are aware of these patterns. Figure 2 underlines this problem by displaying adjusted data of weekly gate counts at Münster University Library for the years 1998 to 2000.

Hardly any week or even longer time frame can be identified as a reliable basis for purposive sampling over several years, as many weeks show varying gate counts over the years in question, and periods of high use blend into periods of lower use. Furthermore, experienced members of staff in user services were asked to determine periods of average in-library use intensity. As seen in Figure 2, gate counts in the periods chosen by staff still vary between +15.8 and –20.5 percent from the mean. Staff in other libraries may even come to different results. Thus, the significantly smaller variation of values indicates that staff judgement can in fact improve the sample, but it is not a very solid foundation for statistical reporting and comparisons.

RANDOM SAMPLING OVER TIME

While nonrandom sampling cannot be counted on for precision, the "accuracy" of random samples can be measured in terms of error and confidence level. The following examples apply different methods of random sampling to reference and other use statistics. As the methods were applied to different library settings, the results and boundaries were generally not compared except where indicated.

A description of the "purest" sampling method, a simple random sample of opening hours throughout the year, can be found in Maxstadt.[12] For the fiscal year 1986/87, staff at Louisiana State University Libraries calculated a sample size of 52 hours (of 4,103 hours of service a year) setting a confidence level of 90 percent and error boundaries of ± 10 percent. With an increased sample size of 60 hours, the actual overall error range was later determined as ± 11.23 percent. The yearly total of reference questions was estimated by linear extrapolation of the sample count.

To avoid any bias or service delays, additional library staff were assigned to collect the sample data. If no extra staff are available, this method may be criticized because the hourly count as practiced here requires a great deal of coordination, especially in large libraries with several service points.

Kesselman and Watstein[13] describe the use of additional information to stratify the sample and thereby reduce its variation, compared to a simple random sample. Based on fully counted reference statistics at New York University's Bobst Library from the year 1982/83, weekly reference counts were stratified in high, medium and low activity. Given a 95 percent confidence limit and an error of ± 400 ($\approx$ 10%) a sample size of 15 weeks was calculated, which represented the number of weeks in each of the classes or "strata." The yearly total was estimated by linear extrapolation of the weighted class means.

It was recognized, however, that the stratification of reference weeks may vary from year to year for a number of reasons, academic or school holidays being the most obvious. Consequently, library staff may find it difficult to determine in advance whether information from previous years is still reliable. In the Bobst Library case, the sample mean of medium weeks was higher than the one of high weeks. The problem was solved by merging both into one stratum, thereby losing some of the expected improvement.

Starting from the procedure chosen at Bobst Library, Lochstet and Lehman[14] developed a correlation method that makes use of a highly significant, almost linear direct correlation (+.957) between weekly reference statistics values and door counts as found by staff at Thomas Cooper Library, at the University of South Carolina in 1996. In this case, the door count was used as a boundary distribution to extrapolate the reference sample values and estimate the yearly total.

The correlated total and the total sampled from the same weeks differed by only .05 percent. The standard error with the correlation method, however, was considerably high. The authors recommend collecting and correlating data of two variables for one or even two years to provide a substantial set of comparable data before the correlation method can be regarded as a functional alternative. After an accurate correlation coefficient is obtained, however, it is expected that the amount of time spent on recording reference statistics can be significantly reduced. Only a small random sample of a few weeks will be needed to verify that the correlation has not changed.

Staff at Münster University and Regional Library in Germany examined whether the correlation method used at Thomas Cooper Library could be extended to certain datasets from the library system. At first all in-library usage data were regarded as possible high correlates to the gate count because all these activities could only be initiated by persons who had

TABLE 1 Correlation between Weekly Gate Count and Data from Automated System (Münster University Library, 1999/2000)

	Visits	Reference	Reservations (in library)	Reservations (remote)	Account information	Renewals	Textbook loans	Normal loans
Visits	1.000							
Reference	.876**	1.000						
Reservations (in library)	.802**	.751**	1.000					
Reservations (remote)	.437**	.347	.269**	1.000				
Account information	.800**	.765**	.796**	.220**	1.000			
Renewals	.523**	.512*	.568**	.256**	.759**	1.000		
Textbook loans	.473**	.383	.558**	.117	.312**	.140*	1.000	
Normal loans	.506**	.057	.656**	-.019	.508**	.283**	.483**	1.000

**The correlation is significant at the 0.01 level (2-sided).
*The correlation is significant at the 0.05 level (2-sided).

previously entered the library. Second, the data to be analyzed should be collected automatically by the library system, i.e., available with only minimal staff input. Weekly gate counts (and reference questions) were then correlated with the selection of automated data shown in Table 1. The highest correlation values (> +.75) with gate counts and reference were found in (a) user-initiated reservations and (b) accesses to user accounts from PC workstations inside the library.

In contrast, loans and reservations from workstations outside the library premises are obvious examples of unsuitable correlates. While loans differ in their seasonal patterns from library visits over a year, users frequenting the automated system from outside the library are unlikely to be included in the gate count on the same day; yet it seems likely that remote use can also show high correlation values, e.g., online reference with virtual visits of the library Web site.

Seemingly corresponding data may in fact be pure coincidence as the correlation coefficient only measures the nature and extent, but not the causal connection ("direction") of a relationship between two variables. Before high correlation values can be used, it is therefore important to preselect possible correlates carefully and analyze them for logical consistency, and to monitor the correlation values over a longer period of time to ensure that the correspondence is not purely accidental.

CONCLUSIONS

- Sampling procedures have always been widely applied in libraries because the full count of some data was impossible or too costly. The introduction of sampling in international statistical reporting reflects a general shift of focus from input to output measures, many of which can only be counted in sample form.

- From the point of data collection management, it seems useful to choose a week as the sampling unit. "Normal" weeks, when selected by judgement, may be difficult to anticipate even from data collected over several years, and the precision of judgement sampling cannot be calculated in terms of error and confidence level.

- It is likely that certain usage data show significant correlation and can provide useful information for estimating totals. The significance of the correlation, however, should be revised at regular intervals as correlation only indicates the extent, not any causal connection, of a relationship between variables.

- Due to the lack of comparable data, it seems unreasonable to recommend an overall "best" or "most appropriate" sampling method for international statistical reporting. Libraries are therefore asked to apply sampling methods carefully with respect to all possible sources of error, and their regional and national institutions will have to monitor and actively supervise the quality of data delivered to them.

NOTES

1. Ben-Ami Lipetz, "Catalog Use in a Large Research Library," *Library Quarterly* 42, no. 1 (1972). Abraham Bookstein, "Sampling from Card Files," *Library Quarterly* 53, no. 3 (1983).

2. F. Wilfrid Lancaster, *If You Want to Evaluate Your Library* ... 2nd ed. (Champaign, IL: University of Illinois, Graduate School of Library and Information Science, 1993): 145–51.

3. Rowena Cullen and Alistair Gray, "A Method for Taking a Reliable Statistical Sample of Reference Inquiries in a New Zealand Public Library System," *Journal of Library Administration* 22, no. 1 (1995).

4. Herman H. Fussler and Julian L. Simon, *Patterns in the Use of Books in Large Research Libraries* (Chicago: University of Chicago Press, 1969).

5. Maurice B. Line and Alexander Sandison, " 'Obsolescence' and Changes in the Use of Literature with Time," *Journal of Documentation* 30 (September 1974).

6. Sharon L. Baker and F. Wilfrid Lancaster, *The Measurement and Evaluation of Library Services*, 2nd ed. (Arlington, VA: Information Resources Press, 1991), 51–75.

7. *ISO 2789:1991: Information and Documentation–International Library Statistics*, 2nd ed. (Geneva: International Standards Organisation, 1991), 3.

8. *ISO 2789:2003: Information and Documentation–International Library Statistics*, 3rd ed. (Geneva: International Standards Organisation, 2003), 15.

9. "ANSI/NISO Z39.7-2004: Information Services and Use: Metrics & Statistics for Libraries and Information Providers—Data Dictionary: Appendix: Methods of Measurement," *NISO*, http://www.niso.org/dictionary/appendices/appendixa/.

10. Cullen and Gray, "Method for Taking a Reliable Statistical Sample," 116.

11. John M. Maxstadt, "A New Approach to Reference Statistics," *College & Research Libraries* 49 (February 1988).

12. Ibid.

13. Martin Kesselman and Sarah B. Watstein, "The Measurement of Reference and Information Services," *Journal of Academic Librarianship* 13, no. 1 (1987).

14. Gwenn Lochstet and Donna H. Lehman, "A Correlation Method for Collecting Reference Statistics," *College & Research Libraries* 60, no. 1 (1999).

SUMMARY

"The strength of survey research is in answering questions of fact and in assessing the distributions of the characteristics of populations."[26] It does not permit causal inferences, although it can facilitate the analysis of relationships between variables, particularly correlational relationships. Survey research is typically weak on internal control or validity, but, if based on random sampling, it is strong in external validity. This is because survey research generally concerns itself with naturally occurring variables in natural settings.

However, the only reliable way to ensure that the results of survey research can be generalized from a sample to a population or beyond a single study is to draw a representative sample. The most common, and one of the best, techniques for selecting a representative sample is simple random sampling. Depending on certain characteristics of the population, or on the purpose of the research, other probability techniques may be preferable in a given situation.

Other closely related concerns include the size of the sample and sampling error. There are formulas for estimating these properties, but, again, the nature of the population and the purpose of the research should be considered. There are no absolute criteria for sample size and sampling error. What is satisfactory for one study may not be for another. There may even be occasions where non-probability sampling is preferable to probability sampling, but the researcher should keep in mind that the generalizability of studies using nonprobability samples is open to serious question.

NOTES

1. Claire Selltiz, Lawrence S. Wrightsman, and Stuart W. Cook, *Research Methods in Social Relations*, rev. ed. (New York: Rinehart and Winston, 1959), 55.

2. Ibid., 65.

3. Paul D. Leedy, *Practical Research: Planning and Design*, 2nd ed. (New York: Macmillan, 1980), 76.

4. Gary Golden, *Survey Research Methods* (Chicago: ACRL, 1982), 5.

5. John C. Flanagan, "The Critical Incident Technique," *Psychological Bulletin* 5 (1954): 327–58.

6. Paul D. Leedy and Jeanne Ellis Ormrod. *Practical Research: Planning and Design*, 8th ed. (Upper Saddle River, NJ: Pearson Merrill Prentice Hall, 2005), 209.

7. Ibid., 208.

8. Charles H. Busha and Stephen P. Harter, *Research Methods in Librarianship: Techniques and Interpretations* (New York: Academic Press, 1980), 79–87.

9. Arlene Fink, *How to Conduct Surveys: A Step-by-Step Guide*, 3rd ed. (Thousand Oaks, CA: Sage, 2006).

10. Ibid., 140.

11. Earl R. Babbie, *The Practice of Social Research*, 12th ed. (Belmont, CA: Wadsworth/Cengage Learning, 2010), 197.

12. Matthias Schonlau, Ronald D. Fricker, and Marc N. Elliott. *Conducting Research Surveys via E-mail and the Web* (Santa Monica, CA: Rand, 2002), 19–20.

13. Babbie, *The Practice of Social Research*, 2010).

14. Ibid., 193.

15. Ibid.

16. Edward Lakner, "Optimizing Samples for Surveys of Public Libraries: Alternatives and Compromises," *Library & Information Science Research* 20, no. 4 (1998): 329.

17. Babbie, *The Practice of Social Research* 2010, 219.

18. Pete Capre, "Social Media: Short-Term Craze or Long-Term Phenomenon?" *SSI Survey Sampling International*, http://www.surveysampling.com/en/ssicompass/december-2008/social-media-short-term-craze-or-long-term-phenomenon.

19. Babbie, *The Practice of Social Research* 2010, 197.

20. Chava Frankfort-Nachmias and David Nachmias, *Research Methods in the Social Sciences*, 7th ed. (New York: Worth Publishers, 2008), 164.

21. Helena C. Kraemer and Sue Thiemann, *How Many Subjects? Statistical Power Analysis in Research* (Newbury Park, CA: Sage, 1987).

Peter Hernon, "Determination of Sample Size and Selection of the Sample: Concepts, General Sources, and Software," *College & Research Libraries* 55 (March 1994): 171–79.

Jacob Cohen, *Statistical Power Analysis for the Behavioral Sciences*, 2nd ed. (Hillsdale, NJ: Lawrence Erlbaum Associates, 1988).

22. David Nachmias and Chava Nachmias, *Research Methods in the Social Sciences*, 2nd ed. (New York: St. Martin's Press, 1981).

23. Ian S. Simpson, *Basic Statistics for Librarians*, 3rd ed. (London: Library Association, 1988), 44.

24. Abraham Bookstein, "How to Sample Badly," *Library Quarterly* 44 (April 1974): 124–32.

25. Ibid., 132.

26. Louise H. Kidder, *Research Methods in Social Relations*, 4th ed. (New York: Holt, Rinehart and Winston, 1981), 80.

5

Data Collection Techniques

This chapter will deal with three frequently used data collection techniques—the questionnaire, the interview, and observation. (See Chapter 7, Qualitative Research Methods, for additional information about interviews, observation, and content analysis.) These methods for gathering data are most commonly, but not exclusively, used in survey research. They are data collection techniques or instruments, not research methodologies, and they can be used with more than one methodology. Observation is the possible exception, in that some texts do treat observational research as both a technique and a methodology. Regardless, their purpose is to collect data. Achievement tests, aptitude tests, and so on are, of course, often used to collect data for educational research and to assess or evaluate performance, ability, knowledge, and behavior. Readers wishing to learn more about that type of data collection tool should refer to texts by Gay, Mills, and Airasian.[1]

THE QUESTIONNAIRE

Pre-Questionnaire Planning

The planning that should precede the design of a questionnaire is not that different from the planning that should go into the early development of a research study. The process will be given here in brief outline form as a way of reviewing the major steps and of emphasizing decisions that should be made before the data collection instrument is selected or designed.

1. Define the problem (and purpose).
2. Consider previous, related research, the advice of experts, and so on.
3. Hypothesize a solution to the problem (or at least identify research questions, the answers to which will shed some light on the problem).
4. Identify the information needed to test the hypothesis. This step should include deciding which aspects of the problem will be considered

and planning ahead to the presentation and analysis of the data. Deciding how the data will be organized, presented, and analyzed can significantly influence what types of data will have to be collected. It may be useful at this point to construct so-called dummy-tables, or tables presenting the important variables with hypothetical values, to help anticipate possible problems regarding presentation and analysis.

5. Identify the potential respondents or subjects. As noted earlier, practical questions should be asked at this time, such as, "Are the potential respondents accessible? Are they likely to respond?"

6. Select the best or most appropriate technique for collecting the necessary data. It is here that the researcher should consider the relevant advantages and disadvantages of the questionnaire, interview, observation, and other techniques in relation to the more general methodology to be used.

To some extent, research findings are affected by the nature of the data collection technique used. In fact, findings strongly affected by the technique can lose their validity. Consequently, a researcher may elect to use two or more techniques and methods to test hypotheses and/or measure variables; this process often is referred to as *triangulation*. Burgess believed that triangulation implies "the notion of three points of view within a triangle;"[2] therefore, Gorman and Clayton suggest using the term, "mixed methods" "to allow the researcher to use a range of methods, data, investigators and theories within any study."[3] For example, information about library use could be collected with questionnaires, interviews, documentary analysis, and observation. Consistent findings among the different data collection techniques would suggest that the findings are reasonably valid. Discrepancies among the results would indicate a need for further research. Morgan provides a discussion of the different approaches for combining qualitative and quantitative methods, as well as identifying the challenges of combining the two methods.[4]

Advantages of the Questionnaire

The questionnaire, which the *American Heritage Dictionary of the English Language* defines as "a form containing a set of questions, especially one addressed to a statistically significant number of subjects as a way of gathering information from a survey,"[5] offers several important advantages over other techniques or instruments for collecting survey data. Among them are the following:

1. The questionnaire, especially the mail, email, and Web-based questionnaire, tends to encourage frank answers. This is in large part because it is easier for the researcher to guarantee anonymity for the respondent when using a mail questionnaire. In addition, the respondent can complete the questionnaire without the researcher's being

present. Thus the questionnaire can be quite effective at measuring attitudes (see number 4 below for another consideration).

2. The characteristics of the questionnaire that help to produce frank answers also eliminate interviewer bias. This is not to say that the questions could not be worded in a biased manner, but that there is no style of verbal presentation which can influence the response. (The problem of biased questions is a serious one and will be treated in greater detail later.)

3. Another way of stating the second advantage is that the fixed format of the questionnaire tends to eliminate variation in the questioning process. Once the questions have been written in their final version and included in the questionnaire, their contents and organization will not change. However, this does not rule out the possibility of respondents interpreting the same question in different ways.

4. The manner in which a mail questionnaire is distributed and responded to also allows it to be completed, within limits, at the leisure of the participants. This encourages well thought out, accurate answers. On the other hand, if the researcher is more interested in obtaining spontaneous or immediate reactions, as in an attitudinal survey, then the relatively large amount of time allotted for completion of the questionnaire could be a disadvantage.

5. Questionnaires can be constructed so that quantitative data are relatively easy to collect and analyze.

6. Questionnaires can facilitate the collection of large amounts of data in a relatively short period of time. Questionnaire-based surveys of several thousand people are not unusual, and responses typically are expected within one to two weeks.

7. Last, but not least, questionnaires are usually relatively inexpensive to administer.

Disadvantages of the Questionnaire

While the advantages of the questionnaire seem to outweigh the disadvantages, there are several of the latter that should be noted:

1. Use of the mail questionnaire eliminates personal contact between the researcher and the respondent. However, this also can be seen as an advantage, for, as stated earlier, the absence of direct contact eliminates interviewer bias from the questioning process.

2. The mail questionnaire does not permit the respondent to qualify answers to ambiguous questions or, at least, makes it more difficult. On the other hand, the more difficult it is for respondents to qualify answers, the more likely the researcher is to obtain consistent responses.

3. Studies have shown that persons who are highly opinionated regarding the subject of a questionnaire are more likely than others to be

motivated enough to complete and return it. This phenomenon tends to result in a biased sample or return, as the less opinionated members of the sample will be underrepresented and may well have certain characteristics in common.

4. Questionnaires may be more difficult for uneducated participants to complete, again possibly resulting in a biased return. The researcher can minimize this problem by keeping his or her audience in mind when developing the questionnaire and writing the questions.

5. In general, there simply seems to be a resistance to mail questionnaires. In the extreme case, this can result in some participants attempting to "sabotage" a survey by purposefully responding incorrectly to some questionnaire items. This problem can be alleviated through appropriate research design, specific techniques of which will be mentioned later.

6. Nonresponse rates are relatively high for mail, email, and Web-based questionnaires, although Web-based surveys often first use another survey method to recruit participants. Since survey respondents are usually female, more educated, and older than those who do not respond to surveys, nonresponses reduce the sample size and may introduce sampling error by eliminating a subset of the population. The researcher should correct for sampling bias incurred from nonresponse or minimize nonresponse rates by combining several data collection techniques.[6]

7. If the questionnaire is distributed electronically, it will reach only those who have access to and are comfortable using email and Web technology.

CONSTRUCTING THE QUESTIONNAIRE

Proper construction of the questionnaire is essential to its success. In general, the researcher must consider his or her information needs and the characteristics of the participants. The former concern will be dealt with first.

Type of Question According to Information Needed

In selecting or writing specific types of questions, the researcher must first consider what kind of data he or she needs. The major types of questions, according to the kind of information needed, include the following:

1. Factual questions: questions used to ascertain such things as the respondent's age, gender, and so on. They are probably the most straightforward type of questionnaire item.

2. Opinion and attitude questions: questions intended to determine a person's ideas, inclinations, prejudices, convictions, and so on.

(Questionnaires used for an attitudinal survey are usually known as "attitude scales" or "indexes.") They tend to be considerably more subjective than factual questions and are more difficult to validate externally.

3. Information questions: questions designed to measure the respondent's knowledge about some topic. They typically require the greatest response time.

4. Self-perception questions: questions quite similar to attitude questions, but restricted to one's opinions about himself or herself.

5. Standards of action questions: questions used to determine how respondents would act in certain circumstances. For example, one may ask library patrons how they would react to a new library service or a change in hours.

6. Questions about actual past or present behavior: questions that potentially fall within some of the categories of questions already identified but tend to be narrower in that they focus on behavior. For example, the kind of information gathered to describe past or present behavior could be factual, attitudinal, or informational in nature. Behavioral questions also tend to be rather subjective but usually become more valid as they become more specific. Data on past and present behavior can serve to some extent as a predictor of future behavior.

7. Projective questions: questions that allow respondents to answer questions indirectly by imposing their personal beliefs, attitudes, and so on onto others. In other words, they permit the respondent to indicate how he or she would react to some question or situation by reporting how peers, colleagues, and so on would react in the same situation. This technique can be particularly useful for eliciting responses on a topic about which participants may be reluctant to express their own, true feelings openly or directly. For example, certain public librarians could be asked how their colleagues feel about censorship, with the researcher assuming that the attitudes of the respondents are similar to the attitudes of the colleagues. The researcher must be aware, however, that such measures may be weak in validity as indicators of the characteristics they are designed to measure.

   Projective questions are considered to be a type of indirect method of questioning people and as such require only minimal cooperation on the part of the individuals being studied. Hoyle, Harris, and Judd discuss a variety of specific projective methods, as well as several more structured indirect tests.[7] The reader interested in learning more about indirect assessment should consult Hoyle, Harris, and Judd, keeping in mind that the validity and reliability of indirect methods are open to question. Such techniques are probably most appropriate for exploratory research.

All or most of the items in a questionnaire may be focused on one specific topic and, in aggregate, considered to constitute a *scale* for the topic of interest.

In the typical survey in LIS, however, the questionnaire is likely to consist of a variety of questions addressing a number of components of a broader topic.

Type of Question According to Form

In selecting or designing questionnaire items, the researcher must consider the question format that will best obtain the information desired. The form of the question in turn determines the method of response. The researcher must decide which response format will be the easiest for the respondent while still producing adequate, definite, and uniform answers. Whenever possible, it is recommended that consistent response formats be employed. This results in less confusion for the respondent and makes speedier replies possible.

There are two basic types of questions—open-ended questions and fixed-response questions. *Open-ended*, or *unstructured questions*, as the name indicates, are designed to permit free responses from participants rather than ones limited to specific alternatives. They are especially useful for exploratory studies; they "are called for when the issue is complex, when the relevant dimensions are not known, or when the interest of the researcher lies in exploration of a process or of the individual's formulation of an issue."[8]

On the negative side, as there is almost no limit to the possible responses to an open-ended question, their answers are usually more difficult to categorize and analyze than responses to structured questions. Open-ended questions may also discourage responses because they typically take longer to answer.

Examples of open-ended questions are

1. What do you think about the library?
2. Which library services do you value the most?
3. I typically use the library in order to _____.

Fixed-response or *structured questions*, also known as closed questions, limit the responses of the participant to stated alternatives. The possible responses may range from a simple "yes" or "no," to a checklist of possible replies, to a scale indicating various degrees of a particular response.

Structured questions have several advantages and disadvantages in comparison with unstructured questions. Structured questions more easily accommodate precoding in that the possible responses are generally known and stated. The precoding, in turn, facilitates the analysis of the data gathered by the questions. Precoding essentially involves anticipating responses, establishing numerical codes or symbols for the various responses, and including the codes on the questionnaire. An example of a precoded questionnaire item follows:

	Yes	No
Do you have a current library card?	1	2

In this example, the respondent would be asked to circle the number representing his or her answer. A 1 or a 2, whichever the response happens to be, would be entered into the data set for future analysis. (This technique will be discussed in greater detail in Chapter 9, Analysis of Data.) The use of precoded forms is sometimes referred to as direct data entry or DDE. The respondent, in this example, could have been asked to circle "yes" or "no" rather than circle a code. After receiving the questionnaire, the researcher would then have to assign a numerical code to that response and enter it, thus adding an extra step to the analysis process. Golden identified seven different coding schemes: listing, simple factual, bracket, scales, combination, frame of reference, and series.[9]

Other advantages to the structured question format include the fact that responses to structured questions tend to have more reliability than responses to unstructured questions. This occurs because there is a limited set of responses, and thus less potential for variation from test to test. Fixed-alternative questions also have the advantages of being "standardizable," simple to administer, and more easily understood by the respondent in terms of the dimensions along which the answers are sought. Having fixed responses also helps to ensure that the answers are given in a frame of reference that is relevant to the purpose of the inquiry.

Among the disadvantages of the structured question is a real possibility that a limited set of possible replies can force respondents to select inaccurate answers. None of the choices may correspond exactly to the participant's position, or may not allow for qualification. Having an "other" category can alleviate this problem somewhat, but respondents tend to limit their answers to those provided rather than utilizing the "other" option.

Similarly, a closed question may force a statement of opinion on an issue about which the respondent does not have one. The inclusion of a "don't know" or "no opinion" type response can help to provide an indication of no opinion, but again the respondent is inclined to give a more definite response. The omission of possible responses can also introduce bias. For example, in a question asking a library user to check the services he or she uses regularly, the list may be biased toward print rather than electronic resources, or traditional rather than more innovative services, in that more options are provided for one or the other orientation. Again, an "other" category does not completely eliminate this problem.

Providing possible answers can also help the respondent to cover up a certain amount of ignorance. The respondent will be able to provide a reasonable answer even when he or she knows nothing about the subject. Whether this is a problem depends on the nature of the study.

In conclusion, "closed questions are more efficient where the possible alternative replies are known, limited in number, and clear-cut. Thus they are appropriate for securing factual information ... and for eliciting expressions of opinion about issues on which people hold clear opinions."[10] In practice, a combination of structured and unstructured questions can be most efficient. In addition, two surveys, or a survey followed by a survey of a subsample, can effectively utilize both types of questions and thereby complement one another. For example, following a survey based on structured questions, a subsample could be studied in greater depth with unstructured questions.

Structured questions come in a variety of specific formats, including the following:

1. A checklist, each item of which requires a response. (An example is provided for this and each of the other types of structured questions to follow.)

    Have you ever done any of the following while using a library? (Circle one number on each line.)

	Yes	No
a. Asked a reference question?	1	2
b. Checked out a book?	1	2
c. Read a magazine?	1	2
d. Read a newspaper?	1	2
e. Listened to a recording?	1	2

2. A checklist of items, one or more of which represents the "best" answer.
    Which of the following types of library services do you use at least five times a year? (Circle all numbers that apply.)

a. Reference	1
b. Circulation	2
c. Audiovisual	3
d. Periodicals	4
e. Photocopying	5
f. Children's department	6

3. A checklist of items with subdivisions or categories.
    What is the highest grade of school you have completed? (Circle one number.)

Grade school	01	02	03	04	05	06	07	08
High school		09	10	11	12			
College or technical school		13	14	15	16			
Post-graduate			17					

4. A checklist of bracketed or grouped responses.
    How many times did you use a public library during the past 12 months? (Circle one number.)

None	1
1–5	2
6–10	3
11–15	4
16–20	5
21 or more	6

5. Fill in the blank.
    The reference desk is on the _____ floor of the library.

Scaled Responses

A variety of questions utilize scales of one type or another in order to obtain responses. One kind of scale is the *rating scale*. Specific rating scales, with examples, include the following:

1. An itemized rating or specific category scale.

   How important would each of the following items be to you in deciding to use a library? (Circle one number on each line.)

	Of great importance	Of some importance	Of little importance	Of no importance
a. Adequate hours of service	1	2	3	4
b. Multiple copies of best-sellers	1	2	3	4
c. Adequate parking	1	2	3	4
d. Helpful staff	1	2	3	4

   An itemized rating scale often has a category representing "no opinion" or "undecided."

2. A graphic rating scale. (This too is a scale designed to collect ordinal-level data, but, unlike the specific category scale, the graphic scale allows the respondent to check anywhere along a continuum.)

   For each of the following statements, indicate your degree of agreement by placing a checkmark on the continuum.

   a. The library does an adequate job of teaching students how to use its collections.

   Strongly agree   Strongly disagree

   b. The library's collection is usually adequate to meet my needs.

   Strongly agree   Strongly disagree

   The second and third points along the continuum could have been labeled as "Agree" and "Disagree," but doing so might have encouraged respondents to limit their responses to four labeled checkpoints. Such scales typically have from four to seven categories or checkpoints and are often used for measuring attitudes. It may be desirable to include a response for "undecided" or "no opinion." Careful consideration must be given to the placement of such a category, however, in that its location on the continuum determines its point value. (If it were placed in the middle of the graphic scale given above, its value would be three. If placed at the end, its value might be one or five.) If the code for the value is treated as a real number, then the value of statistics such as those representing the average can be misleading and the results of the data analysis difficult to interpret.

3. A rank-order or comparative rating scale.

   Please rank, in order of importance, the following types of library services. (Record "1" for the most important, through "5" for the least important.)

   Library instruction programs ____

   Reference services ____

   Circulation services ____

   Audiovisual services ____

   Study facilities ____

Ranking type questions are not always recommended and should be used carefully. They become especially difficult for the respondent to deal with when many items are listed.

Other scaling methods use multiple responses or measurements and combine the responses into a single scale score. According to Hoyle, Harris, and Judd, *multiple-item scales*, even more so than rating scales, can help to reduce the complexity of data.[11] They also hold more potential for testing hypotheses and are considered to have better validity and reliability. Multiple-item scales can be categorized as differential, summated, and cumulative.

A *differential scale*, often referred to as a Thurstone type scale, utilizes a series of statements or items with equidistances between them. Each item, therefore, receives a value point equidistant from those immediately preceding and following it. The respondent is asked to check each statement with which he or she agrees or the two or three statements that best represent his or her position. Statements about a public library might include the following examples:

Statement	Scale value
I believe the public library is an important agency for educating citizens.	1.0
I believe the public library plays a major role as a cultural agency.	1.5
I believe the public library duplicates educational services provided elsewhere.	7.4
I believe the public library is of value only for recreational reading.	8.2

The statements would represent favorable and unfavorable attitudes toward the public library and would be arranged in a random order. The respondent's overall attitude would be the mean of the scale values of the items with which he or she agreed.

Differential scales do have certain disadvantages. They are time-consuming to develop, in that it is difficult to design questions that truly represent values equidistant from one another. In addition, it is difficult to avoid rater or compiler bias in developing questions utilizing differential scales.

Summated scales also consist of series of statements or items, but no effort is made to distribute them evenly along a continuum. In fact, only items that are favorable or unfavorable to the attitude of interest are used (unless a "no opinion" type of response is included.) The Likert scale is one of the most commonly used summated scales. An example follows:

Item	Strongly Agree	Agree	Disagree	Strongly disagree
A college reference librarian should refer students to sources of information.	SA	A	D	SD
A college reference librarian should teach students how to obtain their own information.	SA	A	D	SD
A college reference librarian should provide students with needed information.	SA	A	D	SD

In this case, the sum of responses to the items favoring the provision of library instruction, minus the sum of responses to the items opposing library instruction, would constitute the scale score. (The response values would be those values assigned to "strongly agree," "agree," and so on.) Likert-type scales are often used with individual, nonsummated scales as well. (See the examples of itemized rating and graphic scales given above.)

The major disadvantage of summated or Likert-type scales is that, since they represent an ordinal scale of measurement, they do not permit one to say anything about the exact amount of differences in attitudes. For example, one could not say that a respondent who checked "strongly disagree" was twice as unfavorable toward some library service as a respondent who checked "disagree." Some do argue that the data collected by a Likert-type scale are, for all practical purposes, interval level, and proceed to analyze the data accordingly. A more conservative, rigorous approach would not permit this assumption.

The third basic category of multiple-item scales utilized in questionnaires is the *cumulative scale*. It consists of a series of statements with which the respondent indicates agreement or disagreement; however, the items are related to each other, so one "should" respond to subsequent items in a manner similar to preceding ones. It is generally assumed that cumulative scales represent the ordinal level of measurement. Examples of cumulative scales include the Bogardus-type scale, used for measuring social attitudes, and the Guttman scale, also known as "scale analysis" or "the scalogram method." As was the case with the Likert scale, all items or statements must be either clearly favorable or unfavorable to the topic. A unique feature of the cumulative scale is that none of the respondents should give a negative response before a positive response or a positive response after a negative response.

A specialized scale which shares some of the characteristics of the summated scales is the *semantic differential scale*. This scale provides pairs of antonyms and synonyms, along with five- to seven-step rating scales. An example follows:

For each pair of items below, what number comes closest to describing the conditions of your public library? (Circle one number on each line.)

	Extre-mely	Moder-ately	Nei-ther	Moder-ately	Extre-mely	
a. Pleasant	1	2	3	4	5	Unpleasant
b. Clean	1	2	3	4	5	Dirty
c. Organized	1	2	3	4	5	Disorganized
d. Helpful	1	2	3	4	5	Unhelpful
e. Available when needed	1	2	3	4	5	Unavailable when needed

To obtain the respondent's overall rating of the library, the researcher would sum the total value of each column and divide by the number (five) of rows.

All of these scales possess one or more weaknesses. As was noted earlier, one common problem relates to the determination of the neutral position when provided. Another concerns the conceptual validity of assigning one value or point that represents a person's attitude along a continuum when, in fact, a wide range of values may be more accurate.

Self-ratings are subject to a variety of limitations resulting from personal bias and the subjectivity of the questions. Ratings by others can suffer from certain *systematic errors* which decrease the validity and reliability of the results. One of these, the *halo effect*, occurs when the respondent generalizes the rating from one item to another in an unconscious attempt to make his or her ratings consistent. This phenomenon is especially likely to occur when a general, all-encompassing question is asked before more specific questions on the same topic. For example, if a participant responds positively to a general question about a library, he or she is more likely to give positive responses to subsequent questions about specific services of the same library. Another constancy error, the *generosity error*, involves the rater's overestimating the desirable qualities of subjects. A third systematic error, the *contrast error*, results when respondents tend to view persons as different from themselves on the trait being rated. A variety of other factors relating to the construction and administering of questions can decrease the reliability of their scales. These problems will be considered later in the text as appropriate.

Having selected a specific form of response, the researcher must make other decisions regarding that particular format. If a researcher had decided to utilize the check answer, he or she must then decide if it would be best to provide dichotomous, multiple-choice, or scaled responses. He or she should be satisfied that a checklist provides enough alternatives, and that the categories are mutually exclusive. In other words, there should be (within limits) a category for every possible response, and no response should require more than one category to contain it. For many fixed-response questions, the researcher must decide whether to provide a "don't know" response option. There is a difference of opinion on the desirability of doing so, but a good case can be made for providing that option when it is reasonable to expect that some respondents will not have an opinion or any knowledge on which to base an answer.

Question Content and Selection

Having decided on the type(s) of questions to be employed in terms of the information needed and the form of response desired, the researcher must next decide what specific questions to ask, and consider their content and wording. The questioner should first ask himself or herself whether a specific question is actually necessary or will be useful. If the answer is "yes," how many questions are needed on that particular topic in order to obtain the necessary information? One should never ask any more questions than are absolutely necessary.

One technique that can help the researcher avoid unnecessary and redundant questions, while asking those that are necessary, is to construct a variable-question matrix. This matrix is simply a table with the questions numbered across one edge and the variables across an adjoining edge. Corresponding boxes or cells are then checked when there is a question about a variable. If several cells are checked for any one variable, it may suggest that more questions are being asked about that topic than is necessary. Too few or no checks for a variable would raise the opposite concern.

Another question that the researcher should ask himself or herself is whether the respondents can be expected to have the information needed to provide an answer. Perhaps a question needs to be more concrete, specific, or related to the respondents' personal experiences. (On the other hand, the question should be general enough that it is free from spurious concreteness or specificity; i.e., it should not be more specific than it sounds.)

In general, a question should not be biased, or at least it should be accompanied by a question designed to balance any emphasis or perspective. The researcher also should avoid questions that are misleading because of unstated assumptions or unanticipated implications.

Last but not least, the researcher should be satisfied that each question asks only one question. This is a common occurrence in questionnaires, and yet it does not receive the attention that it deserves. Consider the following real questionnaire item as an illustration: "Ability to describe the various theories of learning and assess their relevance to particular adult learning situations." In this case, the respondents were asked to rate the degree to which they agreed with this statement. But what if one agreed with "describing the various theories" but disagreed with "assessing their relevance?" Obviously a single response could not represent both of the participants' attitudes. In addition, a question containing more than one concept presents difficulties for subsequent analysis and interpretation.

Question Wording

The way in which the contents of questionnaire items are worded can also affect their validity and reliability. Consider the following two questions:

"Do you think the U.S. should forbid public speeches against democracy?"

"Do you think the U.S. should not allow public speeches against democracy?"

In 1940, the two forms of this attitude question were asked in a "split-ballot" experiment using two comparable national samples. Although there seems to be no real difference between forbidding and not allowing something, in one sample, 54 percent of the respondents said the United States should forbid speeches against democracy, but in the other, 75 percent said the government should not allow such speeches. It appears that the variation in wording significantly affected the responses to essentially the same question. This test was replicated in the mid-1970s, and again there was a difference between samples of about 20 percent.[12]

During the Watergate scandal, Gallup polls never found a majority of Americans to be in favor of "impeaching" President Nixon; however, a majority never failed to favor impeachment when defined as an "indictment" or a decision to bring the president to trial before the Senate. In a *Reader's Digest* poll, when the pollsters asked if "government spending to aid foreign nations should be increased, decreased or kept where it is now," 67 percent said that they wanted spending cut. When asked the same question worded differently—this time in the context of cutting programs to reduce the federal deficit—83 percent favored reducing foreign aid. For discussions of how words can be interpreted differently in library settings, the reader may wish to consult articles written by Bookstein and Kidston.[13]

It is, therefore, a good idea to avoid questions that tend to be misunderstood because of difficult or unclear wording. Such questions can result from the use of biased and emotionally laden terms. In general, it is also a good idea not to use slang, jargon, and technical terms. It is even possible for some words to be objectionable to certain respondents, thereby biasing their answers or resulting in their not completing the questionnaire.

In most cases, questionnaire items should be impersonal, but whether they should request information directly or indirectly depends on the type of information needed. When the researcher doubts that subjects will be willing or able to give accurate information about themselves, indirect methods of collecting data may be necessary. However, the validity of indirect methods tends to be more suspect, and they sacrifice precision and reliability in the interest of breadth and depth of information.

In constructing questionnaire items, one should be careful that the wording used in certain questions does not bias responses to later questions. To help alleviate this problem, as well as others mentioned earlier, it is important to provide clear definitions of key terms where needed. The researcher must avoid making too many assumptions about the respondent's knowledge or the likelihood that all respondents will interpret important terms in the same way.[14]

Sequencing of Questionnaire Items

Even the sequencing of questions can influence how they are answered. Changes in question order can produce "context errors" resulting in substantial differences in responses to the same question. In a 1979 study, a question was asked about whether a pregnant woman should be allowed "to obtain a legal abortion if she is married and does not want any more children."[15] When this question was asked alone, responses were considerably more favorable than when it followed a question about allowing abortion if "there is a strong chance of serious defect in the baby." During the United States presidential campaign in 1992, voters were asked to name their favorite candidate in a two-way race between George H. W. Bush and Bill Clinton and in a three-way race among Bush, Clinton, and Ross Perot. Perot always fared better if the three-way question was asked last rather than first.

Due to the effects of "context," it is important to maintain the same order of questions if a survey is being repeated in order to investigate trends. Within a single study, the researcher should consider whether a question is likely to be influenced by the context of the preceding questions. Also, is the question led up to in a natural way? Does it occur too early or too late with regard to arousing sufficient interest and avoiding undue resistance?

It is generally recommended that questions with a similar context be placed together. Another rule of thumb is to sequence the questions from the general to the specific. Particular topics may dictate other sequences, however. The first question is generally considered to be the most crucial one, and it has a relatively large influence on the response rate. Therefore, it should be clearly related to the topic, interesting, neutral, and easy to answer. The first question should be well constructed, and it is usually desirable for it to be one that all subjects can answer.

Sources of Error

Before continuing with the outline of the procedures for developing a questionnaire, it may be worthwhile to consider some of the types of questionnaire error not already discussed. Some of the more common types of error or bias, not all of which are limited to questionnaires, are the following:

1. Researcher bias—In essence, this bias results from the researcher's unconsciously developing the questionnaire in a manner that will increase the likelihood of obtaining the desired results.

2. Sponsorship bias—This bias results from the researcher's, hopefully unconscious, attempt to produce research results that will please the outside agency funding the research. A researcher may well be suspected of such bias if his or her research is sponsored by an agency with vested interests in certain outcomes.

3. Imperfections of design—Weaknesses in the design of the questionnaire can result in biased or inaccurate responses. Such imperfections

include haphazard sequencing, inadequate instructions, and a failure to explain the purpose and scope of the study.

4. Respondent interpretations—As implied earlier, varying interpretations of the "facts" and key terms by the respondents also can result in inaccurate answers.

5. Time lapse—It has been found that answers to the same question tend to vary over time even when not directly affected by the passage of time. It must be realized that perceptions, attitudes, and so on are not static in most cases.

6. Circumstances—A variety of factors, such as carelessness and mood of the respondent, ambiguous questions, "unthinking" answers, and general resistance to questionnaires, can produce inaccurate responses.

7. Response bias—Error can result from the response rate being low and thus the final sample ends up less representative than originally conceived. Some of the steps that can be taken to minimize response bias include using questionnaires only when one is reasonably certain that the subjects are interested in the topic, making responses confidential or anonymous, sending reminders to complete questionnaires, providing gift or cash incentives to encourage responses (some incentives can be included with an email or Web-based questionnaire by initiating a trigger for the gift when the questionnaire is completed and submitted), and being realistic about eligibility criteria for subjects.

8. Reactive insight—There is a growing concern that, as subjects participate in surveys over time, especially in surveys dealing with sensitive topics, they may begin to rethink their lives, attitudes, and so on. This activity could then result in the participants' being biased in certain areas and less representative of their larger populations.

Preparing the First Draft

Much of the preceding section relates, of course, to the preparation of the first draft of the questionnaire. As was suggested above, the researcher must decide on the sequence of questions that best serves his or her purpose. In some cases, this may result in the questions being sequenced in the most logical arrangement. This may mean ordering the items from the general to the particular, or the best arrangement may be by the subject. For example, a questionnaire about the administration of a library could be categorized by staff, services, collections, budget, and so on. Questions within these sections could then be ordered from the most general to the most particular. When the topic changes noticeably, it is a good idea to provide a lead-in statement as a transition.

On the other hand, the researcher may wish to achieve the optimal psychological sequence, which may not be the same as the most logical arrangement. This can be an important consideration when a questionnaire contains sensitive questions, or questions that ask for rather confidential information, or questions that take a lot of time to answer. Such questions can prompt a person to quit answering a questionnaire and return it partially finished or, worse yet, discard it. But if these questions occur near the end of the questionnaire, the respondent is more likely to go ahead and complete the questionnaire because of the time and effort already invested in it.

In light of the types of errors discussed above, the best psychological sequence may also mean that questions that are likely to bias questions that follow should be located at or near the end of the questionnaire. This will at least reduce the error or bias that they introduce into the study.

In preparing the first draft of the questionnaire, the researcher may decide that some questions are of such a nature that respondents are unlikely to answer them accurately or honestly. In this case, he or she may be well advised to incorporate some "cross-check" questions to determine the reliability of certain questions. Crosscheck questions are those that ask for the same information as one or more others, but each is worded differently. If the respondents answer essentially the same question differently, then one must question their reliability. Keep in mind, however, as was discussed earlier, the wording of a question can affect its responses. In addition, respondents may be irritated, or even insulted, if they detect the use of cross-check questions. Such a reaction can affect their responses to the questionnaire as a whole and bias the results.

Evaluating the Questionnaire

Once the first draft of the questionnaire has been completed, and before it is actually pretested, it is a good idea to get one (or more) expert's opinion of the questionnaire. A person who is expert in research methodology can help to catch methodological weaknesses in the instrument, such as faulty scales, inadequate instructions, and so on. A person who is familiar with the topic of the questionnaire can help in assessing the face validity of the questions. Do they make sense, are they easy to understand, do they ask what they are supposed to be asking?

The Pretest

After obtaining an informal evaluation of the questionnaire, it should be pretested fully. This pretest is sometimes referred to as a "pilot study," although pilot study is actually more synonymous with "exploratory study." A pretest gives the researcher an opportunity to identify questionnaire items that tend to be misunderstood by the participants, do not obtain the information that is needed, and so on. But, in addition to testing the actual questionnaire items, the pretest should include interviews with some or all of the pretest participants or at least incorporate one or more open-ended questions. Interviews and/or open-ended questions are necessary in order for the respondents to have ample opportunity to point out problem questions, poor instructions, and unnecessary or missing questions, and to give their general reactions to the instrument. Pretest participants are sometimes encouraged to call the researcher if they wish to make additional comments about the questionnaire.

The pretest also offers certain advantages beyond helping to refine the data collection instrument. It can permit a preliminary testing of the hypothesis, point out a variety of problems not anticipated relating to design and methodology, facilitate a practice run of the statistical procedures to be used, and perhaps even indicate that the final study may not produce any meaningful results and therefore should be rethought or abandoned.

Ideally, the pretest sample should be as scientifically selected as the sample for the final study. That is, it should be randomly selected and of an adequate size to permit generalizations to the population. In actual practice, pretest samples are seldom so rigorously selected. Sometimes known as "samples of several," they often are in effect nonprobability, convenience samples, selected because of their members' proximity and willingness to participate. But the pretest sample should be reasonably representative of the final study group, or there is little value in conducting the pretest.

Researchers also should be careful that they do not view the pretest as a mere formality. This means that, if the pretest does turn up any problems, the questionnaire should be revised accordingly. If substantial problems are found, resulting in significant revisions, another pretest should be conducted. This process should continue until the researcher is prepared to move to the final study with a questionnaire that does not represent an instrument that is significantly different from the last one pretested.

As the researcher evaluates the results of the pretest, there are some good questions to ask: Did each of the items measure what it was intended to measure? Were all of the words understood? Did all respondents similarly interpret all questions? Did each fixed-response question have an answer that applied to each respondent? Were some questions regularly skipped or answered unintelligibly?

Final Editing

Having been pretested, the questionnaire is ready for final editing before distribution. It is recommended that the title of the study or survey be placed at the top of the questionnaire. The organization will benefit from the employment of an outline format in lettering and numbering sections and questions. The questions on each page should be arranged so that there is adequate white space among them and in the margins. Adequate lines or spaces should be left for responding to open-ended questions. Nothing frustrates the respondent more than being asked to provide answers for which there is inadequate room. One less than ideal solution to this is asking the respondent to use the back side of the page when necessary.

The general rule is that the questionnaire should be as short as possible in order to encourage complete responses. (Other factors, such as the respondent's motivation, which is affected by his or her interest in the topic and probability of benefiting from the study, may make a longer questionnaire feasible.)

Keeping in mind that a reasonable amount of white space is desirable, there are a variety of steps one can take to keep the questionnaire length to a minimum. One, while instructions must be clear, they also should be kept as brief as possible. Two, if the questionnaire is to be mailed, the original questionnaire can be typed in a small font. Three, relatively long questionnaires can be printed on both sides of the sheets, in order to at least minimize the thickness of the instrument. Finally, and for other reasons as well, the questionnaire should ask only for information not already held by the researcher. Unnecessary and redundant questions should be avoided. It is a waste of the respondent's time to supply information already held by the researcher or readily available from other sources, and if the respondent becomes aware of being asked to do so, there is a greater chance that the questionnaire will not be completed and returned.

In order to facilitate accurate, easy responses, the researcher should strive for simplicity in word use and question construction. As much as possible, the questionnaire's response format should be consistent. For example, the respondent should be asked to "circle the number" or "check the appropriate box" throughout as much of the questionnaire as is appropriate. Changing formats can create some confusion as well as increase the response time. (It typically requires more than one format to obtain all needed information, such as age and job, however, and some researchers argue that switching formats helps to keep the respondent alert and to avoid response patterns.) It will generally increase the respondent's accuracy if factual questions are tied to a definite time period. For example, rather than asking a person how often he or she uses a library during a typical year, it may be better to ask how often he or she used the library between January and December of the preceding year.

Other measures that will help both the researcher and the respondent include holding open-ended questions to a minimum in *self-administered* questionnaires. While they may be necessary in certain types of studies, they are more susceptible to inconsistencies in interpretation and unreliable responses. As was indicated earlier, the analysis will be expedited by utilizing as much precoding as possible, and this is not practical with open-ended questions. Some questionnaires are designed to be optically scanned after they are completed.

It may be useful to screen out respondents who should not answer certain questions. This will save response time for the participant and analysis time for the researcher. One technique for doing so involves the use of filter questions or skip patterns. A filter question may, for example, ask the respondent if he or she has used the library's reference service during the preceding 12 months. If the answer is no, then the respondent may be asked to skip the next few questions pertaining to reference services and go on to those asking about the collection. (Skip patterns can easily be automated in an electronic questionnaire by deleting questions if a specific answer is checked or by not allowing an answer to be inserted if the question does not correspond to the previous answer.) A graphic format may be utilized by drawing a line to the next pertinent question so as to avoid any confusion. An illustration of this method follows:

1. Are you a member of the American Library Association?

(1) Yes↓   (2) No→Go to Question 2.

If yes: 1.a. Please indicate the year you first joined. _____ Year

1.b. Has your membership been continuous? ___ Yes ___ No

And finally, the questionnaire should have a thank-you note at the end and repeat the instructions for how and by when the questionnaire should be returned. An accompanying letter might have contained this information but could have been misplaced.

Cover Letter

In most cases, a cover letter should accompany the questionnaire. The basic purpose of the cover letter is to explain briefly the purpose of the study and to stress the importance of each person's responding. In some situations, such as with instruments designed to measure certain values indirectly, it may be necessary to be somewhat vague, if not actually misleading, about the scope of the study. This does present ethical concerns, however, and in general it is best to be open regarding the purpose of the study. It is not easy to conceal the true nature of a study, and if respondents become aware that they have been misled, they are not likely to view the questionnaire favorably. Persons receiving the letter and questionnaire generally appreciate being told how they were selected to participate in the study. Miller and Salkind also suggest including in the cover letter a statement that informs the respondents that by returning the questionnaire they are consenting to participate in the study.[16]

If one can be used legitimately, it is a good idea to employ a letterhead, whether it is a mail or electronic survey, to lend some authority to the study. In addition to, or in lieu of, a letterhead, a second cover letter signed by an influential person within the field of study can help increase the response rate. Cover letters should be written in a friendly, but professional, style.

Persons are more likely to complete the questionnaire if the cover letter stresses the potential usefulness of the study for the respondent. Along those lines, it may help to offer each respondent the results, or at least a summary of the results, of the study. In order to avoid having to distribute any more results than necessary, it is a good idea to ask respondents to indicate whether they wish to receive some report of the study results. Instead of promising to send results of the study to respondents, the researcher may simply emphasize that results will be disseminated via the professional literature or via a Web site and include the URL for the site, or state that the URL will be distributed when the results are available.

Another useful technique for increasing the response rate, as well as helping to ensure frank answers, is to guarantee confidentiality and/or anonymity for all respondents. The researcher should keep in mind, however, that confidentiality and anonymity do not mean the same thing. Confidentiality merely assures the respondent that his or her replies and name will not be associated publicly. Anonymity requires the use of techniques that make it impossible for anyone, including the researcher, to link a respondent with his or her answers. The latter is more difficult to achieve, especially in an electronic environment, and it should not be promised to the respondents unless it is actually going to be provided.

DISTRIBUTION OF THE QUESTIONNAIRE

There are three main methods of administering the survey questionnaire. The questionnaire can be self-administered, which means that the respondents are asked to complete the questionnaire themselves; administered face-to-face to respondents by researchers; or administered to respondents via the telephone by interviewers. The self-administered questionnaire can be mailed or electronically transmitted via email or the Web.

Mail Questionnaire

Unless the questionnaire is designed as a self-mailer, or is to be faxed or emailed back to the researcher, it should be accompanied by a self-addressed, stamped, return envelope. Again, almost anything that will help to encourage responses is worth doing. In deciding when to mail the questionnaire, the researcher should take into account common vacation periods and other such factors that may affect how quickly persons are likely to respond. If one were mailing questionnaires to university faculty members and asking that they be completed and returned within 10 days, it obviously would not be wise to mail them just before semester break. Apparently most librarians prefer to receive work-related questionnaires at the office rather than at home.[17] A timetable can be quite useful for keeping track of when certain activities relating to the distribution of the questionnaire should take place.

Most researchers utilizing a mail (or email or Web-based) questionnaire should expect to have to conduct one or more follow-up mailings in order to reach an adequate response rate. In so doing, the researcher must first decide how long to wait before distributing a follow-up mailing. This decision will depend upon how long the participants were given to respond to the first mailing. The response period should be long enough to avoid rushing the participants but short enough that they do not forget about the questionnaire. One to two weeks is usually considered to be a reasonable period of time.

A second decision relating to the follow-up is whether another copy of the questionnaire should be included with the reminder letter. Once again, any device that will help to increase the number of responses should be considered. Obviously, the more duplicate questionnaires mailed, the greater the costs for the researcher. (The cost of postage is not an issue with the email or Web-based questionnaire; however, there are still costs associated with the researcher's time.) Persons receiving a follow-up with no questionnaire are not likely to take the time to write for another copy if they have lost the first one. Some experts recommend designing the follow-up to be as eye-catching as possible, through the use of clever letters, humorous pictures, and so on. Items such as free pencils, books, and so on are sometimes offered with the follow-up to encourage responses.

Another important decision regarding follow-up mailings concerns whether to send them to all participants in the study or only to those who have not yet responded. In order to avoid sending follow-up questionnaires to all participants, one must maintain some sort of record of returns. The most common method of keeping track of who has returned his or her questionnaire, unless respondents are asked to write their names, is to code each questionnaire. This is usually done by placing somewhere on each questionnaire a number that represents each participant in the survey. When a questionnaire is returned, the code number is noted, and the corresponding name is checked as having returned the questionnaire.

This method, however, has a serious drawback when utilized in a study guaranteeing *anonymity*. People are becoming more aware of this technique and realize that a number or code on their questionnaire probably means the researcher will be able to associate their answers with their names. Consequently, they may well doubt the researcher's promise to maintain anonymity, if given. As a result, they may refuse to answer the questionnaire, or at least the validity of their responses may be weakened.

One method for dealing with the need to maintain a record of who has returned his or her questionnaire, in order to avoid sending follow-up questionnaires to all participants, while still assuring anonymity, involves the use of postcards. A postcard can be sent with each questionnaire with a code number for, or the name of, each participant. No identifier is put on the questionnaire itself. The participant is asked to mail the postcard separately but at about the same time that the questionnaire is returned. The researcher will thus receive something indicating who has returned his or her questionnaire but will not be able to associate a particular response with an individual, or at least not on the basis of code numbers.

Another technique involves removing the respondent's name from a master list upon receipt of his or her questionnaire. Having done so, if any identifier is removed from the questionnaire, there is no longer any way to associate responses with names of respondents. When a follow-up questionnaire is mailed, it is sent only to those names remaining on the master list. (If either of these two techniques is to be used for follow-up mailings, it probably is a good idea to explain it briefly in the cover letter.) Readers particularly interested in follow-up mailings may wish to refer to a work by Erdos.[18]

No matter how many steps one takes to maximize the response to a questionnaire, there is still a good chance that the response rate will be lower than what was desired, especially with a mail questionnaire. One rule of thumb has been that a response rate of at least 75 percent is needed if one is to be able to assume that what was learned about the respondents is reasonably equivalent to what would have been learned about all the individuals included in the survey had everyone responded. Seventy-five percent is a rather high threshold, however, and many surveys have gathered reliable data with lower response rates. The critical issue is how much the nonrespondents differ from those who did respond. An acceptable response rate can be lower for a homogeneous population than for a heterogeneous one. If one is concerned about the response rate, then it is advisable to learn as much as possible about the nonrespondents, at least on the key variables, to determine how much they differ from the respondents. Information can be obtained about nonrespondents by, for example, examining other sources of data such as census reports, checking the findings of studies of the same population, and conducting telephone interviews with nonrespondents.

Electronic Questionnaire

In the relatively recent past, surveys have been designed for participants to enter their responses directly into a computer; however, in the late 1980s and early 1990s email questionnaires were more often used because of the ease of transmission, the immediacy of the delivery, and the low cost of distribution. These early survey instruments were text-based and allowed for no interactivity. They were basically paper questionnaires delivered electronically, or as Pickard states, they are basically "paper-based" questionnaires that utilize a different distribution mechanism.[19] The Web became more available and more popular in the mid-1990s and made multimedia and interactive surveys possible. One can now use dynamic forms that store the responses, download the data, and compile the results. Web-based surveys also make it possible to "micro-target respondents" and to "create multiple surveys simultaneously."[20] According to Baker, a Web survey is typically a survey in which the questionnaire is formatted with HTML and stored on a Web server; respondents are invited to a URL and required to log in or authenticate in some way; questions are presented via the respondent's Web browser; and responses are examined by the survey software and stored on the Web server.[21] Bertot states that there are three components to successful Web surveys—"a database, programming code, and interface."[22] (The software for a Web survey should be able to handle a variety of question types, a variety of answer display options, branches and filters, fills, computations, range and edit checks, and error resolution.)

A literature review conducted by Schonlau, Fricker, and Elliot indicates "that surveys using a mail response mode and surveys using both a mail and Web response mode tend to have higher response rates than those using just an email or Web response mode."[23] In the studies reported, "response rates range from 7 to 44 percent for Web surveys and from 6 to 68 percent for email surveys."[24] Roselle and Neufeld, in a survey reported in 1998, found "that email as a follow-up method is as effective as postal mail in terms of both the speed and size of the survey response."[25] Web surveys can be especially useful for surveying populations for which there is no list and for exploratory research, and they tend to enjoy quicker response times than do paper surveys and take less time to administer.

Although there is a belief that email questionnaires are less expensive than mail questionnaires, this may pertain only to postage and printing costs. Schonlau, Fricker, and Elliot ascertained that Web surveys are more economical than mail surveys when several hundred to a thousand surveys are distributed.[26] They do caution that technical problems and programming costs associated with Web surveys can rapidly increase costs. There also continue to be concerns about the internal and external validity of findings based on data collected in Web surveys.

Email and Web-based surveys can be designed to automate skip patterns and automatically validate answers. Electronic surveys can be designed to skip questions, based on the respondents' answers to previous questions, and to validate the respondents' answers to identify missed questions or unusable answers. These automated functions help to reduce measurement errors.

There are numerous commercial and open source electronic survey tools available. These tools enable researchers to create and administer surveys using a Web interface. The survey responses are stored in databases that can be accessed online or downloaded into software programs. Two popular software programs for Web surveys are SurveyMonkey.com and Zoomerang. Such services allow the researcher to design the Web questionnaire, collect responses, and analyze the results. With Zoomerang, one can design a questionnaire using one of over 100 templates or create his or her own. A third program, The Survey System, offers both Web survey software and full-service hosting. In other words, if the researcher does not have a Windows-based Web server, The Survey System will provide Web site hosting for the survey.

The sources of error for email and Web-based questionnaires include those discussed above for the mail survey. The lack of coverage for Internet surveys is the most readily identifiable source of error. One problem with email surveys is acquiring email address lists, but the Web has made it possible to acquire convenience samples without having to know respondents' email addresses. [27] As more of the population has access to the Web, this error will become less of an issue in the sampling design for Web-based surveys. As noted by Schonlau, Fricker, and Elliot, when developing email and Web-based surveys, the researchers should develop a method for stripping the email addresses of the respondents from their survey to maintain confidentiality and anonymity of the respondents' names. Schonlau, Fricker, and Elliot also recommend that the respondents be assured that all survey data are encrypted and saved to a private server in order to retain the respondents' privacy. [28] Miller and Salkind state that it is possible that someone other than the intended recipient may see the subjects' responses; therefore, the subjects should be informed that while every effort will be made to retain the subject's privacy and confidentiality, it cannot be guaranteed. [29] Also, Web-based surveys are subject to spamming. To avoid this problem a unique, confidential identifier can be assigned to each person being asked to participate in the study or each individual can be given a unique URL for accessing the questionnaire. But the most serious weaknesses of electronic surveys are that email addresses often cannot be randomly dialed and that such surveys under-represent people who do not have computers—i.e., people who tend to have lower income and less education.

Nicholls, Baker, and Martin report that computer-assisted survey research techniques may be more efficient than conventional techniques, without reducing the quality of the data. This is dependent upon the design of survey instruments that adhere to criteria such as the following:

1. Easy to read online
2. Do not often require respondents to leave their computers to find information
3. Do not take up excessive space in electronic mailboxes
4. Are preceded by a separate introductory message
5. Provide adequate instructions, and on the screen where needed
6. Anticipate how different systems will format the questionnaire
7. Minimize cursor movement
8. Do not assume more than basic computer skills. [30]

Electronic questionnaires should be designed using most of the criteria that are discussed in the preceding text. Schonlau, Fricker, and Elliot provide a list of guidelines specifically for developing an electronic questionnaire. [31] They suggest listing only a few questions per screen, using graphics sparingly, and providing an indication of the respondents' progress in answering the survey. [32]

In his workshop cited above, Baker first identified a number of special challenges facing researchers planning to conduct Web surveys. [33] Those challenges included:

1. Different browsers can display screen information differently.
2. Screen resolution can cause problematic scrolling.

3. Screen width (horizontal scrolling can be problematic for participants).

4. Connection speed ("heavy" screens may download especially slowly).

5. Special functions and gadgets such as Flash may not work.

6. Corporate firewalls.

7. Need to provide respondent support (FAQs, email, etc.).

Baker also provided numerous tips and suggestions regarding screen design, question presentation, and implementation. They included:

1. A Web questionnaire, more so than a Web site, must be able to solicit information from participants with varying levels of motivation.

2. Progress indicators tend to work better with short questionnaires.

3. Scrolling (vs. paging) is easy to program, shortens download times, and allows the respondent to view the entire questionnaire; but it eliminates control over the order of completion, tends to result in more unanswered questions, and makes skips and logic more difficult.

4. Factors such as the location of information on the screen; background color; navigation techniques; and font type, size, and color can affect responses.

5. Careful thought should be given to error messages, instructions, definitions, and question format.

6. Question numbering is generally not useful for online questionnaires.

7. The size of the input area is a visual clue to the length of the expected answer.

8. Visual images can help to clarify questions but also can have unintended effects.

9. Things to avoid include document attachments, use of multiple URLs, HTML or graphics, special text formatting, and anything that looks like spam.

10. Appropriate authentication techniques should be used to ensure that only legitimate respondents participate and that each participates only once.[34]

Schonlau, Fricker, and Elliott also provide guidelines for email and Web-based survey design and implementation for those who are interested in more detailed information on this subject.[35] Covey outlines the different methods of developing and administering survey questionnaires in library research.[36] Hsu describes "a software program designed exclusively for the creation of survey questionnaires. Its main goal is to enable a user to create, edit, modify and run online surveys using the markup language system."[37] An article by Gunn addresses, among other matters, the advantages and disadvantages of Web-based surveys, the design of Web-based surveys, the language of Web questionnaires, and Web-based survey respondents.[38] The *Handbook of Research on Electronic Surveys and Measurements* was published in 2006.[39] The WebSM Web site is dedicated to the methodological issues of Web surveys.[40]

THE INTERVIEW

Developing the Interview

The basic steps in developing a *standardized* or *structured* interview are not that different from those for developing most other kinds of survey studies. One of the first steps must be development of the list of questions to be asked, or the *interview schedule*. The techniques for constructing questionnaires and structured interview schedules are quite similar and consequently will not be repeated here. As is true for questionnaires, it is highly recommended that interview schedules be pretested. Again, the pretest should provide the respondents with ample opportunity to comment on the questions.

An additional step in the development of the interview involves the training of interviewers. Even if one is working with experienced interviewers, they need to become familiar with the researcher's particular questions. The same interviewers should be involved in the pretest as in the final interview.

Conducting the Personal Interview

In conducting an interview, the interviewer should attempt to create a friendly, nonthreatening atmosphere. Much as one does with a cover letter, the interviewer should give a brief, casual introduction to the study; stress the importance of the person's participation; and assure anonymity, or at least confidentiality, when possible. The interviewer should answer all legitimate questions about the nature of the study and produce appropriate credentials upon request. He or she should be prepared to respond to such questions as: How did you happen to pick me? Who gave you my name? Why don't you go next door?

When possible and appropriate, the researcher should set up the interview well in advance, and of course the interviewer should appear for the interview punctually. Some researchers recommend sending the list of questions to the participant before the scheduled interview. This may be inadvisable, however, if the interviewer is particularly concerned about obtaining frank, spontaneous responses. Giving respondents a lot of time to consider answers is likely to reduce their candidness.

If the interview has been scheduled ahead of time, it is a good idea to confirm the date in writing and to send a reminder several days before the interview. Audiovisual aids may be used to facilitate the questioning or improve the recording of responses. If the interviewee's responses are to be taped, his or her permission to do so should be obtained in advance.

Following the interview, the researcher may wish to submit a typescript of the questions and responses to the interviewee for confirmation of the accuracy of the answers. It should be made clear, however, that the respondent is not to use this opportunity to revise the meaning or the substance of his or her answers. At this point, if not before the interview, it may be desirable to obtain the interviewee's permission to use the information in the resulting research report.

When asking the questions, the interviewer should avoid rephrasing questions for the interviewee. One of the advantages of interviews is the inherent personal contact, but one must be careful that this does not become a liability.

Expansions or revisions of questions, or unnecessary explanations, in effect result in different questions being asked of different participants. Consequently, comparisons of responses become invalid. For similar reasons, the interviewer should not alter the sequence of the questions from respondent to respondent, nor should he or she omit questions. As was discussed earlier, the context of the question can affect or bias its response. And, as was true for questionnaires, the interviewer should avoid asking more than one question at a time. In contrast to mail, email, or Web-based questionnaires, the reactions of the researcher can affect the respondent's answers. The interviewer must be careful not to show surprise or other emotions as a result of any of the interviewee's responses. Such reactions can bias future responses of the participant.

In obtaining or encouraging responses, the interviewer may find it necessary to repeat certain questions. This should not present a problem so long as the interviewer does not significantly change the wording of such questions. In order to obtain an adequate response from the interviewee, it may on occasion be necessary for the interviewer to ask the respondent to elaborate on his or her reply. If done carefully, this should be legitimate, but one should always avoid putting words into the respondent's mouth. The interviewee's responses should represent his or her thoughts alone, not a combination of his or hers and the interviewer's. To obtain as many responses as possible, the interviewer must also learn how to deal with "don't knows." Often, people need a certain amount of encouragement before they will respond fully to a particular question. There is a fine line, however, between encouraging a response and helping to word it or forcing an answer where there should not be one. Consequently, one should be conservative or cautious in encouraging a response when the interviewee seems reluctant to provide one. Probing for complete answers can take the form of repeating the question (with the caveats given above), making an expectant pause, repeating the respondent's answer, making reassuring remarks, asking for further clarification, and asking neutral questions such as: Anything else? Any other reason? Could you tell me more about that?

As is the case with questionnaires, it is desirable to precode the answer sheets when possible. This is feasible only with fixed or structured responses, of course. Free-answer responses should be recorded verbatim, if at all possible, to facilitate subsequent analysis and to prevent the loss of data. Tape recorders provide one relatively easy method of recording answers word for word. It is a good idea to record responses during the interview and to use the respondent's own words (rather than summaries or paraphrases). If any probes for more complete answers are used, they should be noted.

Disadvantages of the Interview

As with other research methods and techniques, bias presents a real threat to the validity of interviews. Particularly critical is the bias that may be introduced by the interviewer. As was indicated earlier, some interviewer bias can be avoided by ensuring that the interviewer does not overreact to responses of the interviewee. Other steps that can be taken to help avoid or reduce interviewer bias include having the interviewer dress inconspicuously and appropriately for the environment, holding the interview in a private setting, and keeping the interview as informal as possible.

The Internet interview diminishes the chances of introducing some of these biases. The Internet interview utilizes computer-mediated communication (CMC) which allows humans to interact directly with each other in synchronous or real time using monitors, text, and keyboards. Researchers have used Internet interviewing to investigate Internet use and culture, the demographics and characteristics of Internet users, experiences with distance learning, and general human behavior.[41] One of the main biases of Internet interviewing is the unrepresentativeness of the sample since not everyone has access to or uses the Internet.

Rapport and interpersonal relationships are more difficult to develop in an online interview than in person. It is possible to establish a relationship online, but it requires a specific skill and can be more challenging than in a face-to-face or telephone interview. The interview can be quite expensive in terms of travel and long distance telephone costs. An Internet interview is a more cost-efficient and practical method for conducting in-depth interviews if there is an economical telecommunications system and if the interviewers and researchers are comfortable with and knowledgeable of the technology used for the Internet interviews.

As with the electronic questionnaire discussed above, the Internet interview raises legal and ethical issues. Mann and Stewart state, "There is little agreement about how to proceed ethically in a virtual arena, and few research practice conventions are available."[42] It is difficult to authenticate the responses in an Internet interview, which necessitates taking steps to ensure that the appropriate person is participating in the interview.

Advantages of the Interview

In contrast to the mail or electronic questionnaire, the interview does have certain important advantages. Perhaps most important, it almost always produces a better response rate. Thus the sample of persons actually participating in the study tends to represent a large percentage of the original sample and is, therefore, more representative of the population than would be a sample representing a relatively low response rate. Apparently the personal contact of the interview helps to encourage, or put more pressure on, persons to respond fully. Consequently, it is also possible to employ interview schedules of greater length than comparable questionnaires, without jeopardizing a satisfactory response rate.

As was suggested earlier, the personal contact also provides a greater capacity than the mail or electronic questionnaire for the correction of misunderstandings by participants. Again, one must be careful that this capability is not abused and becomes a disadvantage as a result.

It is generally believed that the interview is better at revealing information that is complex or emotionally laden. The use of visual aids can sometimes facilitate presenting and recording complicated information. The data gathered from Internet interviews can be easily uploaded to data analysis software packages.

FOCUS GROUP INTERVIEWS

In contrast to what has been covered thus far, there are less-structured interview techniques available to the researcher. The unstructured interview is more flexible than the structured one and most appropriate in the early stages of an investigation and in qualitative studies. It is generally better for studying perceptions, attitudes, and motivation, but it tends to be more difficult to administer and analyze. Examples of less-structured interviews include the focus(ed) group, the clinical interview or personal history, and the nondirective interview.

The *focus group* is a group interview designed "to explore in depth the feelings and beliefs people hold and to learn how these feelings shape overt behavior."[43] "They are called focus groups because the discussions start out broadly and gradually narrow down to the focus of the research."[44] The focus group interview technique can be used as a self-contained research method or in combination with other quantitative and qualitative research methods. Focus groups are useful for orienting oneself to a new field; developing ideas and concepts or even generating hypotheses based on informants' insights; evaluating different research sites or study populations; developing and refining research instruments, such as interview schedules and questionnaires; and getting participants' interpretations of results from earlier studies. As a self-contained method, focus groups can be used to explore new research areas or to examine known research questions from the participants' perspective, facilitate complex decision making, and identify and address important issues. The focus group interview may be used to replace the questionnaire or individual interviews, if the research questions warrant use of the method.

Library and information agencies can utilize the focus group interview method to develop needs assessment, community analysis, and promotional strategies for new services. Focus group interviews can be utilized in library and information science research to answer research questions concerned with the evaluation of library resources and services, including online public access catalogs and online resources. The method can be used in all types of libraries and indeed has been used in public, academic, special, and state libraries.

The method can also be used to identify the information gathering patterns of scholars and other specific user groups. The participants could be asked to discuss the sources they use to find information, what types of information they find most useful, how they evaluate the information they retrieve, and what resources or tools would facilitate information retrieval for their specific purposes. The literature does not reflect this use of the method.

Focus group interviews have been used in academic, newspaper, hospital, public, and state libraries to gather information on users' perceptions of services and collections.[45] A public library system utilized the method to gather information on the lifestyles of senior citizens in order to identify barriers and methods to increase library use by the elderly.[46] The New York State Education Department used the focus group interview method in conjunction with other methods to evaluate advisory and information referral services.[47] Mellon incorporated focus group interviews in the evaluation of bibliographic instruction by undergraduate students.[48] An LIS program conducted focus groups to identify the need for professional library and information science education within a state and the role of the program in providing such education.[49]

The method can and has been used to gather information about the work and beliefs of practicing librarians. Reference and technical service librarians participated in focus group interviews to identify their perceptions of a need for online authority control systems.[50] In Wisconsin, academic and public library technical services managers and catalogers participated in focus group interviews to assist the researchers in developing hypotheses for an extensive study of the decisions made and the tasks performed by technical services managers and catalogers.[51] The technical services managers and catalogers were asked to describe their typical day on the job, the decisions made during a workday, and how the job had changed over the past two years. The focus group interview method was used as an exploratory approach in this instance to develop a list of tasks performed by technical services managers and catalogers and to assign these tasks to decision levels.

The focus group interview technique has also been used in libraries to evaluate online searching by end users, as well as in the research and development of online public access catalogs.[52] Faculty and undergraduate and graduate students were asked to describe the online library catalogs they had used and their reasons for using the catalogs, to identify the difficulties encountered in the use of the university online catalog, and to discuss the characteristics of an online catalog that they would find useful. The data were used by the library administration to identify necessary improvements to the existing online catalog.[53] Connaway includes readings and a bibliography of the uses of focus group interviews in library and information agencies.[54] Covey outlines how focus group interviews are used in library research.[55]

In designing a focus group interview, the researcher, keeping in mind the objectives of the study, must first decide who will be interviewed. Focus groups typically consist of from 5 to 12 people. Volunteers are often recruited for focus groups (though they may be reimbursed), but it is desirable to select participants who are as representative as possible of their population. Selection of the moderator is equally important. Preferably, the moderator will be an outside person, trained in focus group techniques, with good communication skills.

Focus groups are usually scheduled for one session of one or two hours, but it may be necessary to hold more than one session in some cases. It also may be desirable to break or stratify groups into smaller, more homogeneous groups. For example, college students could be divided into subgroups of undergraduate, graduate, and professional students. The interview should be held in a convenient, comfortable, informal location that is conducive to discussion. It may be necessary to use a room that accommodates audio taping and/or observation behind a one-way mirror. Refreshments may be a good idea.

The focus group session should open with appropriate introductions and "icebreakers" and then shift to the interview itself. The moderator, of course, has the primary responsibility for conducting the interview. He or she should utilize an interview schedule or discussion guide. This guide should not be a list of structured questions, all of which must be posed. Rather, it "should be designed as a projective technique, designed to deliberately stimulate a relaxed free-flow of associations and bypass people's built-in censoring mechanisms."[56]

The moderator asks questions intended to initiate discussion of pertinent issues, but beyond that should "keep guidance and direction to a minimum."[57] He or she should listen to, not edit or judge, participants' comments. The moderator should employ standard techniques for conducting unstructured interviews, such as probing for more complete responses, encouraging everyone to participate, establishing a nonthreatening environment, and not asking leading questions. It is a good idea to assign another person the primary responsibility for recording the content of the interview and to utilize someone else as an assistant and neutral observer.

Notes of the focus group sessions are often taken with the aid of audio recorders, but at some point tape recordings must be transcribed and reduced to a more manageable size. Recorders often use forms to facilitate initial note taking or the summarizing of mechanically recorded data. When taking notes, the recorder should attempt to

1. Trace the threads of an idea throughout the discussion.
2. Identify the subgroup or individual to whom an idea is important.
3. Distinguish between ideas held in common from those held by individuals.
4. Capture the vocabulary and style of the group.
5. Distinguish, if possible, among perceptions, feelings, and insights.[58]

Analysis and Reporting of the Focus Group Data

The information acquired from focus group interviews is generally used to help researchers understand perceptions and attitudes of the target population. The results of focus group interviews cannot be used to generalize to an entire population, as the groups may not be representative of their total populations. Instead, the results give one the opportunity to consider a range of responses to questions.

The focus group interview permits assessment of nonverbal responses and reveals group interaction patterns. The researcher analyzes the data acquired from the moderator's reports and taped interview sessions. The analysis begins with getting an overview or global picture of the entire process and involves consideration of words, tone, context, nonverbal communications, responses, and ideas of the interviewees.

There are then two basic approaches to analyzing focus group data—ethnographic summary and content analysis. The content analysis approach produces numerical descriptions of the data. Content analysis is the tallying of mentions of very specific factors. Mentions can be brief or very extensive and can be weighted.

Ethnography involves establishing rapport, selecting research participants, transcribing observations and conversations, and keeping diaries, although Geertz believes that none of these techniques or procedures adequately defines the venture. He believes ethnography is defined by the kind of intellectual effort it is, "an elaborate venture in 'thick description.'"[59] Reality, as perceived by the observer, is described in such detail that the reader can experience the total event as if he or she had actually been involved in it. The data must be interpreted in a manner that retains this richness. This thick description, including group interactions, is one of the advantages of the focus group interview method. The ethnographic summary and the content analysis approach are not conflicting means of analysis. The combination of the two approaches brings an additional strength to the analysis.[60]

One of the recurring questions that arise with the discussion of the focus group interview technique is that of its validity and reliability as a research method. "Focus groups are valid if they are used carefully for a problem that is suitable for focus group inquiry."[61] If the researcher deviates from the established procedures outlined above and if the research questions do not lend themselves to focus group interview methods, the focus group interviews are invalid. The focus group interview method is similar to other social science methods where validity depends not only on the procedures used but also on the context within which the procedures are used.[62]

The validity of the analysis of the data collected during the focus group interviews is another concern. If content analysis is used as a method of data analysis, "the validity between the classification schemes, or variables derived from it, and the validity of the interpretation relating content variables to their causes or consequences" is crucial.[63] This means that in the dissemination and interpretation of the results, the researcher must ascertain that the findings are not generalizable beyond, nor dependent upon, specific methods, data, or measurements outside the specified study.[64]

Reproducibility, or intercoder reliability, can be determined when the same data are coded with the same results by more than one coder. Intercoder reliability is important in content analysis because it measures the consistency of understandings or meaning held by two or more coders.[65] Intercoder reliability should be determined when analyzing focus group interview data. If one person examines one set of transcripts, while another concentrates on a different set of transcripts, two perceptions and perspectives of discovery can also be included in the reporting of the results.[66]

Other Advantages and Disadvantages
of the Focus Group Interview

The main advantage of focus group interviews is the opportunity to observe a large amount of interactions on a topic in a limited period of time.[67] In contrast to most other techniques, focus group interviews are able to benefit from the interactions of more than one respondent. "In focus groups, people tend to be less inhibited than in individual interviews."[68]

The methodology can also be used with hard-to-reach groups, such as library nonusers, minorities, and children. It is a data gathering technique that can be useful to both practitioners and researchers when they want to find out not only what a specific group thinks, but why the group thinks what it does. The format gives the moderator a chance to probe and to develop questions and discussions not anticipated by the researcher. The results can be analyzed and reported shortly after the data have been collected.[69]

Focus group interviews are quite susceptible to bias caused by the interview setting, the moderator, faulty questions, and an unrepresentative sample. The cost of the sessions can be another disadvantage of the focus group methodology. Each session can cost as much as $2,500.[70] The cost of the session may include gifts and gratuities for the participants, as well as moderator fees, refreshments, and travel expenses. Libraries and other nonprofit organizations can utilize this research technique at a lesser cost by training staff to be moderators, paying mileage only for the participants, using library facilities for the sessions, and offering refreshments to the participants instead of gifts or gratuities.

The success of the focus group interview is dependent upon the skills of the moderator. The moderator must be carefully trained in the technique. If the moderator is not capable of directing the participants' discussions to the research questions, the participants can redirect the focus of the interview. The group experience may intimidate and suppress individual differences, causing some participants to withdraw and not participate in the discussions. Focus group interviews can also foster conformity among group members. The group participants can display a collective pattern of defensive avoidance and practice self-censorship by pressuring any member who expresses strong arguments counter to the group's stereotypes or rationalizations. This can intensify group loyalties and rigidly polarize individual opinions. The focus group interview methodology is vulnerable to manipulation by an influential and willful member of the group. A skillful and trained moderator can control these disadvantages.

"Focus groups should be followed up with statistically sound quantitative research;"[71] they should not be used as the sole basis for making policy decisions. They can provide another type of data for decision making when used in combination with other methods and data analyses.

TELEPHONE INTERVIEWS

Another important type of interview is the telephone interview. Because more and more interviews are being conducted over the telephone, this technique deserves special attention. Like the researcher-administered questionnaire, the telephone interview tends to combine the advantages and disadvantages of the mail questionnaire and the personal interview.

Among the advantages of the telephone interview are the following: (1) it tends to provide significant savings in actual time and cost in contrast to the personal interview; (2) it can be conducted more quickly after an event has occurred; (3) it is generally easier to supervise, train, and monitor the staff for a telephone interview than for a personal interview (telephone interviewing does require some special skills, however, that should be incorporated in the training); and (4) telephone interviews lend themselves to a certain amount of computer assistance. CATI, or computer-assisted telephone interviewing, can build in skip patterns to expedite the interview process and thereby increase the savings in time and money.

CATI is quite popular with survey researchers. There are various CATI practices, but it basically involves the automatic dialing of computer-generated random digit telephone numbers and an interviewer equipped with a headset and the script and questions displayed on a computer monitor. When the respondent answers the telephone, the interviewer begins asking the questions and inputs the respondent's answers into the computer. The data are automatically prepared for analysis.[72] CATI was first introduced in 1971, but gained more popularity in the early 1990s with the introduction of computer-assisted personal interviewing (CAPI), which is similar to CATI, but involves face-to-face interviews.[73]

One major disadvantage of the telephone interview is that the process obviously favors those people who have telephones. The Institute for Social Research at the University of Michigan has estimated that from 9 percent to 10 percent of American adults do not have telephones, and that a high percentage of those who do not are poor and live in rural areas. Consequently, a sample of telephone subscribers would tend to underrepresent poor and rural households, thus producing a bias that may weaken a particular study.

Further aggravating this problem is the fact that unlisted telephone numbers are becoming more common. Computerized, random digit dialing helps to alleviate this problem, however, in that this technique can generate unlisted, as well as listed, telephone numbers. In addition, it can help to ensure the respondent's anonymity. A manual technique known as "added digit dialing" or "add-a-digit sampling" can also help to ease the problem of unlisted numbers. Yet another challenge is the growing use of cell phones; persons using cell phones only, without landline phones in their homes, are particularly difficult to access for a survey. There are concerns that the demographics of wireless-only households are different from those of others. Response rates may be lower for cell phone users than for landline phone owners.

Finally, in comparison with the personal interview, the person being interviewed over the telephone tends to find it easier to terminate the interview before it is finished. Therefore, the response rate tends to be a bit lower for telephone than for personal interviews. Babbie provides a list of survey research techniques that have developed because of advances in technology.[74] Frey has authored a book specifically on survey research by telephone.[75]

In order to summarize some of the advantages and disadvantages of the mail survey, telephone survey, in-person survey, and electronic survey, a chart comparing the three techniques on major criteria is given in Table 5.1.

OBSERVATION AND USABILITY TESTING

Observe means to watch attentively in a scientific or systematic manner. In an observational study, the current status of a phenomenon is determined not by asking but by observing. Observation is sometimes treated as a research method, sometimes as a data collection technique to be utilized with a research method. As a data collection technique, it is used in both basic and applied research and in quantitative and qualitative studies. In applied research, it probably is most frequently used in evaluation. In basic research, it is used with both experimental and survey research designs. Observational methods are central to much qualitative research.

TABLE 5.1 Advantages and Disadvantages of Four Survey Designs

Characteristics of Design	Mail Survey	Phone Survey	In-Person Survey	Electronic Survey
Representative sample				
Opportunity for inclusion is known				
For completely listed populations	High	High	High	Medium
For incompletely listed populations	Medium	Medium	High	Low
Selection within sampling units is controlled (e.g., specific family members must respond)	Medium	High	High	Low
Respondents are likely to be located				
If samples are heterogeneous	Medium	High	High	Low
If samples are homogeneous and specialized	High	High	High	High
Questionnaire construction and question design				
Allowable length of questionnaire	Medium	Medium	High	Medium
Ability to include				
Complex questions	Medium	Low	High	High
Open-ended questions	Low	High	High	Medium
Screening questions	Low	High	High	High
Tedious, boring questions	Low	High	High	Low
Ability to control question sequence	Low	High	High	High
Ability to ensure questionnaire completion	Medium	High	High	Low
Distortion of answers				
Odds of avoiding social desirability bias	High	Medium	Low	High
Odds of avoiding interviewer bias	High	Medium	Low	High
Odds of avoiding contamination by others	Medium	High	Medium	Medium
Administrative goals				
Odds of meeting personnel requirements	High	High	Low	Medium
Odds of implementing quickly	Low	High	Low	High
Odds of keeping costs low	High	Medium	Low	High

Source: Russell K. Schutt, *Investigating the Social World: The Process and Practice of Research,* 5th edition, 2006. Reprinted with permission of Sage Publications, Inc.

Observation is one of the oldest forms of data collection, but, in order to qualify as scientific observation, it should meet certain criteria. Scientific observation should be systematic, objective, and free from bias; quantitative whenever possible; and strong in usability, reliability, and validity.[76]

Advantages of Observational Research

As a data collection technique, observation has several important advantages, including the following:

1. The use of observation makes it possible to record behavior as it occurs.

2. Observation allows one to compare what people actually did with what they said they did. Participants in a study may consciously or unconsciously report their behavior as different from the way it in fact occurred; the observed behavior may well be more valid.

3. Observational techniques can identify behavior, actions, and so on that people may not think to report because they seem unimportant or irrelevant. It can enable the researcher to examine the relative influence of many factors.[77]

4. With observational techniques, a researcher can study subjects who are unable to give verbal reports.

5. The use of observation is generally independent of the subjects' willingness to participate. For example, one could observe how library patrons are using the catalog without asking each patron beforehand if he or she were willing to be observed. There are ethical and sometimes legal implications that should be explored before deciding to observe persons without their permission, or at least their awareness, however.

Limitations of Observational Research

Observational techniques do suffer from a few limitations; some of the more important ones are as follows:

1. It is not always possible to anticipate a spontaneous event and thus be prepared to observe it. Some of the most critical activity at the library's online catalog, for example, may take place when no one is there to observe.

2. The duration of an event affects the feasibility of observing it. The activities at an online catalog are generally short enough to be easily observed; such would not be the case in trying to observe how a faculty member conducts his or her research.

3. Some types of behavior are obviously too private or personal in nature to be observed. This is less of a disadvantage in library-related research, however, than it is in the behavioral sciences.

4. It is generally somewhat more difficult to quantify observational data than other kinds. Behavior simply cannot always be broken down into neat categories.

Unstructured Observation

There are essentially two basic types of observation—structured and unstructured; the latter will be considered first. Unstructured observation is sometimes equated with participant observation, but its most important characteristic reflects the fact that the researcher does not have predetermined sets of categories of behavior to use. Therefore, it is a relatively flexible technique and is particularly useful in exploratory research.

In planning unstructured, observational research, one must take into account the participants or subjects, the setting, the purpose for the subjects' being where they are, the type of behavior to be observed, and the frequency and duration of the behavior. In other words, the researcher must be as well prepared as possible to record accurately the upcoming behavior without going so far as to predesignate specific categories of behavior or to limit the observations to those types of behavior.

The researcher must also decide beforehand what kind of relationship he or she plans to have with the subjects. The observer may be obtrusive—that is, obviously observing certain behavior and known to the subjects—or unobtrusive. If he or she is going to participate in the activities of the subjects, is it going to be in an active or passive role? Finally, the researcher must decide whether the observation will take place with or without the permission of the subjects. Again, ethical considerations come into play here, especially if the observation is to be unobtrusive. (See Chapter 7 for more consideration of these issues.)

In recording unstructured observation, it is best if records are made on the spot and during the event in order to maximize their accuracy. As to techniques, it is best to record observations as unobtrusively as possible, even if the researcher is a participant. Record keeping should not be distracting for the subjects, or it may affect their behavior. Common techniques include taking notes (anecdotal records) and remembering behavior to be recorded later. The latter technique obviously tends to be less reliable and less accurate.

There are steps that can be taken to increase the accuracy of unstructured observations. They include the following:

1. Using two or more observational techniques, such as sound and visual recordings, and then comparing results.
2. Having two or more people observe the same behavior, with the same technique, and then comparing the results.
3. Being careful to distinguish between actual behavior and perceptions or interpretations of the behavior when taking notes. Researcher bias can easily creep in during this stage.
4. Avoiding becoming involved in the activity being observed.

5. Being careful not to take behavior for granted.

6. Obtaining reactions from the participants regarding the accuracy of the observations can be useful in situations where the subjects are fully aware of the role of the researcher. But one would have to be careful that doing so did not affect or bias future behavior of the subjects.

Structured Observation

Structured observation is a more formal technique, often used in quantitative studies in order to provide systematic description or to test causal hypotheses. It may be used in field studies or in laboratory type settings, but it should focus on designated aspects of behavior.

As was the case with unstructured observation, the observer must decide in advance what type of relationship should exist between him or her and the subjects to be observed. Beyond that, the steps involved in planning structured observation are somewhat different from those for unstructured observation.

The most basic step involves developing the observational categories to be employed. (These are set up in advance but may be adjusted later if necessary.) Developing such categories involves defining appropriate, measurable acts, establishing time units or the time length of observations, and anticipating patterns of the phenomena likely to occur. The observer also must decide on his or her frame of reference; for example, will certain behavior be categorized according to a subject's actions or intentions, or by the reactions of others?

Specific techniques used for recording structured observations include the use of rating scales, with which characteristics or behaviors are rated according to the degree to which they are present. Similarly, one may use "all-or-none" or dichotomous categories where the behavior is simply present or absent.

If the researcher can be quite specific about the types of behavior likely to occur, he or she may elect to utilize sheets with checklists of categories to be coded and cells to be checked as their respective categories of behavior occur. Checklists also may employ symbols to represent certain types of behavior in order to speed up the process of recording observations. An example of a checklist of categories is presented in Table 5.2. This is Flanders' system, in which classroom behavior is classified according to ten categories.[78]

The researcher may choose to use mechanical recording instruments or audiovisual equipment to record observations as accurately as possible. Using audiovisual equipment is useful for providing an overall view of some behavior, and it permits the researcher to analyze the behavior more closely and at his or her leisure. It does not systematically record or categorize the data; the researcher must still do this. Having the opportunity to observe again behavior at a more controlled, slower pace can help to avoid overloading the observer, which is one of the most serious threats to observational accuracy. Otherwise, one must be careful not to assign too much activity to be observed to one observer.

TABLE 5.2   Flanders' Category System for Classroom Behavior

Response	1. Accepts Feeling
	2. Praises or Encourages
	3. Accepts or Uses Ideas of Pupils
Teacher Talk Imitation	4. Asks Questions
	5. Lecturing
	6. Giving Directions
	7. Criticizing or Justifying Authority
Pupil Talk	8. Pupil-Talk Response
	9. Pupil-Talk Imitation
Silence	10

Other steps that can be taken to increase the reliability of structured observation, as well as unstructured observation in some cases, include the following:

1. Developing adequate definitions of the kinds of behavior that are to be recorded, and being certain that they correspond to the specific concepts to be studied.
2. Carefully training the observers to ensure that they are adequately prepared and that they have confidence in their ability or judgment to check the appropriate categories.
3. Avoiding observer bias. Generally the observer should take behaviors at their face value and not attempt to interpret their "real" meaning, at least not at the time the observations are made.

The researcher also should be concerned with the validity of the observation, or the extent to which the recorded differences in subjects represent actual differences rather than the observer's perceptions of differences. Some of the measures that can be taken to improve the accuracy of unstructured observations apply to structured observations as well.

Usability Testing

"Evaluating usability involves measuring the degree to which a user can successfully learn and use a system or service . . . usability testing . . . is the observation and analysis of users' behavior while they interact with a system or prototype."[79] Usability testing is a form of human ethnographic observation combined with ergonomics and cognitive psychology and became popular for interface design in the 1980s with the growth of access to computers.[80] It was the catalyst for human-computer interface (HCI) usability studies. The user is involved from the initial design phase through system upgrades.[81]

Usability testing is being used in libraries for the development and evaluation of online catalogs and Web sites. See Prasse and Connaway for an in-depth discussion of the opportunities and challenges presented by usability testing as well as a detailed description for planning and conducting usability tests.[82]

"Some suitable, basic library-related questions for the methodology include:

- What is the best layout for a Web page?
- How can reading from the screen interface be optimized?
- Which online fonts are the best?
- What makes a site difficult to use?

Usability testing also can accommodate more structured, detailed questions, such as:

- Can individual personality or cognitive skills predict Internet use behavior?
- Can library collection holdings and library data be represented geographically in a way that users are able to understand and manipulate the data?
- Can users easily customize and manage discipline-specific content available in an open-source library portal?
- Can users quickly and easily find serials, i.e., newspapers, journals, magazines, etc., from a library's Web site and online catalog?"[83]

As new technologies develop, usability testing will become more important to determine if users are able to navigate through the systems and utilize system functionalities. The results of usability testing can not only influence system design but also "identify topics for library information literacy programs."[84]

SUMMARY

In conducting survey research, the researcher has several data collection techniques at his or her disposal. This chapter has emphasized three of the most commonly used techniques—the questionnaire, the interview, and observation.

Questionnaires and interviews are frequently used for obtaining information about a person's perceptions, beliefs, attitudes, and so on. As the Internet has become more widely available and popular, it is being utilized to distribute questionnaires and to conduct interviews. With the Web survey, more "attention has been focused on the role of the survey interviewer in an automated data collection environment."[85]

With these techniques, heavy reliance is placed on the respondent's report; normally, the investigator has not observed the events in question. This raises the issue of the validity of verbal reports in particular, but the question of validity (and reliability) is important in deciding upon any technique of data collection. Observational methods are best suited for describing and understanding behavior as it occurs. They are less effective for gathering information about a person's perceptions, beliefs, attitudes, and so on.

In developing any of the three data collection techniques, the researcher must make decisions regarding the specific types of questions to be used or the types of behavior to be observed. These decisions are greatly affected by the kinds of information needed and whether the study is exploratory in nature. Throughout the design process, the researcher must be particularly careful not to introduce bias into the study. Even the sequencing of questions can affect their accuracy.

Finally, in selecting a specific technique or instrument, the researcher should weigh the various pros and cons of each method. For example, if one were particularly anxious to achieve a high response rate, he or she might choose the interview over the questionnaire. If cost were the major concern, then the questionnaire would be the obvious choice, other considerations being roughly equal. No one method is likely to be perfect for a given situation, but it should be possible to select one technique as the best alternative, given the objectives, subject, priorities, and limitations of the investigation. Survey data collection techniques may be combined in order to provide richer data.

NOTES

1. L. R. Gay, Geoffrey E. Mills, and Peter W. Airasian, *Educational Research: Competencies for Analysis and Applications* (Upper Saddle River, NJ: Pearson Merrill Prentice Hall, 2006).

2. Robert G. Burgess, *In the Field: An Introduction to Field Research*, Contemporary Social Research Series 8 (London: Allen & Unwin, 1984), 146.

3. G. E. Gorman and Peter Clayton, *Qualitative Research for the Information Professional: A Practical Handbook*, with contributions by Sydney J. Shep and Adela Clayton (London: Facet, 2005), 12.

4. David L. Morgan, "Practical Strategies for Combining Qualitative and Quantitative Methods: Applications to Health Research," in *Emergent Methods in Social Research*, ed. Sharlene Nagy Hesse-Biber and Patricia Leavy, 165–82 (Thousand Oaks, CA: Sage, 2006).

5. *American Heritage Dictionary of the English Language*, 4th ed, s.v. "Questionnaire."

6. Jacquelyn Burkell, "The Dilemma of Survey Non-response," *Library & Information Science Research* 25 (Autumn 2003): 239–63.

7. Rick H. Hoyle, Monica J. Harris, and Charles M. Judd, *Research Methods in Social Relations*, 7th ed. (Fort Worth, TX: Wadsworth/Thomson Learning, 2002).

8. Claire Selltiz, Lawrence S. Wrightsman, and Stuart W. Cook, *Research Methods in Social Relations*, rev. ed. (New York: Holt, Rinehart & Winston, 1959), 262.

9. Gary Golden, *Survey Research Methods* (Chicago: ACRL, 1982), 43–46.

10. Selltiz, Wrightsman, and Cook, *Research Methods in Social Relations*, 262.

11. Hoyle, Harris, and Judd, *Research Methods in Social Relations* 2002, 153.

12. "Questions and Answers," *ISR Newsletter* (Spring–Summer 1982): 6–7.

13. Abraham Bookstein, "Questionnaire Research in a Library Setting," *Journal of Academic Librarianship* 11 (March 1985): 24–28.

James S. Kidston, "The Validity of Questionnaire Responses," *Library Quarterly* 55 (April 1985): 133–50.

14. Abraham Bookstein, "Sources of Error in Library Questionnaires," *Library Research* 4 (1982): 85–94.

15. "Questions and Answers," 7.

16. Delbert C. Miller and Neil J. Salkind, *Handbook of Research Design & Social Measurement*, 6th ed. (Thousand Oaks, CA: Sage, 2002), 123.

17. Marilyn Wurzburger, "Conducting a Mail Survey: Some of the Things You Probably Didn't Learn in Any Research Methods Course," *College & Research Libraries News* 48 (December 1987): 698.

18. Paul L. Erdos, *Professional Mail Surveys*, rev. ed. (Malabar, FL: Robert E. Krieger Publishing, 1983).

19. Alison Jane Pickard, *Research Methods in Information* (London: Facet Publishing, 2007), 198.

20. John Carlo Bertot, "Web-Based Surveys: Not your Basic Survey Anymore," *Library Quarterly* 79, no.1 (2009): 119.

21. Reg Baker, "What They See is What You Get: Nuts and Bolts of Web Surveys" (workshop presented at the 10th General Online Research Conference, Hamburg, Germany, March 10, 2008).

22. Bertot, "Web-Based Surveys," 121.

23. Matthias Schonlau, Ronald D. Fricker, and Marc N. Elliott, *Conducting Research Surveys via E-mail and the Web* (Santa Monica, CA: Rand, 2002), 20.

24. Ibid.

25. Ann Roselle and Steven Neufeld, "The Utility of Electronic Mail Follow-ups for Library Research," *Library & Information Science Research* 20, no. 2 (1998): 153–61.

26. Schonlau, Fricker, and Elliott, *Conducting Research Surveys*, 26.

27. Ibid.

28. Ibid.

29. Miller and Salkind, *Handbook of Research Design & Social Measurement*, 123.

30. William L. Nicholls II, Reginald P. Baker, and Jean Martin, "The Effect of New Data Collection Technology on Survey Data Quality," in *Survey Measurement and Process Quality*, ed. Lars E. Lyberg, Paul Biemer, Martha Collins, Edith de Leeuw, Cathryn Dippo, Norbert Schwarz, and Dennis Trewin (New York: Wiley, 1996), 221–48.

31. Schonlau, Fricker, and Elliott, *Conducting Research Surveys*, 41–50.

32. Ibid.

33. Baker, "What They See is What You Get."

34. Ibid.

35. Schonlau, Fricker, and Elliott, *Conducting Research Surveys*.

36. Denise Troll Covey, *Usage and Usability Assessment: Library Practices and Concerns* (Washington, DC: Digital Library Federation and Council on Library and Information Resources, 2002), 6–14.

37. Jeffrey Hsu, "The Development of Electronic Surveys: A Computer Language-Based Method," *Electronic Library* 13, no. 3 (June 1995): 197.

38. Holly Gunn, "Web-Based Surveys: Changing the Survey Process," *First Monday* 7 (December 2002), http://firstmonday.org/issues/issue7_12/gunn/index.html

39. Rodney A. Reynolds, Robert Woods, and Jason Baker, *Handbook of Research on Electronic Surveys and Measurements* (Hershey, PA: IGI Global, 2006).

40. University of Ljubljana (Slovenia) Faculty of Social Sciences, "WebSM: Web Survey Methodology," http://www.websm.org/.

41. Chris Mann and Fiona Stewart, "Internet Interviewing," in *Handbook of Interview Research: Context & Method*, ed. Jaber F. Gubrium and James A. Holstein (Thousand Oaks, CA: Sage, 2002), 604.

42. Ibid., 609.

43. Alfred E. Goldman and Susan S. McDonald, *The Group Depth Interview* (Englewood Cliffs, NJ: Prentice Hall, 1987), 7.

44. Victoria L. Young, "Focus on Focus Groups," *College & Research Libraries News* 7 (July-August 1993): 391.

45. Barbara M. Robinson, *A Study of Reference Referral and Super Reference in California* (Sacramento: California State Library, 1986).

Charles T. Townley, "Developing Relationships Between Academic Libraries and the State Library of Pennsylvania: A Report of the Research Recommendations" (unpublished consultant's report, report no. ED250542, August 1984).

Debra Wilcox Johnson and Lynn Silipigni Connaway, "Arrowhead Library System, the Older Adult in Rock County: Implications for Library Service" (unpublished consultants' report, March 1991).

Jean Ward, Kathleen A. Hansen, and Douglas M. McLeod, "The News Library's Contribution to Newsmaking," *Special Libraries* 79, no. 2 (Spring 1988): 143–47.

Kathryn Robbins and Ruth Holst, "Hospital Library Evaluation Using Focus Group Interviews," *Bulletin of the Medical Library Association* 78, no. 3 (July 1990): 311–13.

M. K. Scharf and Jean Ward, "A Library Research Application of Focus Group Interviews," in *Association of College and Research Libraries National Conference, Energies for Transition* (Chicago: ACRL, 1986), 191–93.

Richard Widdows, Tia A. Hensler, and Marlaya H. Wyncott, "The Focus-Group Interview: A Method for Assessing Users' Evaluation of Library Service," *College & Research Libraries* 52 (July 1991): 352–59.

Suzanne Walters, *Focus Groups: Linkages to the Community* (Denver: US West Communications, 1988).

46. Johnson and Connaway, "Arrowhead Library System."

47. Marilyn D. Jacobson, *New York State Education Information Centers Program: Summative Evaluation Report*, ED 250542 (Albany: New York State Education Department, 1984).

48. Constance A. Mellon, *Naturalistic Inquiry for Library Science: Methods and Applications for Research, Evaluation, and Teaching* (New York: Greenwood Press, 1990).

49. Roger Verny and Connie Van Fleet, "Conducting Focus Groups," in *Library Evaluation: A Casebook and Can-Do Guide*, ed. Danny P. Wallace and Connie Van Fleet (Englewood, CO: Libraries Unlimited, 2001), 43–51.

50. Liz Bishoff, "Public Access to the Library of Congress Subject Headings" (paper presented at the Annual Conference of the American Library Association, San Francisco, CA, 1987).

51. Debra Wilcox Johnson and Lynn Silipigni Connaway, "Cataloger as Decision Maker" (paper presented at the annual meeting of the Wisconsin Library Association, Appleton, 1990).

52. Debra Wilcox Johnson and Lynn Silipigni Connaway, "Use of Online Catalogs: A Report of Results of Focus Group Interviews" (unpublished consultants' report, report no. 19, 1992).

Karen Markey, *Subject Searching in Library Catalogs: Before and After the Introduction of Online Catalogs* (Dublin, OH: OCLC, 1984).

Kenneth W. Berger and Richard W. Hines, "What Does the User Really Want? The Library User Survey Project at Duke University,"*Journal of Academic Librarianship* 20 (November 1994): 3069.

Sharon W. Schwerzel, Susan V. Emerson, and David L. Johnson, "Self-Evaluation of Competencies in Online Searching by End-Users After Basic Training," in *Proceedings of the Forty-fifth ASIS Annual Meeting*, ed. Anthony E. Petrarca, Celianna I. Taylor, and Robert S. Kohn (White Plains, NY: Knowledge Industry, 1982), 272–75.

53. Neal K. Kaske, "Studies of Online Catalogs," in *Online Catalogs/Online Reference*, ed. Brian Aveney and Brett Butler (Chicago: American Library Association, 1984), 20–30.

Neal K. Kaske and N. P. Sanders, "Online Subject Access: The Human Side of the Problem," *RQ* 19 (Fall 1980): 52–58.

54. Lynn Silipigni Connaway, "Focus Group Interviews: A Data Collection Methodology for Decision Making," *Library Administration & Management* 10 (Fall 1996): 231–39.

55. Denise Troll Covey, *Usage and Usability Assessment*, 15–23.

56. Young, "Focus on Focus Groups," 392.

57. Karen Markey Drabenstott, "Focused Group Interviews," in *Qualitative Research in Information Management*, ed. Jack D. Glazier and Ronald R. Powell (Englewood, CO: Libraries Unlimited, 1992), 85–104.

58. Mary M. Wagner and Suzanne H. Mahmoodi, *A Focus Group Interview Manual* (Chicago: American Library Association, 1994), 10.

59. Clifford Geertz, *The Interpretation of Cultures: Selected Essays* (New York: Basic Books, 1973), 6.

60. David L. Morgan, *Focus Groups as Qualitative Research* (Newbury Park, CA: Sage, 1988), 64–69.

61. Richard A. Krueger, *Focus Groups: A Practical Guide for Applied Research* (Beverly Hills, CA: Sage, 1988), 41.

62. Richard A. Krueger and Mary Anne Casey, *Focus Groups: A Practical Guide for Applied Research* (Thousand Oaks, CA: Sage, 2000), 201–3.

63. Robert Philip Weber, *Basic Content Analysis*, 2nd ed. (London: Sage, 1990), 18.

64. Ibid.

65. Ibid.

66. Morgan, *Focus Groups as Qualitative Research*, 64.

67. Ibid., 15.

68. Young, "Focus on Focus Groups," 391.

69. Krueger, *Focus Groups* 1988, 44–46.

70. Morgan, *Focus Groups as Qualitative Research*, 40.

71. Young, "Focus on Focus Groups," 393.

72. Earl Babbie, *The Practice of Social Research*, 12th ed. (Belmont, CA: Wadsworth/Cengage Learning, 2010), 282.

73. Mick P. Couper and Sue Ellen Hansen, "Computer-Assisted Interviewing," in *Handbook of Interview Research: Context & Method*, ed. Jaber F. Gubrium and James A. Holstein (Thousand Oaks, CA: Sage, 2002), 557.

74. Babbie, *Practice of Social Research* 2010, 281–82.

75. James H. Frey, *Survey Research by Telephone* (Beverly Hills, CA: Sage, 1983).

76. George J. Mouly, *Educational Research: The Art and Science of Investigation* (Boston: Allyn and Bacon, 1978), 216–17.

77. Robert J. Grover and Jack D. Glazier, "A Conceptual Framework for Theory Building in Library and Information Science," *Library & Information Science Research* 8 (1986): 257.

78. Rick H. Hoyle, Monica J. Harris, and Charles M. Judd. *Research Methods in Social Relations*. 7th ed. (Fort Worth, TX: Wadsworth/Thomson Learning, 2002), 375.

79. Michael J. Prasse and Lynn Silipigni Connaway, "Usability Testing: Method and Research," in *Academic Library Research: Perspectives and Current Trends*, ed. Marie L. Radford and Pamela Snelson (Chicago: Association of College and Research Libraries, 2008), 215.

80. Ibid.

81. Elaina Norlin and C. M. Winters, *Usability Testing for Library Websites: A Hands-on Guide* (Chicago: American Library Association, 2002).

82. Prasse and Connaway, "Usability Testing."

83. Ibid., 216.

84. Ibid., 245.

85. Couper and Hansen, "Computer-Assisted Interviewing," 557.

Chapter 6

Experimental Research

In some ways, experimental research is the most rigorous of all research methods and is arguably the best method for testing cause and effect relationships. Yet a review of the literature reveals that it is used in only 8 percent to 10 percent of LIS research studies. Some of the probable reasons why that is the situation will be explored during the course of this chapter; however, before discussing experimental research methods per se, causality, a concept which is crucial to experimental research, will be considered.

CAUSALITY

Simply stated, causality suggests that a single event (the "cause") always leads to another single event (the "effect").[1] Anderson states, "causes and consequences concentrate on the relationships between phenomena—how one phenomenon affects another."[2] In the social sciences, at least, the focus is normally on a variety of determining factors, which increase the probability of a certain event occurring, rather than on a single factor. Goldhor even argues that the "demonstration of causality in any rigorous sense is philosophically impossible," and he suggests that causality and "explanation" can be used interchangeably.[3] Yet at least an understanding of causality is essential to the proper testing of causal hypotheses or relationships and is useful in designing research studies to be as rigorous as possible.

The Conditions for Causality

In attempting to confirm causality in a relationship, one must consider the so-called conditions or factors that may exist. A *necessary condition* is one that must occur if the phenomenon of which it is a cause is to occur. That is to say, if X, the independent variable, is a necessary condition of Y, the dependent variable, Y will never occur unless X occurs. For example, if library instruction were a necessary condition of effective library use, then the latter would never occur unless library instruction had been provided.

A *sufficient condition* is one that is always followed by the phenomenon which it "causes." In other words, if X is a sufficient condition of Y, then whenever X occurs, Y will always occur. If library instruction were a sufficient condition of effective library use, then after an individual received appropriate library instruction, he or she would begin using the library effectively.

A condition may or may not be both necessary and sufficient for the occurrence of a phenomenon. (If both, Y would never occur unless X had occurred, and whenever X occurred, Y would occur also.) In fact, in the example provided, one can see that it is quite possible for neither condition to exist. Library instruction is probably not a necessary condition for effective library use, as a patron may teach himself or herself to use the library; and it certainly is not a sufficient condition, as effective library use does not always follow library instruction, regardless of how well it is presented.

As was noted earlier, in the social sciences especially, a variety of factors tend to cause or influence any one dependent variable. The example of effective library use is a good case in point. In addition to library instruction, effective library use might be affected by motivation, intelligence, previous experiences, role models, peer pressure, and so on. In short, the researcher rarely finds a single factor or condition that is both necessary and sufficient to cause an event, so he or she is well advised to consider other types of conditions.

One type of condition that can be considered, in addition to necessary and sufficient conditions, is the *contributory condition*. Contributory conditions increase the probability that a certain phenomenon will occur, but they do not make it certain. So, if library instruction were considered to be the factor likely to have the strongest effect on library use, then the other factors named, such as peer pressure, might be considered to be contributory conditions. And in fact, the combination and interaction of all of the relevant factors or independent variables would probably best explain effective library use.

The picture is further complicated by the fact that certain variables will represent contributory conditions in some situations, but not in others. Again, social science concepts tend to be complex and the interaction of variables, or how they affect one another and combine influences, must be taken into account. The conditions under which a given variable is a contributory cause are referred to as *contingent conditions*. In the previous example, the various factors suggested as likely causes of effective library instruction might do so only if the library's services and collections were strong. In other words, the environment may increase or decrease the influence of certain variables.

The researcher should also be aware of the possibility of *alternative conditions* that might make the occurrence of a certain phenomenon more likely. Alternative conditions, in essence, refer to the different forms that a given factor or variable may take and how the factor's influence is affected by its form. Library instruction can be provided in different formats, and it may be that one type of library instruction would promote effective library use and another would not. For example, library orientation may be inappropriate for graduate students and have no real effect on how they use the library, while instruction in the use of the literature of a certain discipline may greatly improve their library use effectiveness. In turn, the alternative conditions would continue to be affected by other contributory conditions, such as how well the library is able to support research in the specific area of graduate study.

A less commonly discussed factor, *mechanism*, refers to the conditions that create the causal connection, or the intervening variables. Consideration of the mechanism helps us to understand how variation in the independent variable(s) results in variation in the dependent variable(s). This condition seems to be conceptually similar to the contingent condition discussed earlier in that it is concerned with the context in which the cause has its effects.

Bases for Inferring Causal Relationships

Unfortunately, as Goldhor implied, it is usually impossible to demonstrate directly that one variable causes another variable, either by itself or in combination with other variables. As a result, the social science researcher normally has to infer a causal relationship between two or more variables based on the data gathered.[4]

One type of evidence for inferring a causal relationship is known as *concomitant variation*. Evidence of concomitant variation, or covariation when there are two variables, indicates that the independent variable (X) and the dependent variable, or assumed effect (Y), are associated in the way predicted by the causal hypothesis. For example, one might have hypothesized that, as the amount of library instruction is increased, the level of library skills will increase.

The relationship just specified is an example of a positive one. A relationship in which both variables decrease simultaneously is in effect a positive relationship as well. Other possible relationships include a negative or inverse relationship, in which, as one variable decreases, the other increases (or vice versa); and a curvilinear relationship, where the degree to which one variable affects the other tends to diminish beyond a certain point.

In the case of a hypothesis that predicts that the independent variable is a contributory condition of the dependent variable, the "logical consequence" would be that Y would appear in more cases where X is present than in cases where it is not present. So, if it were hypothesized that library instruction is a contributory condition of effective library use, then persons who had received library instruction would be more likely to be effective library users than those who had not received library instruction. But one would not be able to assume that every person who had received library instruction would be an effective library user. Other types of causal hypotheses (e.g., X is a necessary cause of Y) would call for other patterns of associations between the independent and the dependent variables.

A second basis for inferring a causal relationship between two variables relates to the *time order* of occurrence of the variables. To establish the necessary time order requires evidence that the dependent variable did not occur before the independent variable. One could not support a hypothesis predicting a necessary causal relationship between library instruction and effective library use if it were found that the effective library use was occurring before the patrons received any library instruction.

The third basis for inferring a causal relationship is nonspuriousness or evidence *ruling out other factors* as possible causes of the dependent variable. However, such evidence merely helps to provide a reasonable foundation for inferring that X is or is not a cause of Y. It cannot absolutely confirm a relationship because the researcher may have overlooked one or more other factors that are actually the determining conditions. The process of ruling out other factors, or controlling for the effects of extraneous variables, will be considered further in upcoming sections of this chapter.

In conclusion, there are certain conditions that should exist, and certain kinds of inferences that must be made, in order to support causal relationships. The most effective method for collecting the necessary evidence, or testing a causal hypothesis, is the experiment.

CONTROLLING THE VARIABLES

Certain characteristics or capabilities are essential to the experimental research method. Virtually all quantitative research requires the measurement of variables, but experimental research necessitates the control and manipulation of certain variables as well. In addition, the variables must vary under different conditions, or have at least two values; otherwise, they are not variables. The independent variable is the experimental variable. It also is referred to as the cause or causal variable and the predictor variable. It is the variable that the researcher manipulates. (Organismic variables are variables such as age and income, which are often treated as independent variables but over which the researcher has no real control.) The dependent variable is often known as the effect, the subject variable, or the criterion variable. It is "caused," or at least affected, by the independent variable.

True experimental manipulation also requires the use of at least one experimental group and one comparison or control group, each consisting of an appropriate number of subjects. The experimental group receives the experimental treatment, and the comparison group receives no treatment, thereby creating an independent variable with at least two values. The dependent variable is represented by the measurement of the effect of the experimental treatment, and several dependent variables or measures of effect may be used.

If one were conducting an experiment to measure the effect of library instruction on library use, library instruction would be the independent variable and library use would be the dependent variable. The two values for library instruction could be the provision of instruction to the experimental group and no instruction for the comparison group. The dependent variable could be measured by a tally of the frequency of library use for the members of both groups. Another dependent variable could be represented by types of reference questions asked by members of the two groups.

One of the difficulties in exerting adequate control in an experiment relates to the fact that there typically are a variety of extraneous independent variables that conceivably are influencing or causing the dependent variable(s), in addition to the one or ones being investigated. (Extraneous variables can also influence both the independent and the dependent variables and thus create a spurious association between them.) In order to isolate the effects that the experimental variable or variables are having, the researcher must control the extraneous independent variables, which could include, in the most recent example, assignments made by instructors, increased "marketing" by the library, and so on.

There are three major techniques for controlling the influence of extraneous variables, two of which are intended to equate the experimental and comparison groups prior to the experiment. One technique involves holding the other variables constant by matching or selecting subjects with the same traits for the experimental and comparison groups. That is, as a subject is selected for the experimental group, another one which is quite similar on all characteristics or variables that are relevant or capable of affecting the dependent variable, is selected for the comparison group. For example, after a subject had been selected for the experimental group in a study on the effects of library instruction, then a subject with a comparable IQ, previous library experience, GPA, age, and so on would need to be assigned to the comparison group. It is difficult to identify all relevant variables when matching subjects, but the researcher may derive some consolation from the fact that key variables tend to correlate highly with other, unidentified variables.

If the subjects are not completely equivalent going into the experiment, the extraneous variables may be controlled statistically during the analysis stage. However, this approach is less reliable than others, as it is done ex post facto, or after the experiment. No amount of statistical control can completely undo the preceding effects of other factors. And it is effective at all only if the relevant extraneous variables are identified and properly measured.

Random Assignment

The third and best technique for equating two or more groups before the experimental treatment begins is referred to as random assignment or randomization (not to be confused with random sampling or selection). It is a procedure used after the sample is selected but before the experimental treatment is applied. It involves randomly assigning the subjects in the total sample to the experimental and comparison groups. Specific techniques used for random assignment are often essentially the same as those used for selecting random samples. The researcher may elect, for example, to draw names from a hat, use a table of random numbers, or employ a computer to generate a list of random numbers.

One can assume, however, that the groups are equivalent only within certain probability levels. But "equating" the experimental and comparison groups is essential for making causal inferences about the effects of the experimental treatment. It improves the external validity, or generalizability, of the experiment, as well as its internal validity, or the dependability of the results. Random assignment does not necessarily control for the effects of the experimental setting. The researcher must take other steps to eliminate or minimize the influence of such factors as the mode of instruction, quality of tests, and interaction of subjects.

INTERNAL VALIDITY

Briefly defined, internal validity "refers to the possibility that the conclusions drawn from experimental results may not accurately reflect what went on in the experiment itself."[5] Stated more positively, it is "the conclusiveness with which the effects of the independent variable are established in a scientific investigation, as opposed to the possibility that some confounding variables may have caused the observed results."[6]

Generally speaking, the greater the control the experimenter has over the experiment, including the extraneous variables, the greater the internal validity. The greater the control, however, the more artificial or unnatural is the setting and the lower the external validity. (This relationship will be referred to again when discussing experimental designs.)

Threats to Internal Validity

Internal validity is crucial to the dependability of the results of an experiment, and it is closely related to replicability. It indicates the extent to which the experiment adequately tested the treatment under study by helping to rule out rival explanations and ensuring freedom from bias. In short, internal validity provides confidence that the observed effect on the dependent variable is actually due to the independent variable.

Unfortunately, a number of factors can jeopardize the internal validity of experimental research. Those factors most frequently cited in standard texts are as follows:

1. History, or specific events, in addition to the experimental treatment or variable, which occur between measurements of the dependent variable. During an experimental study of the effects of library instruction on the frequency of library use, subjects might be exposed to some event or influence such as a midterm exam that would encourage them to use the library more than usual. The researcher might then be uncertain about how much of the increase in library use was caused by the midterm exam and how much by the library instruction provided.

2. Maturation, or processes *within* the subjects operating as a function of time such as growing older, or more mature. During the course of the experiment just referred to, the subjects might naturally develop into more frequent library users regardless of any library instruction received.

3. Testing, or the effects of taking a test upon the scores of a subsequent testing. In a library instruction experiment, students would tend to do better on a second test of library skills simply because they had already taken the test.

4. Instrumentation, or the process wherein changes in the techniques used for the measurements, or changes in the persons making the measurements, affect a second set of measurements or observations. For example, if a pretest on library use measured use as the number of *volumes* borrowed, and a second test measured it as the number of *titles* borrowed, then the second measurement would probably be different simply because the method of measurement had been changed.

5. Statistical regression, or the statistical phenomenon wherein extreme scores obtained on a first test tend to gravitate toward the mean on

subsequent tests. This is especially significant where groups have been selected on the basis of their extreme scores. If subjects in one group made extremely high scores on a test of library skills, and subjects in a second group earned exceptionally low scores, the odds are that many of the subjects in both groups would tend to be closer to the mean score on a retest. Again, this event would confound the effects of any library instruction provided between tests.

6. Biases in differential selection of subjects for the comparison groups. If a researcher selected students for the comparison group (the group not receiving any library instruction) who were not likely to evidence much use of the library, then he or she would be guilty of biasing the experiment in favor of the experimental treatment. The students in the experimental group (those receiving library instruction) would probably use the library more than those in the comparison group, with or without library instruction, but it might appear that library instruction was having a positive effect.

7. Experimental mortality, or the differential loss of subjects from the comparison group. If during the course of an experiment, students who tended to be infrequent library users, perhaps because of their area of study, dropped out of the comparison group, then the remaining members might produce scores higher than would be normal. Such an occurrence would suggest that library instruction was having less effect than it actually was because the difference in scores between the experimental and comparison groups would be less than expected.

8. Interaction of selection and other sources of invalidity. The results of interaction can be mistaken for the effects of the experimental variable. For example, the students selected for the experimental group might have been exceptionally receptive to library instruction because they had matured intellectually during the experiment. Therefore, their retest scores would be higher than their pretest scores, and the gain probably would be attributed to the library instruction received. At least some, if not all, of the increase in test scores could have resulted, however, solely from the intellectual maturation that had taken place.

To repeat, these threats to internal validity, if not controlled, may well produce effects confounded with the effect of the experimental stimulus.[7] Types of experimental designs that can help to control these extraneous variables will be discussed later.

EXTERNAL VALIDITY

Before taking up specific types of experimental designs, external validity, the second type of validity important to successful experimental research, will be considered. External validity is important because it relates to "the possibility that conclusions drawn from experimental results may not be generalizable to the 'real' world."[8] Hoyle, Harris, and Judd define external validity as "the extent to which one can generalize the results of the research to the populations and settings of interest in the hypothesis."[9]

Threats to External Validity

Unfortunately, as Campbell and Stanley note, the question of external validity is never completely answerable.[10] (As is the case with internal validity, certain experimental designs can help to maximize external validity.) The major factors jeopardizing external validity, or representativeness, are as follows:

1. The reactive or interactive effect of testing. This occurs when a *pretest* increases or decreases the subject's sensitivity or responsiveness to the experimental variable, and thus makes the results unrepresentative of the general, or unpretested, population from which the subjects were selected. If a student were pretested on his or her library skills, given library instruction for one semester, and then tested again on library skills, there is probably a good chance that the skills would be higher on the retest. However, the researcher would have to question how much of the increase in skills was due to the pretest's making the student more aware of, for example, library services and resources and therefore more likely to improve his or her library use with or without the library instruction.

2. The interaction effects of selection biases and the experimental variable. This threat is similar to the sixth listed threat to internal validity. It simply means that one must be careful not to select experimental subjects who are likely to be more receptive to the experimental variable than is the general population. For example, if one selected English honors students for an experiment on the effects of library instruction, there is a chance that they would be more motivated to utilize library instruction than more average students. Consequently, the ability to generalize the results of the study to other, more typical, students would be diminished.

3. The reactive effects of the experimental arrangements can prevent the researcher from being able to generalize about the effect of the experimental variable on persons exposed to it in nonexperimental settings. In other words, the experimental environment, or elements thereof, might have been influencing the subject along with, or instead of, the experimental treatment. Behavior in the laboratory has a tendency not to represent accurately what would happen in similar circumstances in real life. A well-known example of this phenomenon is the classic Hawthorne study, in which workers became more productive whenever they were studied, regardless of whether their working conditions improved or worsened, simply because they were aware that they were being observed.

4. Multiple treatment interference may occur whenever more than one experimental treatment is applied to the same subjects basically because the effects of prior treatments do not entirely disappear. For example, if a student were given different types of library instruction, one after another, they would tend to have a cumulative effect on the student's library skills. Consequently, it would be difficult for the researcher to distinguish between the effects of any one mode of library instruction and those of the others.

In summary, the threats to external validity are basically interaction effects, involving the experimental treatment and some other variable. On the other hand, the factors jeopardizing internal validity are those that directly affect the dependent variables or scores. They are factors which by themselves can produce changes which might be mistaken for the results of the experimental treatment.[11]

EXPERIMENTAL DESIGNS

In spite of the challenges associated with creating equivalent groups, controlling for the threats to internal and external validity, and establishing adequate control over the experimental setting, experimental research holds significant potential for the resolution of library-related problems. As has been noted, the testing of causal hypotheses increases our ability to explain why certain phenomena occur, and experimental research may be the method best equipped for such testing. Survey research methods, for example, are not able to provide the researcher with enough control over extraneous variables to be able to say with any certainty that one variable is the direct cause of another. In a survey of students' library usage, we could ask them why they used the library, but data gathered in that manner would at best allow us to establish associational relationships. For a number of reasons, even including a desire to please the researcher, the subject might attribute more influence to the library instruction than was warranted.

As was indicated earlier, a variety of designs can be employed for experimental research, and the stronger they are, the better they can minimize or control the various threats to internal and external validity. Some of the designs appropriate for true experiments, or those experiments designed to investigate causal relationships while exercising considerable control and utilizing random assignment, will be considered first.

True Experimental Designs

1. **The Pretest-Posttest Control Group Design**. One of the classic, true experimental designs is usually referred to as the pretest-posttest control group design. As will be seen after a few examples, the standard names of basic designs tend to describe them rather well, but diagrams point out their major features even more clearly. The diagram for this design appears as follows:

$$R \quad O_1 \quad X \quad O_2$$
$$R \quad O_3 \quad \quad O_4$$

In this illustration, and in the others to follow, the X symbolizes the experimental treatment or independent variable or cause. The O represents the process of observation or measurement of the dependent variable or effect. These observations can take the form of questionnaires, tests, interviews, and so on. Each row represents one group of subjects; the left-to-right direction indicates the temporal order, and Xs and Os vertical to one another occur simultaneously. The R indicates that the subjects in the group so designated have been randomly assigned to their treatment, or lack of treatment.

Therefore, this first diagram indicates that there are two groups, both randomly assigned. Both groups have been pretested and retested, but only the first group received the experimental treatment. The random assignment means that the two groups should be equivalent, or nearly so. This experimental design is considered strong because it controls for all eight of the threats to internal validity. For example, history is controlled because historical events that might have produced a change from O_1 to O_2 would also produce a comparable change from O_3 to O_4. In other words, due to random assignment, the groups are equivalent and should be equally affected by historical events, especially if the experiment is controlled as carefully as possible. For example, a study conducted as a double-blind experiment, in which the person(s) administering the experimental treatment does not know who the subjects are and the subjects do not realize they are part of an experiment, will be proportionately stronger in internal validity. In our library instruction study, assignments given to students outside the experimental setting should have similar effects on both groups. The other threats to internal validity would be controlled in essentially the same manner.

The pretest-posttest control group design is not as effective at controlling the threats to external validity. The interaction of testing and X remains a concern, because attitudes and behavior may be affected by the pretest. The design's ability to control the interaction of selection biases and X is questionable. It should account for differences between the experimental and control groups, but the results may still be atypical due to the nature of the subjects selected. This design's control of reactive arrangements is probably less than satisfactory also. There remains a good possibility that phenomena such as the Hawthorne effect may influence the effect of X. Multiple treatment interference is not an issue here because only one experimental treatment is involved.

In summary, this particular design is stronger in internal validity than in external validity. This suggests that the researcher could be confident that the experimental treatment, not extraneous variables, caused the measured effects; however, he or she would have to be cautious in generalizing the results to other groups as they might have been unique for those particular subjects.

2. **The Solomon Four-Group Design**. A second standard, true experimental design is referred to as the Solomon four-group design. It is diagrammed as follows:

$$
\begin{array}{cccc}
R & O_1 & X_1 & O_2 \\
R & O_3 & & O_4 \\
R & & X_2 & O_5 \\
R & & & O_6 \\
\end{array}
$$

As can be seen, this design involves four randomly assigned, or equivalent, groups, two of which receive the experimental treatment, and two of which are given posttests only.

This design "scores" the same on internal validity as does the pretest-posttest control group design because it controls all eight threats. It is better than the pretest-posttest control group design in controlling the factors that jeopardize external validity in that it is able to control the interaction of pretesting and X. It can do this because one experimental group and one control group are not pretested, thus allowing the researcher to measure the effects of the experimental treatment without the "contamination" of a pretest. It also benefits from the fact that the effect of X can be determined in four ways: the differences between O_2 and O_1, O_2 and O_4, O_5 and O_6, and O_1 and O_3. In short, this design is somewhat stronger than the pretest-posttest control group design and should be used in preference to it when possible.

3. **The Posttest-Only Control Group Design**. The posttest-only control group design diagrams the same as the last two groups of the Solomon four-group design and appears as follows:

$$R \quad X \quad O_1$$
$$R \qquad\quad O_2$$

This design is not used as frequently as it deserves to be, perhaps because of its lack of a pretest. Yet one can assume that the two groups are equivalent at the start of a study because of the random assignment, and a pretest should not be necessary to confirm that assumption. In fact, this design achieves the same control of internal and external validity as does the Solomon four-group design, but without the necessity of establishing four groups. Therefore, it is in some ways preferable to the Solomon four-group design, as well as to the pretest-posttest control group design. Not having pretests, however, precludes the researcher's being able to calculate differences in the dependent variable before and after the experiment, or gain scores.

4. **Factorial Designs**. The three preceding designs are examples of designs capable of accommodating only one independent and one dependent variable. Factorial designs can deal with two or more independent variables and one dependent variable. They tend to be higher in external validity than other true experimental designs because they can consider more independent variables and can measure interaction. As can be seen in the following example, a factorial design contains every possible combination of the independent variables.

$$R \quad X_1 \quad X_2 \quad O_1$$
$$R \quad X_1 \qquad\quad O_2$$
$$R \qquad\quad X_2 \quad O_3$$
$$R \qquad\qquad\quad O_4$$

Not only would this design allow the researcher to measure the specific effects of the two independent variables on the dependent variable, but it should give some indication of the interaction of X_1 and X_2. In other words, it controls for multiple treatment interference.

A simpler factorial design is as follows:

$$R \quad X_1 \quad O_1$$
$$R \quad X_2 \quad O_2$$
$$R \qquad\quad O_3$$

This is a multivariate equivalent of the posttest_only control group design. It does not measure the interaction of treatments, but that should be unnecessary, as no one group receives more than one treatment. (There may be some situations, such as in library instruction experiments, however, where one would be interested in knowing if the different modes of instruction had any cumulative effects on library skills or use.)

True Experiments and Correlational Studies

Having discussed the essential criteria for true experimental research and having looked at a few examples of true experimental designs, it should be kept in mind that it is not always possible to assign people to experimental treatments in a laboratory-like setting. For example, if one were designing a study to test the effects of library instruction provided to English literature students on their use of the library, in most cases it would not be possible to assign particular students to the sections designated to receive and not to receive library instruction. Probably, the researcher would have to accept the two groups as they were already constituted. Thus, there would be no assurance that the two groups were equivalent.

Consequently, much social science research is correlational, or associational, in nature. This type of research may well permit one to predict change in one variable based on knowledge about another variable, but it would not allow the establishment of a causal relationship between the variables. Correlational studies tend to be relatively high in external validity but relatively low in internal validity and, therefore, less able to account for rival explanations of a relationship.

Essentially true experiments can be conducted in real-life settings, assuming the controls are adequate. Such experiments are often referred to as field experiments. They tend to be less artificial than laboratory type experiments but may still lose validity if the subjects are aware that they are being studied.

Reiterating a point made earlier, properly conducted true experiments should be high in internal validity. This means that the researcher should be able to be quite confident that the experimental treatment was the cause of the observed effect. True experiments have less external validity, however. That is, true experiments are poor representations of natural situations. More specifically, they provide a relatively artificial test of the hypothesis, tend to be low in generalizability, and often produce relatively little descriptive data about the population, unless the subjects are unusually representative.

Difficulties to be Avoided

In order to design an experiment that will be as reliable and valid as possible, the researcher should attempt to avoid the following:

1. Relying too heavily on a single experiment
2. Using poorly designed or faulty data collection instruments
3. Not identifying all of the variables that may affect the results
4. Not choosing subjects that are as representative of the population as possible
5. Introducing experimenter bias
6. Introducing subject bias
7. Making the subjects aware of the hypothesis being tested through unconscious signaling or behavior
8. Using an insufficient number of subjects

Evaluating the Experiment

In evaluating the design and results of an experiment, there are several points that the researcher should consider. One, the experiment should have the ability to test a null hypothesis, which suggests that there is no relationship between the variables being studied. Two, the experiment should be sensitive. That is, it should be able to detect relatively small effects or differences. Increasing the number of subjects, which decreases the chance of random or experimental error, and exerting additional control, such as by matching subjects, helps to increase the experiment's sensitivity. The selection of subjects can be facilitated with the use of power charts, which provide the number of subjects for each group, given the effects of power or sensitivity of the experiment, the effect size, and the significance level.[12] "The experiment is planned so that the size of each treatment group provides the greatest sensitivity that the effect on the outcome is actually due to the experimental manipulation in the study."[13] The formulas used for determining optimal sample sizes for surveys are of limited use for experiments.

In evaluating the results of the experiment, the researcher should assess the reliability of the data and its external validity, or generalizability. Last, but not least, the significance or importance of the results should be considered.

Preexperimental Designs

If random assignment of subjects and laboratory-like control are not possible, it will be necessary for the researcher to use a preexperimental or quasi-experimental design. Preexperimental designs, which will be considered first, are those designs which not only lack random assignment but which have few observation points as well. A few examples of preexperimental designs follow.

1. **The One-Shot Case Study**. The one-shot case study, which can be diagrammed simply as $X\,O$, is an extremely weak design. As there is only one group, there is no basis for comparison of subjects who have received and have not received the experimental treatment.

   With neither random assignment nor pretests, this design is susceptible to numerous alternative influences or threats to its internal validity. It is threatened particularly by history, maturation, selection biases, and experimental mortality. Regarding external validity, this design is unable to control for interaction between selection biases and the experimental variable. For practical reasons, however, the one-shot case study is used fairly frequently.

2. **The One-Group Pretest-Posttest Design**. The one-group pretest-posttest design represents a slight improvement over the one-shot case study, because it incorporates a pretest, or one more observation point. It appears as follows:

$$O_1 \quad X \quad O_2$$

If posttest scores are higher than the pretest scores, this design should rule out selection biases as a rival explanation. It does not, however, control for the effects of history, maturation, testing, instrumentation, interaction of selection and other factors, and quite possibly statistical regression. It also is about as weak as the one-shot case study at controlling threats to external validity.

3. **The Static-Group Comparison**. Another preexperimental design, which improves a bit more on the preceding designs, known as the static-group comparison, diagrams as follows:

$$\begin{array}{ccc} \text{Group 1} & X & O_1 \\ \hline \text{Group 2} & & O_2 \end{array}$$

As can be seen, this design utilizes two groups rather than one, each of which is observed once. The line, however, as well as the absence of R's, indicates that the groups occurred naturally and were not based on random assignment. In other words, "this is a design in which a group which has experienced X is compared with one which has not, for the purposes of establishing the effect of X."[14] An example of naturally occurring groups might be two English literature classes, to which the researcher was unable to assign particular students and which had already experienced some level of an experimental variable such as library instruction. Since the researcher was unable to create two equivalent groups, there is no assurance that the two groups had experienced the same amount of the experimental variable or that the experimental treatment actually produced the differences, if any, in the final group scores. Differences in group scores might have resulted entirely because one or the other group was atypical.

Consequently, as the researcher using this design cannot be certain whether X actually caused O, or natural selection did, the static-group comparison is at best a correlational design. The X represents what the subjects naturally brought to the study, and the researcher can only ascertain that there is some sort of association between the variables in question. In fact, the static-group comparison is often considered to be a survey design.

To its credit, the static-group comparison does control relatively well for several threats to internal validity. Those controlled are history, testing, instrumentation, regression, and possibly maturation. It is not considered to be capable of controlling the threats to external validity.

Quasi-Experimental Designs

A type of experimental design which represents an improvement over preexperimental designs, including those just considered, is the quasi-experimental design. Quasi-experimental designs usually include naturally occurring groups, but they often involve more than one group and typically have more observation points than do preexperimental designs. The employment of naturally occurring groups means there is no random assignment of subjects to the control and experimental groups.

Quasi-experimental designs are not as strong as those for true experiments. As they do not have randomly assigned treatment and comparison groups, comparisons must be made with nonequivalent groups or with the same subjects in one group prior to and after treatment. In most cases the independent variable(s) cannot be fully manipulated by the researcher. Quasi-experimental designs also have less control than do true experiments but are able to rule out more threats to internal validity than preexperiments. In fact, if the quasi-experimental design is strong enough to rule out many of the threats to internal validity, it may be used to infer cause and effect.[15] A few examples of quasi-experimental designs follow.

1. **The Time-Series Design**. The time-series design is an example of a single-group quasi-experimental design. It takes this form:

   $$O_1 \quad O_2 \quad O_3 \quad O_4 \quad X \quad O_5 \quad O_6 \quad O_7 \quad O_8$$

   As a comparison will reveal, this design represents an extension of the one-group pretest-posttest design (O_1 X O_2). The longer sequence of observation points helps to control additional factors jeopardizing internal validity, such as maturation and testing, because it allows one to examine trends in the data before, at the time of, and after the experimental treatment. (Graphing the Xs and Os can help to reveal any patterns that might exist.) For example, if one were testing the library skills of students and learned that their skills were regularly rising even before X, or library instruction, was applied, one would have to question the apparent effects of library instruction.

   The time-series is still relatively weak in external validity. It does possibly control for interaction of selection biases and reactive arrangements.

2. **The Equivalent Time-Samples Design**. A second single-group quasi-experimental design, the equivalent time-samples design, employs two

equivalent measurements, one when the experimental variable is present and another when it is not, and then repeats the sequence. This design diagrams as follows:

$$X_1 \quad O \quad X_0 \quad O \quad X_1 \quad O \quad X_0 \quad O$$

This type of design is particularly useful where the effect of the experimental treatment is expected to be of transient or reversible character (e.g., library instruction, environmental conditions within the library, and so on.). This arrangement is relatively high on internal validity but low on external validity because of the effects of multiple treatment interference.

3. **The Pretest-Posttest Nonequivalent Control Group Design**. This multiple-group design has some of the features of the static-group comparison and the one-group pretest-posttest design. As can be seen from the following diagram, it provides pretest information and a comparison group, but the groups are not fully matched or randomly assigned and thus cannot be assumed to be equivalent.

$$\begin{array}{ccc}
\text{Group 1} & O_1 & X & O_3 \\
\hline
\text{Group 2} & O_2 & & O_4
\end{array}$$

(The comparison group would be selected for its similarity to the experimental group, however.) Its major advantage over the static group comparison is that one can measure preexisting differences between the groups. It is widely used in educational research.

4. **The Multiple Time-Series Design**. A second multiple-group, quasi-experimental design is the multiple time-series design. It is the multiple-group counterpart of the time-series design and could be diagrammed thus:

$$\begin{array}{ccccccccc}
\text{Group 1} & O_1 & O_2 & O_3 & O_4 & X & O_5 & O_6 & O_7 & O_8 \\
\hline
\text{Group 2} & O_1 & O_2 & O_3 & O_4 & & O_5 & O_6 & O_7 & O_8
\end{array}$$

Assuming that the groups were exposed to the same historical conditions, this design should control for the effects of history. It is considered to be a useful design for conducting research in schools.

Ex Post Facto Designs

Ex post facto designs represent a weaker type of quasi-experimental design. They are designed to simulate real experimentation by using a static-group type comparison such as

$$\begin{array}{cc}
X & O \\
\hline
& O
\end{array}$$

to accomplish a pre-X equation of groups by matching on pre-X characteristics *after* the members of the groups have experienced the experimental variable. Perhaps, for example, one has assumed the directorship of a library soon after the library gave some sort of library instruction to all first-year English students. It might be tempting to try to determine whether the library skills of those students were better than those of other first-year students not given library instruction. The experimental group, those students who received library instruction, is in effect already established. In order to *simulate* a real experiment, the librarian must attempt to establish a comparison group of students equivalent to those in the "experimental group." It would be necessary, therefore, to identify students comparable to those students who had received library instruction. The librarian must try to match the two groups of students on every relevant trait, such as previous training in library skills. As Mouly states, "this is experimentation in reverse, and it is very difficult to match subjects on enough variables to rule out other influences."[16] The researcher has no control over events that have already occurred and can never be certain how many factors might have been involved.

In spite of the fact that quite a few significant studies have employed ex post facto analysis, such designs are considered to be quite weak. Yet they sometimes represent the only feasible approach for investigating a particular question. Specific types of ex post facto analysis include case studies and the so-called causal-comparative studies.

Web-Based Experiments

Web-based or Internet-based experiments are becoming more common, especially in some of the social sciences. This technique allows researchers to collect large amounts of data from widely dispersed people and locations at minimal cost. On the other hand, Web-based experiments have relatively weak internal controls and thus are not well suited for the conduct of true experiments. One good resource for designing a Web experiment can be found at http://wextor.org.[17] This free tool guides the researcher through the process of creating the customized Web pages needed for an experiment. Additional information about the methodology of Web-based experiments can be found in a 2007 article by Reips.[18]

SUMMARY

Experimental research is generally considered to be the most rigorous of the basic research methods. Unlike historical and survey methods, experimental research is considered capable of supporting causal relationships. It is able to do so primarily because, at least in the case of true experiments, it employs equivalent comparison groups, permits manipulation of the experimental variable, and controls alternative causes of the dependent variable. Experimental methods can be used to examine questions such as the effect of certain types of resources on the success of reference transactions, the effect of changes in facilities on user behavior, and users' reactions to certain characteristics of reference staff.

Experimental studies have been criticized for being artificial and for not reflecting real-life situations. However, designs, other than true experimental designs, can be used to allay this problem. One of these alternatives, the preexperimental design, is the weakest type of experimental design, but it is higher in external validity. The second alternative, the quasi-experimental design, represents a compromise between preexperiments, which are low in internal validity, and true experiments, which are high in internal validity. Stated somewhat differently, it is a compromise between maximizing internal validity and external validity. It is a good choice of design when a natural setting must be used, when random assignment of subjects is not feasible, and when the independent or experimental variable cannot be manipulated fully (e.g., when the independent variable represents a demographic variable or a process of natural selection).

There are an almost unlimited number of quasi-experimental designs; the researcher is not restricted to those already developed by others but may create his or her own. The amount of control built into a quasi-experimental design can vary, but it is almost always less than that of true experimental designs. Consequently, the results of quasi-experimental designs tend to be more subject to incorrect interpretation.

NOTES

1. Claire Selltiz, Lawrence S. Wrightsman, and Stuart W. Cook, *Research Methods in Social Relations*, rev. ed. (New York: Holt, Rinehart & Winston, 1959), 80.

2. James A. Anderson, *Communication Research: Issues and Methods* (New York: McGraw-Hill, 1987), 9.

3. Herbert Goldhor, *An Introduction to Scientific Research in Librarianship* (Urbana: University of Illinois, Graduate School of Library Science, 1972), 87.

4. Ibid.

5. Earl R. Babbie, *The Practice of Social Research*, 12th ed. (Belmont, CA: Wadsworth/Cengage Learning, 2010), 240.

6. Louise H. Kidder, *Research Methods in Social Relations*, 4th ed. (New York: Holt, Rinehart & Winston, 1981), 447.

7. Donald T. Campbell and Julian C. Stanley, *Experimental and Quasi-Experimental Designs for Research* (Chicago: Rand McNally, 1963), 5.

8. Babbie, *Practice of Social Research 2010*, 242.

9. Rick H. Hoyle, Monica J. Harris, and Charles M. Judd, *Research Methods in Social Relations*, 7th ed. (Fort Worth, TX: Wadsworth/Thomson Learning, 2002), 32.

10. Campbell and Stanley, *Experimental and Quasi-Experimental Designs*, 5.

11. Ibid., 16.

12. Geoffrey Keppel, *Design and Analysis: A Researcher's Handbook*, 4th ed. (Upper Saddle River, NJ: Prentice Hall, 2004).

13. John W. Creswell, *Research Design: Qualitative, Quantitative, and Mixed Methods Approaches*, 3rd ed. (Thousand Oaks, CA: Sage, 2009), 157.

14. Campbell and Stanley, *Experimental and Quasi-Experimental Designs*, 12.

15. Hoyle, Harris, and Judd, *Research Methods in Social Relations*, 126.

16. George J. Mouly, *Educational Research: The Art and Science of Investigation* (Boston: Allyn and Bacon, 1978), 257.

17. Ulf-Dietrich Reips, Thomas Blumer, and Christoph Neuhaus, "Wexstor: Ten Steps to your Experimental Design," http://wextor.org/wextor/en/.

18. Ulf-Dietrich Reips, "The Methodology of Internet-Based Experiments," in *The Oxford Handbook of Internet Psychology*, ed. Adam N. Joinson, Katelyn McKenna Tom Postmes, and Ulf-Dietrich Reips (Oxford: Oxford University Press, 2007), 373–90.

Chapter 7

Qualitative Research Methods*

Lynn Westbrook

The theories and techniques associated with the naturalistic paradigm and qualitative research methods have become accepted enough to engender a political, ideological, and even economic backlash.[1] Despite recent efforts to deny the value of qualitative work, it continues to pervade modern sociological research production.[2] Library and information science (LIS) research makes substantial use of this approach to address complex questions, such as those associated with human-information interaction. This chapter reviews the following elements: the underlying principles of naturalistic work, ethical concerns, data gathering techniques, data analysis tools and methods, developing grounded theory, ensuring analytic integrity, and the presentation of findings.

Raya Fidel's excellent "guided tour through the world of such research"[3] provides an invaluable context for information scholars considering the use of these methods. She cites exemplary studies throughout, but they are representative rather than exhaustive. For a taxonomic, annotated bibliography of qualitative studies in LIS as well as detailed discussions of primary data gathering and data analysis techniques as they are applied in information settings, see Gorman and Clayton's *Qualitative Research for the Information Professional*.[4]

UNDERLYING PRINCIPLES OF NATURALISTIC WORK

In virtually every area of LIS research, from system design to user-education evaluation, the series of factors that finally lead a user to an interaction with some part of an information system is increasingly complex. Naturalistic work seeks

*This chapter is a revised and expanded version of Lynn Westbrook, "Qualitative Research Methods: A Review of Major Stages, Data Analysis Techniques, and Quality Controls," *Library & Information Science Research* 16, no. 3 (1994): 241–54. It is presented by permission of Elsevier Publishing. The author is grateful to the editors, Professor Glynn Harmon, and Professor Phillip Doty for their feedback on this chapter as it developed.

out all aspects of that complexity on the grounds that they are essential to understanding the behavior of which they are a part. The values and context inherent in every human activity are posited as necessary to any analysis.[5] The flexibility and sensitivity of the human instrument are critical to understanding this complexity, but rigorous efforts are required to make effective use of those qualities.

The critical realism approach provides additional insights, positing that both the physical and conceptual (a.k.a., "material" and "ideational") components of reality are essential to understanding and, eventually, improving the human condition. This "critical reality" perspective builds from a philosophical foundation in that it requires research to explain the human condition more holistically than can be done by naïve realism's focus on the material (a.k.a., "positivism"). Critical realism asserts that the separation of the physical and conceptual is impossible in human activity, thereby denying the strictly stratified or dual approach to understanding individuals, societies, and interactions between the two.[6]

Naturalism as a Research Paradigm

When defined as a research paradigm, rather than as a research method, naturalism is an approach that posits reality as holistic, based in the perceptions of individuals and communities, and continually changing. Theory formation requires an organic, continuous process designed to understand phenomena rather than to test hypotheses. The research goal centers on understanding, discovering, and explaining rather than on predicting or testing.

Critical theory underpins many aspects of qualitative research that developed from the Marxist approach to social research by pushing for wide analytic lenses that more fully account for the social, cultural, political, and economic complexities of modern society. The drive to mitigate or even dissolve social injustice underpins the choice of research questions, methodology, and analysis.[7] The constructivist approach to making those choices asserts that individuals and groups actually construct reality which can, therefore, be properly understood only from the perspective of the context in which they function.[8]

Feminist theory, for example, builds from the following premises: (a) that the role of women is inherently worth study (e.g., fully including women in studies of health information); (b) that women are not merely victims of patriarchal systems or individual men (e.g., deliberately seeking out the ways in which domestic violence survivors assert or protect their independence); (c) that women's experiences, not scholarly consensus, should generate research questions about women; (d) that research on women should benefit women, not just men; and (e) that the critical theory and reflexive approaches to deliberate, thoughtful use of the human instrument as a subjective and critical component of research design improve on the artificial and inaccurate effort to maintain an objectivity that actually undermines both rigor and accuracy.[9]

The basic premises underlying the naturalistic paradigm (e.g., research is not politically or morally neutral, methods are determined by research questions, the scientific method is one means–not the sole means–of adding to knowledge) are under systemic attack in several recent publications by social conservatives.[10] Responses to these critiques point out that the political, governmental, and social forces of the past decade have encouraged other politically motivated policies in multiple arenas. They note, for example, the emphasis on teaching creationism (a.k.a., "intelligent design"), the refutation of global warming studies, and the general refusal to incorporate unpalatable facts into policy making (e.g., the 9/11 attacks were not instigated by Iraq) as part of a systemic approach to research and the use of data in the U.S. government. When a politically conservative ideology drives government-funded research, then qualitative research is underfunded and even actively decried. From this political perspective, the bias of qualitative work generates an emphasis on alternative voices, support for social justice studies, and resistance against straightforward solutions to complex problems, therefore the inevitably invalid results obviously prohibit any significant funding.[11]

Certainly the extremes of the naturalistic paradigm stir debate. Critics assert that qualitative researchers' understanding and description of people are generally limited to those with whom they have a political or ethical sympathy, commonly those people who have been in some way discriminated against or socially oppressed.[12] Some qualitative work deliberately refuses to analyze or question the perspectives of marginalized populations to the same degree that it examines the perspectives of those with higher social status on the grounds that the former have such experiential validity that their view is inviolable, while the latter's views are inherently suspect.[13] Qualitative work that relies entirely or heavily on interviews lacks the context of action and observable behaviors that are commonly identified as the justification for eschewing the large, random samples available via the survey method.[14] Taking the premise that all individuals construct their own socially rooted realities, some qualitative scholars working from standpoint epistemology may insist that directly contradictory accounts carry similar weight or import as a result of their equal truth and accuracy.[15] Standpoint epistemology may, for example, require judging both domestic abuse survivors' narratives and their abusers' narratives as equally accurate, social and personal constructions of an assault.

Naturalism in LIS Research

The naturalistic paradigm only recently has been accepted in the applied or "professional" schools.

> The professional schools of social work ... and information studies have always lagged behind the academic disciplines in accepting new theoretical and methodological trends. ... Because of their marginal position, people in these fields tend to be conservative—the imitators rather than the innovators.[16]

Nevertheless, resultant theories (such as Mellon's "library anxiety")[17] and major studies[18] have opened the doors for qualitative work in LIS[19] to such an extent that the critical focus is on the quality rather than the method of these studies, as has always been the case with quantitative works. With almost 20 percent of high-profile journal articles classed as qualitative and almost 16 percent classed as a mixture of both quantitative and qualitative, no significant shift in the balance of LIS methodologies appears.[20]

An exemplary wellspring of literally hundreds of qualitatively based studies in information seeking is the extensive work of Brenda Dervin. Her sense-making approach to understanding communication, decision making, and information-seeking behaviors provides a sound theoretical basis for a great deal of LIS research.[21]

In any research setting, the research problem determines the research approach and the choice of methods. No single approach fits every problem; a reasoned choice must be made. The direct continuity between research question and research design is essential and requires, therefore, clear explanation.[22] In LIS, qualitative research is usually most useful when the information-interactions concerns are so new, so complex, or so unexplored that researchers are working to understand the cognitive, affective, and behavioral aspects of the phenomenon. If enough is known of an area to sustain a priori patterning, hypothesis formation, or even theory explication, then the positivist approach with its more quantitative methods might be used. If so little is known of an area that the simple identification of what is not known becomes problematic, then an effective application of the naturalistic approach with its more qualitative methods provides valuable insight. In between these two extremes lie a range of mixed methods approaches.

Role of Mixed/Multi Method Research

Of course, in many research situations a reasoned, effective combination of the positivist and naturalist approaches provides the most complete or insightful understanding. Using the positivist approach for segments of a research problem that support hypothesis testing and the naturalistic approach for areas that are yet to be so well understood, for example, can maximize the benefits of both approaches. Given the rapidly changing environment of LIS work, this positivist/naturalist decision requires a focus on what best answers the research problem. Still relatively rare in LIS research, most social science scholars accept mixed-methods work as an addition to their paradigmatic tool kit.[23]

A mixed-methods or multi-methods approach, in some cases, provides the necessary array of data.[24] The mixed-methods approach posits as a false dichotomy the absolute, forced choice of either qualitative or quantitative methods. Sometimes considered the third paradigm, the mixed-methods' deliberate recognition of a full spectrum of externally and internally realized phenomena speaks to, for example, usability testing in LIS.[25] Conceptualizing methods as exploratory or confirmatory, rather than as qualitative or quantitative, supports the deliberate and effective combination of methods.[26]

Four basic principles guide mixed method design:

1. Determine and adhere to the theoretical impetus underpinning the project.
2. Work to account for the impact of the method that is brought into the primary methodological thrust.
3. Drive the design decisions from the assumptions of the base method.
4. Employ only the essential data sets.[27]

These principles encourage the meshing or linking of methods, which is more appropriate than integrating them because it encourages a more thoughtful and deliberate approach to building from the strengths of different methods as they relate to research questions.[28]

Starting from the purpose of the study and moving on to delineate specific research questions, scholars who employ multiple-methods approaches gain particular clarity from remembering the impetus behind their original planning. The nine broad research purposes include: predicting; adding to existing knowledge; impacting on a personal, institutional, or social level; measuring change; understanding phenomena; testing new ideas, approaches, solutions, or hypotheses; generating new ideas, approaches, solutions, or hypotheses; informing stakeholders, participants, and other constituents; and examining the past.[29]

ETHICAL CONCERNS

As in any research involving human beings, a number of ethical concerns demand careful attention. (See Chapter 3 also for consideration of ethical concerns.) Naturalistic settings compound the usual issues of participant confidentiality and harmless involvement. University and grant-funding sources' human subject review committees (institutional review boards) usually consider both of these issues, but qualitative researchers must take particular responsibility for them when no outside review is required.[30]

Participant confidentiality, rather than participant anonymity, generally dominates in qualitative research. The face-to-face involvement of interviews, general observation, focus groups, and participant observation preclude any pretense of participant anonymity. Even written documents, such as questionnaires and journals, can contain such revealing information that identification of some participants is relatively easy. Therefore, the goal of confidentiality becomes crucial. Using pseudonyms, removing identifying details, and keeping careful records, the researcher does everything possible to ensure that the participants will never be identified to anyone outside of the study team.

This confidentiality is just as important for information-seekers as it is for any other population. They have an absolute right to their privacy within the context of the study. People may reveal illegal or immoral behaviors, such as plagiarism, copyright infringement, or theft of library materials. They may reveal gaps or weaknesses in their knowledge, understanding, or appreciation of the fundamentals of information-seeking; that revelation may imperil their status in the workplace or home. For example, junior faculty could find their tenure status jeopardized by public revelation of their inability to manage the information of their discipline. Therefore, confidentiality must be rigorously protected.

The consent form that many participants must sign should spell out the mechanisms by which that confidentiality will be protected and the extent to which it will be breached. For example, if a transcription service is hired to handle taped interviews, then someone outside the study team will be hearing the tapes. The schedule for destruction of notes, tapes, computer files, and other records should be included.

Informed consent becomes problematic when dealing with populations that have limitations on effective implementation of their free choice (e.g., the illiterate, those who do not easily speak the same language as the researcher, and those who are commonly subjected to external authority rather than allowed to make their own choices, such as children) and research questions in which the extent of the information elicited is so uncertain that participants might be surprised by what emerges.[31]

Harmless involvement is the second ethical issue to consider. While confidentiality is meant to ensure that participants are not harmed by the revelation of their studied words or actions, this issue refers to any harm that might ensue as a result of simply participating in the study. For example, in a study of the differing levels of reference accuracy between support staff and librarians, it would be necessary to consider patron involvement. It would not be unreasonable to assume that patrons whose complex reference questions are answered only by support staff would be "harmed" to the extent that their questions would be less accurately answered than they might have been.

An ethical and trustworthiness issue arises regularly in life history work and it is inherent in most face-to-face qualitative work, namely the balance point between supporting participant revelation and shaping that revelation. In some cases "participants want to feel that they are being understood and that what they say holds special meaning for the researcher."[32] Researchers must balance or carefully move between states of intentional listening, with all the deliberate use of follow-up questions such listening requires, and immersion in the participant's tale, with all the potential for personal connection and validation that such immersed action can generate.

Even those who do not participate in the study may be affected by it. They might hesitate to approach an online public access catalog (OPAC) that prominently displays a sign indicating that those who use the system will have their searches logged and studied. They may choose to do without help or information rather than risk becoming involved in a study.

Feminist research raises ethical concerns from a political and social perspective. Feminist research is rooted in attention to the power dynamics of sex and gender with full awareness of the interplay of power dynamics in race, ethnicity, politics, economics, culture, and education.[33] Postcolonial, postmodern, and transnational approaches to these examinations of power dynamics have pushed discussions among all qualitative researchers, whether they self-identify as feminist or not, of the ethical dilemmas inherit in establishing rapport, providing reciprocity, and being open to empathy between researcher and participant. At what point does a sort of emotional exploitation occur? At what point is rapport disingenuous?[34] These questions become particularly critical in participatory action research in which the researcher contextualizes efforts to contribute to solutions of real-world problems by immersing and actively participating in the contexts of the problems, partnering with those whose lives are impacted by and enmeshed in the problems.[35]

Whether imposing definitions or encouraging participants to self-define their race, ethnicity, culture, or sexual orientation, researchers must be sensitive to the social, political, economic, and situational factors which influence all such categorization efforts.[36] Historical and cultural studies require decisions about who speaks for a period or for a culture and how those determinations are made. Who is included as "representative," and why are others excluded? Finally, is the material shared by those who are heard a matter of "personal or public" history?[37]

Balancing the possible benefits of the study against the possible harm to the participants requires minimizing the latter and maximizing the former. Research questions and data analyses that focus primarily on the "deficits" of a particular community or population may well lack the premise of "fairness" demanded by any ethical standard. Focusing on deficits can minimize strengths, reinforcing biases and creating an unbalanced picture of the phenomenon in question.[38] The impact of narrative, participant-directed interviewing in which participants are encouraged to share their stories of difficult situations requires particular ethical consideration. While sharing difficult narratives can be empowering, cathartic, and even affirming for some, it requires interviewers who respect both the disturbing content and potentially negative consequences for participants who, essentially, relive traumatic times in their lives.[39] Since very few information-seeking situations involve actual physical or significant psychological harm to individuals, most studies are able to manage research ethics with the application of careful analysis.[40]

Contrasting consequential ethics and nonconsequential ethics provides a framework for many LIS decisions in the field. Consequential ethics argue that the results of an act determine its ethical value. That is, good consequences outweighing harmful consequences are the hallmark of an ethical act. The problem for qualitative researchers following this approach is that determining the consequences in advance is almost impossible, much less determining how each participant would analyze the balance of good and harm on a personal level.[41] Nonconsequential ethics argue that consequences are not the determinant of ethical actions but rather principles (e.g., honesty), the Kantian maxim (act such that the maxim of the action might become universal law), or rules (e.g., confidentiality will not be broken).[42] Qualitative researchers employing nonconsequential ethics use abstracts as their guide while simultaneously striving to fully respect those study participants most immediately affected by their ethical stance. Consider the following example. While studying information behaviors of medical researchers, a qualitative researcher realizes that two faculty members at different institutions are working on opposite halves of the same puzzle and could probably generate more productive cancer research if they knew of each other's work. The consequential ethics perspective would push the researcher to break all confidentiality bonds by informing the two of each other's work in the expectation that global good could result from an earlier and more complete piece of cancer research. The nonconsequential ethics perspective could push the researcher to maintain confidentiality without reference to the preferences of the participants or the needs of cancer patients in general.

DATA GATHERING TECHNIQUES

The act of gathering data for a qualitative study is an evolving process rooted in ongoing analysis. It involves more than obtaining discrete units of information. Simply holding a preset number of interviews, for example, does not constitute meaningful data gathering. Instead, the researcher engages in reiterative, cyclical movement between data gathering and data analysis. Initial interviews might well, for example, spark a tentative point of analysis that would then be fed back into the interview protocol. The next interviews, by virtue of that tentative data analysis effort, would be somewhat deeper than their predecessors. Thus data gathering is envisioned as a process rather than a procedure; it requires analytic judgment rather than a preplanned routine. "Design remains flexible throughout the study because you have to work out questions to examine new ideas and themes that emerge during [data gathering]."[43]

That is not to imply that qualitative data gathering lacks planning and preparation. In addition to the exercise of thoughtful judgment during the process, the researcher must exercise care in planning two crucial elements: sampling and data gathering techniques, both of which are discussed below.

Finally, although this forum does not allow extensive discussion of the point, it must be noted that almost all data gathering is, to some extent, socially constructed. The interaction between two or more people is created within the social contexts of the individuals involved. Their contact involves factors that are beyond the control of the researcher and the participants, such as their race, age, sex, gender, socioeconomic class, and more. Those factors influence the rapport, trust, and honesty of both parties. The hierarchical nature of the research relationship means that the participant is often in a subordinate position.[44] The impact of those factors on a constructed, hierarchical relationship and on decisions regarding both ethics and data integrity must not be underestimated.

Sampling

No single formula provides the "correct" sample size for a qualitative study. The depth, complexity, and "richness" of the data are critical, but identifying a representative sample is not even a consideration since the purpose of the research is to understand, not to generalize. The two criteria for determining the right number of interview participants are sufficiency and saturation. Sufficiency refers to the effort to include all the subpopulations involved. Researchers should include two or more participants in demographic categories (e.g., race, gender, age), contextual subgroups (e.g., first-year, sophomore, junior, and senior high school students), and locations (e.g., on-site and remote-site workers).[45] Saturation refers to the point at which the critical elements of the study have become "saturated," i.e., until further exemplars fail to add new nuance or to contradict what is understood. For example, in a study of the reasons behind library anxiety among first-semester doctoral history students at a major research university, a researcher might interview ten of the forty-member population, choosing those ten carefully to include as many known variables among participants as possible such as race, sex, and area of study. If participants eight through ten yielded no new information, then there would be little point in insisting on a larger sample.

The standard of saturation will not, however, answer all questions regarding sample size. A second key factor must be involved, namely the nature of the research question being asked. Consider again the question of library anxiety among doctoral history students.

1. A phenomenological study might seek to understand the nature of the anxiety as felt by those students. In that case, the researcher needs

only a small sample (five to eight), but each person must be studied in great depth.

2. An ethnographic study might seek to describe the in-library behavior of those students. The researcher would, therefore, need a larger sample of the student population (15 to 20) plus some data from those who interact with the students, such as reference librarians and circulation staff.

3. A grounded theory study might seek to describe the social and psychological processes that those with library anxiety go through in their use of the library. The researcher would again need a larger sample (15 to 20), although it would consist only of the students themselves.[46]

In each case, the nature of the research question affects the sample size.

Related to saturation and the nature of the research question, a third element is required in each sampling decision, namely the purpose of the first sample. "In purposeful sampling, members of the sample are deliberately chosen based on criteria that have relevance to the research question rather than criteria of randomness of selection."[47] Rather than planning "the sample," the researcher might think of "the first sample." Since the sample is used to gather data which immediately undergo initial analysis, there is always the possibility that something will be learned which changes the study parameters. In that case, the first sample may be adjusted, augmented, enlarged or otherwise modified to meet the new parameters. This multistage approach to sampling requires that a decision be made about the purpose of the first sample.

The most common sampling techniques in qualitative studies follow the thread of "purpose." Rather than the probabilistic sampling of a positivist approach, the naturalist approach starts with a purpose for working with one type of participant rather than with another. In LIS research, the following methods may be most useful:

1. Maximum variety sampling. This method seeks as heterogeneous a sample as possible and is useful when seeking to identify patterns and commonalities that exist across otherwise divergent individuals.[48] This is analogous to the classic, experimental sampling technique known as "stratified random sampling" in that population variables are identified, as much as possible, in advance so that a deliberate effort can be made to maximize heterogeneity.

2. Extreme case sampling. This method selects participants who appear to "exemplify characteristics of interest"[49] in order to clarify the critical issues in an area. For example, those who experience severe cases of library anxiety might be interviewed and observed to help identify key factors in that issue.

3. Intensity sampling. This technique identifies participants who have a great deal of experience (rather than an extreme experience) with a phenomenon.[50] For example, in a study of reference librarians' use of tagging Web sites for research purposes, those who have used this technique for a substantial period would be selected over novices when taking an intensity sample.

4. Snowball sampling. This method identifies participants who are linked through shared experiences, perspectives, or other factors. Participants point the researcher towards other individuals in the same population. People who use library computer labs to play forbidden, group-based, computer games might be identified through snowball sampling.

Subsets of purposive sampling used in life history work include each of the previous methods as well as the critical case technique in which participants are chosen on the basis of specific critical incidents that pertain to the phenomena in action, even if those incidents are rare.[51]

Several other purposive sampling techniques are available to the researcher including opportunistic, convenience, criterion, operational construct, and combination techniques.[52] When integrated with the concept of saturation and a clear idea of the nature of the research question, the techniques provide several viable options. (For more on sampling, see Chapter 4.)

Finally, the use of a single or extremely limited set of cases can prove fruitful in specific circumstances. Case studies are particularly useful when examining policy implications, program impact, or complex but limited communities.[53] In addition to gathering baseline factual data (e.g., number of instances or individuals, duration of phenomena, funding levels), the primary work in a case study comes from seeking to identify the key issues (e.g., barriers and supports for information literacy), the stakeholders and actors (e.g., undergraduates and their faculty), and their experiences, belief systems, expectations, mental models, and values.[54] The former is generally susceptible to planning, but the latter may require emergent design in which data are gathered when the opportunity presents.[55] Case studies typically entail the use of several data gathering techniques since their primary value is in their depth rather than their potential for generalizability. Mixed and/or triangulated methods, participants, and data formats foster enriched data analysis by providing multiple perspectives on complex matters.[56]

Observation

Observation is a broad category of data gathering in which the naturalistic researcher must choose a point of balance between observing and participating. Carefully documented watching and/or listening may be augmented with judicious interviewing and the collection of artifacts.[57] The real-time work in a natural setting requires researchers to practice a high degree of flexible anticipation of the unexpected.[58] LIS scholars have made good use of participant observation for some time.[59]

A potentially effective means of deepening the field's understanding of human behavior, observation requires careful efforts to prepare, gather data, respect participants, and analyze date. Researchers are expected to:

1. Use the extant research literature as one means of providing background, insight, and questions.
2. Gain access to a community with integrity.

3. Choose a sample which most effectively addresses the research questions.

4. Deliberately identify and follow a chosen researcher role.

5. Document data collection with care, detail, and reflection.

6. Thoughtfully meet all ethical obligations, particularly those which are unexpected.

7. Leave the field ethically.

8. Analyze the resulting data accurately, honestly, and fully.[60]

A casual or ad hoc approach to observation can impinge on people's lives, adding to the standard, scholarly obligations to maintain rigorous quality control criteria.

Employing observation requires decisions on two points, the researcher's role and the use of additional data. First, there are four different positions on a continuum of roles that researchers play when using the observation technique: complete participant, participant-as-observer, observer-as-participant, and complete observer.[61] This variety allows use of whatever perspective will best answer the research question[62] thereby providing a "here-and-now experience in depth."[63] Much observation includes some degree of questioning, perhaps even formal interviewing, as well as incorporation of artifacts such as papers, search records, or journals.[64]

The primary advantage of observation is the opportunity it provides to determine how well the observed and self-reported data match. Verifying that people are doing what they think and/or report they are doing can often be accomplished through observation.[65] Observation can also help counter the ill effects of time order, history, and maturation.[66]

Although only unobtrusive observation in the natural setting, with all its attendant ethical and logistical difficulties, can negate the impact of the observer on the observed, much can be accomplished through properly conducted general observation. As much as possible, the point of observation is to understand what occurs without introducing new stimuli or manipulating the participants.[67] Of necessity, in some settings or with some research questions, the observation must be highly structured. In every case, however, the researcher works to slip into the natural setting with minimal impact on the participants.[68]

Focusing the observational field starts with a review of the full setting and narrows to those phenomena most central to the research question.[69] The observer considers activities, attitudes, and relationships in all their variation[70] through multiple observations.[71]

The setting and purpose determine the observation structure and format. Anything from stationing a video camera in front of the reference desk to blending in as a parent at a storytelling session could constitute observation. (In every case the ethical concerns mentioned earlier must be carefully addressed.) For much LIS research, the setting varies along the following four continua:

1. Number of participants—e.g., settings can be crowded (as in a busy branch library) or sparsely populated (as in a quiet map library).

2. Public vs. private—e.g., settings can be as public as a reference desk or as private as a professor's office.

3. Size of the observable actions—e.g., settings can be limited to small actions, such as keyboard motions, or they can focus on large actions, such as routes taken through the library building.

4. Staff or public—e.g., settings can involve library staff, the public, or some combination thereof.

The choice of observation techniques depends on the setting and purpose of the research. An ethnographic approach requires moving into the setting as deeply as possible while disturbing the participants as little as possible. Participant observation of the use of self-revelation by reference staff, for example, would require the researcher to appear as a patron to the librarians under study. Unobtrusive observation in a public setting requires the researcher to fade quietly and naturally into the surroundings. Unobtrusive observation can be disguised (researcher becomes part of the community while hiding the research), field-based (researcher manipulates a setting or situation in order to observe behaviors), or indirect (researcher "observes" the artifacts or traces of behavior); reactive observation (direct or structured) can be continuous monitoring (observation that continues constantly for a set period of time) or spot sampling (selective observations taken over a period of time); participant observation involves open, direct interaction and observation as part of the group.[72] Observing the instances of peer instruction at OPACs in a school library would require the researcher to sustain a believable, probable, unobtrusive activity near the terminals. Obtrusive observation requires the researcher to build enough rapport with the participant(s) to overcome the natural reactions that anyone might have to the activity. Observing the search strategies employed on Google searches among a group of corporate librarians, for example, would require the researcher to develop a relationship with each individual which is informal enough to promote easy conversation yet formal enough to reinforce the nonjudgmental nature of the interaction.

The continuum of participation includes seven levels ranging from none at all (e.g., analyzing artifacts of human behavior), to passive, to observation-focused work (i.e., the engaged stranger whose interest is clear), to moderate membership (e.g., selective participation in the minor aspects of the community's activities), to active membership (e.g., fuller participation in the community without fully sharing their values, norms, or beliefs), to complete participation (i.e., full participation in the community), and finally to complete membership (i.e., accepted into the group as a full partner in decision making and activity).[73]

Interviews

In all their variety, interviews are a valuable qualitative method for researchers who make effective choices along the continuum between structured and unstructured interviews.

> The structured interview is the mode of choice when the interviewer *knows what he or she does not know* and can therefore frame appropriate questions to find it out, while the unstructured interview is the mode of choice when the interviewer *does not know what he or she doesn't know* and must therefore rely on the respondent to tell him or her.[74]

Other choices can be made among common interview formats including critical incident interviews (taking place at the end of an event, such as an online search), in-depth interviews (often taking place over the course of an hour or more), and focus group interviews.[75] (The critical incident technique is useful in LIS for understanding key information interactions and generally includes three stages: ask participant to recall a specific incident of a particular type; ask for a description of the incident; ask what made it positive or negative.)[76]

Format of the initial data also plays a role in determining the most effective use of interview data. LIS professionals have an established use of online synchronous interviews (chat), online asynchronous interviews (email), and virtual focus groups[77] that can augment or even replace the in-person or telephone interview. Finally, a choice must be made as to the number of people involved in the interview: one, a small group, or a larger group.

Focus groups (see Chapter 5 also) are not an easy means of gathering a large amount of narrative data. Obtaining a representative or purposive sample is much more difficult than gathering a convenience or self-selected sample. Moderating a focus group takes great skill and energy; the resulting tapes and notes are often difficult to transcribe accurately and fully. Nevertheless, focus groups provide two substantive opportunities that must be considered carefully. First, they allow participants to create, develop, explicate, and even moderate their own ideas by stimulating engaged analysis via comparisons and contrasts with other participants. Second, they allow marginalized or low-power individuals to develop a greater sense of rapport, ease, and engagement–with a correspondingly higher degree of revelation–by forming a community within which the skillful moderator must function.[78] An effectively moderated focus group generates a high degree of self-revelation from participants who focus on their own narratives rather than responding solely to a researcher's preset questions.

The researcher guides and even directs the focus of a focus group;[79] this can be done personally or via a properly trained moderator. Even if the intent is for the participants to determine what is discussed, the researcher is responsible, to whatever extent is possible, for ensuring that all views are heard. This requires involving everyone and making sure that the discussion is not dominated by an individual or by a cluster of individuals. If people have been gathered to address a particular phenomenon, then the researcher is responsible for keeping the focus on that topic. These efforts need not undermine the carefully nurtured informality that strengthens trust. Common techniques for building that trust include using an unscripted introduction, responding nonverbally to input, and posing questions in an improvised manner.[80] Broaching complex questions early in the focus group meeting can generate substantive responses from participants; the focus group moderator can respond to such initial answers by calling for clarification, further exploration, and exemplars. Once discussion is well launched on the larger questions, the tighter questions can be slipped in where useful.[81]

Interviewing's primary strength is its ability to range over a time period, thereby capturing more than the single instant of an isolated action.[82] This flexible technique allows the investigator to probe, to clarify, and to create new questions based on what has already been heard. Well conducted, in-depth interviews develop narratives along the lines of most immediacy for the participant while also providing the researcher with the opportunity to include focused questions that fill in gaps, clear up ambiguities, explore new lines of inquiry, and make connections among statements.[83] The thoughtful sequencing of different mechanisms for eliciting information includes the use of direct questions when following up on topics that a participant has identified as critical, silence that allows people the time needed to reflect on a topic, and structured questions to pull an interview back on track.[84]

Interviewing can be quite appealing to the informants even when payment is not employed as an incentive. The opportunity to share experiences with an engaged, responsive, and attentive professional can be rewarding in itself. Additionally, the act of verbalizing experiences and explaining processes can generate insights that are fruitful on a personal or professional level.[85] Finally, the satisfaction of contributing to the larger social good that is inherent in any serious research project can be more immediate and visceral for interview participants who get to meet the researcher.[86]

A set of four questioning techniques strengthens the depth of the resultant data. Comparison questions focus on similarities, while contrast questions focus on differences.[87] Of course, narrative (i.e., focused on stories, anecdotes, the flow of an overall experience) and episodic (i.e., focused on specific, concrete, limited experiences) interviewing techniques encourage human-centered service and resource design in LIS by focusing on client perspectives of information work.[88] Probe questions explore the unknown background of a statement, while clarifying questions elucidate details or factors of a statement in order to further explicate it.[89] Probe questions that follow the main questions could be of the following types:

1. Continuation–follows up on the same participant to elicit more details, complete a train of thought that was interrupted, complete a description; they are open-ended in that they might lead to new topics.

2. Elaboration–solicit further analysis or explanation of a specific point; they are focused in and only add to an area without leading to new topics.

3. Clarification–used to clear up the interviewer's own understanding of the participant's comments; they might involve language, culture, or simply clarification.

4. Steering probes–these are designed to move the interview back into the areas of interest or away from areas that are being avoided.

5. Sequence probes–these are designed to elicit explanations of how phenomena progress in a step-by-step or staged fashion.

6. Evidence probes ask people to explain the basis for their viewpoints, opinions, or beliefs.

7. Slant probes seek to identify, often indirectly, the participant's bias, perspective, world view, or mental model of a phenomenon, group, or situation.[90]

Effective questions are framed so as to build upon the shared understanding, whether personal or cultural,[91] between researcher and participant. That shared understanding can ease participants' concerns regarding ego-threatening questions, their ability to remember certain types of information, and their tendency to generalize.[92] Establishing rapport and the restating of informants' observations are two useful techniques in these more delicate situations.[93]

Digital interviews, when properly used, can 1) be more cost and time efficient to administer and analyze, 2) reach participants not readily reached by other means (e.g., people with limited phone access, disabilities, time constraints, or certain types of social, political, personal, or economic constraints), and 3) encourage full responses from participants who can choose their own time to answer in the setting of their choice after the possibility, at least, of considering the questions they were asked.[94] At their best, these tools can still be limited in their efficacy by 1) a lack of access to people with no, unsafe, or limited Internet access[95] and 2) a lack of immediately asked, probe questions in email interviews.[96] Also, like all text-based data gathering tools, these assume a literacy level that is not always available in all populations. Using these tools effectively requires tactics that focus on the participants' needs, e.g., embedding questions in an email rather than attaching them[97] and clarifying questions with meticulous wording that does not overly limit the responses.

Documents: Questionnaires, Diaries, Journals, Papers, and More

Finally, the written word can be a source of narrative or qualitative data. Materials written by participants diverge in their format, content, and impetus. Since these data sources are well documented elsewhere, this section provides only a general overview.

Questionnaires vary by means of delivery (in-person, telephone, mail, email, WWW, and point-of-contact) and format (open-ended questions, attitudinal scales, multiple choice questions, ratings, and rankings). This is perhaps the most thoroughly studied form of data gathering.

Each means of delivery has its advantages and disadvantages. An in-person questionnaire allows the researcher to clear up any obvious misunderstandings on the spot, but it is time consuming. A telephone questionnaire allows contact with distant participants, but it is difficult to convince people to complete one without advance, written preparation. Mailed questionnaires are relatively simple to conduct, but require significant followup to produce sufficient response rates. (See Fowler for methods of writing such questionnaires and increasing the response rate.)[98] Although they are the bane of digital communities, email and Web-based questionnaires are cheap to conduct; of course, they reach a very limited portion of many populations. Some WWW sites have embedded questionnaires for their users and those are often productive, assuming all users have equal facility in responding, and that individuals do not submit multiple forms. Finally, point-of-contact questionnaires (commonly found in libraries at the reference or circulation desk) are simple and affordable but do limit responses to those who choose to or who can be persuaded to complete the forms on site. Obviously, questionnaires that are deeply embedded in the daily context of the participant are somewhat more likely to generate naturalistic responses than are highly artificial instruments.

The format variations of questionnaires also have their strengths and weaknesses. The use of open-ended questions provides participants with a greater forum for expressing their responses, but it can intimidate those who do not feel comfortable or confident in their answers, do not have the time to devote to the complexities of answering, or do not have a great facility with written or spoken communication in the language used. An extensive literature discusses the use of attitudinal or Likert-type scales, rankings, and ratings. Producing ordinal level data, they are not qualitative techniques at all. Finally, multiple-choice questions can be designed to help participants identify their own answers out of a full range of possible answers. The trick here, of course, is to either provide a "full" range of responses or to sufficiently encourage respondents to write in any additional items.

In addition to questionnaires, participants can sometimes be persuaded to keep written, audio, or visual records of their activities, thoughts, motivations, emotions, and decisions throughout the life of an information-seeking interaction or project. Carol Kuhlthau's early work, for example, involved the use of self-reported, written records from high school students.[99] These documents can provide great depth and detail when participants fully engage in the project. Among their obvious disadvantages are the tendency to reveal only what the participants choose to share with the researcher and the tendency to be incomplete (due to factors such as time, stress, or shame) on those points of extreme difficulty which are often most crucial to the researcher. To minimize these weaknesses, self-reported documents are often used in careful conjunction with other data-gathering techniques. Kuhlthau, for example, included interviews and observations in her research design.[100]

Event sampling provides a variation on this approach that focuses participant attention on the specific areas of most interest to the researcher. In this situation "participants are asked to monitor and describe ongoing activity according to schedules and formats defined and regulated by the investigator."[101] By getting people to explicate what just happened to them, investigators minimize distortions of memory and retrospection. Obviously, the question under review must center on discrete, defined events or moments so that such recording effort becomes reasonable and recall efforts are relatively straightforward.

Finally, the naturally generated end products of various information interactions can be obtained for research purposes. For example, the I-Search paper is a fairly common format among high school and college populations in which students report the problems and solutions encountered during the information search, as well as the more traditional information on the topic at hand. Those papers lack the artificial nature of a research-induced diary but do include all the self-reported problems of an assigned, course-related document. They can be particularly revealing when combined with interviews.

DATA ANALYSIS TOOLS AND METHODS

Two principles of qualitative data analysis recur in virtually all descriptions of it. First, analysis is an ongoing process that feeds back into the research design right up to the last moment of data gathering. Second, whatever theory, model, or working hypothesis eventually develops must grow naturally from the data analysis rather than standing to the side as an a priori statement that the data will affirm or repute.

Because its purpose is to understand rather than to predict, qualitative research requires a cyclical approach in which the collection of data affects the analysis of the data which, in turn, affects the gradual formation of theory which, in turn, affects the further collection of data. This integration of data collection and analysis is central to qualitative work.[102] The coding of observed behavior exemplifies most immediately the interplay of data gathering and data analysis because the very act of choosing rudimentary coding terms refocuses the mental lens with which people are viewed.[103]

Discourse Analysis

Presently, the majority of LIS qualitative work seeks to understand populations within their information-interaction contexts; a key subset of this work employs discourse analysis. Working from a more sociological perspective these scholars eschew the constant comparison approach to content analysis in favor of a focus on "knowledge formations, which organize institutional practices and societal reality on a large scale."[104] Discourse analysis, developed by Michel Foucault, has the "capacity to track historically the origins of and challenges to mainstream ideas and to illustrate marginalized ideas" through an open, conceptualized process of discovery that centers on analysis of power dynamics.[105]

Discourse analysis can be linguistically or culturally based. The purpose of linguistic-based discourse analysis is "to gauge the efficacy of linguistic exchanges aimed at accomplishing particular objectives." The purpose of culture/social-based discourse analysis is "to study the circuitous routes taken by what is said [and how it] refutes, borrows, opposes, adopts, manipulates, ignores, appropriates, and buries what has been said." Both approaches have value in LIS by providing us with new ways to examine, understand, identify facets of, and question the interactions between practitioners and clients as well as between information organizations and the society in which they function.[106] This approach is still in development within LIS.

Content Analysis Basics

One of the most commonly used data analysis techniques of qualitative research, content analysis "uses a set of procedures to make valid inferences from text. These inferences are about the sender(s) of the message, the message itself, or the audience of the message."[107] Content analysis is based on the premise that the many words from interviews, observations and documents can be reduced to, or organized into, categories in which words or word units (e.g., paragraphs) share the same central meaning or connotation. Content analysis is applied in qualitative, quantitative, and mixed-methods studies.[108] Data in text, image, or mixed formats that are appropriate for content analysis require "cohesion, intentionality, acceptability, informativity, situationality, and intertextuality."[109]

The classification procedure that is used to accomplish this organization or reduction must be consistent so that anyone with training and the requisite coding documentation (e.g., a coding manual, detailed memos) would get essentially the same results.[110] Data analysis involves "working with data, organizing it, breaking it into manageable units, synthesizing it, searching for patterns, discovering what is important and what is to be learned, and deciding what you will tell others."[111]

Content Analysis Terms

Before exploring the techniques of content analysis, it is necessary to review a few of the basic terms relating directly to coding.

1. A *datum* "is a unit of information that is recorded in a durable medium, distinguishable from other data, analyzable by explicit techniques, and relevant to a particular problem."[112] These units may be any of the following: physical (pages), syntactical (words, sentences, paragraphs), referential (objects, events, persons, acts), propositional (words which are required to conform to a certain structure), and thematic (require a deep understanding of the language).[113]

2. *Categories* organize each datum by grouping it in with others that share similar denotations or connotations.[114]

3. *Themes* then cluster categories that share some commonality, such as reference to a single issue.

Additional terminology is needed to delineate among the various supporting documents that maximize coding fidelity, accuracy, and consistency:

1. *Field notes* contain as much as possible of what the investigator says, experiences, and remembers from being in the field, as well as notes on affective responses to experiences and initial analytic comments.[115] These field or observation notes come in various formats including the following: running notes, field experience logs or diaries, and notes on thematic units.[116] Field notes must be kept in a structured, detailed format that captures as much of the observable data as possible. A common method is to take notes on a stenographic pad with raw notes in the left column and annotations, insights, questions, and comments in the right column.[117] Field notes should answer six essential questions as much as possible, both during and after the data gathering:

   a. What are people doing and/or trying to do?
   b. What are the ways, means, strategies, and tactics they employ to do this?
   c. How do they frame, word, discuss, describe, and conceptualize both what they're doing and how they do it?
   d. What are their explicit and implicit assumptions about both goal and process?
   e. What did the researcher actually observe, and what do the field notes add to an understanding of that observation?
   f. Why were these field notes made and these particular items included?[118]

2. *Memos* are brief, informal essays written by the investigator to capture some part of the coding process that has been inductively recognized. Beginning with the first data gathering and continuing to the final report, memos record the development of the coding schema by noting the reasoning and impetus behind researcher choices on data gathering.[119] Analytic and conceptual, rather than strictly factual, memos highlight insights, questions, possibilities, and reflections on the entire data gathering process.[120]

3. The *coding manual* contains the final results of decisions made on the choice, definition, hierarchy, and relationships of codes. The units of analysis, the elements of classification, and the rules for applying the codes comprise the manual. Carefully written to serve as a record as well as an application tool, the manual will be revised until its application is consistent and meaningful.[121]

The Constant Comparative Method of Content Analysis

The constant comparative method, codified by Glaser and Strauss,[122] is generally recognized as one of the most effective means of qualitative content analysis. It involves joint coding and analysis during the continual review of data to gradually form categories. Originally the constant comparative method was "described in four stages: (1) comparing incidents applicable to each category, (2) integrating categories and their properties, (3) delimiting the theory, and (4) writing the theory."[123] These categories are carefully defined and made mutually exclusive so that relationships can be identified between those elements that fall into the categories. Several cycles of these comparisons[124] gradually delimit the dimensions, boundaries, and relationships of the codes.[125] This method is designed

> to guarantee that two analysts working independently with the same data will achieve the same results; it is designed to allow, with discipline, for some of the vagueness and flexibility that aid the creative generation of theory.[126]

Like other methods, comparative analysis can be used to generate substantive theory and formal theory.[127] Substantive theory refers to specific areas, such as OPAC use and Internet search strategies. Formal theory refers to conceptual areas, such as information-seeking patterns and relevance criteria.

Coding Data

Among the many advantages of coding are that it:

(1) both follows upon and leads to generative questions; (2) fractures the data, thus freeing the researcher from description and forcing interpretation to higher levels of abstraction; (3) is the pivotal operation for moving toward the discovery of a core category or categories; and so (4) moves

toward ultimate integration of the entire analysis; and (5) yields the desired conceptual density (i.e., relationships among the codes and the development of each). . . .[128]

Coding lies at the heart of the constant comparative method in that units of data are compared to each other in terms of their fit into the developing coding scheme. Coding does not descriptively paraphrase the interview or observation notes; instead it identifies the main categories as well as associated subcategories so that, eventually, all units of data can be organized according to these codes.[129] These categories must be pertinent and functional[130] in order to develop the properties of each category, thereby increasing the explanatory power of the resulting analysis.[131]

Immediately following an interview or observation period, the investigator must organize and complete the field notes so that initial analysis can begin.[132] Periods of preliminary data analysis are interpolated between periods of data gathering. This analysis consists, in part, of fleshing out skeletal field notes and reviewing the results to locate any preliminary patterns that might begin to emerge.[133] For example, researchers must take care to value the silences in conversations, interviews, and focus groups. Their connotation, denotation, and meaning are more difficult to code and analyze than words, but strong field notes help researchers fully appreciate the information provided in these silences.[134]

Line-by-line coding constitutes the initial stage of data analysis. When no new codes are generated in new data sets, then the selective coding begins with an effort to focus on refining particularly striking code categories. The resorting of data through these stages builds greater understanding of participants' perspectives, particularly when line-by-line coding is used. Codes are then grouped in categories that move from analytic to conceptual to theoretical. Diagrams, mapping, flowcharts,[135] and mindmaps,[136] help track relationships; memos track reasoning, insights, and questions. The process ends when theoretical development (and, therefore, code and category development) is no longer productive because the point of saturation has been reached. Sorting well-developed memos, polishing diagrams, and integrating the process documentation with the findings and theoretical results constitute the final phase of work in preparation for sharing the study.[137]

Three different types of coding generally follow the progression of a classic grounded theory analysis. *Open coding* is the initial, provisional work done on an unrestricted basis to produce concepts that fit the data.[138] *Axial coding* takes place during the latter portions of open coding as major categories emerge from the data. By focusing on one category in terms of its conditions, consequences, and other features, the researcher develops cumulative knowledge about the category as well as its subcategories and related categories.[139] *Selective coding* takes place as soon as open and axial coding have begun to establish core categories. At this point, even if the other two methods are still in use, everything gradually becomes subservient to the core categories.

Coding requires an iterative process of identifying themes, identifying subthemes, pulling out critical themes/sub-themes for deeper analysis, structuring a hierarchical set of codes, developing those codes and their definitions into a documented codebook, applying the codes, linking codes, and using the linkages and themes to develop theory. The codebook in which the rules for this work are recorded is essential and must be kept meticulously. Codebook entries require six basic components for each code: the code (usually a word or brief phrase), a simple definition (usually a phrase to use in confirming that the coder is indeed considering the correct code), a full definition (complete and lucid), use characteristics (an explanation of when to apply the code and, possibly, examples), nonuse parameters (an explanation of when *not* to apply the code and, possibly, references to related codes with examples), and an example (one quintessential example as well as, perhaps, additional examples that help illustrate the boundaries of the use characteristics).[140]

The principle of saturation is critical in data analysis. A category can be considered saturated when no new information about it develops out of the data. Once a category is as fully understood as possible in all of its ramifications and detail, then the continuous assignment of new data to that category becomes unnecessary for the generation of theory.

Coding Techniques

Only experience can translate the mechanics of coding guidelines into efficient, effective methods, but several techniques facilitate that process. Initially, during open coding, the researcher should look for terms used by the participants, using those terms as major coding terms.[141] Once the categories are firmly in mind, the focus moves to understanding each day's observations and interviews. As that understanding develops, recoding data to move beyond the initial open coding becomes critical.[142] No single mechanism exists for determining the categories in which the data are sorted; therefore, identification of categories should be limited until initial field experience is completed.[143]

After leaving the field but prior to final data analysis, additional techniques are useful. For example, if a memo becomes central to the theory, then the researcher can saturate the redeveloped category or property that is the point of the memo.[144] Memos, from theoretical to methodological, have their own special guidelines. Two of the most common are to memo fully and carefully on a regular basis[145] and to indicate in memos when saturation has been reached.[146]

Although categories generally evolve from the data, several types of categories are quite common in coding. Bogdan and Biklen, for example, noted ten such category types (e.g., settings, situations, perspectives, processes, activities, events, strategies, and relationships),[147] whereas Lofland and Lofland formulated eleven "thinking units"[148] (e.g., roles, relationships, practices) that could be used as coding categories.

To manage all of these codes, memos, and data, researchers used to keep separate items on note cards that could then be organized and reorganized as needed. Today, of course, there are several software packages that do all of this. Computer software can be used for the obvious tasks (e.g., writing, editing, and transcribing data, memos, and audit trail materials; and searching on the resulting documents) as well as specialized tasks that make data analysis less cumbersome and, therefore, more accurate (e.g., recording, altering, consolidating, and organizing codes and the data to which they are applied). Some of the more advanced software can support the development of theory, models, diagrams, and inductive analysis by grouping, linking, displaying, and mapping data and analysis points.[149] Software also can be used to support the development of theory (e.g., identify patterns and relationships, link segments of data, integrate data).[150] Atlas, NVivo, MAXqda, and HyperResearch are among the more common packages. Two free packages are available from the Centers for Disease Control and Prevention. AnSWR supports analysis of text-based, qualitative data, particularly that gathered by large teams for complex projects; it permits integration of quantitative data, codebook development, intercoder reliability testing, and multiple report formats.[151] "CDC EZ-Text is a software program developed to assist researchers create, manage, and analyze semi-structured qualitative databases. Researchers can design a series of data entry templates tailored to their questionnaire."[152,153]

Once the categories have formed, certain guidelines assist in their application. Entries can be continuous rather than dichotomous in their intensity. Some codes may be directional (e.g., preferring or avoiding a search tool). Some data may be coded in two categories where one is the main category and the other is a subcategory.[154] Dual or multiple coding is appropriate when multiple meanings (connotations or denotations) are involved.[155]

Clustering groups categories that share some observed qualities or, alternatively, partitions them into mutually exclusive classes whose boundaries reflect differences in the observed qualities of their members.[156] For example, in a study of information-seeking behavior among faculty, a researcher might cluster interview statements that have to do with technology; similarly, a researcher might partition those statements that have to do with people from those which deal with objects.

Both codes and clusters may be referred to as "emergent" in that they are not firmly determined in advance of data gathering. However, they are not genuinely inherent in the data alone. The researcher's perspective, experience, research questions, and expectations interact with the data to create them.[157]

A variation on this approach is the use of typologies. Typologies are high level, macro categories of people or phenomena. As a single aspect of data analysis, typologies group like items and characterize the groupings. Creating typologies is a five-step process that involves: 1) identifying the primary domain that merits classification, e.g., people, objects, or behaviors. 2) coding the data for relationships and qualities (e.g., kinds, parts, results, reasons, places, uses, methods, steps, and characteristics). 3) seeing if the data can be grouped into categories that share two or more codes, for example experienced searchers who expect to reword searches at least twice. 4) creating meaningful labels for the categories that emerge from this analysis and 5) codifying the typology with full descriptions of the named categories as well as exemplars.[158]

Moving from Codes to Theory

The process of moving from coding to theory or pattern generation is ongoing, but when saturation has been reached it is necessary to leave the field and begin the final analysis.[159] After all the data are finally coded, analysis gradually reveals a framework of patterns and contrasts from which, in some cases, theory can be developed. "The truly emergent integrating framework, which encompasses the fullest possible diversity of categories and properties, becomes an open-ended scheme, hardly subject to being redesigned."[160] Generalizing and reducing terminology gain a parsimony of variables as well as a scope in the applicability of the theory to a wide range of situations.

"Delimiting the theory"[161] curbs what could become an overwhelming task, and it occurs at two levels: the theory and the categories. First, the theory solidifies in the sense that major modifications become fewer and fewer as the analyst compares the next incidents of a category to its properties. Second, categories become theoretically saturated. The process of delimiting theory may involve sorting data within categories, reviewing categories for overlap, and looking for relationships among categories.[162]

Organizing data by categories, themes, and concepts can provide a framework that supports the move from coding to theory. Data can be organized by 1) categories (i.e., their basic properties) making sure that the categories develop from the data, are mutually exclusive, cover all the data, and fit into similar levels of analysis; 2) themes (i.e., their broad threads of overarching meaning) making sure that the themes develop from the categories or from a theoretical approach, pervade the majority of the data, or when in a minority, bear significant weight; and then by 3) concepts (i.e., explanations) making sure that the concepts develop from the themes and are borne out by study of the categories.[163] Techniques for organizing data on all three levels include, in addition to those already discussed, seeking comparisons and contrasts within the data, generating—then testing themes and/or concepts against the raw data, seeking inconsistencies and variations that push the borders of any pattern, visualizing organizational relationships through such tools as diagrams, and constantly writing out memos on this process as a whole.[164]

Insuring Coding Integrity

During coding, three techniques help ensure the integrity of the work. First, the acceptable reliability level must be established prior to test coding and met regularly before final coding.[165] Reproducibility (i.e., inter-coder reliability) is a minimum standard. "Double-coding the same transcripts is essential. . . . get code-recode consistencies over 90 percent before going on."[166] An 85 percent inter-coder reliability rating is the minimal goal for "good agreement."[167] If a single researcher is doing the coding, then intra-coder reliability must be established at the same rate. "Stability is the degree to which a process is invariant or unchanging over time. Stability becomes manifest under test-retest conditions . . ."[168]

Second, face validity (i.e., the correspondence between investigators' definitions of concepts and their definitions of the categories that measured them) is necessary but far from sufficient. Construct validity requires that a category or code should appear to measure the construct it is intended to measure.[169] A well-constructed and detailed coding manual, replete with definitions and examples, should tie consistently to memos to create a lucid explanation of each code and category.

Finally, in some situations, other sources can be used to confirm inferences from data, codes, and categories. These may include contextual experiences, established theories, related studies, and representative interpreters. "A content analysis is valid to the extent its inferences are upheld in the face of independently obtained evidence."[170]

DEVELOPING GROUNDED THEORY

The grounded theory approach, while not the only theoretical option, stands out as central to the naturalistic paradigm because it develops models, hypotheses, and theory directly and primarily from the data without reference to pre-existing concepts or theories.[171] Grounded theory work values the process of continuously developing, refining, and enhancing theory in recognition of the contributions that other studies, perspectives, and minds can make to the original effort.[172] The explanations of these theories are "grounded" in the "details, evidence, and examples"[173] of the data.

Originated by Glaser and Strauss in 1967, grounded theory is both a method of developing theory and a category of theory, namely that which develops from this method.[174] Crossing most developments of and variations on grounded theory is the originators' premise that explanatory, if not predictive, theory can be constructed through systematic, deliberate iterations of data gathering, data analysis, and mid-level theory generation. The reflexive accretion of code development, data gathering, and category development gradually lead to an inductively generated theory.[175]

Variations in the means of developing grounded theory emphasize different expectations. Over the past 40 years, the originators of this approach have taken the work in different directions. Both Glaser and Strauss use open coding of words and lines but with their tightest definitions; they differ in most other respects. Glaser intends to generate theory through discovery by using the constant comparison method, relevant literature, and analysis of entire sections of data. Strauss intends to verify theory through axial coding at three structured levels of data analysis (including work at the paragraph level), identifying category relationships, and some minimal use of literature at later stages of data analysis.[176]

Strauss and Corbin[177] urge the use of axial coding wherein emergent categories are viewed as axes with their properties and dimensions carefully specified, subcategories related to each other, and overarching relationships explicated. They use comparative analysis to look for similarities and differences, bringing out the properties and dimensions of the coding scheme.[178] They expect coding to lead to categories that, in turn, lead to theoretical categories that are followed by mid-level theory development. However, Glaser urges the use of emergent coding without forcing data into relationships; he "insists that theoretical codes must earn their way into the analysis"[179] and that theoretical coding must, therefore, follow development of higher-order categories. The abductive approach that underpins both implementations of grounded theory requires scholars to gather data as one means of determining the viability of a nascent theory while remaining open to the potential value of alternative theories.[180]

Although not necessarily generalizable or predictive in nature, grounded theory does have concrete value[181] in its progression towards explaining human behavior.[182] The current practice of grounded theory development posits the research process context as crucial to both data analysis and theory generation. Power relationships, socio-economic dynamics, world view, personal bias, and situations frame all actors involved, including researchers, as well as the communities to which those actors belong. Data are constructed, the researcher creates coding categories rather than discovering them in the data, and understanding is more likely than explanations.[183] Applications are tentative and can only be made in other settings if multi-site studies have been extensive or if a fit is made between two similar settings. A working hypothesis that evolves from a grounded theory could be explored if the fit between two contexts is strong enough to make transferability feasible.[184] Some of these hypotheses may later be tested in a quantitative approach, but many will describe an ongoing process of mutual shaping so complex that verifying any single hypothesis thereof is meaningless.

Among the advantages of a grounded theory approach are that it "promotes the development of theoretical accounts and explanations which conform closely to the situations being observed, so that the theory is likely to be intelligible to, and usable by, those in the situations studied . . ."[185] Grounded theories are likely to reflect the complexity of that which is studied rather than oversimplifying it.

In the continuing thread of Anselm Strauss's development of work on grounded theory, three types of analytic maps provide useful means of generating theory: situations (both human and non-human elements), social worlds, and analytic axes. The resulting diagrams, charts, and maps help delineate relationships among data points.[186]

ENSURING INTEGRITY

Ensuring integrity is no more difficult for naturalistic work than it is for positivist work, but again, the means differ. Field studies can be models of rigor, requiring the researcher to develop and apply systematic mechanisms for documenting all aspects of the research process.[187] For example, positivists use techniques such as random sampling to support generalizability, while naturalists use techniques such as prolonged contact to support transferability. Given the necessity of research within whatever setting is most natural for the participants, the investigator can not escape bias and so must recognize its impact upon the study in much the same way that a positivist recognizes the impact of an artificial laboratory setting upon a participant's response.[188] Central to this methodology is the belief that "the human instrument is as capable of refinements as any other variety."[189] More than recognizing internal bias, qualitatively-centered researchers make active use of their world view and perspectives.

The techniques discussed below focus on ensuring the integrity, trustworthiness, and value of naturalistic data gathering and analysis as well as the theory or working hypothesis that results from them. As with the positivist paradigm, there are no guarantees of results that are both meaningful and unbiased.

Primary Techniques

Particularly when used in concert, the following techniques strengthen the credibility of findings:[190]

1. Coordinated collection of sufficient data is ensured through the use of prolonged engagement, persistent observation, and triangulation. Extending the time in the field and increasing the number of observations provide more data. Triangulation requires the planned, deliberate gathering of different types or formats of data, perhaps from different populations.[191] Triangulation is not an automatic validation strategy[192] but it can be, when properly executed, one of several strategies for arguing that a study has sought and obtained layers of knowledge about a complex phenomenon. Researchers can plan for triangulation of data (multiple formats, e.g., photos and email), investigators (in data gathering, data analysis, or the ideally iterative interplay between the two), methods (focus group, interviews, and self-reporting diaries with the same people on the same phenomenon), and theories[193] as well as populations.

2. Peer debriefing requires submitting the research process and resultant analysis to an unaffiliated and perhaps critical peer for rigorous review and open input.[194] Some scholars find it more useful to seek out supportive peers who give constructive feedback rather than oppositional peers who play the devil's advocate.[195]

3. Member checks take the study participants, participants, and stakeholders as a critical audience. A member check seeks to provide meaningful feedback on all matters from those most involved with the human activity under study[196] by opening up a discussion on the research process, codes, categories, insights, models, theories, and the overarching analysis.[197] It can be either formal or informal. One technique, for example, is to use cards that participants rearrange, rename, discard, revise, and otherwise manipulate. This process helps participants refine, clarify, organize, and verbalize their understanding of the phenomenon.[198] Feedback from participants provides new insights and can be useful in clarifying misconceptions, but the ultimate analysis is still the responsibility of the researcher.[199] Study participants do not have final, overarching, unexamined insight into their own contributions to the study, much less to the study as a whole. They, too, have bias, perspective, situational, and contextual impact factors, as well as power dynamics that influence their process of evaluating and understanding the data analysis provided by the researcher. Their input on researchers' conclusions can provide additional data but does not absolutely, automatically invalidate or affirm the researcher's own analysis.[200]

4. Negative case analysis requires developing and revising a theory, model, or hypothesis until it accounts for every known case.[201] Although that ideal may not really be possible, if the analysis can account for even 60 percent of the cases, then the finding is worth consideration.[202]

5. Although difficult for the resource-poor investigator, referential adequacy can be valuable. This technique requires the investigator to set aside a segment of the data prior to final analysis. Once the analysis is completed then these archived data are retrieved and examined in light of the results with an eye to inconsistencies and gaps.[203]

6. Coordinating data gathering systematically, however flexibly, requires establishing structural corroboration or coherence, audits,[204] self-transcription,[205] explicit recording instructions,[206] and a methodological log.[207]

7. Finally, watching for and noting the impact of researchers' bias, perspective, and expectations require reflexive journals and a personal log.

Additional Techniques

In addition to the standard techniques, Miles and Huberman listed twelve tactics for "confirming meanings, avoiding bias, and assuring the quality of conclusions,"[208] namely: counting, noting patterns or themes, seeing plausibility, clustering, making metaphors, splitting variables, subsuming particulars into the general, factoring, noting relations between variables, finding intervening variables, building a logical chain of evidence, and making conceptual or theoretical coherence.

Elfreda Chatman's (1992) techniques for seeking reliability, which she defined as "to the degree to which observations are reported as consistent with some phenomenon during the life span of the inquiry,"[209] were varied. She did each of the following: consistently took notes, immersed herself in the setting, exposed herself to multiple situations, and built on what she learned from other research studies.

PRESENTATION OF FINDINGS

The material in Chapter 11 of this volume explains all of the critical points regarding the presentation of general research findings. However, there are five points specific to the presentation of qualitative research findings that bear mention.

First, in almost any forum it may be necessary to explain the concepts behind naturalistic methods. Although more and more reviewers are familiar with the naturalistic paradigm, there are still those who require authors to provide a basic primer for readers. In writing a journal article, for example, an author may be required by reviewers to fully explain the paradigmatic approach underlying all of the research design decisions. Researchers who work from a positivist perspective and use experimental techniques can take all of that background for granted. In giving conference presentations, it may be possible to assume a greater knowledge of the issues depending on the nature of the group being addressed.[210]

Second, qualitative research requires great detail and explication of both data gathering and data analysis, as does sound quantitative research, with care taken to recognize that the quality controls must be adjusted to context. That context and the adjustments must be explained, e.g., choice of setting, demographics of participants, process by which codes and coding themes developed, means of recording and organizing data, and means of establishing trust with participants.[211] Process details, exemplars, and timelines should be written up fully enough to provide readers with sufficient information to make their own determinations regarding the validity, bias, perspective, consistency, accuracy, and/or depth of the data gathering and analysis. The disciplined rigor needed to make effective use of the "human instrument" must be delineated in specific terms for the reader.

Third, one ethic of particular value to qualitative research requires the researcher to make some return to the community. For example, offering to share findings in a public forum with those who participate or might have participated in the study is common. Sometimes a copy of the findings is presented to individual participants who request the information. While quantitative scholars may disseminate their findings primarily through academic journals, qualitative scholars must make a concerted effort to frame an additional report, i.e., one which meets the needs of study participants.

Fourth, in almost every case, researchers must make active, careful decisions about "giving voice" to the participants. Within the context of the research problem, an effort to facilitate participants' interest in having their perspectives understood should be considered.[212] "Qualitative researchers have for some time begun to question the ethics of representing the voices of others, interpreting narrative accounts, and the privileging that occurs in the decisions that we make in the questions that we ask (or fail to ask), interpretations that we map onto (or miss), and the ways in which participant voices are portrayed and presented."[213]

Finally, if research is simply to help us understand the world, then the act of scholars publishing solely for other scholars in the same field makes a modest contribution to that goal. However, if the purpose of research is to start with understanding primarily as a fulcrum with which to improve the world, then scholars have an ethical obligation to reach practitioners, educate the public, inform scholars in relevant fields, involve research and funding partners in both the research process and the dissemination process, and become part of the policy discourse.[214] This political, activist, reformist, or developmental approach to research stands in contrast to the role of researcher as an observer who is separated from and not part of the world of the observed. Findings that are shared, presented, published, and indexed becomes the embodiment of those choices.

SUMMARY

As LIS scholars lead the information community's development of information systems and services for users, they must maintain a solid grounding in the purpose behind their work. Understanding what users encounter as they move through the complex, multidimensional, and dynamic experience of information interactions provides that solid grounding. Qualitative research methods enrich and augment the toolbox of LIS research approaches. Applied research of human experience centers on problems of such complexity that no single paradigmatic approach can suffice. The naturalistic/constructivist paradigm that underpins qualitative research and the scientific/positivist paradigm that underpins quantitative research provide—when properly employed—data, insights, models, hypotheses, and theories that move society towards solutions that work in the lives of individuals.[215] Both on its own and as a judiciously incorporated element of the mixed methods approach, qualitative research serves LIS well. However, for any research question, integrating methodologies in a coherent research design to take advantage of the most effective means of moving towards an applied solution is the goal. "Claims that quantitative methods are the sole, or at least the primary, effective methodology [in LIS] ignore the nature of the phenomena in question and constitute ineffective argument."[216] These six, deceptively simple "rules" for social research serve both scholar and participant well throughout the process.

1. Surprise should be possible.
2. Look for and report differences that make a difference.
3. Build reality checks into the data gathering.
4. Replicate where possible.
5. Compare like with like.
6. The method is servant, not master.[217]

Narrative (discourse based analysis), phenomenological (lived experience analysis), grounded theory (theory driven analysis), ethnographic (community based analysis), and case study (individual case analysis) approaches to qualitative design all bring value to LIS.[218] Scholars, practitioners, and students must choose the most effective approach for their research question. Beyond their own immediate projects, they should also consider potential connections with the work of others. Practical innovations in practice, policy, and application often develop from integrating and/or sequencing the use of qualitative and quantitative methods, facilitating the move from initial theory development into the steady progression of hypothesis testing[219] for improvements in the information experiences.

NOTES

1. Norman Denzin and Michael Giardina, "Introduction: Qualitative Inquiry and the Conservative Challenge," in *Qualitative Inquiry and the Conservative Challenge*, ed. Norman Denzin and Michael Giardina (Walnut Creek, CA: Left Coast Press, 2006), passim.
   Martyn Hammersley, *Questioning Qualitative Inquiry: Critical Essays* (Los Angeles: Sage, 2008).
2. *The Sage Handbook of Social Research Methods*, ed. Pertti Alasuutari, Leonard Bickman, and Julia Brannen (Los Angeles: Sage, 2008).
3. Raya Fidel, "Qualitative Methods in Information Retrieval Research," *Library & Information Science Research* 15 (1993): 219–47.
   See also: Philip Hider and Bob Pymm, "Empirical Research Methods Reported in High-profile LIS Journal Literature," *Library & Information Science Research* 30, no. 2 (2008): 108–14.

4. G. E. Gorman and Peter Clayton, *Qualitative Research for the Information Professional: A Practical Handbook*, 2nd ed., with contributions by Sydney J. Shep and Adela Clayton (London: Facet Publishing, 2005).

5. Yvonna S. Lincoln and Egon G. Guba, *Naturalistic Inquiry* (Newbury Park: Sage, 1985), 114.

6. Kathryn Dean, Jonathan Joseph, John Michael Roberts, and Colin Wight, *Realism, Philosophy and Social Science* (New York: Palgrave MacMillan, 2006), 2–11.

7. Jerry Willis, *Foundations of Qualitative Research: Interpretive and Critical Approaches*, with Muktha Jost, and Rema Nilakanta (Thousand Oaks, CA: Sage, 2007), 44–48.

8. Ibid., 53–54.

9. Ibid., 58–59.

10. See for example: Hammersley, *Questioning Qualitative Inquiry*.

11. Denzin and Giardina, "Introduction: Qualitative Inquiry," passim.

12. Hammersley, *Questioning Qualitative Inquiry* 25.

13. Ibid., 27.

14. Ibid., 30.

15. Ibid., 34–35.

16. Robert Bogdan, foreword to *Naturalistic Inquiry for Library Science: Methods and Applications for Research, Evaluation, and Teaching*, by Constance Ann Mellon (New York: Greenwood Press, 1990), xiii.

17. Constance Mellon, "Library Anxiety: A Grounded Theory and Its Development," *College & Research Libraries* 47 (March 1986): 160–65.

18. See, for example: Nadia Caidi, Susan MacDonald, "Information Practices of Canadian Muslims Post 9/11," *Government Information Quarterly* 25 (2008): 348–78.

19. Theresa Maylone, ed., "Qualitative Research," *Library Trends* 46, no. 4 (1998): 597–768.

20. Hider and Pymm, "Empirical Research Methods Reported," 112.

21. Brenda Dervin, Lois Foreman-Wernet, and Eric Lauterbach, eds., *Sense-Making Methodology Reader: Selected Writings of Brenda Dervin* (New York: Hampton Press, 2003).

22. Isadore Newman, Carolyn Ridenour, Carole Newman, and George DeMarco, Jr., "A Typology of Research Purposes and its Relationship to Mixed Methods," in *Handbook of Mixed Methods in Social and Behavioral Research*, ed. Abbas Tashakkori and Charles Teddlie (Thousand Oaks, CA: Sage, 2003), 170–71.

23. Raya Fidel, "Are We There Yet?: Mixed Methods Research in Library and Information Science," *Library & Information Science Research* 30, no. 4 (2008): 265.

24. See, for example, the following: Elizabeth B. Fitzpatrick, Anne C. Moore, and Beth W. Lang, "Reference Librarians at the Reference Desk in a Learning Commons: A Mixed Methods Evaluation," *The Journal of Academic Librarianship* 34, no. 3 (2008): 231–38.

Nahyun Kwon, "A Mixed-Methods Investigation of the Relationship Between Critical Thinking and Library Anxiety Among Undergraduate Students in their Information Search Process," *College & Research Libraries* 69, no. 2 (2008): 117–31.

25. Fidel, "Are We There Yet?" 265–72.

Marilyn Domas White and Emily Marsh, "Content Analysis: A Flexible Methodology," *Library Trends* 55, no. 1 (2006): 22–45.

26. Anthony Onwuegbuzie and Nancy Leech, "On Becoming a Pragmatic Researcher: The Importance of Combining Quantitative and Qualitative Research Methodologies," *International Journal of Social Research Methodology* 8 (2005): 382.

27. Janice Morse, "Principles of Mixed Methods and Multimethod Research Design," in *Handbook of Mixed Methods in Social and Behavioral Research*, ed. Abbas Tashakkori and Charles Teddlie (Thousand Oaks, CA: Sage, 2003), 193–95.

28. Jennifer Mason, "Mixing Methods in a Qualitatively Driven Way," *Qualitative Research* 6 (2006): 9–25.

29. Newman, Ridenour, Newman, and DeMarco, Jr., "A Typology of Research Purposes," 173–79.

30. Celia Fisher and Andrea Anushko, "Research Ethics in Social Science," in *The Sage Handbook of Social Research Methods*, ed. Pertti Alasuutari, Leonard Bickman, and Julia Brannen (Los Angeles: Sage, 2008), 95–109.

31. Ibid., 100.

32. Robert V. Labaree, "Encounters with the Library: Understanding Experience Using the Life History Method," *Library Trends* 55, no. 1 (2006): 128.

33. Andrea Doucet and Natasha Mauthner, "Qualitative Interviewing and Feminist Research," in *The Sage Handbook of Social Research Methods*, ed. Pertti Alasuutari, Leonard Bickman, and Julia Brannen (Los Angeles: Sage, 2008), 331–36.

34. Ibid.

35. Willis, *Foundations of Qualitative Research*, 264.

36. Fisher and Anushko, "Research Ethics in Social Science," 103.

37. Marija Dalbello, "A Phenomenological Study of an Emergent National Digital Library, Part I: Theory and Methodological Framework," *Library Quarterly* 75 (2005): 400.

Geoffrey C. Bowker and Susan Leigh Star, *Sorting Things Out: Classification and Its Consequences* (Cambridge, MA: MIT Press, 2000).

38. Fisher and Anushko, "Research Ethics in Social Science," 104.

39. Jane Elliott, *Using Narrative in Social Research: Qualitative and Quantitative Approaches* (London: Sage, 2005), 135–37.

40. For more, see the following: Elizabeth Buchanan, "Ethics, Qualitative Research, and Ethnography in Virtual Space," *Journal of Information Ethics* 9, no. 2 (2000): 82–87.

41. Mark Israel and Iain Hay, *Research Ethics for Social Scientists: Between Ethical Conduct and Regulatory Compliance* (London: Sage, 2006), 13–14.

42. Ibid., 14–16.

43. Herbert Rubin and Irene Rubin, *Qualitative Interviewing: The Art of Hearing Data*, 2nd ed. (Thousand Oaks, CA: Sage, 2005), 45.

44. Andrea Fontana and James Frey, "Interviewing: The Art of Science," in *Handbook of Qualitative Research*, ed. Norman Denzin and Yvonna Lincoln (Thousand Oaks, CA: Sage, 1994), 369.

45. Irving Seidman, *Interviewing as Qualitative Research: A Guide for Researchers in Education and the Social Sciences*, 3rd ed. (New York: Teachers College Press, 2006), 55.

46. For more of this perspective on sampling, see: Janice Morse, "Designing Funded Qualitative Research," in *Handbook of Qualitative Research*, ed. Norman Denzin and Yvonna Lincoln (Thousand Oaks, CA: Sage, 1994), 220–35.

47. Jana Bradley, "Methodological Issues and Practices in Qualitative Research," *Library Quarterly* 63, no. 4 (1993): 440.

48. Morse, "Designing Funded Qualitative Research," 220–35.

49. Ibid., 229.

50. Ibid., 220–35.

51. Labaree, "Encounters with the Library," 125.

52. Michael Quinn Patton, *Qualitative Evaluation and Research Methods*, 2nd ed. (Newbury Park, CA: Sage, 1990), 169–83.

53. Linda Mabry, "Case Study in Social Research," in *The Sage Handbook of Social Research Methods*, ed. Pertti Alasuutari, Leonard Bickman, and Julia Brannen (Los Angeles: Sage, 2008), 214.

54. Ibid., 215.

55. Ibid., 216.

56. Ibid., 218–22.

57. Margaret LeCompte, Judith Preissle, and Renata Tesch, *Ethnography and Qualitative Design in Educational Research*, 2nd ed. (New York: Academic Press, 1993), 196.

58. Danny Jorgensen, *Participant Observation: A Methodology for Human Studies* (London: Sage, 1989), 82.

59. Raya Fidel, "The Case Study Method: A Case Study," *Library & Information Science Research* 6 (July 1984): 275.

60. Lynda M. Baker, "Observation: A Complex Research Method," *Library Trends* 55, no.1 (2006): 171–89.

61. Raymond Gold, "Roles in Sociological Field Observation," in *Issues in Participant Observation*, ed. George McCall and J. L. Simmons (Reading, MA: Addison-Wesley, 1969), 33. See also: Elfreda Chatman, *The Information World of Retired Women* (Westport, CT: Greenwood Press, 1992).

62. Morris Schwartz and Charlotte Schwartz, "Problems in Participant Observation," *American Journal of Sociology* 60 (1955): 349.

63. Lincoln and Guba, *Naturalistic Inquiry*, 273.

64. William Whyte, "On Making the Most of Participant Observation," *American Sociologist* 14, no. 1 (1979): 56.

See, for example, the following study which combined observation with a structured interview guide: Chatman, *The Information World of Retired Women*, 1992.

65. LeCompte, Preissle, and Tesch, *Ethnography and Qualitative Design*, 197.

66. Norman Denzin, *The Research Act: A Theoretical Introduction to Sociological Methods*, 3rd ed. (NJ: Prentice Hall, 1989), 30.

67. Patricia Adler and Peter Adler, "Observation Techniques," in *Handbook of Qualitative Research*, ed. Norman Denzin and Yvonna Lincoln (Thousand Oaks, CA: Sage, 1994), 378.

68. Constance A. Mellon, *Naturalistic Inquiry for Library Science: Methods and Applications for Research, Evaluation, and Teaching* (New York: Greenwood Press, 1990), 40.

69. Jorgensen, *Participant Observation*, 84.

70. Paul Diesing, *Patterns of Discovery in the Social Sciences* (London: Routledge & Kegan Paul, 1972), 19.

71. Ibid., 291.

72. Michael Angrosino, *Naturalistic Observation* (Walnut Creek, CA: Left Coast Press, 2007), 32–41.

73. Baker, "Observation," 174–79.

74. Lincoln and Guba, *Naturalistic Inquiry*, 269.

75. Jorgensen, *Participant Observation*.

76. Marie Radford, "The Critical Incident Technique and the Qualitative Evaluation of the Connecting Libraries and Schools Project," *Library Trends* 55, no.1 (2006): 46.

77. Lokman Meho, "E-Mail Interviewing in Qualitative Research: A Methodological Discussion," *Journal of the American Society for Information Science and Technology* 57, no. 10 (2006): 1284.

78. Janet Smithson, "Focus Groups," in *The Sage Handbook of Social Research Methods*, ed. Pertti Alasuutari, Leonard Bickman, and Julia Brannen (Los Angeles: Sage, 2008), 358–59.

79. Claudia Puchta and Jonathan Potter, *Focus Group Practice* (London: Sage, 2004), 6.

80. Ibid., 46.

81. Ibid., 64.

82. Barney G. Glaser and Anselm L. Strauss, *The Discovery of Grounded Theory: Strategies for Qualitative Research* (New York: Aldine de Gruyter, 1967), 273.

83. Whyte, "On Making the Most of Participant Observation," 57.

84. Steinar Kvale, *InterViews: An Introduction to Qualitative Research Interviewing* (Thousand Oaks, CA: Sage, 1996), 133–35.

85. Whyte, "On Making the Most of Participant Observation," 60.

86. Chris Argyris, "Creating Effective Relationships in Organizations," *Human Organization* 17, no. 1 (1958): 39.

87. Jorgensen, *Participant Observation*, 88.

88. Jessica Bates, "Use of Narrative Interviewing in Everyday Information Behavior Research," *Library & Information Science Research* 26 (2004): 15–28.

89. Patricia Dewdney and Roma Harris, "Community Information Needs: The Case of Wife Assault," *Library & Information Science Research* 14 (1992): 5–29.

90. Herbert J. Rubin and Irene S. Rubin, *Qualitative Interviewing: The Art of Hearing Data*, 2nd ed. (Thousand Oaks, CA: Sage, 2005), 164–72.

91. Herbert Clark and Michael Schober, "Asking Questions and Influencing Answers," in *Questions about Questions: Inquiries into the Cognitive Bases of Surveys*, ed. Judith M. Tanur (New York: Russell Sage Foundation, 1992), 18.

92. Raymond Gorden, "Dimensions of the Depth Interview," in *Reader in Research Methods for Librarianship*, ed. Mary Lee Bundy, Paul Wasserman, and Gayle Araghi (Washington, DC: NCR, 1970).

93. Jorgensen, *Participant Observation*.

94. Mcho, "E-Mail Interviewing in Qualitative Research," 1285, 1288, and 1290.

95. Ibid., 1292.

96. Ibid., 1290.

97. Ibid., 1290.

98. Floyd J. Fowler, Jr., *Survey Research Methods*, 2nd ed. (Newbury Park, CA: Sage, 1993).

99. Carol Collier Kuhlthau, *Seeking Meaning: A Process Approach to Library and Information Services*, 2nd ed. (Norwood, NJ: Ablex Publishing, 2003).

100. Ibid.

101. Harry Reis and Shelly Gable, "Event-Sampling and Other Methods for Studying Everyday Experience," in *Handbook of Research Methods in Social and Personality Psychology*, ed. Harry T. Reis and Charles M. Judd (Cambridge: Cambridge University Press, 2000), 190.

102. Mellon, *Naturalistic Inquiry for Library Science*, 24.

103. For an in-depth analysis of this relationship, see: Roger Bakeman, "Behavioral Observation and Coding," in *Handbook of Research Methods in Social and Personality Psychology*, ed. Harry Reis T. and Charles M. Judd (Cambridge: Cambridge University Press, 2000).

104. Sanna Talja, "Analyzing Qualitative Interview Data: The Discourse Analytic Method," *Library & Information Science Research* 21, no. 4 (1999): 459–77.

105. Carol Grbich, *Qualitative Data Analysis: An Introduction* (London: Sage, 2007), 146–50.

106. John M. Budd, "Discourse Analysis and the Study of Communication in LIS," *Library Trends* 55 (2006): 80.

107. Robert Phillip Weber, *Basic Content Analysis*, 2nd ed. (London: Sage, 1990), 9.

108. White and Marsh, "Content Analysis," 22.

109. Ibid., 27–28.

110. Weber, *Basic Content Analysis*.

111. Robert C. Bogdan and Sari Knopp Biklen, *Qualitative Research for Education: An Introduction to Theories and Methods*, 5th ed. (Boston: Allyn and Bacon, 2007), 147.

112. Klaus Krippendorff, *Content Analysis: An Introduction to Its Methodology* (London: Sage, 1980), 53.

113. Ibid., 61–63.

114. Weber, *Basic Content Analysis*, 37.

115. Mellon, *Naturalistic Inquiry for Library Science.*

116. Yvonna S. Lincoln and Guba, *Naturalistic Inquiry.*

117. Catherine Marshall and Gretchen B. Rossman, *Designing Qualitative Research*, 4th ed. (Thousand Oaks, CA: Sage, 2006), 98–99.

118. David Silverman and Amir Marvasti, *Doing Qualitative Research: A Comprehensive Guide* (London: Sage, 2008), 216–18.

119. Matthew Miles and Michael Huberman, *Qualitative Data Analysis: A Sourcebook of New Methods*, 2nd ed. (Beverly Hills: Sage, 1994), 71.

120. Ibid., 69.

121. Charles Smith, "Content Analysis and Narrative Analysis," in *Handbook of Research Methods in Social and Personality Psychology*, ed. Harry T. Reis and Charles M. Judd (Cambridge: Cambridge University Press, 2000).

122. Glaser and Strauss, *The Discovery of Grounded Theory.*

123. Barney Glaser, "The Constant Comparison Method of Qualitative Analysis," *Social Problems* 12 (Spring 1965): 437–39.

124. Krippendorff, *Content Analysis.*

125. Mellon, *Naturalistic Inquiry for Library Science*, 72–73.

126. Glaser and Strauss, *The Discovery of Grounded Theory*, 103.

127. Ibid., passim.

128. Anselm Strauss, *Qualitative Research for Social Scientists* (New York: Cambridge University Press, 1987), 55–56.

129. Ibid., passim.

130. Guido Stempel, "Content Analysis," in *Research Methods in Mass Communication*, 2nd ed., ed. Guido Stempel and Bruce Westley (Englewood Cliffs, NJ: Prentice Hall, 1989).

131. Glaser and Strauss, *The Discovery of Grounded Theory*, 24.

132. Lincoln and Guba, *Naturalistic Inquiry.*

133. Ibid.

134. Lisa A. Mazzei, *Inhabited Silence in Qualitative Research: Putting Poststructural Theory to Work* (New York: Peter Lang, 2007).

135. Juliet Corbin and Anselm Strauss, *Basics of Qualitative Research*, 3rd ed. (Los Angeles: Sage, 2008), 107–41.

136. Norvell Northcutt and Danny McCoy, *Interactive Qualitative Analysis: A Systems Method for Qualitative Research* (Thousand Oaks, CA: Sage, 2004), 81.

137. Kathy Charmaz, "Reconstructing Grounded Theory," in *The Sage Handbook of Social Research Methods*, ed. Pertti Alasuutari, Leonard Bickman, and Julia Brannen (Los Angeles: Sage, 2008), 471–73.

138. Strauss, *Qualitative Research for Social Scientists.*

139. Ibid.

140. Kathleen MacQueen, Eleanor McLellan-Lamal, Kelly Bartholow, and Bobby Milstein, "Team-Based Codebook Development: Structure, Process, and Agreement," in *Handbook for Team-Based Qualitative Research*, ed. Greg Guest and Kathleen MacQueen (Lanham, MD: Altamira Press, 2008), 119–23.

141. Strauss, *Qualitative Research for Social Scientists.*

142. Glaser and Strauss, *The Discovery of Grounded Theory.*

143. Ibid., 34.

144. Ibid., passim.

145. Miles and Huberman, *Qualitative Data Analysis*, 2nd ed., 71.

146. Earl R. Babbie, *The Practice of Social Research*, 12th ed. (Belmont, CA: Wadsworth/Cengage Learning, 2010).

147. Bogdan and Biklen, *Qualitative Research for Education*.

148. John Lofland and Lyn Lofland, *Analyzing Social Settings: A Guide to Qualitative Observation and Analysis*, 2nd ed. (Belmont, CA: Wadsworth, 1984).

149. Eben Weitzman, "Software and Qualitative Research," in *Collecting and Interpreting Qualitative Materials*, 2nd ed., ed. Norman Denzin and Yvonna Lincoln (Thousand Oaks, CA: Sage, 2003), 310–39.

150. Ann Lewins and Christina Silver, *Using Software in Qualitative Research: A Step-by-Step Guide* (Los Angeles: Sage, 2007), 12–14.

151. Centers for Disease Control and Prevention, "AnSWR: Analysis Software for Word-based Records," http://www.cdc.gov/hiv/topics/surveillance/resources/software/answr/index.htm.

152. Centers for Disease Control and Prevention, "CDC EZ-Text," http://www.cdc.gov/hiv/topics/surveillance/resources/software/ez-text/index.htm.

153. For more on computer-assisted data analysis, see: Raymond Lee and Lea Esterhuizen, "Computer Software and Qualitative Analysis: Trends, Issues, and Resources," *International Journal of Social Research Methodology* 3, no. 3 (2000): 231–43.

Linda Gilbert, "Going the Distance: 'Closeness' in Qualitative Data Analysis Software," *International Journal of Social Research Methodology* 5, no. 3 (2002): 215–28.

Sharlene Nagy Hesse-Biber, "Unleashing Frankenstein's Monster? The Use of Computers in Qualitative Research," in *Approaches to Qualitative Research: A Reader on Theory and Practice*, ed. Sharlene Nagy Hesse-Biber and Patricia Leavy (New York: Oxford University Press, 2004).

Lewins and Silver, *Using Software in Qualitative Research*.

154. Weber, *Basic Content Analysis*.

155. Matthew Miles and Michael Huberman, *Qualitative Data Analysis: A Sourcebook of New Methods*, 1st ed. (Beverly Hills, CA: Sage, 1984), 64.

156. Krippendorff, *Content Analysis*.

157. Yvonna S. Lincoln, "Insights into Library Services and Users from Qualitative Research," *Library & Information Science Research* 24 (2002): 13.

158. Carol A. Bailey, *A Guide to Qualitative Field Research*, 2nd ed. (Thousand Oaks, CA: Pine Forge Press, 2007), 143–49.

159. Margot Ely et al., *Doing Qualitative Research: Circles within Circles* (London: Falmer Press, 1991).

160. Glaser and Strauss, *The Discovery of Grounded Theory*, 41.

161. Ibid., passim.

162. Lincoln and Guba, *Naturalistic Inquiry*.

163. Peter Woods, *Successful Writing for Qualitative Researchers*, 2nd ed. (London: Routledge, 2006), 25–32.

164. Ibid., 32–36.

165. Weber, *Basic Content Analysis*.

166. Miles and Huberman, *Qualitative Data Analysis* 1984, 64.

For additional insights and alternative reliability approaches see the following: Kimberly Neuendorf, *The Content Analysis Guidebook* (Thousand Oaks, CA: Sage, 2001).

167. MacQueen, McLellan-Lamal, Bartholow, and Milstein, "Team-Based Codebook Development," 131.

168. Krippendorff, *Content Analysis*, 130.

169. Weber, *Basic Content Analysis*, 2nd ed.

170. Krippendorff, *Content Analysis*, 155.

171. Steven J. Taylor and Robert Bogdan, *Introduction to Qualitative Research Methods*, 2nd ed. (New York: John Wiley and Sons, 1984), 126.

172. Glaser and Strauss, *The Discovery of Grounded Theory*, 32.

173. Rubin and Rubin, *Qualitative Interviewing*, 1st ed., 4.

174. Charmaz, "Reconstructing Grounded Theory," 461.

For insights into the application of mid-level theories to LIS research, see the following: Herbert L. Poole, *Theories of the Middle Range* (Norwood, NJ: Ablex Publishing, 1985).

175. Charmaz, "Reconstructing Grounded Theory, 462.

176. Grbich, *Qualitative Data Analysis*, 72.

177. Corbin and Strauss, *Basics of Qualitative Research*.

178. Ibid., 195.

179. Charmaz, "Reconstructing Grounded Theory," 466.

180. Ibid., 467.

181. Glaser and Strauss, *The Discovery of Grounded Theory*.

182. Mellon, *Naturalistic Inquiry for Library Science*, 2–3.

183. Charmaz, "Reconstructing Grounded Theory," 469–70.

184. Lincoln and Guba, *Naturalistic Inquiry*, 124.

185. Barry Turner, "Some Practical Aspects of Qualitative Data Analysis: One Way of Organizing the Cognitive Processes Associated with the Generation of Grounded Theory," *Quality and Quantity* 15, no. 3 (1981): 226–27.

186. Adele Clarke, "Situational Analysis: Grounded Theory Mapping After the Postmodern Turn," *Symbolic Interaction* 26 (2003): 553–76.

187. Patricia Dewdney, "Recording the Reference Interview: A Field Experiment," in *Qualitative Research in Information Management*, ed. Jack D. Glazier and Ronald R. Powell (Englewood, CO: Libraries Unlimited, 1992), 122.

188. Mellon, *Naturalistic Inquiry for Library Science*.

189. Lincoln and Guba, *Naturalistic Inquiry*, 194.

190. Ibid., 301.

191. Ibid., 306–7.

192. Uwe Flick, "Triangulation in Qualitative Research," in *A Companion to Qualitative Research*, ed. Uwe Flick, Ernst von Kardoff, and Ines Steinke, trans. Bryan Jenner (London: Sage, 2004), 179.

193. Ibid., 179–81.

194. Lincoln and Guba, *Naturalistic Inquiry*, 308.

195. Ely et al., *Doing Qualitative Research*.

196. Ibid.

197. Lincoln and Guba, *Naturalistic Inquiry*, 314.

198. Northcutt and McCoy, *Interactive Qualitative Analysis*, 98–99.

199. Sherryl Kleinman, *Feminist Fieldwork Analysis* (Los Angeles: Sage, 2007), 112.

200. Silverman and Marvasti, *Doing Qualitative Research*, 322.

201. Lincoln and Guba, *Naturalistic Inquiry*, 309.

202. Ibid., 312–13.

203. Ibid., 313.

204. Ibid., passim.

205. Mellon, *Naturalistic Inquiry for Library Science*.

206. Krippendorff, *Content Analysis*.

207. Lincoln and Guba, *Naturalistic Inquiry*.

208. Miles and Huberman, *Qualitative Data Analysis*, 1st ed., 215.

209. Chatman, *The Information World of Retired Women*, 8.

210. For more on writing, see the following: Harry R. Wolcott, *Writing Up Qualitative Research*, 2nd ed. (Thousand Oaks, CA: Sage, 2001).

Adrian Holliday, *Doing and Writing Qualitative Research* (London: Sage, 2002).

211. Adrian Holliday, *Doing and Writing Qualitative Research*, 2nd ed. (London: Sage, 2007), 8–9, 42–58.

212. For more on these points, see the following: Amanda Coffey and Paul Atkinson, *Making Sense of Qualitative Data: Complementary Research Strategies* (Thousand Oaks, CA: Sage, 1996), chap. 5.

Mellon, *Naturalistic Inquiry for Library Science*, chap. 5.

213. Lisa Mazzei and Alecia Youngblood Jackson, "Introduction: The Limit of Voice," in *Voice in Qualitative Inquiry: Challenging Conventional, Interpretive, and Critical Conceptions in Qualitative Research*, ed. Lisa Mazzei and Alecia Youngblood Jackson* (London: Routledge, 2009), 2.

See also: Carol Gilligan, Renée Spencer, M. Katherine Weinberg, and Tatiana Bertsch, "On the Listening Guide: A Voice-Centered Relational Method," in *Emergent Methods in Social Research*, ed. Sharlene Nagy Hesse-Biber and Patricia Leavy (Thousand Oaks, CA: Sage, 2006), 253–71.

214. Paul Bywaters and Gayle Letherby, "Extending Social Research," in *Extending Social Research: Application, Implementation and Publication* (Berkshire, England: Open University Press, 2007), 3–18.

215. Adriana Baban, "Reconceptualization of the Division Between Quantitative and Qualitative Research Methods," *Cognition, Brain, Behavior: An Interdisciplinary Journal* 12 (2008): 337–43.

216. John M. Budd, "What We Say about Research: Rhetoric and Argument in Library and Information Science," *Library Quarterly* 76 (2006): 223.

217. Glenn Firebaugh, *Seven Rules for Social Research* (New Jersey: Princeton University Press, 2008), 1, 36, 64, 90, 120, and 207.

218. John W. Creswell, *Qualitative Inquiry & Research Design: Choosing Among Five Approaches* (Thousand Oaks, CA: Sage, 2007), 53–84.

219. Robert Smith, *Cumulative Social Inquiry: Transforming Novelty into Innovation* (New York: Guilford Press, 2008).

Historical Research

A number of researchers, including some historians, have argued that historical research cannot be considered true scientific research because it does not
permit enough precision and objectivity. In other words, it does not have the
rigor of such research methods as experimental and survey methods. Others
argue that historical research can meet the standards of inquiry of other methods.[1] Regardless, there is a consensus that historical research has much to
contribute to library and information science.

NATURE AND VALUE OF HISTORICAL RESEARCH

"As used by the Greeks, history meant an inquiry designed to reconstruct past
events, and, in a sense, historical research can still be defined as a scholarly
attempt to discover what has happened."[2] Currently, historical research, or
"documentary research" as it is sometimes labeled (although historical research
is not limited to documents), typically goes beyond mere description and
attempts to interpret the facts as reconstructed. In other words, the historian
attempts to give meaning to the facts in light of a relevant theory. The basic purposes of historical research are to "provide a clear perspective of the present"
and to facilitate planning for the future by identifying general principles applicable to recurring situations.[3] Tosh and Lang refer to this as "historical awareness," which is based on three principles—difference, context, and process.[4]
Difference is the "recognition of the gulf which separates our own age from all
previous ages."[5] Context means that the setting for the subject of the enquiry
must be retained.[6] Process is "the relationship between events over time," which
makes the events more relevant "than if they were viewed in isolation."[7]

Chronology

It may be useful, at this point, to distinguish true historical research from
chronology. *Chronology* can be defined as simply the describing of events in the
order of their occurrence, a process similar to the older concept of historical

research. Chronology is important, however, as it represents the first step in the process of historical research and provides material or data for the steps to follow.

In contrast, true historical research, or *historiography* or intellectual history, is concerned with analyzing and interpreting the meaning of historical events within their contexts. It is the process by which a researcher is able to reach a conclusion as to the probable truth of an event in the past by studying objects available for observation in the present.[8]

History has two dimensions, both of which are important to the interpretation of historical data. One dimension is *historical time*, or the chronology which takes into account the spacing of events and patterns. A good example of such a chronology, which is sometimes referred to as a time line, is *Libraries in the U.S. Timeline*, compiled by Wiegand for the American Library Association in 1999.[9] The second dimension is *historical space*, or where events occurred (i.e., geographical location).

Importance of Historical Research to Librarianship

In addition to fulfilling the basic purposes noted above, historical research can make specific contributions to the advancement of library and information science. As Busha and Harter indicate, historical research can contribute to the body of knowledge about librarianship; it can increase our understanding of how, when, and why past events occurred; and it can expand our appreciation of the significance of these events.[10] Busha and Harter also quote Harris, who stated that "a clear understanding of the historical definition of the functions of libraries may well contribute to increased communication between libraries."[11] Harris notes that Shera has argued that library history allows librarians better to understand the present and to fulfill their social responsibility more effectively.[12] More specifically, as Gorman and Clayton note, historical research can help to gain historical understanding of the long-term development of library collections, inform budgetary decision making, provide a basis for decisions concerning services, and inform an investigation of changing information culture.[13]

According to the Library History Round Table of the American Library Association:

> A knowledge of history and an understanding of historical methodology are indispensable elements in the education of library and information professionals. A knowledge of history provides a necessary perspective for understanding the principles and practices of library and information science. Many of the most important issues of our day—including, for example, intellectual freedom, fees for service, service to minorities, access to government information, the role of new technologies, and the place of women in the profession—can only be understood in the light of their historical contexts. And the research process, an essential component of contemporary professional education and practice, can be significantly informed by awareness of both historical precedents and historical methodology.[14]

Both Davis and Shiflett call for the inclusion of library and information science history in LIS program curricula.[15] They believe that LIS professionals must know and understand the history of the profession in a historical context of society and culture in order to become leaders instead of merely practitioners. By studying history, LIS professionals will look beyond practice and will "strive continuously to raise the standards of the profession and improve the system in which it functions."[16]

Shiflett suggests utilizing sense-making methodology to teach and learn history.[17] This approach would enable both teachers and students to "make retrospective sense of the situations in which they find themselves and their creations."[18] In short, a knowledge and understanding of good historical research can help librarians build on the past in an efficient, effective manner to avoid reinventing the wheel and to develop new theories and systems to advance the profession.

Types of Historical Research

Hillway identifies six different types of historical research or documentary study:

(1) biographical research, (2) histories of institutions and organizations, (3) the investigation of sources and influences, (4) editing and translating historical documents, (5) studying the history of ideas, and (6) compiling bibliographies. The extent to which these different types are employed depends on the nature of the inquiry and the subject field. Whether they represent true historical research, or the mere compilation of facts, depends on the manner in which they are conducted.[19]

This also may be an appropriate place to note that the manner in which a historian collects and interprets his or her data may be somewhat influenced by the historical school of thought to which he or she adheres. Students of historical research have identified a number of trends in U.S. historiography, for example, ranging from the "providential" perspective of the seventeenth and eighteenth centuries to the more recent "new social history." As Winkler suggests, historians are moving away from new social history and back to an earlier school of thought known as the narrative mode.[20] At the same time, she concludes that narrative history, with its emphasis on how the account is written, is not replacing new social history, with its use of social science–type analysis. What is happening, according to Winkler, is that scholars are becoming more willing to accommodate a diversity of approaches to conducting and reporting historical research.

SOURCES OF HISTORICAL INFORMATION

The data gathered in historical research can come from a wide variety of sources. Among the more commonly used are the following:

1. Official records, such as laws, deeds, annual reports of organizations, charters, and so on
2. Newspapers and other periodicals
3. Eyewitness accounts of events

4. Archives

5. Manuscripts

6. Letters and personal diaries

7. Biographies, autobiographies, and memoirs

8. Historical studies

9. Literary writings

10. Oral evidence

11. Memorials

12. Catalogs

13. Schedules, agendas, and so on

14. Archaeological and geological remains (nondocuments).

Virtually all written sources of historical information can be categorized as either primary or secondary documents. *Primary* sources represent the data which lie closest to the historical event. They are considered to include the testimony of eyewitnesses, or observations made with one of the other senses or by some mechanical device. In most cases, primary sources are the written record of what the writer actually observed, or the firsthand expression of his or her thoughts. *Secondary*, or secondhand, sources may be considered virtually everything not viewed as primary. Everything that historians and others have written about the past are secondary sources and include most textbooks, journal articles, histories, and encyclopedias. The use of primary sources tends to ensure the integrity of a study and to strengthen its reliability. Their use provides the only solid base for conclusions reached in documentary research.[21] According to Bates, primary sources "are the raw materials of historical interpretation."[22] They are critical for the consideration of complex historical issues.

Library-related primary sources may include official records, government documents, manuscripts, newspaper articles, letters, and statistics, but whether these sources are truly primary depends on whether they represent firsthand accounts. (Readers particularly interested in sources for library-related research should see Shiflett's article in the Spring 1984 issue of *Library Trends*).[23] Statistics, for example, could be based on other, primary sources and thus become secondary sources themselves. In other words, the distinction between primary and secondary sources is not as clear-cut as it might first appear, and it can vary with the authority. Primary sources are defined as being contemporary with the event or thought to which they refer, but different people can define "contemporary" differently. Some prefer a broader definition which recognizes different levels of "primary." For example, a report of a conversation that occurred a week ago would no doubt be primary. A report of the conversation written 20 years later for an autobiography might be considered primary as well, but somewhat less so than the more immediate account. And what about the increasing number of electronic facsimiles? According to Duff and Cherry, some users have expressed concern about the authenticity of Web-based digital copies of original documents.[24] Others, however, view facsimiles, whether electronic or photographic, as primary resources for all practical purposes.

It is seldom possible, or even desirable, for a historical researcher to base his or her work entirely on primary sources. In fact, secondary sources may provide important insights and conceptual development not available elsewhere. By synthesizing the existing research literature, secondary sources help to round out the setting or fill in the gaps between primary sources of information and can suggest topics for future research. Because secondary sources do not represent eyewitness accounts, the researcher should keep in mind their limitations and avoid an overreliance on such materials, however. In evaluating secondary data sources, for example, the researcher should ask questions about the qualifications of the person responsible for the data collection, what data were collected and what they were intended to measure, when the information was collected, the methods that were used to collect the data, and the consistency of the data with data from other sources.

EVALUATION OF HISTORICAL SOURCES

In selecting specific sources of data for a historical study, it is critical that they be evaluated properly. The researcher should want to know if the sources are relevant to the study, substantial enough to be worthwhile, and competent (i.e., genuine, accurate, and reasonable). The assessment of the last criterion—competency—should involve two basic processes: external criticism and internal criticism.

External Criticism

External criticism, or the gathering of external evidence, is done to determine if a source in fact provides authentic, primary data. Are the author, the place, and the date of writing what they purport to be? The process of external criticism is crucial to the credibility of historical research. External criticism may be used interchangeably with textual criticism and usually takes into account the provenance, or origin, of a document. In other words, can the document be traced back to the office or person who supposedly produced it? Scholars have long debated the true authorship of at least some of Shakespeare's plays. More recent examples of works whose authenticity has been disputed include de la Pena's diary as it relates to the demise of Davy Crockett, d'Ancona's manuscript about his travels in thirteenth century China, and even Clement Moore's poem, " 'Twas the Night Before Christmas."

External criticism often cannot prove the authenticity of a source, but it can provide reasonable confidence that a particular source is authentic. To assess the authenticity of a work, the investigator may use bibliographical techniques (see the section on bibliographical research later in this chapter) or draw upon expertise in a number of auxiliary disciplines such as linguistics, epigraphy (the study of inscriptions), genealogy, paleography, and heraldry. He or she may need to utilize certain techniques of the physical sciences such as chemical analysis of paper and ink. The contents of the document should be examined for consistency with known facts and with information available to the author at the time the document was written. In short, external criticism can involve physical, textual, and bibliographical analysis.

Internal Criticism

Having decided that a document or source is genuine, the researcher should then confirm the validity and reliability of its contents. He or she is concerned, at this point, with what the source says (i.e., its meaning, accuracy, and general trustworthiness). Internal criticism is generally more challenging than external criticism, and it too is often difficult, if not impossible, to achieve with absolute certainty. Many old documents no longer exist in their original forms, and there is no guarantee that their contents have not changed somewhat as they have been copied, translated, and republished over the years. (See the fuller discussion of descriptive bibliography below.)

Babbie states that the more sources that "point to the same set of 'facts'," the more accurate the research findings. He cautions historical researchers to "always be wary of bias" in the data sources and, if possible, encourages obtaining "data from a variety of sources representing different points of view"[25] concerning a topic or event. These measures will increase the validity and reliability of the research.

Some evidence of internal validity and reliability can be gained by considering the reputation and integrity of the author, allowing for the circumstances under which a document was written, and comparing "facts" within a document with the writings of other authors considered to be authoritative. Shafer recommends asking the following questions, among others, when evaluating the internal evidence of a document:

1. Do the real meanings of words differ from their literal meanings?
2. How well could the author have observed the things he or she is reporting?
3. Are there internal contradictions?
4. Are any statements inherently improbable?
5. Are factual data in agreement with standard reference works?
6. Does the document seem to call for further corroboration?[26]

Additional questions could include the following: Did the historian have full access to all of the relevant documents, or were some withheld from him or her? Was the author of the document biased? Finally, what significance does the document have as a source of information? Aminzade and Laslett also have identified a list of questions for historians to use when reading and evaluating documents.[27]

BASIC STEPS OF HISTORICAL RESEARCH

Different historians may espouse somewhat different procedures of historical research. For example, one school of thought may emphasize the collection and description of facts, while another may emphasize the interpretation stage. Some believe that a historical study should be guided by a formal hypothesis; others argue for a more flexible methodology such as the source-oriented approach. In the latter case, the historian examines a source or group of sources relevant to his or her interests and extracts whatever is of value, allowing the content of the source to determine the nature of the inquiry.[28] But there seems to be a consensus that historical research generally should meet the same criteria and follow the same procedures as the other basic methods of scientific research.[29] In other words, historical research tends to involve the following steps:

1. Identification of a problem of historical significance
2. Collection of background information (i.e., literature review of the secondary sources)
3. Formulation of a hypothesis when possible (more on this later)
4. Gathering of evidence or data (including verification of the authenticity of the primary sources and the validity and reliability of their contents)
5. Organization and analysis of the pertinent data (more often qualitative than quantitative)
6. Interpretation of the findings or the drawing of conclusions

In short, true historical research tends to resemble a scientific method of inquiry or a problem-oriented approach.

The Hypothesis in Historical Research

Generally speaking, the most significant and useful results of any basic research lie in the generalizations or principles which are derived from the factual data. Consequently, historical research, as well as other types of research, tends to benefit from the incorporation of a hypothesis. Indeed, "the hypothesis is a natural and useful device" in the historical method.[30]

More specifically, the use of a hypothesis in historical research helps to increase the objectivity of the study and minimize researcher bias. It also guides the researcher in the collection, analysis, and interpretation of data by indicating what is relevant to the study. The hypothesis provides a basis for considering various factors in relation to one another and for synthesizing them into a generalization or conclusion that puts their overall significance in focus.[31] In effect, the use of the hypothesis in historical research amounts to an application of theory.

For example, one could hypothesize that academic libraries have been used to a greater extent when they have had substantive library instruction programs than when they have not. Based on this hypothesis, the researcher will know that, at the very least, he or she will need to collect historical data on use and library instruction programs for one or more academic libraries in order to "test" the relationship expressed.

In essence, the hypothesis would be tested by ascertaining the factual truth of specific, relevant events and organizing them to determine whether the presence of the independent variable seemed to have any effect on, or contributed to, the dependent variable. In the example just given, the researcher would attempt to determine whether libraries were more heavily used during periods when they had active library instruction programs than when they did not. The measurement of these two variables would be based on how they were operationally defined. (As is the case with other research methods, however, one test cannot really prove a hypothesis, but it can lend support to or increase confidence in it.)

It tends to be more difficult to test historical hypotheses than those developed in other types of research. This is largely because historical research is ex post facto in nature, and the researcher obviously has no control over the relevant variables, as they have already occurred. One "cannot re-enact the past but only interpret it."[32] Nor can the historian always anticipate the facts that he or she will uncover as the examination of sources proceeds. Consequently, the historical hypothesis may have to be employed in a more flexible manner than is the case for more structured research.

Causal hypotheses are particularly complex and difficult to establish in historical research, but in spite of being inherently difficult to deal with, causality is often thought to be important to consider in a historical study. Beard stated that "no historical account that goes beyond the form of a chronicle can be written without the assumption of causal connection. And no historical chronicle exists in which assumptions of this character are not important."[33]

More specifically, considering causality tends to improve the formulation of the hypothesis and the strategies for collecting data. It also promotes the development of generalizations and basic principles. In short, the consideration of causality forces the researcher to move beyond mere description and to reflect on why certain relationships seem to exist. On the other hand, not all historians are in agreement that consideration of causality (and hypotheses) is essential to good historical research.

Collecting the Data

"While historical research is similar to the reviews of literature which precede other forms of research, the historical approach is more exhaustive, seeking out information from a larger array of sources. It also tracks down information that is much older than required by most reviews and hunts for unpublished material not cited in the standard references."[34] In fact, one of the greatest challenges facing the historian is the extent to which his or her research relies on unpublished materials. Many such documents are housed in archives which have developed arrangement and description techniques that differ from those of libraries, and the historian should be well versed in how to identify and access archival collections.

The data collection technique for historical research, or at least for documentary research, basically involves putting together in a logical fashion the evidence derived from documents or records. This process also often involves the comparing and reconciling of information gathered from two or more sources. Indeed, the use of a variety of sources is considered to be one of the hallmarks of historical research. It is important to note, however, that, owing to the great volume of data typically collected, it is essential to organize the data as systematically as possible. Before beginning a historical study, the researcher should have a specific plan for the acquisition, organization, storage, and retrieval of the data. *Tertiary* sources, such as library catalogs and periodical indexes, are routinely used to identify and access resources. The use of note cards, bibliography cards, multiple files, and so on can be quite helpful when gathering data from the resources. Storing notes in database files provides automatic search capabilities and enables the researcher to code the data for content analysis. Electronic files can also facilitate the use of computer software and programs for data analysis and for translating, collating, and comparing documents.

Shafer, in his chapter on collecting historical evidence, begins with a discussion of recording bibliographical information.[35] He notes how critical good bibliographic records are to the overall process. In the third and final section of his chapter, Shafer discusses the mechanics of making and analyzing research notes. He stresses the importance of using standard methods and provides some examples of research notes. Next, Shafer reviews some of the standard bibliographical aids used by historians, including library catalogs, bibliographies, government publication guides and indexes, newspaper and journal indexes, national bibliographies, manuscript and archival guides, dissertation indexes, guides to reference books, booksellers' catalogs, and guides to locations such as union lists. According to Tibbo, other guides to primary resources commonly used by historians now include repository Web sites, bibliographical utilities, and Web search engines.[36]

The Presentation of Findings

In writing the historical report, the researcher should take care to be objective and to preserve intellectual honesty. This is not to suggest that historical researchers are more prone to partiality than others, but to serve as a reminder that historical research is often rather subjective in nature and thus relatively susceptible to researcher bias. The report is normally directed to the knowledgeable scholar, and the facts and interpretations should be presented so that the reader can evaluate conclusions in light of documented evidence. It goes without saying that the data should be related to the purpose of the study, and that clear and unambiguous expression is important.

"The dual aspect of the historical enterprise—the effort to establish what happened and the attempt to explain why things happened in the way they did— explains the twofold task in historical writing: 1) to convey a sense of time or to show chronological development, 2) to analyse and explain the interrelationships of the events studied, to detect underlying patterns, to unify the various elements in a satisfactory whole, which provides a response to the initial research problem, using an analytical style or an approach by topic."[37] Thus historical writings are represented by a variety of literary forms which combine description, narrative, and analysis in different ways and proportions. Description and narrative tend to suffice when the historian merely desires to recreate the past, while analysis is necessary for interpretation of the past. The nature of the subject matter also may influence the literary form of the report.

LIBRARY HISTORY

Historical research conducted in library and information science has often been referred to as "library history." Shiflett defines library history as "a rubric that covers a myriad of topics associated with libraries and other information systems. Its major form consists of the traditional library, but it also includes the history of any activity or event that might be part of the domain of library and information science."[38] Busha and Harter note that library history is "commonly applied to an account of events that have affected any library or group of libraries, as well as to the social and economic impacts of libraries on their communities."[39] (A related, but narrower, area of inquiry is the history of the book.) According to Irwin, since libraries function within a larger context, library historians should be concerned with "the history not only of scholarship in its narrower sense, but of human civilization and culture and literacy."[40]

Unfortunately, the fact that the history of library and information science has been given a special label seems to suggest that it is a special type of history. Some would even argue that it has been an inferior type of history or historical research. In 1952, Shera pointed out that library history had evidenced "an excessive preoccupation with antiquarian detail and a provincial point of view."[41] In 1965, Bartlett argued that "there is never a dearth of library history, but ... its existence has been consistently marred by a tragic shortage of quality."[42]

A review of the more recent literature of library history, however, suggests that the quality of historical research in library and information science has improved. (See Davis and Tucker for a comprehensive guide to the literature of American library history.)[43] As far back as 1978, Kaser pointed out that "we are vastly better equipped today with sound, rigorous, scholarly understanding than we were a few years ago."[44] Shiflett stated, "The condemnation of library history as mere antiquarianism is only valid if the short view of history is held."[45]

As to the future of library history, there continues to be a need for more historical research that considers libraries and other information systems in broad contexts. Almost 40 years ago Hagler pointed out there is a need for more unified interpretations of library history based on comprehensive visions.[46]

BIBLIOGRAPHICAL RESEARCH

Another area of scholarly work that some consider to be a special type of historical research is bibliographical research. Others would argue that bibliographical research does not represent true research, at least as prescribed by the scientific method of inquiry. Most would concede, however, that bibliographical research that takes the form of descriptive bibliography certainly comes closer to being true research than does systematic or enumerative bibliography. The latter is not even considered to be true bibliographical research. There is no question, however, that both types of bibliographical work are important scholarly endeavors which, at the very least, support the work of "true" researchers or historians.

Systematic Bibliography

Persons involved in the compilation of systematic or enumerative bibliographies are concerned with the book (and other materials) as an intellectual entity. Their purpose is to assemble information about individual works into a logical and useful arrangement. The results are one of the following compilations or lists:

1. Universal bibliography—a bibliography that includes everything published or issued in a subject field regardless of date of publcation.

2. National bibliography—a bibliography that lists everything published (and possibly distributed) in a given country.

3. Trade bibliography—a bibliography compiled primarily to aid the book trade by supplying information as to what books are in print or for sale; when, where, and by whom they were published; and their price.

4. Subject bibliography—a bibliography that lists materials relating to a specific topic.

Descriptive Bibliography

In contrast to systematic bibliography, descriptive bibliography is concerned with the book as a physical entity or material object. As was noted above, it resembles true research more than does systematic bibliography. Sir Walter Greg, quoted in Eaton, once defined descriptive bibliography as follows:

> Bibliography is the study of books as tangible objects. It examines the materials of which they are made and the manner in which these materials are put together. It traces their place and mode of origin, and the subsequent adventures which have befallen them. It is not concerned with their contents in a literary sense, but it is certainly concerned with the signs and symbols they contain (apart from their significance) for the manner in which these marks are written or impressed is a very relevant bibliographical fact. And, starting from this fact, it is concerned with the relation of one book to another; the question of which manuscript was copied from which, which individual copies of printed books are to be grouped together as forming an edition, and what is the relation of edition to edition.[47]

A more succinct definition found in the *Oxford English Dictionary* defines bibliography as "the systematic description and history of books . . ."[48]

An important function of descriptive bibliography is to describe the "ideal copy," or primary document, and its variants. This process can be broken down into more specific bibliographical research, including the following:

1. Analytical bibliography, which is concerned with the physical description of the book in order to determine the details of the physical process of its manufacturing.

2. Textual bibliography, which focuses on certain textual variations between a manuscript and the printed book or among various editions. It is more concerned with the author's words than with the physical aspects of the book.

3. Historical bibliography, which deals with the identification of original editions and the placing and dating of individual books.

Other terms that are sometimes used to represent specific types of descriptive bibliography, or are used as synonyms, include comparative, technical, and critical bibliography.

As was pointed out earlier, descriptive bibliographical research is a scholarly activity which may be thought of as historical research in and of itself, but it is also of critical importance to all historians needing assurance of the authenticity and accuracy of their documentary resources. As Ronald McKerrow stated,

> bibliographical evidence will help us to settle such questions as that of the order and relative value of different editions of a book; whether certain sections of a book were originally intended to form part of it or were added afterwards; whether a later edition was printed from an earlier one, and from which; whether it was printed from a copy that had been corrected in manuscript, or whether such corrections as it contained were made in proof, and a number of other problems of a similar kind, which may often have a highly important literary bearing. It will indeed sometimes enable us to solve questions which to one entirely without bibliographical knowledge would appear quite incapable of solution.[49]

Readers interested in learning more about the process of bibliographical research should consult the literature on historical research, reference, and bibliography, including works by Wynar,[50] Robinson,[51] Bowers,[52] Harmon,[53] and Beal.[54] Those interested in examples of bibliographical research may wish to read Eaton's benchmark article in *Library Trends*.[55]

PROBLEMS IN HISTORICAL RESEARCH

A variety of problems are common to most types of research but tend to be particularly important in historical research, including the following:

1. Deciding how much data are enough. This tends to be a relatively subjective decision. At one time, historians generally attempted to collect virtually all relevant data; they now tend toward a more selective approach. Yet the historian must continue to avoid an overreliance on an insufficient amount of data or evidence. Using too little information can lead to the "argument from silence."[56] In other words, the researcher must be careful not to assume that some event did not occur simply because he or she is not aware of some record of the event.

2. Improperly selecting data. Briefly stated, the historian must avoid improper or faulty selection of data, including such tactics as ignoring some data, exaggerating others, and so on. Such action will significantly increase the bias in a study.

3. Relying too heavily on secondary sources of information. This is particularly likely in studies not dealing with relatively recent events.

4. Investigating an overly broad problem. This is difficult to avoid because historical issues tend to be complex.

5. Failing to evaluate adequately the historical data and their sources. (These techniques were addressed in an earlier section.)

6. Failing to interpret the data. As was noted earlier, historical research is most productive when the researcher attempts to synthesize or integrate the facts into meaningful generalizations.

7. Reading the present into the past even though the historical data may not support such an interpretation.

Other problems in historical research and criteria for evaluating historical research can be drawn from the general research guidelines discussed earlier in this work. In addition, Mouly has pointed out several criteria for evaluating historical studies, most of which have already been presented.[57] He, and others, emphasize the desirability of a writing style that will attract as well as inform. He calls for a report that will make a significant contribution on the basis of new knowledge and not simply represent "uninspired hackwork." Finally, Mouly asks that the historical study reflect scholarliness. Again, such criteria are not unique to historical research, but they do seem to receive more attention in this area.

SUMMARY

"Though the methods of historical investigation can be shown to be the appropriate counterparts of the methods used in other sciences to investigate the phenomena that specially concern them, there appears to be a general reluctance to accord to historical conclusions the kind of logical validity that the conclusions of other sciences are deemed to possess."[58] This may be the case because historical research is ex post facto in nature. The historical researcher must work from evidence back to the event. In addition, the historian is usually in the situation of having to investigate exceptionally complex phenomena. Consequently, it is especially difficult for the historian to support causality within a relationship, or even to draw conclusions with a very high level of confidence. For these reasons, it is generally considered advisable for the historical researcher to follow some sort of scientific method of inquiry, including the formulation and testing of a hypothesis and the analysis and interpretation of data. Such processes help to distinguish true historical research from mere chronology.

Regarding the collection of data, it is important for the researcher to draw upon primary, rather than secondary, sources as much as possible. It is also crucial that the researcher establish the internal and external validity of his or her sources. Bibliographical research methods are often used for evaluating the latter.

The criteria for evaluating historical research are much the same as those for other methods of research. It is particularly important that historical research be well presented in a readable but scholarly style. There is a continuing need for genuine historical research in library and information science, and the better its presentation, the more impact it is likely to have. To paraphrase Arthur Bestor, there is no logical reason why historical knowledge cannot, in principle, be as exact as knowledge in other sciences and, therefore, make a real contribution to the advancement of the field.[59] Those interested in more information about historical research in LIS should refer to Gorman and Clayton, who provide a detailed discussion and examples of historical investigation in information organizations.[60]

NOTES

1. George J. Mouly, *Educational Research: The Art and Science of Investigation* (Boston: Allyn and Bacon, 1978), 157.

2. Ibid.

3. Ibid., 158.

4. John Tosh and Sean Lang, *The Pursuit of History: Aims, Methods and New Directions in the Study of Modern History*, 4th ed. (London: Pearson Longman, 2006), 9–11.

5. Ibid., 9.

6. Ibid., 10.

7. Ibid., 11

8. Herbert Goldhor, *An Introduction to Scientific Research in Librarianship* (Urbana: University of Illinois, Graduate School of Library Science, 1972), 98.

9. Wayne Wiegand, comp., *Libraries in the U.S. Timeline* (Published by the American Library Association and the ALA Public Information Office, December 1999; inserted in *American Libraries* 30, no. 11 (December 1999).

10. Charles H. Busha and Stephen P. Harter, *Research Methods in Librarianship: Techniques and Interpretations* (New York: Academic Press, 1980), 92.

11. Michael H. Harris, ed., *Reader in American Library History* (Washington, DC: NCR Microcard Editions, 1971), 1.

12. Jesse H. Shera, "On the Value of Library History," *Library Quarterly* 22 (July 1952): 240–51.

13. G. E. Gorman and Peter Clayton, *Qualitative Research for the Information Professional: A Practical Handbook*, with contributions from Sydney J. Shep and Adela Clayton, 2nd ed. (London: Facet Publishing, 2005), 161.

14. Library History Round Table, American Library Association, "Statement on History in Education for Library and Information Science,"http://www.ala.org/ala/mgrps/rts/lhrt/governance/lhrtpositions/historyeducation.cfm.

15. Donald G. Davis, Jr., "Ebla to the Electronic Dream: The Role of Historical Perspectives in Professional Education," *Journal of Education for Library and Information Science* 39, no. 3 (Summer 1998): 229–35.

Lee Shiflett, "Sense-Making and Library History," *Journal of Education for Library and Information Science* 41, no. 3 (Summer 2000): 254–59.

16. Derek Bok, *Higher Learning* (Cambridge, MA: Harvard University Press, 1986), 168–69.

17. Shiflett, "Sense-Making and Library History," 254–59.

18. Karl Weick, *Sensemaking in Organizations* (Thousand Oaks, CA: Sage, 1995), 14.

19. Tyrus Hillway, *Introduction to Research*, 2nd ed. (Boston: Houghton Mifflin, 1964), 159.

20. Karen J. Winkler, "Disillusioned with Numbers and Counting, Historians Are Telling Stories Again," *Chronicle of Higher Education* 28 (June 1984): 5–6.

21. Hillway, *Introduction to Research*, 147.

22. Rolland E. Stevens, ed., *Research Methods in Librarianship: Historical and Bibliographical Methods in Library Research* (Urbana: University of Illinois, Graduate School of Library Science, 1971), 11.

23. Orvin L. Shiflett, "Clio's Claim: The Role of Historical Research in Library and Information Science," *Library Trends* 32 (Spring 1984): 385–406.

24. Wendy M. Duff and Joan M. Cherry, "Use of Historical Documents in a Digital World: Comparisons with Original Materials and Microfiche," *Information Research* (October 2000), http://informationr.net/ir/6-1/paper86.html.

25. Earl R. Babbie, *The Practice of Social Research*, 12th ed. (Belmont, CA: Wadsworth/Cengage Learning, 2010), 356.

26. Robert J. Shafer, ed., *A Guide to Historical Method*, 3rd ed. (Homewood, IL: Dorsey Press, 1980), 166–67.

27. Ron Aminzade and Barbara Laslett, "Reading and Evaluating Documents," in *The Practice of Social Research*, 12th ed., ed. Earl Babbie (Belmont, CA: Wadsworth/Cengage Learning, 2010), 357.

28. Tosh and Lang, *The Pursuit of History*, 54.

29. Mouly, *Educational Research*, 159.

30. Shafer, *A Guide to Historical Method*, 176.

31. Mouly, *Educational Research*, 160.

32. Goldhor, *An Introduction to Scientific Research*, 111.

33. Ibid., 109–10.

34. Stephen Isaac and William B. Michael, *Handbook in Research and Evaluation: A Collection of Principles, Methods and Strategies Useful in the Planning, Design, and Evaluation of Studies in Education and the Behavioral Sciences*, 3rd ed. (San Diego, CA: EdITS, 1995), 49.

35. Shafer, *A Guide to Historical Method*.

36. Helen R. Tibbo, "Primarily History in America: How U.S. Historians Search for Primary Materials at the Dawn of the Digital Age," *The American Archivist* 66, no. 1 (Spring/Summer 2003): 9–50.

37. Gorman and Clayton, *Qualitative Research for the Information Professional*, 175.

38. Shiflett, "Clio's Claim," 402.

39. Busha and Harter, *Research Methods in Librarianship*, 93.

40. Raymond Irwin, *The Golden Chain: A Study in the History of Libraries* (London: H. K. Lewis, 1958), 3–4.

41. Shera, "On the Value of Library History," 249.

42. Richard A. Bartlett, "The State of the Library History Art," in *Approaches to Library History*, ed. John D. Marshall (Tallahassee: Florida State University Library School, 1965), 19.

43. Donald G. Davis, Jr. and John M. Jucker, *American Library History: A Comprehensive Guide to the Literature* (Santa Barbara, CA: ABC-Clio, 1989).

44. David Kaser, "Advances in American Library History," in *Advances in Librarianship*, vol. 8, ed. Michael H. Harris (New York: Academic Press, 1978), 192.

45. Shiflett, "Clio's Claim," 388.

46. Ronald Hagler, "Needed Research in Library History," in *Research Methods in Librarianship: Historical and Bibliographical Methods in Library Research*, ed. Rolland E. Stevens (Urbana: University of Illinois, Graduate School of Library Science, 1971), 132.

47. Thelma Eaton, "Bibliographical Research," *Library Trends* 13 (July 1964): 44.

48. *The Oxford English Dictionary*, 2nd ed., vol. 2, prepared by J. A. Simpson and E. S. C. Weiner (Oxford: Clarendon Press, 1989), 169.

49. Eaton, "Bibliographical Research," 44–45.

50. Bohdan S. Wynar, *Introduction to Bibliography and Reference Work*, 4th ed. (Rochester, NY: Libraries Unlimited, 1967).

51. A. M. Robinson, *Systematic Bibliography* (London: Clive Bingley, 1979).

52. Fredson Bowers, *Principles of Bibliographical Description* (New Castle, DE: Oak Knoll Books, 1994).

53. Robert B. Harmon, *Elements of Bibliography: A Guide to Information Sources and Practical Applications*, 3rd ed. (Lanham, MD: Scarecrow Press, 1998).

54. Peter Beal, *A Dictionary of English Manuscript Terminology, 1450–2000* (Oxford: Oxford University Press, 2008).

55. Eaton, "Bibliographical Research," 44–45.

56. Goldhor, *An Introduction to Scientific Research*, 107.

57. Mouly, *Educational Research*, 170.

58. Stevens, *Research Methods in Librarianship*, 111.

59. Ibid.

60. Gorman and Clayton, *Qualitative Research for the Information Professional*, 160–81.

Chapter 9

Analysis of Data

A knowledge of basic statistics is imperative both to the research producer and research consumer in library science, just as it is imperative to the research producer and consumer in any social science or in any field which relies on empirical evidence for the development of principles.[1]

Statistical analysis, or "statistics," is concerned with the development and application of methods and techniques for organizing and analyzing data (usually quantitative) so that the reliability of conclusions based on the data may be evaluated objectively in terms of probability. There are two major areas or types of statistics—theoretical and applied. The former is concerned with the mathematical aspects of statistics; the latter involves the practical applications of statistics and is the focus of this chapter.

This text will not attempt to teach readers how to conduct a statistical analysis; it will indicate the kinds of things that statistical analysis can and cannot do while emphasizing the care that should be exercised in using statistics. Specific examples will be given for the major types of analysis; in no way do they represent a comprehensive listing of all of the statistical tests that may be employed. Readers looking for other relatively nonmathematical, nonthreatening introductions to statistics may wish to refer to Norman and Streiner;[2] Spirer, Spirer, and Jaffe;[3] Rowntree;[4] and Jaeger.[5] Texts written primarily for library and information professionals include ones by Simpson;[6] Hafner;[7] Hernon et al.;[8] Hernon;[9] Boyce, Meadow, and Kraft;[10] and Stephen and Hornby.[11] The *Dictionary of Statistics and Methodology* is an excellent resource for "nontechnical definitions of statistical and methodological terms used in the social and behavioral sciences."[12]

ROLE OF STATISTICS

Generally speaking, statistical analysis may be used to accomplish four basic purposes. One, statistics may indicate the central point around which a mass of data revolves. Two, they may show how broad or diverse the spread can be for a mass of data. Three, statistics may reveal how closely or distantly certain features within the mass of data are related, as well as whether a relationship even exists. Four, they may indicate the degree to which the facts might have occurred by mere chance, or whether there is a probability of their having been influenced by some factor other than pure chance.[13] (The last function is accomplished with statistical tests of the hypothesis.)

In short, the basic purpose of statistical analysis is to summarize observations or data in such a manner that they provide answers to the hypothesis or research questions. Statistics facilitate drawing general conclusions based on specific data. Stated somewhat differently, "the field of statistics involves methods for describing and analyzing data and for making decisions or inferences about phenomena represented by the data."[14] Both methods, even the second one, are essentially methods of analysis and should be distinguished from interpretation. Interpretation of the results follows the analysis stage, and its purpose is to search for the broader meaning of the results by linking them to other available knowledge.

CAUTIONS IN USING STATISTICS

In addition to keeping in mind that the statistical analysis cannot do the interpretation, the researcher should be aware of other concerns in using statistics. For example, the nature of the data to a large extent determines the statistical techniques that can be used legitimately. That is to say, certain techniques are appropriate for use with categorical data, others with ordinal data, and so on. Specific examples illustrating this principle will be given later. Second, the more controlled the research setting, the less is the need, in general, for certain statistical techniques. Most, if not all, of the important relevant variables are already controlled, and replication of the study is less likely to produce different results. Fennick describes the problems associated with statistics that are not used properly and provides interesting and understandable examples.[15]

Statistics are necessary for most research studies involving quantitative data and are particularly crucial at the sampling and analysis stages. The analysis process should be planned well in advance in order to anticipate problems that may be encountered. In fact, the analysis of a study is shaped, to a considerable extent, before the data are collected.

The anticipation of the analysis process determines what kinds of data will be needed. For example, a researcher may wish to determine if there is a significant difference between the average frequency of library use of students who have and have not received library instruction. In order to do so, he or she will need to employ an appropriate statistical test, such as the difference of means test. As the difference of means test requires interval level data, the researcher will need to be certain to measure the frequency of library use on an interval scale. Simply ranking users as high, moderate, low, and so on would not be adequate in this case. Once the data have been collected, there is little potential for changing them, and the researcher is at that point limited to certain statistical techniques.

The conceptual development of a research study should not, however, be dictated by the statistical techniques to follow. In the example given above, the researcher should decide what is the most valid measure of library use and then utilize the best statistical methods available. He or she should not decide to use factor analysis, for example, and then proceed to force the data into that technique, regardless of its appropriateness. Sophisticated statistical analysis cannot substitute for early, sound conceptual development.

STEPS INVOLVED IN STATISTICAL ANALYSIS

Regardless of the specific techniques or tests employed, there are certain basic steps common to virtually all statistical analyses. Those steps will be discussed briefly before taking a more detailed look at the major types of analysis.

The Establishment of Categories

In order to organize and analyze the data collected for a study, it is necessary to place them in categories. The identification or establishment of categories should take place before the data are gathered. The actual categorization of the data takes place during or after the collection process. In establishing categories, four basic rules or guidelines should be followed:

1. The set of categories or values (i.e., the classification scheme) for any one variable should be derived from a single classificatory principle, which is determined by the research question or hypothesis being investigated. For example, if one were studying the relationship between size of the reference collection and reference performance, two sets of categories would be needed. Reference collection size might well be categorized according to the number of volumes, and would represent a ratio level scale. Reference performance could be categorized according to the percentage of reference questions answered correctly, another ratio scale. Another variable might be the type of reference question. Questions could be assigned to a set of nominal categories, such as directional and research questions.

2. Each set of categories should be exhaustive. That is, it should be possible to place every observation in one of the categories of the set. This does not preclude the use of a miscellaneous or catchall category, such as "other." However, if one finds it necessary to place a substantial number of observations in an "other" category, or if a large percentage of such observations seem to have certain characteristics in common, the establishment of one or more additional categories should be considered. It is generally preferable to establish as many categories as possible and, if necessary, reduce or combine them later.

3. The categories within each set should be mutually exclusive. This means that it should not be possible to place a specific observation correctly in more than one category. Returning to the categorization of reference questions, every reference question received should logically fit into one, but no more than one, of the categories. It should not, for

example, be possible for a question to be placed accurately in both the directional category and the research category. If it is conceivable to do so, then the categories are not adequately defined or the observations are not accurate.

4. Last, but not least, the development of categories should be based on a sound knowledge of the subject matter and an anticipation of likely responses. A person establishing categories for reference questions should have had enough reference experience, and have done enough reading about the topic, to be able to predict the types of questions that will appear in a study and establish categories accordingly.

Coding the Data

Once the categories have been established and data "assigned" to them, it is necessary to convert the new data or responses to numerical codes, so that they can be tabulated or tallied. These codes are, in turn, assigned to specified locations in data files, particularly if computer data analysis is planned. (A codebook is useful for describing the locations of variables and for indicating the codes assigned to the categories or values of each variable.) See the Coding Instructions in Figure 9.1. However, if the original responses are already numerical, such as are test scores, volume counts in libraries, and so on, then they do not need to be assigned new codes, unless they are being recoded or assigned to groupings.

Figure 9.1   Coding Instructions: Daily Client Contact Log Sheet

Item	Variable name/ field name	Codes/Description
Log Sheet Number	PAGENO	enter number in upper right corner log sheets are numbered sequentially
Staff Id	STAFFID	enter number in upper left corner
Log Date	LOGDATE	enter date as one long number example: 1/12/99 = 12299 If no date enter 999999
Site	SITES	enter the number from column
Location	LOCATION	see service location sheet for codes Leave blank if none given
Client ID	ID	enter the id from the column replace any missing letters or numbers using the space bar unless it is obvious that the missing digit should be 0 example: MD578 = MD0578 FD05M = FD05 M

Figure 9.1 (Continued)

Item	Variable name/ field name	Codes/Description
Gender	GENDER	Female = 1
		Male = 2
		Transgender = 3
		Missing, unknown = 9
Birth Year	BIRTH_YR	enter complete year 19xx or 20xx found as 5th and 6th characters in client id if missing or incomplete enter as 9999
Race	RACE	ALWAYS USE CAPS when entering
		AA (African-American)
		AR (Arab-American)
		AS (Asian)
		B (Black)
		H (Hispanic/Latino)
		NA (Native American)
		W (White)
		O (Other)
		UN (Unknown, missing)
Encounter	ENCOUNTR	Face = 1
		Case Management = 2
		Computer = 3
		Case Conference = 4
		Paperwork = 8
		Phone = 10
		Other = 15 (e.g., fax, letter, email)
Risk # 1	RISKB_1	enter first number given or 99 if blank
Risk # 2	RISKB_2	enter second number given or leave blank if none
Risk # 3	RISKB_3	enter third number given or leave blank if none
Risk#4	RISKB_4	enter fourth number given or leave blank if none
HIV Status	STATUS	Positive = 1
		Negative = 2

(continued)

Figure 9.1   (Continued)

Item	Variable name/ field name	Codes/Description
		Unknown = 3
		Missing = 9
Hepatitis C Status	HEPCSTAT	Positive = 1
		Negative = 2
		Unknown = 3

Services Received:

For all services:

checked = 1

not checked = 0

Individual Counseling	S_HE_IC	
Group Counseling	S_HE_GC	
Community and Street Outreach	S_HE_OUT	
Support Group	S_SG	
Info and Referral	S_IR	
Case Management	S_CM	
Counseling andTesting	S_CT	
Transport	S_T	
Needle Exchange	S_NEP	
Institution Outreach	S_INST	
Jail Advocacy	S_JA	
Mobile Advocacy	S_MA	
Preventive Case Management	S_PA	
Hepatitis C Testing	S_HEPC	
Other	S_O	

Materials

Condoms

type	M_CO_SEX	F = 1 M = 2 B = 3
number	M_CO_NO	enter number (if both types enter the total number of condoms)

Kits

Kit 1	M_KIT_1	Use caps only!
Kit 2	M_KIT_2	A, B, D, H, L, P, W, T (note: BT=T)
Kit 3	M_KIT_3	If there are other codes contact data
Kit 4	M_KIT_4	manager

Figure 9.1   (Continued)

Item	Variable name/ field name	Codes/Description
Brochures	M_PR	checked = 1
		not checked = 0
Referrals		
first	REFER_1	enter the number given
second	REFER_2	leave blank if none
third	REFER_3	
fourth	REFER_4	
fifth	REFER_5	
Minutes	MIN	enter number or 999 if missing

One of the most important considerations in coding is reliability. Problems of reliability in coding can result from inadequacies in the data. For example, a poorly worded questionnaire item may not produce enough relevant information for the purpose of the study. Answers to questions that actually ask more than one question are, of course, difficult, if not impossible, to code accurately. Problems with the categories may also lead to a lack of reliability, particularly if they do not meet the basic guidelines outlined above. Inaccuracies can emerge during the coding process itself as a result of observations being assigned to the wrong category. For that reason, it is important to see that coders are adequately trained and to verify or check the accuracy of their work. As was noted in the section in Chapter 5 on questionnaire construction, precoding can help to minimize the amount of coding errors and thus increase reliability.

In actually coding the data, researchers traditionally have transcribed the observations or scores for each individual or case from the data collection instrument to coding or transfer sheets. Once the coding sheets were complete, the researcher, if he or she were analyzing the data manually, could then work directly from them. See the Code Book in Figure 9.2. But if the mass of data was large, or the statistical techniques to be employed were relatively complex and time consuming to conduct, the researcher would probably elect to use a computer to analyze the data. Today, most researchers input their data into computer programs, some of which still utilize a computer card image of 80 columns per record for organizing the data to be analyzed.

Some researchers are able to take advantage of optical scanning for producing data files; however, direct data entry may now be the most common technique for creating data files. It is based on a computer program that displays each question on the screen and prompts the researcher to input the response directly on the screen (and into the computer file). Most survey research organizations use a database management program to control data entry. Most statistical programs now enable downloading a computer data file or entering the data directly into the statistical program using some sort of data editor. More specifically, the

Figure 9.2   Code Book: Internet Training Sessions

Column	Label	Variables
A	ID with author's initials	
B	Rate computer skills	1=poor 2=fair 3=average 4=good 5=excellent
C	Confident before class	1=poor 2=fair 3=average 4=good 5=excellent
D	Confident after class	1=poor 2=fair 3=average 4=good 5=excellent
E	Level of knowledge before class	1=poor 2=fair 3=average 4=good 5=excellent
F	Level of knowledge after class	1=poor 2=fair 3=average 4=good 5=excellent
G	Look for more health info	1=yes 2=no
H	If no, provides explanation	1=explanation
I	Rate instructor	1=poor 2=fair 3=average 4=good 5=excellent
J	Attend another class	1=yes 2=no
K	If no, provides explanation	1=yes
L	Previous guest lectures	
M	Previous Internet training	
N	Come to other programs	1=yes 2=no
O	If no, provides explanation	1=yes
P	Age	1=under 20 2=21–40 3=41–60 4=61–80 5=81+

Figure 9.2   (Continued)

Column	Label	Variables
Q	Gender	1=male 2=female
R	Education	1=high school 2=community college 3=university
S	Computer at home	1=yes 2=no
T	Email	1=yes 2=no
U	Write letters	1=yes 2=no
V	Search Internet	1=yes 2=no
W	other	1=yes Blank if no response

program prompts the person entering data for each response, checks the response to ensure that it is a valid response for that variable, and then saves the response in the proper data file. As discussed in Chapter 5, many researchers are optimizing the opportunities made available to them via the Web. Web-based and email surveys enable the responses to be input into the software program for analysis when respondents submit their questionnaires.

After the data have been prepared and saved as an electronic file, they can then be analyzed using a software program such as those identified later in this chapter. The manuals that accompany these programs explain how to create data files that can be manipulated by the particular software and how to calculate certain statistics by executing appropriate commands. Some of the manuals even explain how to reformat data files originally created for analysis by another software program. Those individuals wanting to read more about the coding process may wish to refer to Golden,[16] Barnes,[17] Hernon,[18] and Vaughan.[19]

ANALYZING THE DATA—DESCRIPTIVE STATISTICS

Once the data are ready to be analyzed, the researcher can choose to utilize descriptive statistics, inferential statistics, or both. Looking first at descriptive statistics, which have been the predominant type of data analysis employed by researchers in library and information science, there are at least six basic functions that they can perform.[20]

One, at the most basic level, the statistical analysis can indicate how many persons, objects, scores, or whatever achieved each value (or fell into each category) for every variable that was measured. These calculations, known as frequency distributions, are usually reported in tables. Common types of frequency distributions include simple or absolute, cumulative, percentage, and grouped distributions.

Two, when it may be difficult to grasp the overall meaning of frequency distribution tables, pictorial representations can be used to portray a variety of characteristics of the cases or individuals with respect to the variable or variables measured. This process typically involves the use of one or more data displays such as bar graphs or charts, pie charts, histograms, and frequency polygons (see Figures 9.3, 9.4, 9.5, and 9.6). Graphic representations generally sacrifice some detail in an effort to improve communication of data, but the loss of detail may well be desirable and justifiable. Graphs are especially useful for displaying the findings of a research study that has a large number of cases. The design of such devices has become easier with the widespread availability of data analysis and spreadsheet programs. Tufte has authored two interesting and useful books about the visual display of quantitative information.[21]

Three, descriptive statistics are capable of characterizing what is typical in a group of cases. Such statistics, referred to as measures of *central tendency*, commonly include the mean, the median, and the mode. The (arithmetic) mean is what is commonly called the average. It is the sum of the scores divided by the total number of cases involved. The median is the value of the middle item when the scores are arranged according to size. The mode refers to the category or score that occurs most frequently.

Four, descriptive statistics can indicate how widely cases in a group vary. These statistics are known as measures of *dispersion* or *variability*; examples include the range of scores (the highest score minus the lowest score), their mean deviation (the arithmetic mean of the absolute differences of each score from the mean), the standard deviation (the square root of the arithmetic mean of the squared deviations from the mean), and the variance (the mean squared deviation).

The standard deviation is one of the most frequently used measures of dispersion, but it is also one of the more difficult to comprehend. As noted

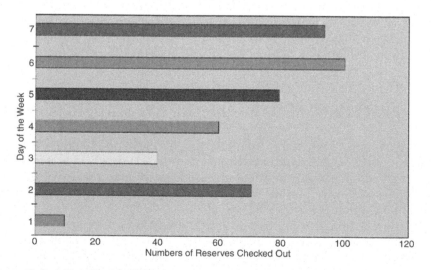

Figure 9.3 A Bar Graph/Chart.

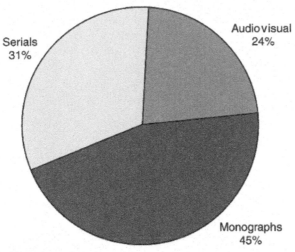

Figure 9.4 A Pie Chart.

above, it reflects the amount of deviation from the mean for the observed scores. Stated differently, it is the positive square root of the variance. Its size increases whenever the size of the deviation scores increases. It is a useful measure of dispersion because, in many distributions of scores, we know what percentage of the scores lie within plus or minus one, two, and three standard deviations. Its usefulness is enhanced because its units of measure are the same as those of the original data. The standard deviation is useful for comparing groups.

Assume, for example, that a survey of a public library's users found that their ages ranged from 3 to 60 years, their mean age was 45, and the standard deviation was three. We would thus know that 67 percent of the users fell between one standard deviation, or three years, or between the ages of 42 to 48, and so on for two and three standard deviations.

Figure 9.5 A Histogram.

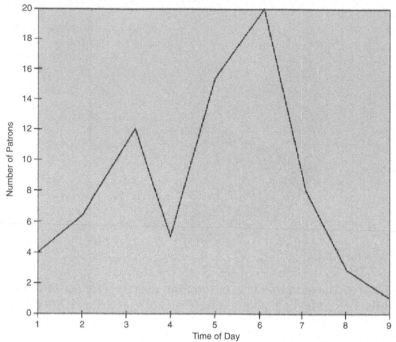

Figure 9.6 A Frequency Polygon.

The formula for the standard deviation is as follows:

$$S = \sqrt{\frac{\sum X_i^2}{N}}$$

where $\sum X_i^2$ equals the total of the squared deviation scores, and N equals the number of cases.

Five, descriptive statistics can measure the relationship between or among the different variables in the data. These are generally referred to as correlational or associational statistics. They have the ability to allow prediction of one variable based on another, but they cannot be used to establish causal relationships. Correlation coefficients are, of course, correlational or descriptive statistics, but they also are often treated as inferential statistics and will be discussed in the section treating that type of statistical test.

Another common type of correlational statistic is the cross-tabulation or bivariate frequency. Bivariate frequencies are the products of tables in which two variables have been cross-classified. The tables consist of rows and columns, where the categories or values of one variable are labels for the rows, and the categories of the second variable are labels for the columns. Usually the independent variable is the column variable, and the dependent variable is the row variable.

The calculation and analysis of bivariate frequencies is an essential step in discovering or testing relationships between variables, so an example of a bivariate table will be presented and discussed next. In reading Table 9.1, one should first note the title and headings in order to learn what information is contained in the table. In this example, the title and headings indicate that the

TABLE 9.1   Frequency of Library Use by Age (hypothetical data)

Library Use Per Year	1–12	13–25	Age 26–50	51+	Total
0–5	6	12	15	40	73
	9%	15%	25%	43%	25%
6–12	10	13	12	35	70
	16%	16%	20%	38%	24%
13–24	25	30	12	10	77
	39%	38%	20%	11%	26%
25+	23	25	20	7	75
	36%	31%	34%	8%	25%
Total	64	80	59	92	295
	100%	100%	100%	100%	100%

table summarizes data on annual frequency of library use and age. It also is apparent that the data have been grouped or categorized in ranges. Each range represents a value for the respective variable. As was indicated earlier, the reader probably can assume that the column variable, age, is the independent variable, and the row variable, library use, is the dependent variable.

The reader next should check at the bottom of the table to see if the source for the data is identified. Knowing the source helps the reader to assess the reliability of the data. If the source is not given at the foot of the table, it should be indicated at the appropriate place in the text. (Remember that every table should be referred to within the text and summarized or highlighted in some fashion.)

Then the reader should determine in which direction the percentages have been calculated. It is important to know whether the percentages have been calculated down the columns or across the rows. This can be learned by noting where the 100 percents have been placed. In Table 9.1, the percentages have been calculated down the columns. It is possible to calculate percentages in both directions.

Finally, the reader should compare the percentage differences in the table in order to determine the extent to which relationships, if any, between the variables exist. Comparisons are always made in the direction opposite to the one in which the percentages were calculated. In Table 9.1, the reader would examine percentages across rows in order to determine whether given levels of library use significantly varied according to age. In looking at the first row, one can see that 9 percent of the persons who were between the ages of 1 and 12 used the library 0 to 5 times, 15 percent of those aged 13 to 25 used the library 0 to 5 times, and so on. An examination of the entire row indicates that the older age groups tended to exhibit less library use, in that higher percentages of them fell into the lowest library use category. The relative percentages in the other rows tend to support this conclusion. The only noteworthy anomaly is represented by the percentage of persons aged 26 to 50 who used the library 25 or more times (34%). (An occasional anomaly does not necessarily weaken a pattern or resulting conclusion, but it generally is worth further consideration for the insights it may provide.)

The figures in the "total" column indicate what percentages of the total number of cases fell into the different ranges of library use. The figures across the "total" row indicate the numbers and percentages of persons who occurred in each age category. The numbers in the final column and row are referred to as marginals, or univariate, frequencies. They are purely descriptive in nature. The numbers within the individual cells are the cross-tabulations or bivariate frequencies. They are the figures that can help to point out relationships, as they represent the cases that have certain values for both variables. For example, the six cases in the first cell represent persons who were aged 1–12 **and** who used the library 0–5 times during the preceding year. By examining such figures, the reader may detect a pattern of covariation, or a relationship between two variables. In this case, use tended to decrease as age increased. Barnes has a useful chapter on preparing and analyzing tables for those wanting to read more about this topic.[22] Most statistical software and spreadsheet programs provide easy methods for displaying statistical analyses in tables and charts.

The sixth basic function that descriptive statistics can perform is to describe the difference between two or more groups of individuals. This is really no more than a special case of showing the relationship between two variables. Such uses of descriptive statistics often involve measures of central tendency. For example, if one had measured the library skills of two groups of students, it could be revealing to compare the mean scores of the two groups. If the two groups had received different types of instruction, such a comparison could help to indicate the superior instructional method.

ANALYZING THE DATA—INFERENTIAL STATISTICS

In contrast to descriptive statistics, which simply summarize and describe the data (though, as indicated above, they can at least suggest relationships), inferential statistics can perform certain more sophisticated functions. They are most commonly used to predict or estimate population *parameters* or characteristics based on random sample *statistics*, and to test hypotheses using tests of statistical significance to determine if observed differences between groups or variables are "real" or merely due to chance. In short, inferential statistics help one to make inferences and judgments about what exists on the basis of only partial evidence.

Using inferential statistics as first described, one could measure the loss rate for a sample of books and then predict the loss rate for the entire population or collection based on the sample statistic. Applying inferential statistics in the second manner, one could test the relationship between loss rate and circulation loan periods by analyzing the difference in loss rates for two groups of books—one housed in a library with a long loan period, and one in a library with a short loan period. In evaluating the difference, if any, it would be necessary to determine if the difference were too large to be due merely to chance, rather than to the effects of different loan periods.

It should be remembered that statistics are used to test the null hypothesis, or the hypothesis of no relationship, as opposed to the research hypothesis, which does predict a relationship (usually a positive one). Null hypotheses are necessary in order to avoid the "fallacy of affirming the consequent" (i.e., we must eliminate false hypotheses rather than accept true ones). In other words, demonstrating that B occurred does not mean that theory A is necessarily true, or caused B. We must eliminate other theories before concluding A is true. Stated yet another way, to support a hypothesis that two or more variables are related, one must first demonstrate that they are not unrelated. Or one must demonstrate that it is safe to conclude that the null hypothesis is wrong so as to conclude that the variables really are related. Demonstrating that the null hypothesis is unlikely to be true before concluding that there is a real relationship also helps to rule out chance as the cause of the relationship.

Accepting the null hypothesis as true means that any observed difference or relationship is not statistically significant and is probably due to chance or sampling error, and that the research hypothesis is not supported. Rejecting the null hypothesis means that the research hypothesis is supported.

Both of these applications of inferential statistics are based on an assumption of random sampling and on probability theory, and the researcher should have a good understanding of their basic concepts. Random sampling was discussed in the chapter on survey research. Probability theory relates to the mathematical likelihood of an event occurring. Central to probability theory is the assumption that, while repeated events will exhibit a certain pattern over time, individual or short-time events tend to differ from overall long-term patterns of events. For example, if we flip a coin enough times in a fair manner, the law of averages should take effect, and we should end up with 50 percent of the flips resulting in heads and 50 percent in tails. On the other hand, ten flips of the coin might well produce as few as three or four or as many as seven or eight heads.

If the difference between the outcome (say six heads) and 50 percent was small, then we might attribute the difference to chance. If nine of ten flips resulted in heads, then we might suspect that something was amiss and that some variable, such as a defective coin, was affecting or biasing the outcomes of the coin flips. Fortunately, "the mathematical theory of probability provides a basis for evaluating the reliability of the conclusions we reach and the inferences we make when we apply statistical techniques to the collection, analysis, and interpretation of quantitative data."[23] As probability theory does play such a crucial role in statistical analysis, the reader is encouraged to consult one or more standard texts on statistics regarding this subject.

Inferential statistics themselves are of two basic types—parametric statistics or tests, and nonparametric statistics or tests. Either type should be used only when certain conditions exist.

Dilevko examined "research articles published between 2001 and 2005 that academic and public librarians are most likely to read" to determine the extent to which inferential statistics were used. He compared these results to the results of studies conducted in the 1970s and 1980s.[24] He reported that there has been "an increase in the use of inferential statistics" in the 475 articles examined. Of the 135 documented uses of inferential statistics in the articles, 36 different inferential statistics were used. The inferential statistics that had more than a total of five occurrences in the articles were: "T-tests (21), chi-square (20), Pearson's r (16), multiple regression (9), one-way ANOVA (9), reliability coefficients (7), and post hoc tests (6)."[25] The majority of the articles using inferential statistics were authored by librarians or library management personnel.

Figure 9.7 A Normal Curve.

Parametric Statistics

Most important, parametric statistics require the assumption of a normal population or distribution. When the data of a normal distribution are plotted on a graph, they should produce a curve that is symmetrical and unimodal (see Figure 9.7); its mean, median, and mode should all coincide; and there should be a constant area, or proportion of cases, between the mean and an ordinate which is a given distance from the mean in terms of standard deviations. In fact, slightly more than two-thirds of the cases should fall within plus or minus (±) one standard deviation of the mean, slightly more than 95 percent within plus or minus two standard deviations, and almost all cases within plus or minus three standard deviations.

However, if the sample drawn from the population has 100 or more cases, the normality assumption can almost always be relaxed. That is, a normal population is not required, as the sampling distribution of sample means is likely to be normal. In fact, "no matter how unusual a distribution we start with, provided N [the sample size] is sufficiently large, we can count on a sampling distribution that is approximately normal."[26] It is sampling distributions, not populations, that form the basis for tests of significance. (See the section on sampling error in Chapter 4 for a definition of the "mean of the sampling distribution.")

If the sample size falls somewhere between 50 and 100, and if there is evidence that departure from normality is not great, then statistical tests of this type can be used with some confidence. If the sample is less than 30, the researcher should use such tests cautiously unless the approximation to normality is known to be good.[27]

Parametric tests also assume that the variance of each group in question is similar, and that the samples are randomly drawn. In addition, they require that the data being analyzed are primarily interval or ratio level data.

Parametric tests are relatively powerful, or likely to detect a difference between groups if a difference really exists. In other words, the power of a test is directly related to its ability to eliminate false null hypotheses. Power may be defined as 1 minus the probability of a type II error. (A type II or "beta error" is the error of failing to reject a null hypothesis when it is actually false; a type I or "alpha error" is the error of rejecting a true null hypothesis. When the probability of one type increases, the other decreases.)

Some examples of frequently used parametric tests include the following:

1. Z test—this test, using standard scores, tests the difference between a group's results and the results that would be expected due to chance alone. Or, stated somewhat differently, it is used to determine whether the mean of a sample is significantly different from the mean of the population from which it is taken. (A standard, or Z, score is a score that is relative to the mean and measured in standard deviation units. It equals the deviation from the mean divided by the standard deviation.) A Z test could be used, for example, to decide whether the physical condition of a sample of books selected from a library's collection is representative of the physical condition of the entire collection in general.

2. Student's t-test—a test that can be used in place of the Z test where there is still only one group but where, in contrast to the Z test, the standard deviation of the population is not known.

3. Difference of means—a commonly used statistical test which utilizes the t statistic, and which determines if the statistical difference between the mean scores of two groups is significant. It does not require that the population standard deviations be known. (For an example of how the difference of means t-test might be used, see the section later in this chapter on selecting appropriate statistical tests.)

4. Analysis of variance—a statistical test which represents an extension of the difference of means test. It utilizes the F statistic, and it tests for differences among the means of more than two samples or groups. Analysis of variance (ANOVA) can be used with only two groups but would produce the same results as a t-test in that case. Multiple analysis of variance (MANOVA) is designed for situations where one needs to test relationships that involve more than one dependent variable.

5. Post hoc tests—these test "the statistical significance of differences between group means" that have an overall difference calculated after an ANOVA or a regression analysis (RA) has been done.[28]

   a. Tukey's HSD (Honestly Significant Difference) test—this test is used to examine the pattern of mean difference and can be used with more than two groups. The HSD score is the within group variability and is part of the ANOVA result. It is compared with all of the possible pairs of means to determine if there is a significant difference between the HSD score and each mean difference.

   b. Scheffé Test—a test of significance used for multiple comparisons of means in an ANOVA. It is good for comparing unequal cell sizes and "tends to err on the side of underestimating significance."[29]

6. Reliability coefficient—a statistic that indicates the reliability of a measurement, i.e., a test, scale, etc. They range from 0 (completely unreliable when observed variance is attributed to random error) to 1.0 (completely reliable).

   a. Cronbach's —"a measure of internal reliability or consistency of the items in an instrument that have more than two answers, such as Likert scales.[30]

b. Kuder-Richardson—"measures the internal consistency or reliability of tests in which items have only two possible answers,"[31] such as yes/no or true/false.

7. Pearson's product-moment correlation coefficient (r)—this test generally is referred to as simply the correlation coefficient; it measures the degree of linear association between two variables or the extent to which changes in one value correspond with changes in another value. It can range from −1 to +1. A negative coefficient indicates a negative relationship, or, as one variable increases, the other decreases (or vice versa). A positive value indicates a positive relationship, or, as one variable increases, the other increases, or they both decrease. A coefficient of 0, or near 0, means that there is little or no linear relationship between the variables. Use of this statistic requires interval level data. Referring back to our concern about the physical condition of books, we could measure the correlational relationship between the number of times certain books are borrowed and the number of times they must be repaired.

Relationships between two variables can be plotted on a graph, which is usually called a scattergram. A straight line can then be plotted that relates specific values of one variable to values of the other. In the graph below (Figure 9.8), the scores of one of the variables are represented on the abscissa (horizontal line), and the scores of the second variable are represented on the ordinate (vertical line). For example, the X value on the horizontal axis could be the number of items checked out; the Y value on the vertical axis could be length of visit. When two variables are highly correlated, the plotted points tend to be very close to the straight line, and as was noted above, the correlation

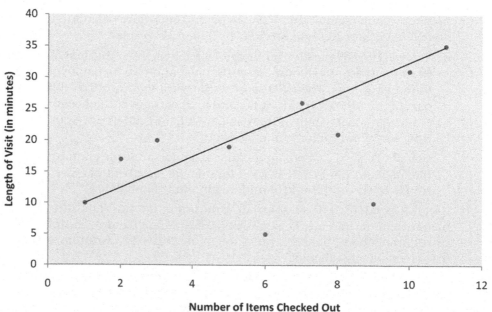

Figure 9.8 A Scatter Diagram with a Regression Line.

coefficient would be close to 1. This line is called a line of regression, and the equation of this line is called a regression equation.

A major aim of quantitative research is prediction. When two variables are correlated, regression equations can be used to predict what value of variable Y would most likely be associated with a given value of X. Regression analysis itself is considered next.

8. Regression—a type of analysis that, as is the case for correlation, can be used for descriptive and inferential purposes. In the former case, Pearson's correlation coefficient is used as the basis for developing a simple linear regression equation to predict the value of one variable when the value of the other variable is known. As an inferential technique, linear regression can be used to generalize findings from a sample to the population from which the sample was randomly selected. For example, using data collected from a sample, one could predict that a certain percentage increase in the median age of a library's population would result in a certain percentage increase in the use of the library.

Regression, and correlation, analysis can be used with two variables or "can readily be extended to include any number of interval scales [variables], one of which can be taken as dependent and the remainder independent."[32] Utilizing multiple regression analysis, one could measure a number of characteristics of reference librarians and use those as a basis for predicting how successful a reference librarian would be in answering reference questions.

Nonparametric Statistics

In contrast to parametric statistics, nonparametric statistics are considered to be distribution-free. That is, they do not require the assumption of a normal population and, therefore, are often used with smaller samples. As they involve weaker assumptions, they are less powerful than the parametric tests and require larger samples in order to yield the same *level of significance*. (The level of significance is the probability of rejecting a true hypothesis. It usually is set at .05 or .01, which means that the null hypothesis, or the prediction of no relationship, is to be rejected if the sample results are among the results that would have occurred no more than 5%, or 1%, of the time. Stated somewhat differently, a significance level of .05 means that there is a 5% probability that the researcher will reject a hypothesis that is actually true.)

Nonparametric tests are usually, but not always, used with ordinal level data. Five common examples are as follows:

1. Chi-square test (X^2)—this test is useful for determining if a statistically significant relationship exists between two categorical variables. If the population is known to be normally distributed, chi-square can be treated as a parametric statistic and frequently is used for causal, comparative studies. The process for calculating a chi-square is essentially the same as described in the section on bivariate frequencies, and it produces the same kind of cross classification. It can indicate only if there is a significant relationship; statistics such as Cramer's V must

be used to determine the strength of any relationships. Returning again to our concern about the physical condition of a library's book collection, we might use a chi-square test to determine whether there is a significant relationship between the location of books and their condition (as assigned to categories). Pearson's chi-square test is the best known one.

2. Mann-Whitney U-test—this is one nonparametric equivalent of the difference of means test, and is used to test for a significant difference between two groups. It cannot be used unless the population is symmetric about its median.

3. Wilcoxon Sign test—this test can be used instead of the Mann-Whitney when the data are not symmetrical. It also is useful in determining the significance of the difference between two correlated groups.

4. Spearman rank-order correlation, or Spearman's ρ—this is a nonparametric correlation coefficient that can be calculated for ranked or ordinal level data. It is interpreted in the same manner as Pearson's correlation coefficient.

5. Kruskall-Wallis test—a nonparametric alternative to analysis of variance; it is appropriate when one has a number of independent random samples and an ordinal scale level of measurement.

Selecting the Appropriate Statistical Test

As has been indicated for most of the examples given above, the various statistical tests must meet certain conditions before being appropriate for use. For example, certain tests call for a normal population, others for a particular level of measurement (see Chapter 2 for a consideration of the basic measurement scales). Most of the examples presented here were intended for the analysis of either one group or two groups. There are also statistical tests intended for more than two variables; such techniques are referred to as multivariate analyses and include multiple regression and factor analysis. One also should consider the primary purpose of the research in choosing statistics; that is, whether it is descriptive or analytical in nature. Other questions relate to the need to distinguish between independent and dependent variables and to the sampling method used.

These and other kinds of questions should be answered before selecting a statistical test. Otherwise, an inappropriate test may be used and thereby invalidate the results of the analysis. The selection of a proper statistic can be facilitated by using some sort of decision tree to systematize the process. An example of the use of decision trees in selecting appropriate statistical tests can be found in a booklet published by the SAS Institute.[33] In using this guide, one starts by noting how many variables are involved, and then continues along the "branches" of the decision tree, answering questions at each decision point. Eventually one arrives at a box which will contain a statistical technique, measure, or test appropriate to the situation. The same information is available in most standard statistical texts but in a less compact, sequential format. Computer programs which will help the researcher select the appropriate statistical test are available as well.

Let us now work through an example of how a statistical test might be selected, and used, to test a hypothesis. Suppose an experiment had been conducted to test the effect of bibliographic instruction (BI) on the library skills of certain university students. The researcher established two groups of randomly selected students. One group of students was given BI during the course of the study; one group received no instruction. At the end of the experiment, the library skills of the students in both groups were measured with a test. The mean test score of the experimental group (instruction) was 85; the mean score of the control group (no instruction) was 65. Thus the difference between mean test scores was 20. The research hypothesis for the study predicted that there would be a significant difference between the mean scores. The implicit null hypothesis was that there would not be a statistically significant difference.

In this scenario, two groups have been observed (i.e., we have calculated the mean library skills scores for two groups of subjects). We are assuming that the two groups were drawn independently from a normally distributed population (all of the students enrolled at the university) in terms of their library skills, but we do not know what the standard deviation for the population is. The test scores represent ratio-level data. We determine prior to the study that BI would be considered the independent variable and library skills (scores) the dependent variable. Thus the difference of means t-test is identified as an appropriate and legitimate statistic for testing our hypothesis.

As indicated, there is a difference of 20 points between the mean test scores of the two groups. The question is whether 20 points represent a statistically significant difference. In order to answer this question, we must first select the significance level and critical region to be used with the test. Assume we selected the .01 level of significance, which means that the test would have a 1 percent chance of rejecting the null hypothesis when it is actually true. Or, as stated earlier, it is the probability of making a type I error.

In selecting the *critical region*, the researcher is deciding whether one or both tails of the sampling distribution will be used to determine whether the hypothesis will be accepted or rejected. (If normal, the sampling distribution would resemble the curve in Figure 9.7.) If the researcher is able to predict the direction of the relationship, he or she is well advised to use a one-tailed test so all of the critical region can be concentrated in one end of the curve. If the direction of the relationship cannot be predicted, a two-tailed test is preferable. In this case, we expect BI to increase library skills, so we elect to use a one-tailed test. Since our significance level is .01, the critical region would be the extreme right 1 percent of the curve or distribution. If our outcome falls into that area, then we would reject the null hypothesis, with a 1 percent chance of having made an error.

Next, we must calculate the value of "t" for our difference of means test. This can be done using the appropriate formula or computer program. Once computed, the t value must be checked in a table of t values to determine whether it is statistically significant (or a computer program can do this for us). If the value is equal to or greater than the value in the table for the appropriate level of significance and "degrees of freedom,"* then it is deemed statistically significant or not likely to have occurred by chance. Therefore, the researcher is

---

*For many statistical tests, the number of degrees of freedom (df) is defined as one less than the size of the sample, or $n-1$.

justified in rejecting the null hypothesis of no relationship and at least tentatively accepting the research hypothesis. We conclude, therefore, that BI does appear to have a positive impact on the library skills of certain university students. A t value lower than the corresponding one in the table would, of course, dictate the opposite conclusion. Gerhan has written an article to help reference librarians understand how statistical significance is employed by the researchers they assist.[34]

CAUTIONS IN TESTING THE HYPOTHESIS

In using statistics to test hypotheses, one must always keep in mind that statistical inferences are based on probability, and one can never rely on statistical evidence alone for a judgment of whether a hypothesis is true. Such a decision must be based on the presuppositions or conceptual basis of the research as well.

It is also important to remember that a single statistical "acceptance" of a hypothesis does not prove it to be true with absolute certainty. It is seldom if ever possible to accept a hypothesis outright as the single correct one, since there are a large number of additional hypotheses which also could be accepted. One simply decides, based on the statistical results, that a hypothesis should not be rejected. This does provide, of course, some support for the hypothesis. In fact, there is a growing interest in *meta-analysis*, which generally refers to a set of statistical procedures used to summarize and integrate many studies that focused on the same issue. It represents a numerical rather than narrative method of relating findings and is considered to be more objective, reliable, and rigorous than the latter.

According to Trahan, the term meta-analysis is used to refer to a variety of methods that have the following points in common:

> A research question of interest, on which a large quantity of experimental data has accumulated, is identified. An exhaustive literature search is performed to locate experimental studies on the topic. These studies are then analyzed and coded for their various methodological features. Effect sizes are computed from the reported numerical results of the studies. These effect sizes are combined to produce an overall result. The results are then analyzed on the basis of the coded study features to determine if any of these features had a consistent effect on the study outcomes.[35]

Trahan also describes a pilot study that indicated that it is feasible to integrate data from library and information science research using meta-analytic methods. Lopez-Lee analyzes meta-analytic articles written by policy makers and social scientists.[36] He concludes that meta-analysis can either blur the distinctions between the studies or provide misleading conclusions. An article by Chow provides a critique of meta-analysis.[37] An older, but still useful, Sage publication presents an overview of meta-analysis in social research.[38]

Even when statistical tests, the results of other studies, and so on suggest that there is a consistent difference or relationship between groups or variables, this finding still does not explain the reason for the relationship. In order to make causal inferences, one must meet assumptions over and above those required for establishing the existence of a statistical relationship.

As an example of this point, one must always be aware of possible spurious relationships. "An apparent relationship between two variables, X and Y, is said to be spurious if their concomitant variation stems, not from a connection between them, but from the fact that each of them is related to some third variable or combination of variables that does not serve as a link in the process by which X leads to Y."[39] In other words, X is not a determining condition of Y. For example, if some variable (Z) occurred before both X and Y, and was in fact causing both of them, then the relationship between X and Y would be spurious. (If Z serves as a link between X and Y, then an indirect relationship exists.) This phenomenon is also referred to as *confounding* the dependent and independent variables. Again, only a sound understanding of the conceptual basis for an apparent relationship can explain its nature; statistics alone cannot.

Other caveats regarding the use of statistics include the fact that a statistically significant result is not necessarily socially or practically significant. Differences of a few thousand volumes between two university library collections could produce significant statistical differences, but in the context of multimillion volume collections, such a difference holds little if any practical significance.

Finally, "weighted data, missing data, small sample sizes, complex sample designs, and capitalization on chance in fitting a statistical model are sources of potential problems in data analysis."[40] When one of these situations exists, statistics should be used with extra caution.

STATISTICAL ANALYSIS SOFTWARE

"Today, quantitative analysis is almost always done by computer programs such as SPSS and MicroCase."[41] Depending upon the methodology, the data are often inherently numerical and easily uploaded into statistical software packages. With the use of online questionnaires, the data can be transported into statistical software programs as soon as the respondents submit the completed survey. Numerical data can be submitted into statistical software programs on personal computers (PCs) and servers. As computing power increases, statistics programs are continually being updated.

Using a statistical software package via servers is an efficient technique for analyzing large amounts of data. An example of such a statistical package is BMDP software.[42] It can be used for a variety of statistical analyses and is not limited to medical research.

Another comprehensive computer system for data analysis is known as SAS,[43] (originally Statistical Analysis System). It tends to be used most frequently by researchers and IT staff in technical fields, but the system can in fact be used for virtually all kinds of data; SAS can be operated through a graphical interface, or via application programming interfaces (APIs). Minitab[44] is a relatively easy-to-use, statistical and graphical analysis software package which allows for extensive use of alphabetic data. MicroCase,[45] another statistical analysis and data management system, was developed for social science researchers and is available for personal computers (PCs).

Probably the most popular statistical package is IBM's SPSS (Statistical Package for the Social Sciences).[46] The SPSS system is a comprehensive, versatile, and relatively easy to use computer program for statistical analysis, report writing, tabulation, and general purpose data management. It provides a suite of modules containing numerous statistical procedures, from simple tables to multivariate analyses. Other SPSS features include a conversational software system which allows interaction between the data and the user, a variety of data import and export modes, and support for Python scripting.

These and other statistical analysis programs are even more widely available in basic versions for PCs, regardless of operating system. The IBM SPSS Statistics 18 (formerly PASW Statistics Base 18) includes a basic set of SPSS-suite modules for calculating a number of standard statistics as well as programs for more advanced statistics, graphic analysis, and data management.[47] The *SPSS Base 16.0 User's Guide* is one of the best and easiest manuals to use, and it provides a lot of information normally found in statistics texts.[48] There are numerous versions of the guide, based upon operating system and on whether the program will be used on a PC or a server. Persons wishing to use an abbreviated guide to SPSS should consult the *SPSS 16.0 Brief Guide*.[49] Numerous other editions and versions of the SPSS publications are available.[50]

The SAS Base system for PCs supports statistical analysis as well as report writing in a variety of formats, and data management and retrieval. SYSTAT is another comprehensive statistics, graphics, and data management software package.[51] SYSTAT, as is true of some of the other packages developed for the PC, provides statistical and graphics capabilities comparable to those available with mainframe programs; a free student version is available. *StatPac for Windows*, a software package that was developed for marketing and survey research, provides modules containing many of the basic and advanced statistical methods used in library and information science research.[52]

Some basic statistical tools are completely available online, such as the Rice Virtual Lab in Statistics,[53] which Bauer reviewed.[54] An online statistics text and resource list, and a simple analysis lab into which a user may paste small data sets also are available online.

In using computers for statistical analysis, one should be careful that the ease of doing so does not waste the researcher's time. With the possible exception of some exploratory research, the investigator should avoid indiscriminately generating all sorts of analyses without any consideration of relevant concepts, theories, and hypotheses. As is the case with manual analyses, the researcher should be certain that he or she has a thorough understanding of the statistical procedures used. Computers cannot think; they will merely do what they are told to do, or, as the saying goes, "garbage in, garbage out." A book by Nardi[55] is intended to assist readers in the interpretation of basic statistics, graphs, and tables that are commonly found in academic writing.

ANALYSIS OF NONQUANTIFIED DATA

It is worth noting briefly at this point that not all research data are susceptible to quantification, and such data do not lend themselves to statistical analysis. Yet they may still have a contribution to make to the analysis and interpretation of the results of a study, and should not be dismissed perfunctorily. Indeed, studies intended to gather qualitative type data have been enjoying a resurgence, and there are research methods and techniques specifically designed to gather nonquantitative or qualitative data.

The analysis of qualitative data differs from the analysis of quantitative data not only in the nature of the data but also in the nature of the process. For example, qualitative analysis is not perceived as a separate phase as in quantitative research. In fact, "qualitative researchers have frequently suggested that research design, data collection and analysis are simultaneous and continuous processes."[56]

One of the major objectives of qualitative data analysis is the generation of concepts. The general process typically involves immersing oneself in the data, looking for patterns, identifying surprising events, and being sensitive to inconsistencies. One of the key activities of qualitative analysis is the coding of data. Coding, which is similar to indexing, is a critical process since it serves to organize the raw information that has been collected, and because it represents the first step in the conceptualization of the data.

As has been noted elsewhere in this text, it may be desirable to combine quantitative and qualitative methods in a single study. Doing so would, of course, also necessitate combining quantitative and qualitative data analysis techniques. Chapter 7 of this book presents additional information about qualitative research methods and data analysis, including statistical software packages. A book edited by Glazier and Powell provides an introduction to qualitative research and gives examples of qualitative research studies in library and information management.[57]

SUMMARY

Statistical methods are generally used for descriptive purposes and for statistical inference. Descriptive statistics deal with the tabulation of data; their presentation in tabular, graphical, or pictorial form; and the calculation of descriptive measures. Inferential statistics are used for making inductive generalizations about populations, based on sample data, and for testing hypotheses. Both types of statistics permit interpreting quantitative data in such a way that the reliability of conclusions based on the data may be evaluated objectively by means of probability statements.

The typical basic steps in statistical analysis are categorizing the data, coding the data, and calculating the appropriate statistics. Descriptive statistics, if calculated, can characterize what is typical in a group, indicate how widely cases in the group vary, show the relationships between variables and groups, and summarize the data. Inferential statistics can estimate population parameters and test the significance of relationships between and among variables.

Certain inferential statistics are classed as parametric statistics, and they require the assumption of a normal population. Others are considered nonparametric or distribution-free statistics. The requirements for using specific statistics of either kind tend to vary somewhat, and the researcher should carefully avoid using statistical tests inappropriately.

There are cautions in utilizing statistics. Perhaps the most important principle to keep in mind is that statistics, whether generated manually or by a computer, cannot substitute for early, sound conceptual development of the research design and statistical analysis. Even the most sophisticated, comprehensive computer statistical packages simply "crunch" numbers, with no real regard for the underlying theories and hypotheses. It is left to the researcher to determine which statistical techniques represent valid methods of analyzing the data. The final interpretation of the analysis must be done by the investigator; statistics can only facilitate the process

NOTES

1. Danny P. Wallace, "The Use of Statistical Methods in Library and Information Science," *Journal of the American Society for Information Science* 36 (November 1985): 403.

2. Geoffrey R. Norman and David L. Streiner, *PDQ Statistics*, 3rd ed. (Hamilton, Ontario: B. C. Decker, 2003).

3. Herbert F. Spirer, Louise Spirer, and A. J. Jaffe, *Misused Statistics*, 2nd, rev. exp. ed. (New York: M. Dekker, 1998).

4. Derek Rowntree, *Statistics without Tears: A Primer for Non-Mathematicians* (1981; repr., Boston: Pearson, 2004).

5. Richard M. Jaeger, *Statistics: A Spectator Sport*, 2nd ed. (Newbury Park, CA: Sage, 1990).

6. Ian S. Simpson, *Basic Statistics for Librarians*, 3rd ed. (London: Library Association, 1988).

7. Arthur Wayne Hafner, *Descriptive Statistical Techniques for Librarians*, 2nd ed. (Chicago: American Library Association, 1998).

8. Peter Hernon, Hae-young Rieh Hwang, Barbara D. Farah, Andrew J. Golub, Pat K. Bryant, Li-Ling Kuo, and Maya De, edited by Charles McClure, *Statistics for Library Decision Making: A Handbook* (Norwood, NJ: Ablex Publishing, 1989).

9. Peter Hernon, *Statistics: A Component of the Research Process*, rev. ed. (Norwood, NJ: Ablex Publishing, 1994).

10. Bert R. Boyce, Charles J. Meadow, and Donald H. Kraft, *Measurement in Information Science* (San Diego: Academic Press, 1994).

11. Peter Stephen and Susan Hornby, *Simple Statistics for Library and Information Professionals*, 2nd ed. (London: Library Association Publications, 1997).

12. Paul W. Vogt, *Dictionary of Statistics and Methodology: A Nontechnical Guide for the Social Sciences*, 3rd ed. (Thousand Oaks, CA: Sage, 2005), xvii.

13. Paul D. Leedy, *Practical Research: Planning and Design*, 2nd ed. (New York: Macmillan, 1980), 141.

14. Chava Frankfort-Nachmias and David Nachmias, *Research Methods in the Social Sciences*, 7th ed. (New York: Worth Publishers, 2008), 320.

15. John H. Fennick, *Studies Show: A Popular Guide to Understanding Scientific Studies* (Amherst, NY: Prometheus, 1997).

16. Gary Golden, *Survey Research Methods* (Chicago: ACRL, 1982).

17. Annie S. Barnes, ed., *Social Science Research: A Skills Handbook* (Bristol, IN: Wyndham Hall Press, 1985).

18. Hernon, *Statistics*.

19. Liwen Vaughan, *Statistical Methods for the Information Professional: A Practical, Painless Approach to Understanding, Using, and Interpreting Statistics*, ASIST Monograph Series (Medford, NJ: Information Today, 2001).

20. Wallace, "The Use of Statistical Methods," 402–10.

21. Edward Tufte, *Envisioning Information* (1990; repr., Cheshire, CT: Graphics Press, 2006). Edward Tufte, The Visual Display of Quantitative Information 2nd ed. (Cheshire, CT: Graphics Press, 2001).

22. Barnes, *Social Science Research.*

23. David V. Huntsberger and Patrick Billingsley, *Elements of Statistical Inference*, 4th ed. (Boston, MA: Allyn and Bacon, 1977), 71.

24. Juris Dilevko, "Inferential Statistics and Librarianship," *Library & Information Science Research* 29, no. 2 (2007): 209.

25. Ibid., 217.

26. Hubert M. Blalock, Jr., *Social Statistics*, rev. ed. (New York: McGraw-Hill, 1979), 183.

27. Ibid., 187.

28. Vogt, *Dictionary of Statistics and Methodology*, 241.

29. Ibid., 288.

30. Ibid., 71.

31. Ibid., 166.

32. Blalock, *Social Statistics*, 451.

33. Frank M. Andrews, Laura Klem, Terrence N. Davidson, Patrick M. O'Malley, Kathleen B. Welch, and Willard L. Rodgers, *Selecting Statistical Techniques for Social Science Data: A Guide for SAS Users* (Cary, NC: SAS Institute Inc., 1998).

34. David Gerhan, "Statistical Significance: How It Signifies in Statistics Reference," *Reference & User Services Quarterly* 40, no. 4 (2001): 361–74.

35. Eric Trahan, "Applying Meta-Analysis to Library Research and Information Science Research," *Library Quarterly* 63 (January 1993): 81–82.

36. David Lopez-Lee, "Indiscriminate Data Aggregations in Meta-Analysis: A Cause for Concern Among Policy Makers and Social Scientists," *Evaluation Review* 26, no. 5 (2002): 520–44.

37. Siu L. Chow, "Meta-Analysis of Pragmatic and Theoretical Research: A Critique," *Journal of Psychology* 121 (May 1987): 259–71.

38. Gene V. Glass, Barry McGaw, and Mary L. Smith, *Meta-Analysis in Social Research* (Beverly Hills, CA: Sage, 1981).

39. Claire Selltiz, Lawrence S. Wrightsman, and Stuart W. Cook, *Research Methods in Social Relations*, rev. ed. (New York: Holt, Rinehart & Winston, 1959), 424.

40. Andrews et al., *Selecting Statistical Techniques*, 1.

41. Earl R. Babbie, *The Practice of Social Research*, 12th ed. (Belmont, CA: Wadsworth/Cengage Learning, 2010), 422.

42. Statistical Solutions, "BMDP Statistical Software Package: ANOVA, Regression, Survival Analysis, Time Series, Nonparametric Analysis," http://www.statistical-solutions-software.com/products-page/bmdp-statistical-software/.

43. SAS Institute, Inc., "SAS Business Analytics and Business Intelligence Software," http://www.sas.com/.

44. Minitab Inc., "Minitab Statistical and Process Management Software for Six Sigma and Quality Improvement," http://www.minitab.com/.

45. Microcase, Wadsworth/Cengage Learning, "Microcase," http://microcase.com/index.html.

46. SPSS Inc., an IBM Company, "SPSS: Data Mining, Statistical Analysis Software, Predictive Analysis, Decision Support Systems," http://www.spss.com.

47. SPSS Inc., an IBM Company, "SPSS Statistics," http://www.spss.com/media/collateral/statistics/pasw-statistics-specs.pdf.

48. SPSS Inc., an IBM Company, *SPSS Base 16.0 User's Guide* (Chicago: SPSS Inc., 2007).

49. SPSS Inc., an IBM Company, *SPSS 16.0 Brief Guide* (Chicago: SPSS Inc., 2007).

50. See, for instance, SPSS, Inc., *SPSS 18.0 Integrated Student Version for Business Statistics* (Englewood Cliffs: Prentice Hall, 2010); Paul R. Kinnear and Colin D. Gray, *SPSS 17 Made Simple* (Hove: Psychology, 2009); Alan Bryman and Duncan Cramer, *Quantitative Data Analysis with SPSS 14, 15, and 16: A Guide for Social Scientists* (London: Routledge, 2009).

51. Systat Software, "SYSTAT: Statistical and Graphical Software," http://systat.com/.

52. StatPac Inc., "StatPac Survey Software Online Surveys Overview," http://www.statpac.com/survey-software.htm.

53. Rice Virtual Lab, "Rice Virtual Lab in Statistics (RVLS)" (last update 12/3/08) http://onlinestatbook.com/rvls.html.

54. Kathleen Bauer, "Resources for Library Assessment," *College & Research Libraries News* 62, no. 1 (2001): 12–14.

55. Peter M. Nardi, *Interpreting Data: A Guide to Understanding Research* (Boston: Allyn and Bacon, 2006).

56. Alan Bryman and Robert G. Burgess, eds., *Analyzing Qualitative Data* (London: Routledge, 1994), 217.

57. Jack D. Glazier and Ronald R. Powell, eds., *Qualitative Research in Information Management* (Englewood, CO: Libraries Unlimited, 1992).

10

Writing the Research Proposal

VALUE OF RESEARCH PROPOSALS

The best research is well planned, and a key step in carrying out such planning is the preparation of a research proposal. The development of the proposal can help to reduce wasted effort and provide a more efficient, problem-free study by encouraging the researcher to clarify the exact nature of the investigation. In developing the research proposal, the investigator should specify the procedures which he or she expects to follow; and in doing so, the researcher will be better prepared to carry out all of the necessary, relevant steps. It is also useful, at this time, to indicate the progress to be expected at various stages of the project. While the deadlines indicated by such a timetable will not always be met, the attempt to meet them should result in a more punctually conducted study. Also, the proposal can provide the basis for discussing the strengths and weaknesses of the proposed project, facilitate the identification of conceptual and theoretical errors, and help to point out weaknesses in selected designs and methods.

In addition, the research proposal is useful for announcing one's research intentions and therein providing enough detail about the proposed project to prevent misinterpretations about the research goals and techniques to be employed. Research proposals are required of doctoral students as an indication that they are prepared to conduct their research properly, and that the topic is worthy of investigation. Last, but not least, proposals are usually necessary for applying for outside funding or grants for research projects.

ORGANIZATION AND CONTENT OF A TYPICAL PROPOSAL

The format of a research proposal will vary somewhat according to the purpose of the proposal and the institutions involved, but the major components are generally the same and are presented below in the order in which they usually occur.

Title Page

Most sponsoring agencies specify the format for the title page, and may even provide a special form. Likewise, universities usually specify the format to be followed by doctoral students. Regardless of the format used, the title of the proposal should accurately reflect the contents and the scope of the suggested study.

Abstract

Most research proposals, with the possible exception of dissertation proposals, should provide a short summary or abstract of about 200 words. The abstract should touch on every major component of the proposal except the budget, if there is one. Some readers read only the abstract and others rely on it for a quick overview of the proposal. Some sponsoring agencies use the abstract to weed out unsuitable proposals and to disseminate information. Consequently, the writing of the abstract should be done with care.

Table of Contents

A table of contents is not always deemed necessary, especially for brief proposals, but it is useful for presenting an overview of the organization of the proposal. In addition to outlining the major components of the proposal, it may provide lists of illustrations, tables, appendices, and so on.

Introduction and Statement of the Problem

An introduction is not always considered necessary, as it tends to duplicate information that follows. But an opening statement characterizing what is being proposed can help to introduce the subject to the reader. Some authors use introductions to outline the major components of the proposal. If included, it should be brief and avoid unnecessary redundancy.

The first section of the typical proposal, if there is not a separate problem section, also introduces the problem to be studied and provides a brief historical background for the problem where appropriate. If the problem warrants being divided into subproblems, they are identified at this point. This section also should indicate the importance of the proposed study, or why a solution is needed, and identify anticipated benefits and their significance. "It is imperative to make the case for the project and to specifically state its importance to the knowledge base and research literature"; therefore, "the proposal should include a justification for the research."[1]

To obtain the background provided in this section, and possibly elsewhere in the proposal, a variety of sources of information may be consulted. The following list includes some of the types of background information often needed for writing a research proposal. Examples of common sources of such information in the field of library and information science are also included below.

1. Terminology: *The ALA Glossary of Library and Information Science*, edited by Heartsill Young (American Library Association, 1983); *Observer's Dictionary of Library Science Information and Documentation in Six Languages* (Observer Scientific, 1973); *Harrod's Librarian's Glossary and Reference Book*, 10th ed., edited and compiled by Ray Prytherch (Ashgate, 2005); *Dictionary of Information Science and Technology*, edited by Carolyn Watters (Academic Press, 1992); *Concise Dictionary of Library and Information Science*, 2nd ed., edited by Stella Keenan and Colin Johnston (Bowker-Saur, 2002); *Dictionary of Information and Library Management*, 2nd ed., edited by Janet Stephenson (A. & C. Black, 2006); *Dictionary for Library and Information Science*, edited by Joan M. Reitz (Libraries Unlimited, 2004); and *ODLIS Online Dictionary of Library and Information Science*, edited by Joan M. Reitz (2002) http://lu.com/odlis/.

2. Brief background: *Encyclopedia of Library and Information Science*, 3rd ed., edited by Marcia Bates, vol. 1–4 (CRC Press, 2010), also available online, with the purchase of the print version; *Encyclopedia of Library and Information Science*, vol. 1–73 (Marcel Dekker, 1968–2003), also available online, with the purchase of the print version; *Encyclopedia of Librarianship*, 3rd ed., edited by Thomas Landau (Hafner, 1966); *ALA World Encyclopedia of Library and Information Services*, 2nd ed., edited by Robert Wedgeworth (Adamantine Press, 1986); and *Encyclopedia of Information Science and Technology*, edited by Mehdi Khosrow-Pour, vol. 1–5 (Idea Group Reference, 2005).

3. Trends: *Library Trends* (1952–, quarterly) and the *Annual Review of Information Science and Technology* (ASIST, 1966–).

4. Statistics:

   a. Agencies regularly gathering and publishing statistics about libraries or librarians:

   i. Association for Library and Information Science Education—*Library and Information Science Education Statistical Report*, 1980–, annual.

   ii. Association of Specialized and Cooperative Library Agencies—*The State Library Agencies*, 10th ed., 1993; *The Report on Library Cooperation*, 7th ed., 1990.

   iii. American Library Association (ALA). A number of units within ALA are concerned with collecting and reporting library-related statistics. The Office for Research and Statistics has issued several statistical reports, as well as a series of research monographs. The Public Library Association has published the *Public Library Data Service Statistical Report* on an annual basis since 1988. The Association of College and Research Libraries regularly compiles and publishes *Academic Library Trends and Statistics*.

   iv. Association of Research Libraries—*ARL Statistics*, annual (published as the Gerould statistics from 1907–08 through 1962–63; *ARL Annual Salary Survey*, 1973–.

   v. Bowker Company—*American Library Directory*, 1923–, biennial; *Bowker Annual of Library and Book Trade Information*, 1956–.

vi. National Center for Education Statistics (NCES), U.S. Department of Education—periodically collects statistics from school, public, and academic libraries. The frequency and titles of the reports vary. Originally the statistics on public libraries and public school libraries were referred to as LIBGIS reports. They are now collected by the Institute of Museum and Library Services (IMLS), (http://harvester.census .gov/imls/index.asp) and published as the Public Libraries Survey (PLS). The statistics on academic libraries were distributed as HEGIS reports but are now known as IPEDS (Integrated Postsecondary Education Data System). The IPEDS data are available online at http://nces.ed.gov/pubsearch/pubsinfo.asp?pubid=2010310. ALS, the Academic Library Survey, was once part of IPEDS but became a separate survey in 1999. LIBGIS essentially became FSCS— the Federal-State Cooperative System for public library data. The NCES program for collecting data on schools and their libraries is the Schools and Staffing Survey (SASS).

vii. Special Libraries Association—results of its salary survey are published every two years with annual updates.

viii. American Association of School Librarians—collects data on school library media centers.

b. Other sources of statistics:

ix. State library agencies—most state libraries collect statistics on public libraries. The Library Research Service (LRS) of the Colorado State Library gathers and reports statistics on libraries of that state. The LRS and the University of Denver, Library and Information Science Program, maintain a Web site (http://www.lrs.org/) which includes information on research and statistics. For the past few years, IMLS has released its annual State Library Agencies Report.

x. Individual libraries—a few libraries collect data on a regional or national level. Reports of individual libraries can be useful also, but the lack of standardization presents some problems for analysis.

xi. Library research centers—the Center for Informatics Research in Science and Scholarship (CIRSS), formerly the Library Research Center (LRC), of the University of Illinois Graduate School of Library and Information Science. Its Web site (http://cirss.lis.illinois.edu/index.html) includes information about the Center's current projects.

xii. The "Bibliography of Statistics of National Scope on Libraries in the United States, 1829–1999" is posted on the Web site of Robert Williams at: http://www.libsci.sc.edu/bob/LibraryStatistics/Library StatisticsGuide.html.

xiii. Sirsi's Normative Data Project (NDP) for Libraries collects data from hundreds of member public libraries on collections, circulation transactions, user demographics, library income, and other operational measurements. It can be accessed by subscribers at: www.library normativedata.info.

5. Biographical information: *ALA Membership Directory* (1950–, annual—combined with the *ALA Handbook of Organization since* 1980); *Who's*

Who in Library and Information Services (ALA, 1982); *Dictionary of American Library Biography*, edited by Bohdan S. Wynar (Libraries Unlimited, 1977; second supplement edited by Donald G. Davis Jr., 2003); and *Directory of Library and Information Professionals* (Research Publications, 1988).

6. Directory-type information: American Library Directory; The ALA Handbook of Organization (annual; during 2009–10 ALA is transitioning this to an Online Handbook of Organization); Directory of Special Libraries and Information Centers, 3 vols. (Gale Research, 1996); and the Web sites of some organizations that list their members.

7. Bibliographical data: See the indexes cited in the Review of Related Research section of this chapter.

Other miscellaneous resources include ALA's *Library Technology Reports*, reports of the Council on Library and Information Resources, ARL *SPEC Kits*, and *CLIP Notes*, published by ACRL.

Review of Related Research

The review of related research, or literature review, is in effect an expansion of the historical background presented in the problem section. It cites and briefly reviews the related research studies that have been conducted. Nonresearch reports and "opinion pieces" should generally be excluded from consideration unless they are particularly insightful or represent all that have been written on the problem. It is desirable, if not essential, that related research in other fields be cited as well. In some cases, the research done in other fields will be all that exists of any real importance. In other words, this section of the proposal describes the foundation on which the proposed study will be built by discussing work done by others, evaluating their methodologies and findings, and stating how the proposed research will differ. The literature review should be selective (the final report often contains additional works or information) and should group the cited studies in some logical fashion.

It is in this section that the theoretical or conceptual framework is established for the subsequent stages, particularly the development of the hypothesis. The literature review helps to suggest the best approach to seeking a solution to the problem. Before continuing with the research study, it is essential to know what has already been done. Unfortunately, bibliographic control of LIS research, particularly research in progress, is not always well maintained; however, there are several publications that do identify in-progress and completed research. A selective list follows:

1. *The Bowker Annual of Library and Book Trade Information*, New York: Bowker, 1956–. Annual. Includes sections on funding and grants and research and statistics.

2. *Library Literature & Information Science Full Text* (formerly *Library Literature*), New York: Wilson, 1934–. Bimonthly. Cites journal articles,

books, and other published research studies. Available electronically and in paper.

3. *Library, Information Science, & Technology Abstracts (LISTA)*. London: Library Association, 1969–. Bimonthly. Provided free by EBSCO. Another basic index. Available in electronic and paper formats.

4. *Library and Information Science Abstracts (LISA), San Diego: ProQuest, 1969–. An international abstracting and indexing tool designed for library professionals and other information specialists.*

5. *Resources in Education (RIE)*, Washington D C: United States Department of Education, 1966–2002. Monthly. An important source of unpublished research reports in the areas of education and library science. Together with the *Current Index to Journals in Education*, it constituted the printed equivalent of the ERIC computer data base. However, the clearinghouse has been reorganized, and these publications ceased in 2002.

6. *ProQuest Dissertations & Theses (PQDT)*, formerly *Dissertation Abstracts International*, Ann Arbor, MI: UMI ProQuest, 1938–. Available only in electronic format, sometimes with full text of the theses.

7. *Information Research Watch International*, London: Bowker-Saur, 2000–. The print equivalent is published six times per year, and the electronic version is updated monthly. This journal is intended for those who need to keep abreast of research and development work in librarianship, information science, archives, documentation, and the information aspects of other fields. Its coverage is international. Each entry provides an overview of a research project and information about personnel, duration, funding, and references. Formerly *Current Research in Library and Information Science* and before that *RADIALS Bulletin*, London: Bowker-Saur, 1981–1999. Quarterly. An annual compilation titled *Current Research for the Information Profession* is distributed by the American Library Association.

8. *Library and Information Research* (formerly *Library and Information Research News*), London: CILIP, 1970s–. A quarterly publication that includes papers, news, and book reviews. It is available on the Web at http://lirg.org.uk.

9. "Research News," a column in the *Canadian Journal of Information and Library Science (CJILS)*. Reports news on LIS research in Canada, including work being done by Canadians abroad and LIS work that relates to Canada. The column also announces winners of Canadian research awards.

10. *New Review of Information Networking*, London: Taylor & Francis (formerly *New Review of Information and Library Research*). An annual publication that promotes current research of interest to information professionals, with a strong emphasis on technological subjects.

11. Social Science Research Network (SSRN) is a Web site that encourages the early distribution of research results by publishing submitted abstracts and the dissemination of scholarly papers. It is available at: http://www.ssrn.com/.

12. *Inspec*, Stevenage, England: Institution of Engineering and Technology, 1969–. An international bibliographic database that contains over 11 million abstracts and indexing to journal articles, conference proceedings, and other literature. Its audience includes librarians and information scientists.

Professional associations are also possible sources of information about research in progress and recently completed research. Within the American Library Association, the Library Research Round Table (LRRT) is particularly concerned with research. Its objectives are to extend and improve library research; to offer programs aimed at describing, criticizing, and disseminating library research findings; and to educate ALA members about research techniques and their usefulness in obtaining information with which to reach administrative decisions and solve problems. ALA's Office for Research and Statistics can also serve as a source of information about current research in progress. It appears that a growing percentage of the papers presented at professional conferences are reports of research. ALISE (Association for Library and Information Science Education) sponsors a research grant award that requires that recipients present progress reports at ALISE conferences, a research paper competition, and a doctoral forum for the exchange of research ideas.

An online database, *Federal Research in Progress*, is available through several online database providers and occasionally includes records of library-related research being performed under the sponsorship of U.S. government agencies. All records include title, principal investigator, performing organization, and sponsoring organization. Most records also include a description of the research, progress reports, and subject descriptors. Many reports of completed research and research in progress are available on the Web. Some reports of funded research projects are available only on the Web.

Research Design

Returning to the outline of a typical research proposal, the next section usually is devoted to a description of the proposed research. Almost always written for the specialist rather than the lay person, it includes the following elements:

1. Goals and objectives—A goals and objectives section, identified as such, is not always included at this point. If it is, a few statements emphasizing the major purposes of the research method to be employed should suffice.

2. Hypothesis—At this time, the major research hypothesis, or hypotheses, should be stated. This section also will include minor or secondary and alternative hypotheses, if any have been developed. As discussed earlier, the researcher may have concluded that the development and testing of formal hypotheses is not feasible at this stage of the research. Thus, he or she may decide instead to pose one or more research questions to be answered.

3. Assumptions—Basic assumptions are usually given after the hypothesis statement. These are needed to help support the hypothesis

and, therefore, logically occur at this point. They should directly relate to the hypothesis and build the case for the hypothesis, not the methodology.

4. Definitions—The operational or working definitions for key terms and terms that are used in a unique way logically follow the hypothesis and assumptions. There is some disagreement as to how much detail should be provided here, rather than in the section describing the data collection instrument, but the operational definitions should at least tell what is to be observed and imply how. For example, an operational definition of library use may specify that external circulations are to be measured by analyzing circulation records. Many researchers prefer to incorporate the hypothesis, assumptions, and definitions in the problem section but may repeat them here.

5. Methodology—The next large section in the typical proposal describes the research methodology. In brief, this is where the researcher describes how the study will be organized and the situation in which the hypothesis will be tested. The researcher also should provide details in this section on the techniques and tools that will be used to collect data. This should include a description of the kind of data that will be collected to test the hypothesis, including the criteria for admissibility of data; whether it will be limited to primary or secondary data; the likely sources of these data; and the type(s) of data collection methods or tools (e.g., questionnaire, interview, etc.) to be used to gather the data. If a pretest is to be made, it too should be described at this point. Readers interested in analyses of methodologies used by previous researchers may wish to consult articles by Lundeen,[2] Peritz,[3] Nour,[4] Feehan et al.,[5] Powell,[6] and Fidel.[7]

6. Treatment of the data—Next, the researcher should describe how he or she proposes to analyze the data to be collected. This part of the proposal generally does not need to be very specific; for example, the specific statistical tests, if any, to be employed in the analysis probably do not need to be itemized here. But at least the general kinds of analysis to be used (e.g., descriptive, bivariate, multivariate, inferential, etc.) should be specified along with the rationales for using them. "Dummy tables" may be provided at this point to illustrate how the data will be categorized and analyzed. If computer statistical packages are to be utilized in the analysis, it probably is advisable to specify them.

Institutional Resources

It may be useful to describe relevant institutional resources that are available to support the proposed research project. Such a section is particularly advisable for grant proposals requesting external funding. Items in this section may include computer facilities, library resources, and survey research personnel and facilities.

Personnel

A section describing personnel to be employed in the study may be necessary only for grant proposals, or for projects involving a relatively large number of people. Funding agencies often encourage or require collaboration. "Collaboration is an important aspect of any project and encourages researchers to address differences," which "often lead to significant new insight and innovation."[8] A personnel section is rarely needed for individual research projects, such as dissertation research, though funding agencies often require the submission of a resume for the principal investigator (PI). If a personnel section is included, it should provide relevant background information about the research staff, emphasizing their qualifications and what they can contribute to the project. Costs relating to personnel will be covered in the following discussion of the budget.

Budget

The budget has two main functions. First, it estimates, as realistically as possible, the costs of completing the objectives of the proposed research. The reader will use the budget details to determine whether the proposed research is economically feasible and realistic. Second, the budget provides a means to monitor the project's financial activities over the life of the project. In this way, it is possible to determine how closely the actual progress in achieving the objectives is being made relative to the proposed budget.

Before considering some of the specific items that should be included in a proposed budget, there are several general points or guidelines worth mentioning, keeping in mind that only grant proposals are likely to have a budget section. Regarding time and personnel, the most common approach to estimating these factors is to list the various stages of the project (such as developing the data collection tools and data analysis) and to calculate how much time and how many staff hours will be required for each. Such estimates usually are based on experience and similar studies, but it should be remembered that almost every operation takes longer than expected. In fact, some researchers argue that the estimates should provide additional time for snags or problems, up to an additional 50 percent of the initial estimates.

Budgets are more likely to be underestimated than overestimated, because the researcher may not realize how much work is actually involved. In addition, researchers tend to get carried away with collecting data or following new leads and, in the process, collect too much irrelevant data. Also, the researcher is anxious to receive approval of the budget and proposal and is prone to underestimating for that reason. A certain amount of budget flexibility is desirable, and underestimating costs reduces that potential.

In order to decrease the likelihood of underestimating the budget, it is advisable for the researcher to check the currentness of the figures at the last minute. It is also desirable to build in a hedge against inflation, or to increase the figures for subsequent years of a multiyear proposal by a reasonable percentage. Explanations for how the major budget figures were calculated should be provided.

Another guideline or rule of thumb worth noting is that the budget should be fitted to the research project, not vice versa. In other words, one should not decide how much money he or she has available or is likely to obtain, and then design a study within those constraints. Instead, the researcher should design the study to investigate the problem as well as possible, and then determine how much such an investigation will cost. Perhaps the project can then be reduced, if necessary. Determining the budget before designing the study is comparable to selecting a methodology before identifying the problem to be studied. Also, the amount of time and personnel needed for the different stages of a research project will depend to some extent on the type of study being proposed. For example, an exploratory study typically requires a relatively greater amount of time for data analysis than does a more focused study where the researcher has a better defined notion of what he or she is examining.

A typical budget will usually contain at least the following items:

1. Salaries and wages—Personnel costs are determined essentially by translating the time and staffing into appropriate salaries and wages. Usually included here are fringe benefits, if paid, and the costs of any contractual services, such as a consultant's fee.
2. Space—Itemized here are the costs, if any, of providing space for the project. For example, the rental of an office would be included here.
3. Equipment—Equipment costs, whether purchased or rented.
4. Materials and supplies—Provided here are the costs for consumable materials and items such as miscellaneous office supplies.
5. Travel expenses.
6. Support services—Expenses related to the use of services and facilities such as computers and photocopiers.
7. Miscellaneous expenses—Additional costs related to telephone service, purchase of books, postage, and so on.
8. Indirect costs—Costs that cannot directly be identified with a particular project, such as library services, utilities, accounting, maintenance, secretarial support, and so on. These are often figured as a percentage of salaries and wages or of modified total costs. This figure is usually somewhere between 30 percent and 70 percent of direct costs. The exact percentage, and the basis for figuring it, usually is established or negotiated by the institution with which the researcher is affiliated and the funding agency.
9. Budget summary—If the budget is relatively long, it may be advisable to provide a summary of the budget, listing major items only.

A sample of a typical 12-month budget is presented in Table 10.1. In this example, the first column represents the proposed contribution of the funding agency; the second column, the support to be provided by the researcher's organization; and the third column, the total. (Usually, the greater the proportion the parent organization is prepared to provide, the greater are the chances of obtaining outside funding.)

TABLE 10.1   Sample 12-Month Budget

	Sponsor	U-M	Total
Personnel			
Project Director, 25%, Academic Year	$ 15,000	$ 0	$ 15,000
Project Associate, 10%	0	3,000	3,000
Research Assistant, 50%	9,000	0	9,000
Clerk-Typist, 50%	7,000	0	7,000
Subtotal	$ 31,000	$ 3,000	$ 34,000
Staff Benefits (31% of S & W)	$ 9,610	$ 930	$ 10,540
Subtotal	$ 40,610	$ 3,930	$ 44,540
Consultants			
John Smith, $200/day, 2 days	$ 400	$ 0	$ 400
Equipment			
Methometer	$ 2,000	$ 0	$ 2,000
Materials and supplies			
Glassware	$ 200	$ 0	$ 200
Chemicals	200	0	200
Subtotal	$ 400	$ 0	$ 400
Travel			
Project Director consultation with sponsor, Ann Arbor to Washington, DC and return. 1 person, 2 days			
Airfare	$ 700	$ 0	$ 700
Per Diem @ $100/day	200	0	200
Local Transportation	25	0	25
Subtotal	$ 925	$ 0	$ 925
Total Direct Costs	$ 44,335	$ 3,930	$ 48,265
Indirect costs			
(52% of modified total direct costs)	$ 22,014	$ 2,044	$ 24,058
Grand Total	**$ 66,349**	**$ 5,974**	**$ 72,323**

Reprinted from *Proposal Writer's Guide* by Donald E. Thackrey (Ann Arbor: University of Michigan, Division of Research Development and Administration, 1996, 8). Since this was published in 1996, the figures are dated and below today's costs.

Anticipated Results

Returning to the outline of the research proposal, the next common section is an evaluation of expected project results, or the likely impact of the study. This information is particularly important for grant proposals, as the potential funding agency must be convinced of the value of the research project.

Limitations of the Study

Typically, the last section of the text of a research proposal points out the limitations of the project. While the researcher does not want to be negative at this point, it is important to note, in a few concise statements, the limitations imposed by the research method, setting, and so on. In essence, the researcher is stating what the research can and cannot do; he or she is not denigrating the value of the study.

Back Matter

Immediately following the text, the writer usually provides the list of references or cited works. If there are fewer than six, they often are inserted in the text; if more, a separate section is probably warranted. After the list of references, the writer may choose to provide a bibliography which will list all the works consulted in writing the proposal and possibly other suggested readings. In a short proposal this is usually unnecessary.

If the author wishes to provide the reader with additional information that is not crucial to the text, then he or she may wish to include one or more appendices. This should not be overdone, however, especially in grant proposals. If there is any doubt about the need to include some information in an appendix, then it is probably best to omit it.

At this point, or perhaps earlier, the researcher may elect to provide a timetable outlining the dates by which he or she expects to have completed certain stages of the proposed study. Or, if not given in a separate section, this information may be integrated throughout the text or even provided as a separate document. Regardless of how it is presented, the development of a timetable is an important exercise in that it sets deadlines for the project and thereby helps to keep it on schedule.

CHARACTERISTICS OF A GOOD PROPOSAL

As Leedy and Ormrod state, "Research demands that those who undertake it be able to think clearly, without confusion."[9] Therefore, it is important that a research proposal be a straightforward document that includes only that information which contributes to an understanding of the problem and its proposed solution. While it should be well written, its primary purpose is to communicate clearly, not to be a literary masterpiece. To that end, the language should be clear and precise and represent conventional prose; the proposal should be clearly and logically organized, and it should make ample use of headings and subheadings.

The general format should be attractive, conform to external mechanics of good form (such as margins and pagination), and should be neat and free of typographical errors. The proposal should represent a high level of scholarship, as evidenced by insight into the problem, imagination in the design of the study, adequate grasp of research and statistical tools, and display of a scientific attitude. Most funding agencies now accept or require electronic proposals and submissions.

FEATURES THAT DETRACT FROM A PROPOSAL

Unfortunately, numerous features of a proposal may diminish its effectiveness. Such weaknesses are always to be avoided, but they are particularly crucial when applying for funding. Some of these deficiencies are obvious, though still surprisingly common. For example, proposals are sometimes guilty of not conforming to the guidelines of the funding or approving agency, or of not addressing the research area or interests of the agency. (That is not to say the researcher should not be creative, however, in identifying possible sources of funding.) Proposals also suffer if they are not complete. It is not unusual for research proposals to lack a clear and explicit budget, for example. It is essential, of course, that grant proposals meet the submission deadline if there is one.

In 2002, The National Institute of Child Health and Human Development, part of the National Institutes of Health (NIH), listed the most common reasons for the rejection of research proposals. Although this list is no longer available on the NIH web site, the information is still relevant to grant writing. The most common reasons for rejection include:

a. Lack of new or original ideas

b. Diffuse, superficial, or unfocused research plan

c. Lack of knowledge of published relevant work

d. Lack of experience in the essential methodology

e. Uncertainty concerning the future directions of the research.[10]

There are many other characteristics that may weaken a proposal, some as minor as the font size. It is important that applicants adhere to the funding agency's description and guidelines for formatting specifications, such as font size, spacing, page limits, and so on.[11] A list of the reasons for grant proposals having been rejected by the NIH is presented in Table 10.2.

OBTAINING FUNDING FOR LIS RESEARCH

If one is planning to seek external funding for a research project, there are a variety of resources to which the researcher can turn for guidance.

If the proposal has been written at the request of a specific funding agency (i.e., in response to a RFP, or request for proposal) or in response to a clear indication that a funding agency is interested in proposals on a topic, seeking funds is relatively easy. The agency should be contacted at an early stage and asked for whatever advice they are able to give as the proposal develops. In most cases the agency will send material describing what it wants and appropriate application forms. In some cases, an agency will refer you to previous projects they have funded and/or volunteer to critique drafts of your proposal. The amount of help an agency is willing to give varies widely. In any case it is important to be aware that assistance in developing a proposal is not a promise that the proposal will be funded. Agencies may deliberately encourage several people to prepare

TABLE 10.2   Why Grant Proposals Are Unsuccessful

The National Institutes of Health (NIH), a major provider of project grants to colleges and hospitals, approves less than half of the grant applications it receives. (The NIH Web site, www.nih.gov, includes grant guidelines and funding opportunities.) A study of applications rejected by the NIH includes more than 50 categories for the rejection of proposals. The figure to the right in the listing below indicates the percentage of proposals which were rejected for that specific reason. Since proposals are normally turned down on more than one ground (in this study, an average of four reasons were cited), the percentages add up to more than 100 percent. The most often cited reasons for rejection were questionable project designs, inadequate explanation of the research in the proposal, and the questionable competence of the investigator. Budgets were seldom a problem.

Class I: Nature of Research

Problem is of insufficient importance or biologically irrelevant	11.8
Proposal is repetitive of previous work	9.6
Theory is outmoded or questionable	1.0
Experimental purpose or hypothesis is vague	12.7
Problem is more complex than investigator realizes	1.7
Research is based on hypothesis that is doubtful or unsound	4.0
Proposed research is based on conclusions that may be unwarranted	2.7
Too little science: problem is more developmental than research	2.3
Problem is scientifically premature and warrants at most a pilot study	7.7

Class II: Approach

Assumptions are questionable; evidence for procedures is questionable	14.6
Approach is not rigorous enough, too naive, too uncritical	11.6
Approach is not objective enough	2.7
Validity is questionable; criteria for evaluation are weak or missing	0.6
Approach is poorly thought out	6.1
Application is poorly prepared or poorly formulated	15.5
Proposal is not explicit enough, lacks detail, or is too vague or general	32.8
Rationale for the approach is poorly presented	3.9
Methods or scientific procedures are unsuited to stated objective	16.5
The design is too ambitious or otherwise inappropriate	13.1
The approach lacks scientific imagination	13.1
Some administrative or practical problems are unsolved	1.9
Unethical or hazardous procedures will be used	1.6
Controls are either inadequately conceived or inadequately described	6.5
The procedure is not well enough organized, coordinated, or planned	6.7

TABLE 10.2   (Continued)

Some problems are not realized or dealt with adequately	16.9
The overall design is unsound, or some techniques are unrealistic	35.5
Approach will not produce useful new insights	3.5
The results will be confusing, difficult to interpret, or meaningless	14.4
The emphasis is on data collection rather than on data interpretation	5.3

Class III: Investigator

Investigator does not have adequate experience for this research	31.6
Investigator is unskilled in scientific method	4.0
Investigator has produced too few publications during the research	6.4
Articles are of generally low quality	3.5
Results from previous year's support are inadequate	9.3
The investigator's knowledge or judgment of literature is poor	20.2
The investigator is spreading himself or herself too thin	1.5

Class IV: Other

The investigator needs more liaison with colleagues in this field	10.5
The project will rely on insufficiently experienced associates	0.5
The institutional setting is unfavorable	2.4
The overall budget is too high	7.5
The budget for personnel is too high	2.4
The budget for equipment is too high	0.7
The budget for other items is too high	0.6
The overall budget is too low	1.2

Source: National Institutes of Health. Reprinted from *Federal Grants and Contracts Weekly,* March 31, 1981.

requests so that they can pick the one they judge to make the best use of available funds.[12]

In lieu of a relatively firm commitment from a funding agency, it is necessary to identify likely sources of support. As Lynch notes, both informal and formal sources should be used to get ideas. Individuals working in the same subject area are possible sources of suggestions for funding.[13] Professional organizations may also be able to give useful advice. In considering and applying to potential funding agencies, it is important to identify organizations that would appear to have an interest in, and something to be gained from, one's proposed research. On the other hand, one should be imaginative in identifying such agencies and not restrict efforts to only the most obvious organizations.

For those persons needing information about granting foundations and agencies and about specific grants, there are numerous standard works available. These include the *Catalog of Federal Domestic Assistance, Annual Register of Grant Support, The Foundation Directory, The Grants Register, Directory of Research Grants,* the daily *Federal Register, The Foundation 1000* (formerly *Source Book Profiles*), the *Foundation Reporter* (formerly *Taft Foundation Information System*), and the *Commerce Business Daily.* DIALOG offers a computer database titled "GRANTS," an abstract file of sources of grants in a wide range of subject areas. It lists active grant offerings from associations, private foundations, commercial agencies, and government agencies. "GRANTS" is produced by Oryx Press and corresponds to the printed work *Directory of Research Grants.* Other databases include the *Sponsored Programs Information Network (SPIN), The Foundation Directory,* and the *Illinois Researcher Information System (IRIS);* grants available from every U. S. government agency are collected on the Web site www.grants.gov. Indeed, an increasing amount of information about grants can be found on the Internet. Among other resources found there are documentation for grant applications, subject guides to funding agencies often with their home pages, and various discussion lists. There is a listserv called GRANTS-L, which includes information on sources of government and non-profit funding for scholarly research. Various workshops and seminars on obtaining grants are regularly held throughout the country.

One article, "Library Grant Money on the Web: A Resource Primer," published in *Searcher,* provides descriptions and URLs for grant funding agencies and resources.[14] Gerding's more current article about the explosion of grant information on the Web reviews a large number of URLs; the author also maintains a Web site of "Library Grants" and has co-authored a book on the subject.[15] Bauer not only describes how to seek grant funding proactively and to develop a grant proposal, but also describes the various government and private funding sources and their differences.[16] Waters lists grant sources and foundations that have funded libraries, thereby identifying potential sources for future funding.[17] Other publications with information about grants and funded research in library and information science include the following:

1. *The Big Book of Library Grant Money, 2007: Profiles of Private and Corporate Foundations and Direct Corporate Givers Receptive to Library Grant Proposals,* Detroit, MI: Taft Group/Chicago: American Library Association, 2007.

2. Jeffrey A. Falkenstein, *National Guide to Funding for Libraries and Information Services,* 8th ed., New York: Foundation Center, 2005.

3. "Research on Libraries and Librarianship" (annual report of the Office for Research and Statistics, American Library Association), *Bowker Annual Library and Book Trade Information,* New York: R. R. Bowker.

4. Dawn V. Kight and Emma B. Perry, "Grant Resources on the Web," *College & Research Libraries News* (July/August 1999): 543–45.

5. Penny Kyker, "Selected World Wide Web Sites for Library Grants and Fund-Raising," *Library Administration & Management* 12 (Spring 1998): 64–71.

6. Laura A. Sullivan, "Grant Funding for Libraries," *Bottom Line: Managing Library Finances* 20, no. 4 (2007): 157–60.

After identifying possible research agencies, Lynch and others recommend gathering as much information as possible about the agencies' interests and what they have supported in the past.[18] In addition, it is usually advisable to contact the potential grantors at an early date to inform them of one's intent to apply for support and to provide the agency with a brief, written description of the proposed research. Feedback gained at this stage can help to assess the interest of the organization, refine the project, and expedite consideration of the formal proposal to follow. Personal contact at this point can be especially beneficial.

According to an older yet still relevant article published in the *Chronicle of Higher Education*, grant officers are in agreement that foundations look at three basic qualities when reviewing grant proposals: the significance of the problem proposed for investigation, the quality of the proposed solution, and the research records of the persons planning to carry out the research. The article includes a list of reference collections operated or coordinated by the Foundation Center, a nonprofit organization established in 1956.[19] According to the Grantsmanship Center, reviewers of proposals are most interested in the purpose and definition of the project, the priority of the project, the financial information, the background of the requesting organization, personnel, and evaluation of the project. A workshop document prepared by the University of Michigan's Division of Research Development and Administration listed nine questions that a foundation is likely to ask when reviewing a proposal:

1. Is the proposal problem solving?
2. Is the problem important?
3. Is this the appropriate foundation?
4. Is the proposal innovative?
5. Will the project become self-supporting?
6. Can the proposing group do the work?
7. Is the project demonstrative (i.e., can it be used as a model)?
8. How will the program be evaluated?
9. Is the amount of money requested sufficient?

Another key to obtaining funding is identifying research areas that are considered timely. From time to time, "inventories" of needed research studies have been produced and may be of some assistance in the identification of topics likely to be seen as relatively high priorities by funding agencies. Though dated now, a good example of such a document was published in 1981 by Cuadra Associates, for the U.S. Department of Education Office of Libraries and Learning Technologies. Titled *A Library and Information Science Research Agenda for the 1980's*, it reflected the input of 26 library and information science researchers and practitioners.[20] More recent research agendas include:

1. "A Research Agenda for YALSA"[21]
2. "In Search of Practical Applications: A Public Services Research Agenda for University Libraries"[22]
3. ACRL's "Research Agenda for Library Instruction and Information Literacy"[23]

4. "SLA Research Statement"[24]

5. *The Digital Reference Research* Agenda, published in 2003[25] (see also the related 2004 "Digital Reference Research Agenda"[26] and the 2005 publication, "A Conceptual Framework and Open Research Questions for Chat-based Reference")[27]

6. Council on Library and Information Resources (CLIR), "Program and Research Agenda, 2007–2010"[28]

7. "Defining the Medical Library Association Research Agenda"[29]

8. "Leadership: Defining a Research Agenda for Academic Libraries"[30]

9. "Digital Curation and Preservation: Defining the Research Agenda"[31]

10. "Research in School Library Media for the Next Decade"[32]

11. "Research Agenda for Women's Studies Librarianship"[33]

12. The Spring 2003 issue of *Library Trends*, titled "Research Questions for the Twenty-First Century," identifies problems and questions that need to be addressed by research and considers how they might be approached.[34]

SUMMARY

The proposal is as essential to successful research as the outline is to good writing. It represents what should be the careful planning that precedes a well-conceived research study. The proposal should spell out, to a reasonable degree, the details of a proposed research project and serve as a guide to which the researcher may refer as he or she carries out the study.

In terms of format, most research proposals are essentially the same. The elements generally included are the title page, abstract, literature review, hypothesis and assumptions, definitions, research design, data analysis, a budget if appropriate, anticipated results, limitations, and references. A timetable, which can be quite useful in keeping the research project on schedule, may be appended or may be integrated throughout the text of the proposal.

There is a variety of characteristics that can increase the attractiveness of a proposal. Most of these attributes simply result from the proposal's being well written and from the author using an appropriate, effective format. Perhaps most important, the proposal should be clear, straightforward, and succinct.

There is also a variety of features that may detract from a research proposal. They range from unsound hypotheses to excessive budgets, with the most common problems being inexplicit proposals, unsound designs, and unqualified investigators. It is important for any research proposal to be as free of detracting features as possible, but this is particularly crucial for proposals for sponsored research.

NOTES

1. Lynn Silipigni Connaway, "A Research Funding Opportunity for Library and Information Science Faculty: The OCLC/ALISE Library and Information Science Research Grant Program," *Journal of Education for Library and Information Science* 46, no. 3 (2005): 263.

2. Gerald W. Lundeen, "Research Record," *Journal of Education for Librarianship* 24 (Winter 1984): 206–7.

3. Bluma C. Peritz, "The Methods of Library Science Research: Some Results from a Bibliometric Survey," *Library Research* 2 (Fall 1980): 251–68.

4. Martyvonne M. Nour, "A Quantitative Analysis of the Research Articles Published in Core Library Journals of 1980," *Library & Information Science Research* 7 (July 1985): 261–73.

5. Patricia E. Feehan, Gregg W. Lee, and Michael W. Havener, "Library and Information Science Research: An Analysis of the 1984 Journal Literature," *Library & Information Science Research* 9 (July 1987): 173–85.

6. Ronald R. Powell, "Recent Trends in Research: A Methodological Essay," *Library & Information Science Research* 21, no. 1 (1999): 91–119.

7. Raya Fidel, "Are We There Yet?: Mixed Methods Research in Library and Information Science," *Library & Information Science Research* 30, no. 4 (December 2008): 265–72.

8. Connaway, "Research Funding Opportunity," 263.

9. Paul D. Leedy and Jeanne Ellis Ormrod, *Practical Research: Planning and Design*, 8th ed. (Upper Saddle River, NJ: Pearson Merrill Prentice Hall, 2005), 116.

10. National Institute of Child Health and Human Development, "Quick Tips: Most Common Reasons for Disapproval," http://www.nichd.nih.gov/about/cpr/dbs/tip4.htm.

11. Connaway, "Research Funding Opportunity."

12. Mary Jo Lynch, *Proposal Procedures: Guidelines for ALA Units* (Chicago: ALA Office for Research, 1981), 15.

13. Ibid., 16.

14. Bill Becker, "Library Grant Money on the Web: A Resource Primer," *Searcher* 11, no. 10 (November/December, 2003): 8–14.

15. Stephanie Gerding, "Tips and Resources for Finding Grants," *Online* 32, no. 6 (November 2008): 16–21.

Stephanie Gerding, "Library Grants," http://www.librarygrants.blogspot.com/.

Stephanie Gerding and Pamela H. MacKellar, *Grants for Libraries: A How-to-do-it Manual* (New York: Neal-Schuman, 2006).

16. David G. Bauer, *"How To" Grants Manual: Successful Grantseeking Techniques for Obtaining Public and Private Grants*, 4th ed. (Phoenix, AZ: American Council on Education/Oryx Press, 1999).

17. Richard L. Waters, "Fund Raising: Grants and Other Bits of Information," *Public Library Quarterly* 17, no. 3 (1999): 51–54.

18. Lynch, "Proposal Procedures."

19. Suzanne Perry, "Getting a Foundation Grant Takes More Than a Good Idea, Program Officers Say," *Chronicle of Higher Education* 25 (October 1982): 25–28.

20. U.S. Department of Education, Office of Libraries and Learning Technologies, *A Library and Information Science Research Agenda for the 1980's* (Los Angeles: Cuadra Associates, 1981).

21. "A Research Agenda for YALSA," *Youth Services in Libraries* (Spring 1995): 267–71.

22. Barbara A. Dewey, "In Search of Practical Applications: A Public Services Research Agenda for University Libraries," *Journal of Academic Librarianship* (September 1997): 371–79.

23. American Library Association, "Research Agenda for Library Instruction and Information Literacy; the Updated Version," *College & Research Libraries News*

(February 2003): 108–13, http://www.ala.org/ala/mgrps/divs/acrl/about/sections/is/projpubs/researchagendalibrary.cfm.

24. Special Libraries Association, "Putting OUR Knowledge to Work: A New SLA Research Statement June 2001: The Role of Reseaerch in Special Librarianship," June 2001, http://www.sla.org/content/resources/research/rsrchstatement.cfm.

25. R. David Lankes, Scott Nicholson, and Abby Goodrum, *The Digital Reference Research Agenda*, Publications in Librarianship no. 55 (Chicago: Association of College and Research Libraries, 2003).

26. R. David Lankes, "The Digital Reference Research Agenda," *Journal of the American Society for Information Science and Technology* 55, no. 4 (February 2004): 301–11.

27. Jeffrey Pomeranz, "A Conceptual Framework and Open Research Questions for Chat-based Reference," *Journal of the American Society for Information Science and Technology* 56, no. 12 (October 2005): 1288–1302.

28. Council on Library and Information Resources, "Program and Research Agenda, 2007–2010," http://www.clir.org/activities/agenda.htm.

29. Jonathan D. Eldredge, Martha R. Harris, and Marie T. Ascher, "Defining the Medical Library Association Research Agenda: Methodology and Final Results from a Consensus Process," *Journal of the Medical Library Association* 97, no. 3 (July 2009): 178–85.

30. Peter Hernon and Candy Schwartz, "Leadership: Defining a Research Agenda for Academic Libraries," *Library & Information Science Research* 30, no. 4 (December 2008): 243–49.

31. The Warwick Workshop, "Digital Curation and Preservation: Defining the Research Agenda," *Library Hi Tech News* 23, no. 3 (April 2006): 23.

32. Delia Neuman, "Research in School Library Media for the Next Decade: Polishing the Diamond," *Library Trends* 51, no. 4 (Spring 2003): 503–24.

33. Association of College and Research Libraries, Research Committee of the Women's Studies Section, "Research Agenda for Women's Studies Librarianship," 2007, 'http://wikis.ala.org/acrl/index.php/Research_Agenda_for_Women's_Studies_Section.

34. Mary J. Lynch, ed. "Research Questions for the Twenty-First Century," *Library Trends* 51, no. 4 (Spring 2003): 499–686.

Writing the Research Report

Regardless of how well a research project is conceived and conducted, if its findings are not disseminated in some fashion, its value will be negligible. The research report, whether it is an unpublished document or a journal article, in either print or electronic format, remains an important vehicle for the dissemination of research results. The researcher should not consider his or her task complete until the research results have been made available to the appropriate audience, and in the most effective form possible. Meadows, in his book *Communicating Research*, states, "Communication lies at the heart of research."[1] Newman goes so far as to say, "Original scholarship and the publication that emerges from it are the moral obligations of those who accept public money to perform as intellectuals."[2] The Committee on Research and Statistics of ALA, in a June 2001 brochure, points out that "unless the implications of research are communicated to practitioners, the results are of little value."[3]

GENERAL OBJECTIVES OF THE RESEARCH REPORT

The general objectives of the research report are to acquaint the reader with the problem that has been investigated, to present the results of the investigation, and to explain its implications or importance. The report should present the data fully and adequately; the data should support the report's interpretations and conclusions. The report should interpret the data for the reader and demonstrate how the data help to resolve the problem.

In meeting these objectives, the research report should be as well structured and logical as possible. It should be a straightforward document that sets forth clearly and precisely what the researcher has done to solve, or at least to investigate, the research problem. It need not be a literary masterpiece, but it should be readable.

GENERAL OUTLINE OF THE RESEARCH REPORT

In a "Guest Editorial" in *College & Research Libraries*, Connell (2010) provides tips for authors for planning and writing a research paper.[4] She provides a succinct explanation of components that should be included in a typical, thorough research paper. Her suggestions are similar to the more detailed outline that follows. Not all reports will present these items in exactly this order, or even include all of them. Others may include additional points. Most of these items were discussed in some detail earlier and therefore are basically listed here.

The Preliminaries/Front Matter

1. Abstract—A brief summary which restates the problem, the procedures, the main findings, and the major conclusions. It is usually about 200 words or less in length. It is considered optional unless the report or journal format specifically calls for it.

2. Title—The title, in effect, serves as part of the abstract and should, within a reasonable length, be descriptive of the study.

3. Copyright notice—U.S. copyright protection is effective for the life of the author plus seventy years. All U.S. publications automatically receive U.S. copyright protection, but there are possible advantages to be gained from actually registering a publication with the U.S. Copyright Office.

4. Acknowledgments (optional).

5. Table of contents—this is particularly important if the report is relatively long.

6. List of tables (where needed).

7. List of figures (graphic illustrations other than tables).

The Text

1. Introduction and problem
   a. Brief introduction—This is not always considered desirable as it usually summarizes the report and therefore becomes somewhat redundant. It can help to express the purpose of the study at an early point in the report.
   b. Statement of the problem—This section also typically includes a brief review of documents relevant to the problem.
   c. Identification of subproblems, if any
   d. Delimitations of the study
   e. Conceptual definitions of key terms
   f. Abbreviations, if needed
   g. Statement of the need or justification for the study
   h. A note on the organization of the remainder of the report

2. Review of related literature—This review will build on the briefer literature review provided for the problem statement. It should provide the conceptual basis for the hypothesis to follow. It may also draw on related subject fields. If individuals are cited, their authority should be indicated.

3. Conceptual framework of the study—As is true for the proposal, many researchers prefer that this section precede the literature review and often include it in the introductory or problem section.

  a. Hypothesis(es) and/or research questions
  b. Assumptions—These basic assumptions help to support the logic of the hypothesis.
  c. Operational definitions of important concepts

4. Design of the study—The design of the study is broader than the basic research method (e.g., survey), which should already be apparent at this point. The description of the design should be clear and precise about what was done and how it was done.

  a. The population and sampling procedures, if any—This section should include a description of the research locale or setting if important.
  b. Sources of relevant data, including criteria for admissibility
  c. Data collection techniques and instruments
  d. Data analysis techniques.

5. Results

  a. Descriptive statistics, if utilized
  b. Inferential statistics—The section where hypotheses, if any, are tested
  c. Other findings—An optional section of miscellaneous findings or results not directly related to the hypothesis
  d. Summary of results

6. Summary and conclusions

  a. Summary of the study
  b. Interpretations and conclusions
  c. Limitations of the results
  d. Recommendations, if any, for future research

Back Matter

1. References—The list of citations or footnotes, if not provided at the appropriate locations in the text.

2. Bibliography—A list of other "classic" studies and highly relevant items; it also will include the references, if not listed separately.

3. Appendix—The appendix or appendices should include only supplementary material not essential to an understanding of the text.

GUIDELINES FOR ORGANIZING AND PRESENTING THE RESEARCH REPORT

Organization of the Report

In organizing a research report of any length, it is always a good idea to develop and follow a detailed outline. In writing the report, it helps to organize the information by employing appropriate headings. Several manuals of style can be used for guidance in selecting headings.[5] One common approach is to utilize centered headings for the major division (all upper case letters), followed in a logical, hierarchical order by free-standing sideheads (capitals and lower case, underscored); paragraph sideheads (underscored, first word only capitalized, followed by a period); and fourth-level headings (capitals and lower case, underscored).

Footnotes and Documentation

In citing information and ideas borrowed from other works, it is again important to use accepted guidelines or manuals of style. The specific style to be employed may be left up to the author, though many journals and book publishers do prescribe a certain format. Regardless of who determines the style to be used, it is important to be consistent throughout the report.

Another general guideline is that, if material is borrowed from any source, whether it be a direct quotation or a paraphrase, then both the author and the work should be cited. If the quotation, or borrowed data, is extensive, and the report may be published or copyrighted, the writer should secure in writing from the holder of the copyright (usually the publisher) permission to reprint the material. In addition to the footnote or reference, the words "Reprinted by permission of the publisher (or author)" should be placed in an appropriate location or added to the footnote. Plagiarism is, of course, unethical and should be avoided at all costs.

Prose Style of the Report

It is generally recommended that a research report be written in the past tense, as it is a report of events which have already occurred. It is usually suggested that the writer employ the passive voice, which means that no identifiable subject is performing an act, and avoid the first person (see Losee and Worley[6] and Creswell[7] for a differing opinion as well as some other suggestions for writing and presenting the results of research).

The prose itself should be clear, exact, and efficient, and should reflect simple English. Regarding efficiency, Hillway argues that every statement that the writer makes should fall into one of the following four categories: (a) a direct statement of fact, (b) a basic assumption, (c) an expression of expert opinion, or (d) the author's personal opinion. It may be advisable to consider eliminating any other type of statement.[8]

Text Preparation

In preparing the text for the research report, it is again advisable to adhere to standard guidelines. Needless to say, general standards for neatness, accuracy, punctuation, and so on should be met. Aesthetics are also worth considering; for example, ample space should be left for margins and between the headings and text. Word processing and electronic publishing software facilitate the revision process. Electronic dictionaries and spell checkers are useful—but not foolproof—to identify misspellings, and electronic thesauri are helpful in selecting alternative words.

Graphic Presentation of Data

Graphics can in some cases present information more clearly and succinctly than can prose. At the very least, graphic presentations can help to supplement explanations and data presented in the text. There is a whole host of types of graphic presentations available, including statistical tables, line graphs, bar charts, pie charts, flowcharts, pictographs (simple pictures or cartoons), and maps. In using graphic representations, the researcher should remember, however, that they should be used only to facilitate the understanding of data. They are not intended to entertain and should not distract from the purpose of the text. Graphic representations should be kept as simple as possible, and they should be clear and accurate.

When designing graphic representations, the writer should see that each one is referred to in the text. It is also important that they be self-contained. In other words, each graphic should contain a title, an explanation of any symbols used, instructions on how to read or use the graphic, a brief description of what it is intended to show, and an indication of the sources of the data. Graphics should be placed as close as possible to the points in the text where they are first discussed.

Oral Presentations of the Report

Researchers often are invited or required to present their research to others in an oral form. In their book, *Organizing and Managing Your Research: A Practical Guide for Postgraduates*, Phelps, Fisher, and Ellis provide a step-by-step guide to planning, managing, organizing, writing, presenting and publishing research.[9] This book is targeted to students, new researchers, and career researchers. The tips and strategies for presenting research include the following:

1. Preparing the speech
   a. Take as many opportunities as possible to speak in public
   b. Know your audience
   c. Plan the structure
   d. Practice your speech as many times as possible
   e. Have everything you need for your presentation ready well beforehand
   f. Get to know the room you will be in for your presentation
   g. Greet a few people as they arrive
2. Delivering the speech
   a. Control nerves before you start
   b. Have a glass of water at hand
   c. Know the *exact* words you are going to start with
   d. Make an initial impact
   e. Acknowledge your audience

    f. Be confident

    g. Keep your talk very simple with a few main points

    h. Do not read your paper or your slides

    i. Speak slowly and clearly

    j. Use pauses to good effect

    k. Avoid padding your content

    l. Avoid filler words such as um, ah, okay, sort of, you know, etc

    m. Establish eye contact and rapport with your audience

    n. Incorporate some humor or narrative

    o. Manage your time well

    p. Be prepared to be flexible

3. Concluding your speech

    a. Acknowledge people who helped you along the way

    b. Remember to conclude

    c. Use questions and discussion well

    d. Above all, enjoy yourself.[10]

EVALUATING THE RESEARCH REPORT

When reading a report of research, the informed, critical reader will generally look for the following: (a) adequacy of documentation, (b) accuracy of sources, (c) correctness of interpretation of sources, (d) appropriateness of data analysis, (e) basis for conclusions, (f) format and style, and (g) evidence of creativity. But there are many specific criteria worth considering, and they may be categorized according to the major sections of a typical research report. A checklist of such criteria, many of which were taken from Wynar, follows.[11]

SUGGESTED CRITERIA FOR JUDGING A RESEARCH REPORT

1. Background

    a. Is the title descriptive, accurate, and of a reasonable length?

    b. Does the introduction give a clear indication of the general scope of the research?

    c. Is the reason or purpose for the research sufficiently indicated?

    d. Is the problem clearly stated and analyzed into definite subordinate questions or issues where appropriate?

    e. Is the logic of the analysis of the problem sound? In other words, have the critical factors been identified, relationships properly identified, and so on?

    f. What is the hypothesis or research question?

    g. Is the hypothesis of social or theoretical significance, and is it stated so that it can be resolved or tested?

    h. Are the variables clear? Have they been designated as independent and dependent variables where appropriate? Are there any logical consequences or implications?

    i. Are the basic assumptions needed to support the hypothesis made clear?

j. Are adequate operational or working definitions provided?

k. Is the coverage of previous, related research adequate? Is the report related to the earlier studies?

2. Design of the study

a. Does the research design seem adequate and logical for the solution of the problem?

b. Are the reasons for its choice adequately explained?

c. Was the methodology explained in an understandable way so that it can be replicated?

d. If important terms are used in an unusual sense, are they defined?

e. Are the data collected adequate for the solution of the problem? In other words, do we have satisfactory measurements of the relevant variables?

f. Are the data sufficiently quantitative (when appropriate) for the solution of the problem?

g. Are the instruments used by the investigator adequate reflections of the conceptual variables of the study (i.e., do they measure the variables in a reliable and valid manner)?

h. If sampling procedures were used, were they adequately explained?

i. If the sample was supposedly random, was it in fact chosen so that each member of the population had an equal chance of being selected?

j. If the researcher used the sample for generalizing, was it adequate for doing so?

k. How reliable and valid is the design overall?

3. Treatment of the data

a. Are the data presented as an integral part of the logical solution of the problem?

b. What techniques were used to analyze the quantitative (or qualitative) data? Do they seem to be appropriate and effective?

c. Were graphical and/or tabular formats appropriately used to display pertinent data?

d. Is there evidence of care and accuracy in the collection and treatment of the data?

e. Is irrelevant material or information excluded?

f. Do the inferences based on the data seem to be sound?

4. Summary and conclusions

a. Do the conclusions actually serve to answer questions or issues raised in the study?

b. Are all conclusions based essentially on data made known to the reader?

c. Are conclusions free from mere unsupported opinions?

d. Are the limitations or qualifications of the conclusions clearly and concisely expressed?

e. Are applications and recommendations, when included, judiciously made?

f. Can the conclusions be generalized to a larger population?

g. Did the researcher appear to be aware of the theoretical implications, if any, of the research?

h. Did the researcher make recommendations for future research?

5. Appendices
   a. If there is an appendix, is it supplementary in nature, rather than essential to an understanding of the text?
   b. Does it include all original data?
6. Bibliography
   a. Does it appear that one style manual was followed (i.e., is the bibliographic style consistent)?

Other authors have developed similar checklists for evaluating research reports, including Mouly,[12] Busha and Harter,[13] Marchant and Smith,[14] Robbins,[15] and Isaac and Michael.[16] Leedy, in a useful work titled *How to Read Research and Understand It*, guides the reader through the evaluation of actual research reports.[17] A book by Hittleman and Simon is a useful guide for the consumer of research.[18] Pyrczak[19] and Girden[20] are the authors of two of the books devoted to the evaluation of research articles. Paul and Elder have developed a template that can be used to assess the quality of any research paper or project.[21] The major concepts state that "all research:

1. Has a fundamental PURPOSE and goal
2. Addresses a fundamental QUESTION, problem or issue
3. Identifies data, INFORMATION, and evidence relevant to its fundamental question and purpose
4. Contains INFERENCES or interpretation by which conclusions are drawn
5. Is conducted from some POINT OF VIEW or frame of reference
6. Is based on ASSUMPTIONS
7. Is expressed through and shaped by CONCEPTS and ideas
8. Leads somewhere (i.e., has IMPLICATIONS and consequences)."[22]

In reading and evaluating a research report, the reader would be well advised to be particularly watchful for certain common faults. Among these weaknesses are the following:

1. Broad, sweeping statements without sufficient evidence or documentation to support them.
2. A lack of precision in statements, or a tendency to state ideas vaguely.
3. A weak organization and arrangement.
4. A failure to describe fully and clearly the method by which the hypothesis was tested, or even a failure to test the hypothesis.
5. A lack of direct linking of the problem to the hypothesis. As was discussed earlier, the hypothesis should represent at least a partial solution to the problem, and therefore must be related to it.
6. A failure to distinguish adequately between the problem and the purpose of the study. In essence, the problem represents what was studied, and the purpose indicates why it was studied.
7. Incorporating information or materials from some source without clearly indicating how they were derived from that source.

8. Bringing new elements, concepts, or ideas into the summary and/or conclusions without having introduced them earlier in the study.

9. Writing the final report as originally conceived rather than as the findings dictate. In other words, the researcher must be sensitive to the results of the research and not be hesitant to reflect them in the conclusions, even when they are contrary to expectations.[23]

PUBLISHING RESEARCH RESULTS

"Librarians have a fundamental responsibility to contribute to professional communication."[24] "The research process is *not* complete until it has been reported."[25] Libraries cannot benefit from the results of research if they are not published.[26] Or as Hillway stated, "To make his discoveries known to the world, the scholar must accept the task of publication as one of his essential responsibilities."[27] Unfortunately, according to a study conducted by Powell, Baker, and Mika, only 26 percent of librarians publish research results.[28]

Early in the process of "getting published," the would-be author must decide on the format to be employed, the report vehicle, and the likely audience. Among the most common formats are monographs, scholarly articles in journals, papers delivered at professional meetings (often appearing in conference proceedings), unpublished reports such as those collected by ERIC, and dissertations. The last two are not publications in the conventional sense, but unpublished reports sometimes (and dissertations almost always) represent original research.

Researchers who have decided to publish their research results in the journal article format must know the journals (vehicles) in which they might publish; select a subject for a manuscript (essentially done when the research was initiated); determine the methodology and style of writing to employ; write the manuscript; prepare the manuscript for submission (as dictated by the journal's instructions to authors); work with the editor in the review of the manuscript; and, if accepted for publication, tend to the final editing and proofreading of the manuscript and galley proofs.[29]

Regarding the selection of a vehicle and audience, Busha and Harter have a useful section in their book on research methods.[30] They discuss the major types of outlets for written research reports and cite numerous examples. As they note, "the selection of a publication vehicle in which to communicate a research report should depend upon the topic of the study, the nature of the material presented, and the desired audience."[31] Electronic journals are becoming an increasingly common option. In 2005, Davis and Nisonger published an analysis and ranking of LIS journals based on the perceptions of LIS education program deans and directors of large research libraries.[32] The top 21 research journals as rated by LIS deans on their importance for promotion and tenure reviews were, from top to bottom:

1. JASIS&T
2. Library Quarterly
3. Information Processing and Management

4. Library & Information Science Research
5. Journal of Documentation
6. ARIST
7. Scientometrics
8. Library Trends
9. Journal of American Medical Informatics Association
10. MIS Quarterly
11. Libraries and Culture
12. College and Research Libraries
13. Library Resources and Technical Services
14. Information Research
15. Journal of Academic Librarianship
16. School Library Media Research
17. Reference and User Services Quarterly
18. Telecommunications Policy
19. The Information Society
20. Information Systems Research
21. Journal of the Medical Library Association

O'Connor and Van Orden report on the results of a survey of 33 national library periodicals.[33] They focus on identifying an author's chances of having an unsolicited manuscript published and on the review process for selecting manuscripts for publication. They point out the importance of journal editors' publishing the purpose and scope of their periodicals and their methods and criteria for reviewing manuscripts and the importance of prospective authors' being aware of them. More recent articles updating and supplementing the analysis done by O'Connor and Van Orden were published in 1988[34] and 1996.[35]

When journal referees evaluate manuscripts, they generally address criteria similar to those used to evaluate research reports (see the criteria provided earlier in this chapter). A referee's report used by the *Library Quarterly* asks the referee to answer the following questions:

1. Does the study address a significant problem, topic, or issue?
2. Does the work offer fresh insights or original treatment of the problem?
3. Does the author demonstrate a command of the relevant literature?
4. Are the research methods appropriate to the problem?
5. Are there flaws in the methods, arguments, or data analyses?
6. Are the conclusions justified by the results of the analysis?
7. Do the findings confirm, expand, revise, or challenge conventional knowledge or professional consensus?
8. Is the paper well organized and clearly written?
9. Is the paper interesting to read?

Would-be authors wishing to report their research results in book format must follow a procedure not much different from that for publishing a journal article. "The author's major responsibility is to develop the idea, to write the manuscript, and to deliver it to the publisher in an acceptable and readable form."[36] Just as one should take care to select the most appropriate journal, one should shop around for a book publisher. Factors to consider in selecting a publisher include pricing, design, marketing, editorial assistance, production schedule, review process, and royalty arrangements. Those wishing to know more about the book contract may wish to refer to the work by Schuman just quoted.[37] Morris highlights the fundamentals of writing and publishing books and journal articles from the perspective of the school library media specialist.[38]

A book by Schroeder and Roberson provides listings of library-related periodicals, electronic journals and newsletters, publications of state library associations, and refereed journals.[39] St. Clair provides a useful article on publishing library research.[40] Giesecke, former editor of *Library Administration & Management*, describes the different types of publications and journals and the most effective methods for preparing the report based on the type of publication.[41] She also includes information on common mistakes made by authors and provides a helpful checklist. Labaree provides a practical list of tips for academic librarians for getting published in scholarly journals.[42] ACRL's *InPrint: Publishing Opportunities for College Librarians* provides descriptive information about submitting manuscripts and journal data for library and information science journals and related journals.[43] Gordon provides pertinent information on how to integrate writing with practice, how to develop ideas for writing, and how to handle rejections for submitted papers.[44] The New Members Round Table of ALA provides a discussion group, NMRTWriter, dedicated to supporting librarians wishing to write and publish articles and books. The ACRL Research Program Committee sponsored Research Writer's Consultations at the 2009 ALA Annual Conference. Small groups of new or inexperienced writers were matched with an experienced writer or editor who provided guidance and critique.

Graduates of doctoral programs are encouraged to publish their dissertations as books and/or to summarize them for publication in a journal. In doing so, they should remove much of the redundancy typical of dissertations, decrease some of the details regarding previous research and methodology, and relate the work to the concrete world as much as possible. The *Publication Manual of the American Psychological Association* addresses converting a dissertation into an article.[45]

SUMMARY

Unless the results of research are properly communicated, all of the efforts that went into the research are, to a great extent, for naught. The first basic step required for disseminating the results of research is the writing of the report. This report should be a straightforward document that clearly, precisely, and efficiently describes what the researcher has done to investigate a problem.

The research report should be well organized and generally follow a standard, recommended format. The researcher should exercise care in the documentation for and writing of the report. It should be neat and error free. Graphic presentations should be used where appropriate. The writer should be aware of what the informed reader would be looking for and be careful to avoid the common faults of research reports.

In writing the report and looking ahead to its publication, the researcher should keep in mind the audience that it should reach and the method of publication or dissemination likely to be used. It is important to be aware of the review mechanisms of journals and to tailor manuscripts to their criteria and interests. In conclusion, the importance of reporting research results should not be underestimated. The research report, regardless of format, is what communicates specific information to an audience, adds to the general body of knowledge, and hopefully stimulates further research.

NOTES

1. A. J. Meadows, *Communicating Research* (San Diego: Academic Press, 1998): ix.

2. John Newman, "Academic Librarians as Scholars," *College & Research Libraries News* 59, no. 1 (January 1998): 19.

3. American Library Association, "Dissemination of Research in LIS: A Statement by the American Library Association Committee on Research and Statistics," (2001), http://www.ala.org/ala/aboutala/offices/ors/orscommittees/dissemination/dissemination.cfm.

4. Tschera Harkness Connell, "Writing the Research Paper: A Review," *College & Research Libraries* 71, no. 1 (January 2010): 6–7.

5. Paul D. Leedy and Jeanne Ellis Ormrod, *Practical Research: Planning and Design*, 8th ed. (Upper Saddle River, NJ: Pearson Merrill Prentice Hall, 2005), 282–83.

6. Robert M. Losee and Karen A. Worley, *Research and Evaluation for Information Professionals* (San Diego: Academic Press, 1993): 217.

7. John W. Creswell, *Research Design: Qualitative, Quantitative, and Mixed Methods Approaches*, 3rd ed. (Thousand Oaks, CA: Sage, 2009), 86; 193–94.

8. Tyrus Hillway, *Introduction to Research*, 2nd ed. (Boston: Houghton Mifflin, 1964), 265.

9. Renata Phelps, Kath Fisher, and Allan Ellis, *Organizing and Managing Your Research: A Practical Guide for Postgraduates* (Los Angeles: Sage, 2007).

10. Ibid., 260–62.

11. Dan Wynar, *Syllabus for Research Methods in Librarianship* (Denver, CO: Graduate School of Librarianship, 1962), 129–30.

12. George J. Mouly, *Educational Research: The Art and Science of Investigation* (Boston: Allyn and Bacon, 1978), 343–44.

13. Charles H. Busha and Stephen P. Harter, *Research Methods in Librarianship: Techniques and Interpretations* (New York: Academic Press, 1980), 28.

14. Maurice P. Marchant and N. M. Smith, "Research Thrust of Brigham Young University's Library School," *Journal of Education for Librarianship* 20 (Fall 1979): 132.

15. Jane B. Robbins, "The Quality of Published Library and Information Science Research," *Library & Information Science Research* 13 (Spring 1991): 315–17.

16. Stephen Isaac and William B. Michael, *Handbook in Research and Evaluation: A Collection of Principles, Methods and Strategies Useful in the Planning,*

Design, and Evaluation of Studies in Education and the Behavioral Sciences, 3rd ed. (San Diego: EdITS, 1995), 238.

17. Paul D. Leedy, *How to Read Research and Understand It* (New York: Macmillan, 1981).

18. Daniel R. Hittleman and Alan J. Simon, *Interpreting Educational Research: An Introduction for Consumers of Research*, 4th ed. (Upper Saddle River, NJ: Merrill Prentice Hall, 2006).

19. Fred Pyrczak, *Evaluating Research in Academic Journals: A Practical Guide to Realistic Evaluation*, 4th ed. (Glendale, CA: Pyrczak Publishing, 2008).

20. Ellen R. Girden, *Evaluating Research Articles from Start to Finish*, 2nd ed. (Thousand Oaks, CA: Sage, 2001).

21. Richard Paul and Linda Elder, *The Miniature Guide to Critical Thinking: Concepts and Tools*, 4th ed. (Dillon Beach, CA: Critical Thinking Press, 2007).

22. Ibid., 20.

23. Hillway, *Introduction to Research*, 274–75.

24. James G. Neal, "Editorial: The Librarian Research and Publication Imperative," *Library & Information Science Research* 17 (Spring 1995): 199.

25. Jane B. Robbins, "Affecting Librarianship in Action: The Dissemination and Communication of Research Findings," in *Applying Research to Practice*, ed. Leigh L. Estabrook (Urbana-Champaign: University of Illinois, Graduate School of Library and Information Science, 1992), 78.

26. Larry N. Osborne, "Research Record," *Journal of Education for Library and Information Science* 25 (Spring 1985): 318.

27. Hillway, *Introduction to Research*, 156.

28. Ronald R. Powell, Lynda M. Baker, and Joseph J. Mika, "Library and Information Science Practitioners and Research," *Library & Information Science Research* 24 (2002): 49–72.

29. Richard D. Johnson, "The Journal Article," in *Librarian/Author: A Practical Guide on How to Get Published*, ed. Betty-Carol Sellen (New York: Neal-Schuman Publishers, 1985), 21–35.

30. Busha and Harter, *Research Methods in Librarianship*.

31. Ibid., 374.

32. Charles H. Davis and Thomas E. Nisonger, "The Perception of Library and Information Science Journals by LIS Education Deans and ARL Library Directors: A Replication of the Kohl-Davis Study," *College & Research Libraries* 66, no. 4 (July 2005): 341–77.

33. Daniel O'Connor and Phyllis Van Orden, "Getting into Print," *College & Research Libraries* 39 (September 1978): 389–96.

34. John M. Budd, "Publication in Library and Information Science: The State of the Literature," *Library Journal* 113 (September 1988): 125–31.

35. Barbara J. Via, "Publishing in the Journal Literature of Library and Information Science: A Survey of Manuscript Review Processes and Acceptance," *College & Research Libraries* 57 (July 1996): 365–76.

36. Patricia G. Schuman, "From Book Idea to the Contract," in *Librarian/Author: A Practical Guide on How to Get Published*, ed. Betty-Carol Sellen (New York: Neal-Schuman Publishers, 1985), 37.

37. Ibid.

38. Betty J. Morris, "Getting Published: What Every Library Media Specialist Needs to Know," *Knowledge Quest* 26, no. 3 (March/April 1998): 16–17.

39. Carol F. Schroeder and Gloria G. Roberson, *Guide to Publishing Opportunities for Librarians* (New York: Haworth Press, 1995).

40. Gloriana St. Clair, "Improving Quality: An Editor's Advice to Authors," *College & Research Libraries* 54 (May 1993): 195–97.

41. Joan Giesecke, "Preparing Research for Publication," *Library Administration and Management* 12, no. 3 (Summer 1998): 134–37.

42. Robert V. Labaree, "Tips for Getting Published in Scholarly Journals: Strategies for Academic Librarians," *College & Research Libraries News* 65, no. 3 (March 2004): 137–39.

43. Alice Harrison Bahr, Michael J. McLane, and Lynn W. Livingston, *InPrint: Publishing Opportunities for College Librarians* (Chicago: Association of College and Research Libraries, 1997).

44. Rachel Singer Gordon, "Getting Started in Library Publication," *American Libraries* 35, no. 1 (January 2004): 66–69.

45. *Publication Manual of the American Psychological Association*, 5th ed. (Washington, DC: American Psychological Association, 2001): 326–29.

References

Abdullahi, Ismail. *Global Library and Information Science: A Textbook for Students and Educators, with Contributions from Africa, Asia, Australia, New Zealand, Europe, Latin America and the Caribbean, the Middle East, and North America.* München: Saur, 2009.

Adeyami, Nat M. "Library Operations Research—Purpose, Tools, Utility, and Implications for Developing Libraries." *Libri* 27 (March 1977): 22–30.

Adler, Patricia, and Peter Adler. "Observation Techniques." In *Handbook of Qualitative Research*, edited by Norman Denzin and Yvonna Lincoln, 377–92. Thousand Oaks, CA: Sage, 1994.

ALA World Encyclopedia of Library and Information Services. 2nd ed., edited by Robert Wedgeworth. London: Adamantine Press, 1986.

Alasuutari, Pertti, Leonard Bickman, and Julia Brannen, eds. *The Sage Handbook of Social Research Methods.* Los Angeles: Sage, 2008.

Allen, G. G. "Management and the Conduct of In-House Library Research." *Library & Information Science Research* 8, no. 1 (1986): 155–62.

Altman, Ellen, and Peter Hernon, eds. *Research Misconduct: Issues, Implications, and Strategies.* Greenwich, CT: Ablex Publishing, 1997.

American Library Association. "ALA Research Series." http://www.ala.org/ala/professionalresources/publications/alaresearchseries/alaresearchseries.cfm.

_____. "Dissemination of Research in LIS: A Statement by the American Library Association Committee on Research and Statistics." http://www.ala.org/ala/aboutala/offices/ors/orscommittees/dissemination/dissemination.cfm.

_____. *Policy Statement on the Role of Research in the American Library Association.* Chicago: American Library Association, 1970.

_____. "Research Agenda for Library Instruction and Information Literacy; the Updated Version." *College & Research Libraries News* (February 2003): 108–13. http://www.ala.org/ala/mgrps/divs/acrl/about/sections/is/projpubs/researchagendalibrary.cfm.

_____. *Who's Who in Library and Information Services*. Edited by Joel M. Lee, Robert J. Beran, and Sandra Whiteley. Chicago: ALA, 1982.

American Library Association Committee on Research and Statistics. "Dissemination of Research in LIS: A Statement by the American Library Association Committee on Research and Statistics." 2001. http://www.ala.org/ala/aboutala/offices/ors/orscommittees/dissemination/dissemination.cfm.

American Library Association and the American Society for Information Science & Technology. *Directory of Library and Information Professionals*. Woodbridge, CT: Research Publications, 1988-.

ASIS&T: The Information Society for the Information Age. "Mission & Vision." http://www.asis.org/missionvision.html.

Aminzade, Ron, and Barbara Laslett. "Reading and Evaluating Documents." In *The Practice of Social Research*, 12th ed., edited by Earl Babbie. Belmont, CA: Wadsworth/Cengage Learning, 2010.

Anderson, James A. *Communication Research: Issues and Methods*. New York: McGraw-Hill, 1987.

Andrews, Frank M., Laura Klem, Terrence N. Davidson, Patrick M. O'Malley, Kathleen B. Welch, and Willard L. Rodgers. *Selecting Statistical Techniques for Social Science Data: A Guide for SAS Users*. Cary, NC: SAS Institute Inc., 1998.

Angrosino, Michael. *Naturalistic Observation*. Walnut Creek, CA: Left Coast Press, 2007.

Argyris, Chris. "Creating Effective Relationships in Organizations." *Human Organization* 17, no. 1 (1958): 34–40.

Association of College and Research Libraries, Research Committee of the Women's Studies Section. "Research Agenda for Women's Studies Librarianship." 2007. http://wikis.ala.org/acrl/index.php/Research_Agenda_for_Women %27s_Studies_Section.

Association of Specialized and Cooperative Library Agencies. *The State Library Agencies*. Denver: The Association of State Libraries, 1973-.

_____. *The Report on Library Cooperation*. 7th ed. Denver: The Association of State Libraries, 1990.

Baban, Adriana. "Reconceptualization of the Division Between Quantitative and Qualitative Research Methods." *Cognition, Brain, Behavior: An Interdisciplinary Journal* 12 (2008): 337–43.

Babbie, Earl R. *The Practice of Social Research*. 2nd ed. Belmont, CA: Wadsworth, 1979.

_____. *Practice of Social Research*. 8th ed. Belmont, CA: Wadsworth, 1998.

_____. *The Practice of Social Research*. 12th ed. Belmont, CA: Wadsworth/Cengage Learning, 2010.

Bahr, Alice Harrison, Michael J. McLane, and Lynn W. Livingston. *InPrint: Publishing Opportunities for College Librarians*. Chicago: Association of College and Research Libraries, 1997.

Bailey, Carol A. *A Guide to Qualitative Field Research*. 2nd ed. Thousand Oaks, CA: Pine Forge Press, 2007.

Bakeman, Roger. "Behavioral Observation and Coding." In *Handbook of Research Methods in Social and Personality Psychology*, edited by Harry Reis T. and Charles M. Judd. Cambridge: Cambridge University Press, 2000.

Baker, Lynda M., ed. "Research Methods." *Library Trends* 55, no. 1 (Summer 2006).

_____. "Observation: A Complex Research Method." *Library Trends* 55, no. 1 (2006): 171–89.

Baker, Reg. "What They See is What You Get: Nuts and Bolts of Web Surveys." Workshop presented at the 10th General Online Research Conference, Hamburg, Germany, March 10, 2008.

Baker, Sharon L., and F. Wilfrid Lancaster. *The Measurement and Evaluation of Library Services.* 2nd ed. Arlington, VA: Information Resources Press, 1991.

Baldwin, James M. *The Mental Development in the Child and the Race.* New York: Macmillan, 1906.

_____. *Social and Ethical Interpretations in Mental Development.* New York: Macmillan, 1907.

Banks, Julie. "Are Transaction Logs Useful? A Ten-Year Study." *Journal of Southern Academic and Special Librarianship* 1, no. 3 (2000) http://southernlibrarianship .icaap.org/content/v01n03/banks_j01.html.

_____. "Can Transaction Logs Be Used for Resource Scheduling? An Analysis." *Reference Librarian* 63 (Special Report, 1999): 95–108.

Bao, Xue-Ming. "An Analysis of the Research Areas of the Articles Published in *C&RL* and *JAL* Between 1990 and 1999." *College & Research Libraries* 66 (2000): 536–44.

Bar-Ilan, Judit, and Bluma C. Peritz. "Informetric Theories and Methods for Exploring the Internet: An Analytical Survey of Recent Research Literature." *Library Trends* 50 (Winter 2002): 371–92.

Barnes, Annie S., ed., *Social Science Research: A Skills Handbook.* Bristol, IN: Wyndham Hall Press, 1985.

Bartlett, Richard A. "The State of the Library History Art." In *Approaches to Library History*, edited by John D. Marshall, 13–23. Tallahassee: Florida State University Library School, 1965.

Bates, Jessica. "Use of Narrative Interviewing in Everyday Information Behavior Research." *Library & Information Science Research* 26 (2004): 15–28.

Bates, Marcia J. "An Introduction to Metatheories, Theories, and Models." In *Theories of Information Behavior*, edited by Karen E. Fisher, Sandra Erdelez, and Lynne (E. F.) McKechnie, 1–24. Medford, NJ: Information Today, Inc., 2005.

Bauer, David G. "How To" Grants Manual: Successful Grantseeking Techniques for Obtaining Public and Private Grants. 4th ed. Phoenix, AZ: American Council on Education/Oryx Press, 1999.

Bauer, Kathleen. "Resources for Library Assessment." *College & Research Libraries News* 62, no. 1 (2001): 12–14.

Bawden, David. *User-Oriented Evaluation of Information Systems and Services.* Brookfield, VT: Gower, 1990.

Beal, Peter. *A Dictionary of English Manuscript Terminology, 1450–2000.* Oxford: Oxford University Press, 2008.

Beck, Susan E., and Kate Manuel. *Practical Research Methods for Librarians and Information Professionals.* New York: Neal-Schuman Publishers, 2008.

Becker, Bill. "Library Grant Money on the Web: A Resource Primer." *Searcher* 11, no. 10 (November/December, 2003): 8–14.

Bejune, Matthew M. "Wikis in Libraries." *Information Technology & Libraries* 26, no. 3 (Sept. 2007): 26–38.

Berger, Kenneth W., and Richard W. Hines. "What Does the User Really Want? The Library User Survey Project at Duke University." *Journal of Academic Librarianship* 20 (November 1994): 306–9.

Bertot, John Carlo. "Web-Based Surveys: Not Your Basic Survey Anymore." *Library Quarterly* 79, no.1 (2009): 119–24.

Bertot, John Carlo, Charles R. McClure, William E. Moen, and Jeffrey Rubin. "Web Usage Statistics: Measurement Issues and Analytical Techniques." *Government Information Quarterly* 14, no. 4 (1997): 373–95.

Bertot, John Carlo, Charles R. McClure, and Joe Ryan. *Statistics and Performance Measures for Public Library Networked Services.* Chicago: American Library Association, 2001.

Bethlehem, Jelke. *Applied Survey Methods: A Statistical Perspective.* Hoboken: Wiley, 2009.

The Big Book of Library Grant Money, 2007: Profiles of Private and Corporate Foundations and Direct Corporate Givers Receptive to Library Grant Proposals. Detroit: Taft Group; Chicago: American Library Association, 2007.

Bishoff, Liz. "Public Access to the Library of Congress Subject Headings." Paper presented at the Annual Conference of the American Library Association, San Francisco, CA, 1987.

Blalock, Hubert M. Jr. *Social Statistics.* Rev. 2nd ed. New York: McGraw-Hill, 1979.

Blixrud, Julia C. "The Association of Research Libraries Statistics and Measurement Program: From Descriptive Data to Performance Measures." *67th IFLA Council and General Conference: Conference Programme and Proceedings,* 2001. http://archive.ifla.org/IV/ifla67/papers/034-135e.pdf.

Bogdan, Robert C., and Sari Knopp Biklen. *Qualitative Research for Education: An Introduction to Theories and Methods.* 5th ed. Boston: Allyn and Bacon, 2007.

Bok, Derek. *Higher Learning.* Cambridge, MA: Harvard University Press, 1986.

Bookstein, Abraham. "How to Sample Badly." *Library Quarterly* 44 (April 1974): 124–32.

_____. "Questionnaire Research in a Library Setting." *Journal of Academic Librarianship* 11 (March 1985): 24–28.

_____. "Sampling from Card Files." *Library Quarterly* 53, no. 3 (1983): 307–12.

_____. "Sources of Error in Library Questionnaires." *Library Research* 4 (1982): 85–94.

Borbinha, José, ed. *Research and Advanced Technology for Digital Libraries*: 4th European Conference ECDL 2000 Proceedings. New York: Springer, 2000.

Bowers, Fredson. *Principles of Bibliographical Description.* New Castle, DE: Oak Knoll Books, 1994.

Bowker, Geoffrey C., and Susan Leigh Star. *Sorting Things Out: Classification and Its Consequences.* Cambridge, MA: MIT Press, 2000.

Boyce, Bert R., Charles T. Meadow, and Donald H. Kraft. *Measurement in Information Science.* San Diego: Academic Press, 1994.

Bradley, Jana. "Methodological Issues and Practices in Qualitative Research." *Library Quarterly* 63, no. 4 (1993): 431–49.

Braxton, John M., and Alan E. Bayer. "Perceptions of Research Misconduct and an Analysis of Their Correlates." *Journal of Higher Education* 65 (1994): 351–72.

Bryman, Alan, and Robert G. Burgess, eds. *Analyzing Qualitative Data.* London: Routledge, 1994.

Bryman, Alan, and Duncan Cramer. *Quantitative Data Analysis with SPSS 14, 15, and 16: A Guide for Social Scientists.* London: Routledge, 2009.

Buchanan, Elizabeth. "Ethics, Qualitative Research, and Ethnography in Virtual Space." *Journal of Information Ethics* 9, no. 2 (2000): 82–87.

Budd, John M. "An Epistemological Foundation for Library and Information Science." *Library Quarterly* 65, no. 3 (1995): 295–318.

_____. "Discourse Analysis and the Study of Communication in LIS." *Library Trends* 55, no. 1 (2006): 65–82.

_____. *Knowledge and Knowing in Library and Information Science: A Philosophical Framework.* Lanham, MD: Scarecrow Press, 2001.

_____. "Publication in Library and Information Science: The State of the Literature." *Library Journal* 113 (September 1988): 125–31.

_____. "What We Say about Research: Rhetoric and Argument in Library and Information Science." *Library Quarterly* 76 (2006): 220–40.

Budd, Richard, Robert K. Thorp, and Lewis Donohew. *Content Analysis of Communication.* New York: Macmillan, 1967.

Burgess, Robert G. *Field Research: A Sourcebook and Field Manual*. London: George Allen & Unwin, 1982.

_____. *In the Field: An Introduction to Field Research*. Contemporary Social Research Series 8. London: George Allen & Unwin, 1984.

Burke, Mary, Min-min Chang, Charles Davis, Peter Hernon, Paul Nicholls, Candy Schwartz, Debora Shaw, Alastair Smith, and Stephen Wiberley. "Editorial: Fraud and Misconduct in Library and Information Science Research." *Library & Information Science Research* 18 (1996): 199–203.

Burkell, Jacquelyn. "The Dilemma of Survey Non-response." *Library & Information Science Research* 25 (Autumn 2003): 239–63.

Busha, Charles H. "Library Science Research: The Path to Progress." In *A Library Science Research Reader and Bibliographic Guide*. Littleton, CO: Libraries Unlimited, 1981.

Busha, Charles H., and Stephen P. Harter. *Research Methods in Librarianship: Techniques and Interpretations*. New York: Academic Press, 1980.

Buttlar, Lois. "Information Sources in Library and Information Science Doctoral Research." *Library & Information Science Research* 21 (1999): 227–45.

Byström, Katriina. "Task Complexity, Information Types and Information Sources: Examination of Relationships." Ph.D. diss., University of Tampere, 1999.

Byström, Katriina, and Kalervo Järvelin. "Task Complexity Affects Information Seeking and Use." *Information Processing & Management* 31, no. 2 (1995): 191–213.

Bywaters, Paul, and Gayle Letherby. "Extending Social Research." In *Extending Social Research: Application, Implementation and Publication*, 3–18. Berkshire, England: Open University Press, 2007.

Caidi, Nadia, and Susan MacDonald. "Information Practices of Canadian Muslims Post 9/11." *Government Information Quarterly* 25 (2008): 348–78.

Camic, Charles. "Reputation and Predecessor Selection: Parsons and the Institutionalists." *American Sociological Review* 57 (1992): 421–45.

Campbell, Donald T. "Evolutionary Epistemology." In *The Philosophy of Popper*, edited by P. A. Schilpp. LaSalle, IL: Open Court, 1974.

Campbell, Donald T., and Julian C. Stanley. *Experimental and Quasi-Experimental Designs for Research*. Chicago: Rand McNally, 1963.

Capre, Pete. "Social Media: Short-Term Craze or Long-Term Phenomenon?" *SSI Survey Sampling International*. http://www.surveysampling.com/en/ssicompass/december-2008/social-media-short-term-craze-or-long-term-phenomenon.

Carlin, Andrew P. "Disciplinary Debates and Bases of Interdisciplinary Studies: The Place of Research Ethics in Library and Information Science." *Library & Information Science Research* 25, no. 1 (Spring 2003): 3–18.

Case, Donald O. *Looking for Information: A Survey of Research on Information Seeking, Needs, and Behavior*. 2nd ed. Amsterdam: Elsevier/Academic Press, 2007.

Centers for Disease Control and Prevention. "AnSWR: Analysis Software for Word-based Records." http://www.cdc.gov/hiv/topics/surveillance/resources/software/answr/index.htm.

_____. "CDC EZ-Text." http://www.cdc.gov/hiv/topics/surveillance/resources/software/ez-text/index.htm.

Charmaz, Kathy. "Reconstructing Grounded Theory." In *The Sage Handbook of Social Research Methods*, edited by Pertti Alasuutari, Leonard Bickman, and Julia Brannen, 471–73. Los Angeles: Sage, 2008.

Chatman, Elfreda. *The Information World of Retired Women*. Westport, CT: Greenwood Press, 1992.

Cherry, Joan M. "Improving Subject Access in OPACs: An Exploratory Study of Conversion of Users' Queries." *Journal of Academic Librarianship* 18 (1992): 95–99.

Chen, Ching-Chih, ed. *Quantitative Measurement and Dynamic Library Service.* Phoenix, AZ: Oryx Press, 1978.

Childers, Thomas A., and Nancy A. Van House. *What's Good? Describing Your Public Library's Effectiveness.* Chicago: American Library Association, 1993.

Chow, Siu L. "Meta-Analysis of Pragmatic and Theoretical Research: A Critique." *Journal of Psychology* 121 (May 1987): 259–71.

Ciliberti, Anne C., Marie L. Radford, and Gary P. Radford. "Empty Handed? A Material Availability Study and Transaction Log Analysis Verification." *Journal of Academic Librarianship* 24 (July 1998): 282–99.

Clark, Herbert, and Michael Schober. "Asking Questions and Influencing Answers." In *Questions about Questions: Inquiries into the Cognitive Bases of Surveys,* edited by Judith M. Tanur, 15–48. New York: Russell Sage Foundation, 1992.

Clarke, Adele. "Situational Analysis: Grounded Theory Mapping After the Postmodern Turn." *Symbolic Interaction* 26 (2003): 553–76.

Coffey, Amanda, and Paul Atkinson. *Making Sense of Qualitative Data: Complementary Research Strategies.* Thousand Oaks, CA: Sage Publications, 1996.

Cohen, Jacob. *Statistical Power Analysis for the Behavioral Sciences.* 2nd ed. Hillsdale, NJ: Lawrence Erlbaum Associates, 1988.

Collings, Dorothy G. "Comparative Librarianship." In *Encyclopedia of Library and Information Science,* vol. 5, 492. New York: Marcel Dekker, 1971.

Colorado State Library Library Research Service, and the University of Denver, Library and Information Science Program. "Library Research Service: Research and Statistics about Libraries." http://www.lrs.org/.

Concise Dictionary of Library and Information Science. 2nd ed., edited by Stella Keenan, and Colin Johnston. London: Bowker-Saur, 2002.

Connaway, Lynn Silipigni. "Capturing Untapped Descriptive Data: Creating Value for Librarians and Users." Paper presented at the ASIS&T 2006 Annual Conference, Austin, TX, November 8, 2006. http://www.oclc.org/research/presentations/connaway/20061108-asist-untappeddata.ppt.

———. "Focus Group Interviews: A Data Collection Methodology for Decision Making." *Library Administration & Management* 10 (Fall 1996): 231–39.

———. "The Levels of Decisions and Involvement in Decision-Making: Effectiveness and Job Satisfaction in Academic Library Technical Services." Ph.D. diss., University of Wisconsin-Madison, 1992.

———. "Making Data Work Harder." *OCLC Newsletter* (April/May/June 2005): 268. http://www.oclc.org/news/publications/newsletters/oclc/2005/268/downloads/research.pdf.

———. "A Research Funding Opportunity for Library and Information Science Faculty: The OCLC/ALISE Library and Information Science Research Grant Program." *Journal of Education for Library and Information Science* 46, no. 3 (2005): 258–65.

Connaway, Lynn Silipigni, John M. Budd, and Thomas R. Kochtanek. "An Investigation of the Use of an Online Catalog: User Characteristics and Transaction Log Analysis." *Library Resources and Technical Services* 39, no. 2 (April 1995): 142–52.

Connaway, Lynn Silipigni, and Timothy J. Dickey. "Beyond Data Mining: Delivering the Next Generation of Service from Library Data." Paper presented at the ASIS&T 2008 Annual Meeting, Columbus, OH, October 28, 2008. http://www.oclc.org/research/presentations/connaway/asist2008.ppt.

———. "Beyond Data Mining: Delivering the Next Generation of Service from Library Data." In ASIS&T 2008: Proceedings of the 71st Annual Meeting, Vol. 45, 2008: People Transforming Information—Information Transforming People, edited by Andrew Grove and Abebe Rorissa. Silver Springs, MD: American Society for Information Science and Technology, 2008.

_____. "Data Mining, Advanced Collection Analysis, and Publisher Profiles: An Update on the OCLC Publisher Name Authority File." Paper presented at the XXVIII Annual Charleston Conference, Charleston, SC, November 7, 2008. http://www.oclc.org/research/presentations/connaway/charleston2008.ppt.

Connaway, Lynn Silipigni, Brian Lavoie, and Lorcan Dempsey. "Anatomy of Aggregate Collections: The Example of Google Print for Libraries." *D-Lib Magazine* 11, no. 9 (2005). http://www.dlib.org/dlib/september05/lavoie/09lavoie.html.

Connaway, Lynn Silipigni, Brian Lavoie, and Edward T. O'Neill. "Mining for Digital Resources: Identification and Characterizing Digital Materials in WorldCat." In *Currents and Convergence: Navigating the Rivers of Change: Proceedings of the Twelfth National Conference of the Association of College and Research Libraries, April 7–10, 2005, Minneapolis, Minnesota*, edited by Hugh A. Thompson. Chicago: Association of College and Research Libraries, 2005.

Connaway, Lynn Silipigni, and Larry Olszewski. "A Geographical Representation of WorldCat Resources: A Decision Making Tool for Acquisitions and Collection Management." Paper presented at the XXVI Annual Charleston Conference, Charleston, SC, November 10, 2006. http://www.oclc.org/research/presentations/connaway/20061110-charleston-worldmap.pdf.

_____. "OCLC WorldMap: Visualizing Information about Collections and Libraries Worldwide." Paper presented at the OCLC Inclusion Council, Dublin, OH, January 31, 2008. http://www.oclc.org/research/presentations/connaway/worldmapfinal2008-01-31.ppt.

_____. "Visualizing the Globalization of WorldCat." *NextSpace* 9 (2008), http://www.oclc.org/nextspace/009/research.htm.

Connaway, Lynn Silipigni, Edward T. O'Neill, and Eudora Loh. *Changing Global Book Collection Patterns in ARL Libraries*. Washington, DC: Association of Research Libraries, 2006. http://www.crl.edu/sites/default/files/attachments/pages/grn_global_book.pdf.

Connaway, Lynn Silipigni, Clifton Snyder, and Lawrence Olszewski. "Geographical Representation of Library Collections in WorldCat: A Prototype." In *Sparking Synergies: Bringing Research and Practice Together at ASIS&T '05, October 28-November 2, Charlotte, NC*, edited by Andrew Grove. Medford, NJ: Information Today, 2005.

_____. "What in the World: Leveraging Corporate Assets for Internal and External Use." Paper presented at the SLA Annual Conference, Toronto, Canada, June 5–8, 2005. http://www.sla.org/Documents/conf/toronto/Olszewski.doc.

Connell, Tschera Harkness. "Writing the Research Paper: A Review." *College & Research Libraries* 71, no. 1 (January 2010): 6–7.

Converse, W. R. "Research: What We Need, and What We Get." *Canadian Library Journal* 41 (October 1984): 235–41.

Cooley, Charles H. *Human Nature and the Social Order*. New York: Schocken, 1964.

Corbin, Juliet, and Anselm Strauss. *Basics of Qualitative Research*. 3rd ed. Los Angeles: Sage, 2008.

Couch, Carl J. *Information Technologies and Social Orders*. New York: Aldine de Gruyter, 1996.

Council on Library and Information Resources. "Program and Research Agenda, 2007–2010." http://www.clir.org/activities/agenda.htm.

Couper, Mick P., and Sue Ellen Hansen. "Computer-Assisted Interviewing." In *Handbook of Interview Research: Context & Method*, edited by Jaber F. Gubrium and James A. Holstein, 557–75. Thousand Oaks, CA: Sage, 2002.

Covey, Denise Troll. *Usage and Usability Assessment: Library Practices and Concerns*. Washington, DC: Digital Library Federation and Council on Library and Information Resources, 2002.

Cox, Allan B., and Fred Gifford. "An Overview to Geographic Information Systems." *Journal of Academic Librarianship* 23, no. 6 (1997): 449–61.

Crawford, Gregory A. "The Research Literature of Academic Librarianship: A Comparison of *College & Research Libraries* and *Journal of Academic Librarianship*." *College & Research Libraries* 60 (May 1999): 224–30.

Creswell, John W. *Research Design: Qualitative and Quantitative and Mixed Methods Approaches*. 3rd ed. Thousand Oaks, CA: Sage, 2009.

_____. *Qualitative Inquiry & Research Design: Choosing Among Five Approaches*. Thousand Oaks, CA: Sage, 2007.

Cullen, Rowena, and Alistair Gray. "A Method for Taking a Reliable Statistical Sample of Reference Inquiries in a New Zealand Public Library System." *Journal of Library Administration* 22, no. 1 (1995): 113–123.

Dalbello, Marija. "A Phenomenological Study of an Emergent National Digital Library, Part I: Theory and Methodological Framework." *Library Quarterly* 75 (2005): 391–420.

Dalrymple, Prudence W. "A Quarter Century of User-Centered Study: The Impact of Zweizig and Dervin on LIS Research." *Library & Information Science Research* 23 (2001): 155–65.

Danton, J. Periam. *The Dimensions of Comparative Librarianship*. Chicago: American Library Association, 1973.

Davis, Charles H. "Information Science and Libraries: A Note on the Contribution of Information Science to Librarianship." *The Bookmark* 51 (1982): 84–96.

Davis, Charles H., and Thomas E. Nisonger. "The Perception of Library and Information Science Journals by LIS Education Deans and ARL Library Directors: A Replication of the Kohl-Davis Study." *College & Research Libraries* 66, no. 4 (July 2005): 341–77.

Davis, Charles H., and James E. Rush. *Guide to Information Science*. Westport, CT: Greenwood Press, 1980.

Davis, Donald G., Jr. "Ebla to the Electronic Dream: The Role of Historical Perspectives in Professional Education." *Journal of Education for Library and Information Science* 39, no. 3 (Summer 1998): 229–35.

Davis, Donald G., Jr., and John M. Jucker. *American Library History: A Comprehensive Guide to the Literature*. Santa Barbara, CA: ABC-Clio, 1989.

De Bellis, Nicola. *Bibliometrics and Citation Analysis: From the Science Citation Index to Cybermetrics*. Lanham, MD: Scarecrow, 2009.

Dean, Kathryn, Jonathan Joseph, John Michael Roberts, and Colin Wight. *Realism, Philosophy and Social Science*. New York: Palgrave MacMillan, 2006.

deMarrais, Kathleen, and Stephen D. Lapan. *Foundations for Research: Methods of Inquiry in Education and the Social Sciences*. Mahwah, NJ: Erlbaum, 2004.

Denzin, Norman. *The Research Act: A Theoretical Introduction to Sociological Methods*. 3rd ed. NJ: Prentice Hall, 1989.

Denzin, Norman, and Michael Giardina. "Introduction: Qualitative Inquiry and the Conservative Challenge." In *Qualitative Inquiry and the Conservative Challenge*, edited by Norman Denzin and Michael Giardina. Walnut Creek, CA: Left Coast Press, 2006.

Denzin, Norman K., and Yvonna S. Lincoln, eds. *The Landscape of Qualitative Research*. 3rd ed. Thousand Oaks, CA: Sage, 2008.

_____. *The SAGE Handbook of Qualitative Research*. 3rd ed. Thousand Oaks, CA: Sage, 2005.

_____. *Strategies of Qualitative Inquiry*. 3rd ed. Thousand Oaks, CA: Sage, 2008.

DeProspo, Ernest R., Ellen Altman, and Kenneth Beasley. *Performance Measures for Public Libraries*. Chicago: Public Library Association, 1973.

Dervin, Brenda, Lois Foreman-Wernet, and Eric Lauterbach, eds. *Sense-Making Methodology Reader: Selected Writings of Brenda Dervin*. New York: Hampton Press, 2003.

Dewdney, Patricia. "Recording the Reference Interview: A Field Experiment." In *Qualitative Research in Information Management*, edited by Jack D. Glazier and Ronald R. Powell, 122–50. Englewood, CO: Libraries Unlimited, 1992.

Dewdney, Patricia, and Roma Harris. "Community Information Needs: The Case of Wife Assault." *Library & Information Science Research* 14 (1992): 5–29.

Dewey, Barbara A. "In Search of Practical Applications: A Public Services Research Agenda for University Libraries." *Journal of Academic Librarianship* (September 1997): 371–79.

Dickson, Jean. "An Analysis of User Errors in Searching an Online Catalog." *Cataloging & Classification Quarterly* 4, no. 3 (1984): 19–38.

Dictionary of American Library Biography. Edited by Bohdan S. Wynar. Littleton, CO: Libraries Unlimited, 1977. Second supplement, edited by Donald G. Davis, Jr., 2003.

Dictionary for Library and Information Science. Edited by Joan M. Reitz. Westport, CT: Libraries Unlimited, 2004.

Dictionary of Information and Library Management. 2nd ed., edited by Janet Stephenson. New York: A. & C. Black, 2006.

Dictionary of Information Science and Technology. Edited by Carolyn Watters. New York: Academic Press, 1992.

Diesing, Paul. *Patterns of Discovery in the Social Sciences*. London: Routledge & Kegan Paul, 1972.

Dilevko, Juris. "Inferential Statistics and Librarianship." *Library & Information Science Research* 29, no. 2 (2007): 209–29.

Dillon, Andrew. "LIS as a Research Domain: Problems and Prospects." *Information Research* 12, no. 4 supplement (2007). http://informationr.net/ir/12-4/colis/colis03.html.

Dimitroff, Alexandra. "Research Knowledge and Activities of Special Librarians: Results of a Survey." *Special Libraries* 87 (Winter 1996): 1–9.

Diodato, Virgil. *Dictionary of Bibliometrics*. New York: Haworth Press, 1994.

Directory of Special Libraries and Information Centers. 3 vols. Detroit, MI: Gale/Cengage 1963–.

Doucet, Andrea, and Natasha Mauthner. "Qualitative Interviewing and Feminist Research." In *The Sage Handbook of Social Research Methods*, edited by Pertti Alasuutari, Leonard Bickman, and Julia Brannen, 331–36. Los Angeles: Sage, 2008.

Dougherty, Richard M., and Fred J. Heinritz. *Scientific Management of Library Operations*. 2nd ed. Metuchen, NJ: Scarecrow Press, 1982.

Drabenstott, Karen Markey. "Focused Group Interviews." In *Qualitative Research in Information Management*, edited by Jack D. Glazier and Ronald R. Powell, 85–104. Englewood, CO: Libraries Unlimited, 1992.

Draper, Lani, and Marthea Turnage. "Blogmania: Blog Use in Academic Libraries." *Internet Reference Services Quarterly* 31, no. 1 (2008): 15–55.

Duff, Wendy M., and Joan M. Cherry. "Use of Historical Documents in a Digital World: Comparisons with Original Materials and Microfiche." *Information Research* (October 2000). http://informationr.net/ir/6-1/paper86.html.

Dugan, Robert E., and Peter Hernon. "Outcomes Assessment: Not Synonymous with Inputs and Outputs." *Journal of Academic Librarianship* 38 (November 2002): 376–80.

Dyer, Esther R. "The Delphi Technique in Library Research." *Library Research* 1 (Spring 1979): 41–52.

Eaton, Thelma. "Bibliographical Research." *Library Trends* 13 (July 1964): 42–53.

Eisenberg, Michael B. "The State of Research Today." *School Library Media Quarterly* 21 (Summer 1993): 241.

Eldredge, Jonathan D. "Evidence-Based Librarianship: The EBL Process." *Library Hi Tech* 24, no. 3 (2006): 341–54.

Eldredge, Jonathan D., Martha R. Harris, and Marie T. Ascher. "Defining the Medical Library Association Research Agenda: Methodology and Final Results from a Consensus Process." *Journal of the Medical Library Association* 97, no. 3 (July 2009): 178–185.

Elliott, Jane. *Using Narrative in Social Research: Qualitative and Quantitative Approaches.* London: Sage, 2005.

Ely, Margot, Margaret Anzul, Teri Friedman, Diane Garner, and Ann MacCormack Steinmetz. *Doing Qualitative Research: Circles within Circles.* London: Falmer Press, 1991.

Encyclopedia of Information Science and Technology. Edited by Mehdi Khosrow-Pour, vol. 1–5. Hershey, PA: Idea Group Reference, 2005.

Encyclopedia of Librarianship. 3rd ed., edited by Thomas Landau. New York: Hafner, 1966.

Encyclopedia of Library and Information Science. 3rd ed., edited by Marcia Bates, vol. 1–4. New York: CRC Press, 2010.

Encyclopedia of Library and Information Science. Vol. 1–73. New York: Marcel Dekker, 1968–2003.

Engle, Michael. "Creativity and the Research Process in Academic Libraries." *College & Research Libraries News* 48 (November 1987): 629–31.

Erdos, Paul L. *Professional Mail Surveys.* Rev. ed. Malabar, FL: Robert E. Krieger Publishing, 1983.

Falkenstein, Jeffrey A. *National Guide to Funding for Libraries and Information Services.* 8th ed., New York: Foundation Center, 2005.

Feehan, Patricia E., Gregg W. Lee, and Michael W. Havener. "Library and Information Science Research: An Analysis of the 1984 Journal Literature." *Library & Information Science Research* 9 (July 1987): 173–85.

Fennewald, Joseph. "Research Productivity Among Librarians: Factors Leading to Publications at Penn State." *College & Research Libraries* 69 (2008): 104–14.

Fennick, John H. *Studies Show: A Popular Guide to Understanding Scientific Studies.* Amherst, NY: Prometheus, 1997.

Ferrante, Barbara Kopelock. "Bibliometrics: Access in Library Literature." *Collection Management* 2 (Fall 1987): 199–204.

Fidel, Raya. "Are We There Yet?: Mixed Methods Research in Library and Information Science." *Library & Information Science Research* 30, no. 4 (2008): 265–72.

_____. "The Case Study Method: A Case Study." *Library & Information Science Research* 6 (July 1984): 273–88.

_____. "Qualitative Methods in Information Retrieval Research." *Library & Information Science Research* 15 (1993): 219–47.

Fink, Arlene. *How to Conduct Surveys: A Step-by-Step Guide.* 3rd ed. Thousand Oaks, CA: Sage, 2006.

Firebaugh, Glenn. *Seven Rules for Social Research.* New Jersey: Princeton University Press, 2008.

Fisher, Celia, and Andrea Anushko. "Research Ethics in Social Science." In *The Sage Handbook of Social Research Methods*, edited by Pertti Alasuutari, Leonard Bickman, and Julia Brannen, 95–109. Los Angeles: Sage, 2008.

Fisher, William. "When Write is Wrong: Is All Our Professional Literature on the Same Page?" *Library Collections, Acquisitions, & Technical Services* 23 (Spring 1999): 61–72.

Fitzpatrick, Elizabeth B., Anne C. Moore, and Beth W. Lang. "Reference Librarians at the Reference Desk in a Learning Commons: A Mixed Methods Evaluation." *The Journal of Academic Librarianship* 34, no. 3 (2008): 231–38.

Flanagan, John C. "The Critical Incident Technique." *Psychological Bulletin* 5 (1954): 327–58.

Flick, Uwe. "Triangulation in Qualitative Research." In *A Companion to Qualitative Research*, edited by Uwe Flick, Ernst von Kardoff, and Ines Steinke, trans. Bryan Jenner. London: Sage, 2004.

The Florida State University College of Information. "About GeoLib." http://www.geolib.org/about.cfm.

Fontana, Andrea, and James Frey. "Interviewing: The Art of Science." In *Handbook of Qualitative Research*, edited by Norman Denzin and Yvonna Lincoln. Thousand Oaks, CA: Sage, 1994.

Fowler, Floyd J. Jr. *Survey Research Methods*. 2nd ed. Newbury Park, CA: Sage, 1993.

Frankfort-Nachmias, Chava, and David Nachmias. *Research Methods in the Social Sciences*. 7th ed. New York: Worth Publishers, 2008.

Franzozi, Roberto, ed. *Content Analysis*. Thousand Oaks, CA: Sage, 2008.

Freud, Sigmund. *The Future of an Illusion*. Garden City, NY: Doubleday Anchor, 1961.

Frey, James H. *Survey Research by Telephone*. Beverly Hills, CA: Sage, 1983.

Froehlich, Thomas J. "Ethical Considerations of Information Professionals." In *Annual Review of Information Science and Technology*, vol. 27, edited by Martha E. Williams. Medford, NJ: Learned Information Inc., 1992.

Fussler, Herman H., and Julian L. Simon. *Patterns in the Use of Books in Large Research Libraries*. Chicago: University of Chicago Press, 1969.

Garrison, Guy. "A Look at Research on Public Library Problems in the 1970's." *Public Libraries* 19 (Spring 1980): 4–8.

Gass, Saul I., and Carl M. Harris, eds. *Encyclopedia of Operations Research*. Boston: Kluwer, 1996.

Gatten, Jeffery N. "Paradigm Restrictions on Interdisciplinary Research into Librarianship." *College & Research Libraries* 52 (November 1991): 575–84.

Gay, L. R. *Educational Research: Competencies for Analysis and Application*. 2nd ed. Columbus, OH: Charles E. Merrill, 1981.

Gay, L. R., Geoffrey E. Mills, and Peter Airasian. *Educational Research: Competencies for Analysis and Applications*. 8th ed. Upper Saddle River, NJ: Pearson Merrill Prentice Hall, 2006.

Geertz, Clifford. *The Interpretation of Cultures: Selected Essays*. New York: Basic Books, 1973.

Geraeds, Gert-Jan, and Judith Kamalski. "Bibliometrics Come of Age." *Research Trends*, 15 (Jan. 2010). http://www.info.scopus.com/researchtrends/archive/RT15/re_tre_15.html.

Gerding, Stephanie. "Library Grants." http://www.librarygrants.blogspot.com.

_____. "Tips and Resources for Finding Grants." *Online* 32, no. 6 (Nov. 2008): 16–21.

Gerding, Stephanie, and Pamela H. MacKellar. *Grants for Libraries: A How-to-do-it Manual*. New York: Neal-Schuman, 2006.

Gerhan, David. "Statistical Significance: How It Signifies in Statistics Reference." *Reference & User Services Quarterly* 40, no. 4 (2001): 361–74.

Giddens, Anthony. *The Constitution of Society: Outline of the Theory of Structuration*. Cambridge, England: Polity, 1984.

Giesecke, Joan. "Preparing Research for Publication." *Library Administration and Management* 12, no. 3 (Summer 1998): 134–37.

Gilbert, Linda. "Going the Distance: 'Closeness' in Qualitative Data Analysis Software." *International Journal of Social Research Methodology* 5, no. 3 (2002): 215–28.

Gilligan, Carol, Renée Spencer, M. Katherine Weinberg, and Tatiana Bertsch. "On the Listening Guide: A Voice-Centered Relational Method." In *Emergent Methods in Social Research*, edited by Sharlene Nagy Hesse-Biber and Patricia Leavy, 253–71. Thousand Oaks, CA: Sage, 2006.

Girden, Ellen R. *Evaluating Research Articles from Start to Finish.* 2nd ed. Thousand Oaks, CA: Sage, 2001.

Glaser, Barney. "The Constant Comparison Method of Qualitative Analysis." *Social Problems* 12 (Spring 1965): 437–39.

Glaser, Barney G., and Anselm L. Strauss. *The Discovery of Grounded Theory: Strategies for Qualitative Research.* New York: Aldine de Gruyter, 1967.

Glass, Gene V., Barry McGaw, and Mary L. Smith. *Meta-Analysis in Social Research.* Beverly Hills, CA: Sage, 1981.

Glazier, Jack D., and Robert Grover. "A Multidisciplinary Framework for Theory Building." *Library Trends* 50 (Winter 2002): 317–29.

Glazier, Jack D., and Peter M. Hall. "Constructing Isomorphism in an Interorganizational Network." *Humboldt Journal of Social Relations* 22 (1996): 47–62.

Glazier, Jack D., and Ronald R. Powell, eds. *Qualitative Research in Information Management.* Englewood, CO: Libraries Unlimited, 1992.

Goetz, Thomas. "Freeing the Dark Data of Failed Scientific Experiments." *Wired* 15, no. 10 (2007). http://www.wired.com/science/discoveries/magazine/15-10/st_essay.

Gold, Raymond. "Roles in Sociological Field Observation." In *Issues in Participant Observation*, edited by George McCall and J. L. Simmons, 30–39. Reading, MA: Addison-Wesley, 1969.

Golden, Gary. *Survey Research Methods.* Chicago: ACRL, 1982.

Goldhor, Herbert. *An Introduction to Scientific Research in Librarianship.* Urbana: University of Illinois, Graduate School of Library Science, 1972.

Goldman, Alfred E., and Susan S. McDonald. *The Group Depth Interview.* Englewood Cliffs, NJ: Prentice Hall, 1987.

Goodall, Deborah. "It Ain't What You Do, It's the Way That You Do It: A Review of Public Library Research with Special Reference to Methodology." *Public Library Journal* 11 (1996): 69–76.

Gorden, Raymond. "Dimensions of the Depth Interview." In *Reader in Research Methods for Librarianship*, edited by Mary Lee Bundy, Paul Wasserman, and Gayle Araghi, 166–171. Washington, DC: NCR, 1970.

Gordon, Rachel Singer. "Getting Started in Library Publication." *American Libraries* 35, no. 1 (January 2004): 66–69.

Gorman, G. E., and Peter Clayton. *Qualitative Research for the Information Professional: A Practical Handbook.* With contributions by Sydney J. Shep and Adela Clayton. 2nd ed. London: Facet Publishing, 2005.

Gould, Stephen J. *Full House: The Spread of Excellence from Plato to Darwin.* New York: Harmony Books, 1996.

Grazier, Margaret H. "Critically Reading and Applying Research in School Library Media Centers." *School Library Media Quarterly* 10 (Winter 1982): 135–46.

Grbich, Carol. *Qualitative Data Analysis: An Introduction.* London: Sage, 2007.

Grotzinger, Laurel. "Methodology of Library Science Inquiry–Past and Present." In *A Library Science Research Reader and Bibliographic Guide*, edited by Charles H. Busha, 38–50. Littleton, CO: Libraries Unlimited, 1981.

Grover, Robert J., and Jack D. Glazier. "A Conceptual Framework for Theory Building in Library and Information Science." *Library & Information Science Research* 8 (1986): 227–42.

_____. "Implications for Application of Qualitative Methods to Library and Information Science Research." *Library & Information Science Research* 7 (July 1985): 247–60.

Grover, Robert, and Martha L. Hale. "The Role of the Librarian in Faculty Research." *College & Research Libraries* 49 (January 1988): 9–15.

Gunn, Holly. "Web-Based Surveys: Changing the Survey Process." *First Monday* 7 (December 2002), http://firstmonday.org/issues/issue7_12/gunn/index.html.

Habermas, Jurgen. *The Theory of Communicative Action.* Vol. 1, Reason and the Rationalization of Society. Boston: Beacon, 1984.

Hafner, Arthur Wayne. *Descriptive Statistical Techniques for Librarians.* 2nd ed. Chicago: American Library Association, 1998.

Hagler, Ronald. "Needed Research in Library History." In *Research Methods in Librarianship: Historical and Bibliographical Methods in Library Research,* edited by Rolland E. Stevens, 128–37. Urbana: University of Illinois, Graduate School of Library Science, 1971.

Hammersley, Martyn. *Questioning Qualitative Inquiry: Critical Essays.* Los Angeles: Sage, 2008.

Harmon, Robert B. *Elements of Bibliography: A Guide to Information Sources and Practical Applications.* 3rd ed. Lanham, MD: Scarecrow Press, 1998.

Harris, Michael H., ed. *Reader in American Library History.* Washington, DC: NCR Microcard Editions, 1971.

Harrod's Librarian's Glossary and Reference Book. 10th ed., edited and compiled by Ray Prytherch. London: Ashgate, 2005.

Hart, Chris. *Doing a Literature Review: Releasing the Social Science Research Imagination.* London: Sage, 2009.

Hauptman, Robert. *Ethics and Librarianship.* Jefferson, NC: McFarland, 2002.

_____, ed. *Journal of Information Ethics* 5, no. 1 (Spring 1996).

Hayes, Robert M. *Use of the Delphi Technique in Policy Formulation: A Case Study of the "Public Sector/Private Sector" Task Force.* Los Angeles: University of California, Graduate School of Library and Information Science, 1982.

Hernon, Peter. "Determination of Sample Size and Selection of the Sample: Concepts, General Sources, and Software." *College & Research Libraries* 55 (March 1994): 171–79.

_____. "Editorial: Components of the Research Process: Where Do We Need to Focus Attention?" *The Journal of Academic Librarianship* 27 (March 2001): 81–89.

_____. "Editorial: Publishing Research." *The Journal of Academic Librarianship* 22 (January 1996): 1–2.

_____. "Editorial: Research in Library and Information Science–Reflections on the Journal Literature." *The Journal of Academic Librarianship* 25 (July 1999): 263–66.

_____. "Library and Information Science Research: Not an Island unto Itself." *Library & Information Science Research* 14 (January-March 1992): 1–3.

_____. "LIS Extends to the Research Frontier." *College & Research Libraries* 53 (January 1992): 3–5.

_____. *Statistics: A Component of the Research Process.* Rev. ed. Norwood, NJ: Ablex Publishing, 1994.

Hernon, Peter, and Ellen Altman. *Assessing Service Quality: Satisfying the Expectations of Library Customers.* Chicago: American Library Association, 1998.

_____. *Service Quality in Academic Libraries.* Norwood, NJ: Ablex Publishing, 1996.

Hernon, Peter, and Robert E. Dugan. *An Action Plan for Outcomes Assessment in Your Library.* Chicago: American Library Association, 2002.

Hernon, Peter, Hae-young Rieh Hwang, Barbara D. Farah, Andrew J. Golub, Pat K. Bryant, Li-Ling Kuo, and Maya De, edited by Charles McClure. *Statistics for Library Decision Making: A Handbook.* Norwood, NJ: Ablex Publishing, 1989.

Hernon, Peter, and Charles McClure. *Evaluation and Library Decision Making.* Norwood, NJ: Ablex Publishing, 1990.

Hernon, Peter, and Cheryl Metoyer-Duran. "Problem Statements: An Exploratory Study of their Function, Significance, and Form." *Library & Information Science Research* 15 (Winter 1993): 71–92.

Hernon, Peter, and Candy Schwartz. "Can Research Be Assimilated into the Soul of Library and Information Science?" *Library & Information Science Research* 17, no. 2 (Spring 1995): 101–3.

_____. "Editorial: A Need for a Greater Commitment in the Profession to Research and Evaluation." *Library & Information Science Research* 29, no. 2 (2007): 161–62.

_____. "Editorial: Research by Default." *Library & Information Science Research* 31, no. 3 (2009): 137.

_____. "Editorial: We Will Not Rest on Our Laurels!" *Library & Information Science Research* 25, no. 2 (2003): 125–26.

_____. "Editorial: What is a Problem Statement?" *Library & Information Science Research* 29, no. 3 (2007): 307–9.

_____. "Leadership: Developing a Research Agenda for Academic Libraries." *Library & Information Science Research* 30, no. 4 (2008): 243–49.

_____. "Library and Information Science Research: Is It Misunderstood?" *Library & Information Science Research* 15 (Summer 1993): 215–17.

_____. "Reliability and Validity." *Library & Information Science Research* 31, no. 2 (2009): 73–74.

Hernon, Peter, and John R. Whitman. *Delivering Satisfaction and Service Quality: A Customer-Based Approach for Librarians.* Chicago: American Library Association, 2001.

Hesse-Biber, Sharlene Nagy. "Unleashing Frankenstein's Monster? The Use of Computers in Qualitative Research." In *Approaches to Qualitative Research: A Reader on Theory and Practice,* edited by Sharlene Nagy Hesse-Biber and Patricia Leavy. New York: Oxford University Press, 2004.

Hesse-Biber, Sharlene Nagy, and Patricia Leavy. *Emergent Methods in Social Research.* Thousand Oaks, CA: Sage, 2006.

Hider, Philip, and Bob Pymm. "Empirical Research Methods Reported in High-Profile LIS Journal Literature." *Library & Information Science Research* 30, no. 2 (2008): 108–14.

Hildreth, Charles R., and Selenay Aytac. "Recent Library Practitioner Research: A Methodological Analysis and Critique." *Journal of Education for Library and Information Science* 48, no. 3 (2007): 236–58.

Hillway, Tyrus. *Introduction to Research.* 2nd ed. Boston: Houghton Mifflin, 1964.

Hisle, W. Lee. "Top Issues Facing Academic Libraries: A Report of the Focus on the Future Task Force." *College & Research Libraries News* 63 (November 2002): 714, 715, 730.

Hittleman, Daniel R., and Alan J. Simon. *Interpreting Educational Research: An Introduction for Consumers of Research.* 4th ed. Upper Saddle River, NJ: Prentice Hall, 2006.

Hoadley, Irene Braden, and Alice S. Clark, eds. *Quantitative Methods in Librarianship: Standards, Research, Management.* Westport, CT: Greenwood Press, 1972.

Hogan, Sharon A., and Mary W. George. "Cropping Up: Librarians' Desire to Conduct Serious Research." *Research Strategies* 4 (Spring 1986): 58–59.

Holliday, Adrian. *Doing and Writing Qualitative Research.* London: Sage, 2002.

_____. *Doing and Writing Qualitative Research.* 2nd ed. London, Sage, 2007.

Hoyle, Rick H., Monica J. Harris, and Charles M. Judd. *Research Methods in Social Relations.* 7th ed. Fort Worth, TX: Wadsworth/Thomson Learning, 2002.

Hsu, Jeffrey. "The Development of Electronic Surveys: A Computer Language-Based Method." *Electronic Library* 13, no. 3 (June 1995): 195–202.

Hunter, Rhonda N. "Successes and Failures of Patrons Searching the Online Catalog at a Large Academic Library: A Transaction Log Analysis." *RQ* 30 (1991): 395–402.

Huntsberger, David V., and Patrick Billingsley. *Elements of Statistical Inference.* 4th ed. Boston, MA: Allyn and Bacon, 1977.

Ikpaahindi, Linus. "An Overview of Bibliometrics: Its Measurements, Laws, and Their Implications." *Libri* 35 (June 1985): 163–77.

International Standards Organisation. "ANSI/NISO Z39.7-2004: Information Services and Use: Metrics & Statistics for Libraries and Information Providers—Data Dictionary: Appendix: Methods of Measurement." *NISO,* http://www.niso.org/dictionary/appendices/appendixa/.

_____. *ISO 2789:1991: Information and Documentation—International Library Statistics.* 2nd ed. Geneva: International Standards Organisation, 1991.

_____. *ISO 2789:2003: Information and Documentation—International Library Statistics.* 3rd ed. Geneva: International Standards Organisation, 2003.

Irwin, Raymond. *The Golden Chain: A Study in the History of Libraries.* London: H. K. Lewis, 1958.

Isaac, Stephen, and William B. Michael. *Handbook in Research and Evaluation: A Collection of Principles, Methods and Strategies Useful in the Planning, Design, and Evaluation of Studies in Education and the Behavioral Sciences.* 3rd ed. San Diego: EdITS Publishers, 1995.

Israel, Mark, and Iain Hay. *Research Ethics for Social Scientists: Between Ethical Conduct and Regulatory Compliance.* London: Sage, 2006.

Jackson, Mary E., Lynn Silipigni Connaway, Edward T. O'Neill, and Eudora Loh. *Changing Global Book Collection Patterns in ARL Libraries.* Report prepared for the Global Resources Network. http://www.arl.org/resources/pubs/grn_global_book.shtml or http://www.crl.edu/sites/default/files/attachments/pages/grn_global_book.pdf.

Jackson, Sidney L. "Environment: Research." In *A Century of Service: Librarianship in the United States and Canada,* edited by Sidney L. Jackson, Eleanor B. Herling, and E. J. Josey, 341–54. Chicago: American Library Association, 1976.

Jacobson, Marilyn D. *New York State Education Information Centers Program: Summative Evaluation Report,* ED 250542. Albany: New York State Education Department, 1984.

Jaeger, Richard M. *Statistics: A Spectator Sport.* 2nd ed. Newbury Park, CA: Sage, 1990.

Jansen, Bernard J., and Udo Pooch. "A Review of Web Searching Studies and a Framework for Future Research." *Journal of the American Society for Information Science* 52, no. 3 (2001): 235–46.

Jansen, Bernard J., Amanda Spink, and Tefko Saracevic. "Real life, Real Users, and Real Needs: A Study and Analysis of User Queries on the Web." *Information Processing and Management* 36 (2000): 207–77.

Jansen, Bernard J., Amanda Spink, and Isak Taksa. *Handbook of Research on Web Log Analysis.* Hershey, PA: Information Science Reference, 2008.

Järvelin, Kalervo, and Pertti Vakkari. "Content Analysis of Research Articles in Library and Information Science." *Library & Information Science Research* 12, no. 4 (1990): 395–421.

Järvelin, Kalervo, and T. D. Wilson. "On Conceptual Models for Information Seeking and Retrieval Research." *Information Research* 9, no. 1 (2003). http://InformationR.net/ir/9-1/paper163.html.

Johanson, Graeme. "Ethics in Research." In *Research Methods for Students, Academics and Professionals: Information Management and Systems.* 2nd ed., edited by Kirsty Williamson. Wagga Wagga, Australia: Charles Sturt University, Centre for Information Studies, 2002.

Johnson, Debra Wilcox, and Lynn Silipigni Connaway. "Arrowhead Library System, the Older Adult in Rock County: Implications for Library Service." Unpublished consultants' report, March 1991.

_____. "Cataloger as Decision Maker." Paper presented at the annual meeting of the Wisconsin Library Association, Appleton, 1990.

_____. "Use of Online Catalogs: A Report of Results of Focus Group Interviews." Unpublished consultants' report, report no. 19, 1992.

Johnson, Richard D. "The Journal Article." In *Librarian/Author: A Practical Guide on How to Get Published,* edited by Betty-Carol Sellen, 21–35. New York: Neal-Schuman Publishers, 1985.

Jones, Robert A. "The Ethics of Research in Cyberspace." *Internet Research: Electronic Networking Applications and Policy* 4 (1994): 30–35.

Jorgensen, Danny. *Participant Observation: A Methodology for Human Studies.* London: Sage, 1989.

Judd, Charles M., Eliot R. Smith, and Louise H. Kidder. *Research Methods in Social Relations.* 6th ed. Fort Worth, TX: Harcourt Brace Jovanovich College Publishers, 1991.

Jurow, Susan R. "Tools for Measuring and Improving Performance." In *Integrating Total Quality Management in a Library Setting,* edited by Susan R. Jurow and Susan B. Bernard, 1–14. New York: Haworth, 1993.

Kalfatovic, Martin R., Effie Kapsalis, Katherine P. Spiess, Anne Van Camp, and Michael Edson. "Smithsonian Team Flikr: A Library, Archives, and Museums Collaboration in Web 2.0 Space." *Arch Sci* 8 (2008): 267–77.

Kalin, Sally W. "The Searching Behavior of Remote Users: A Study of One Online Public Access Catalog (OPAC)." In *Proceedings of the 54th Annual Meeting of the American Society for Information Science,* edited by Jose-Marie Griffiths, 175–85. Medford, NJ: Learned Information Inc, 1991.

Kantor, Paul B. *Objective Performance Measures for Academic and Research Libraries.* Washington, DC: Association of Research Libraries, 1984.

Kaser, David. "Advances in American Library History." In *Advances in Librarianship,* vol. 8, edited by Michael H. Harris, 188–99. New York: Academic Press, 1978.

Kaske, Neal K. "Research Methodologies and Transaction Log Analysis: Issues, Questions, and a Proposed Model." *Library Hi Tech* 11 (1993): 79–86.

_____. "Studies of Online Catalogs." In *Online Catalogs/Online Reference,* edited by Brian Aveney and Brett Butler. Chicago: American Library Association, 1984.

Kaske, Neal K., and N. P. Sanders. "Online Subject Access: The Human Side of the Problem." *RQ* 19 (Fall 1980): 52–58.

Keily, Lyn. "Improving Resource Discovery on the Internet: The User Perspective." In *Proceedings of the 21st International Online Information Meeting,* 205–12. Oxford: Learned Information, 1997.

Keppel, Geoffrey. *Design and Analysis: A Researcher's Handbook.* 4th ed. Upper Saddle River, NJ: Prentice Hall, 2004.

Kesselman, Martin, and Sarah B. Watstein. "The Measurement of Reference and Information Services." *Journal of Academic Librarianship* 13, no. 1 (1987): 24–30.

Kidder, Louise H. *Research Methods in Social Relations.* 4th ed. New York: Holt, Rinehart and Winston, 1981.

Kidder, Louise H., and Charles M. Judd. *Research Methods in Social Relations.* 5th ed. New York: Holt, Rinehart and Winston, 1986.

Kidston, James S. "The Validity of Questionnaire Responses." *Library Quarterly* 55 (April 1985): 133–50.

Kight, Dawn V., and Emma B. Perry. "Grant Resources on the Web." *College & Research Libraries News* 60, no. 7 (July/August 1999): 543–45.

Kim, Sung-Jin, and Dong Y. Jeong. "An Analysis of the Development and Use of Theory in Library and Information Science Research Articles." *Library & Information Science Research* 28, no. 4 (2006): 548–62.

Kimmel, Allan J. "Ethics and Values in Applied Social Research." In *Applied Social Research Methods*, vol. 12. Newbury Park, CA: Sage, 1988.

Kinnear, Paul R., and Colin D. Gray. *SPSS 17 Made Simple.* Hove: Psychology, 2009.

Klarman, Herbert E. "The Road to Cost-Effectiveness Analysis." *Health and Society* 60 (Autumn 1982).

Kleinman, Sherryl. *Feminist Fieldwork Analysis.* Los Angeles: Sage, 2007.

Knievel, Jennifer, Heather Wicht, and Lynn Silipigni Connaway, "Collection Analysis Using Circulation, ILL, and Collection Data." *Against the Grain* 16, no. 6 (December 2004-January 2005): 25–26.

———. "Use of Circulation Statistics and Interlibrary Loan Data in Collection Management." *College & Research Libraries* 67, no. 1 (2006): 35–49. http://www.ala.org/ala/mgrps/divs/acrl/publications/crljournal/2006/jan/knieval-06.pdf.

Kracker, Jacqueline, and Wang Peiling. "Research Anxiety and Students' Perceptions of Research: An Experiment, Part II. Content Analysis of Their Writings on Two Experiences Using Kuhlthau's Information Search Process at a Large Southeastern University." *Journal of the American Society for Information Science and Technology* 53 (February 2002): 295–307.

Kraemer, Helena C., and Sue Thiemann. *How Many Subjects? Statistical Power Analysis in Research.* Newbury Park, CA: Sage, 1987.

Kraft, Donald H., and Bert R. Boyce. *Operations Research for Libraries and Information Agencies: Techniques for the Evaluation of Management Decision Alternatives.* San Diego: Academic Press, 1991.

Krathwohl, David R. *Methods of Educational & Social Science Research: An Integrated Approach.* 2nd ed. Long Grove, IL: Waveland Press, Inc, 2004.

Krippendorff, Klaus. *Content Analysis: An Introduction to Its Methodology.* London: Sage, 1980.

Krippendorff, Klaus, and Mary Angela Bock, eds. *The Content Analysis Reader.* Thousand Oaks, CA: Sage, 2009.

Kristiansson, Michael René. "Strategic Reflexive Conversation—A New Theoretical-Practice Field within LIS." *Information Research* 12, no. 4 (2007), http://InformationR.net/ir/12-4/colis/colis18.html.

Krueger, Richard A. *Focus Groups: A Practical Guide for Applied Research.* Beverly Hills, CA: Sage, 1988.

Krueger, Richard A., and Mary Anne Casey. *Focus Groups: A Practical Guide for Applied Research.* Thousand Oaks, CA: Sage, 2000.

Kuhlthau, Carol Collier. *Seeking Meaning: A Process Approach to Library and Information Services.* 2nd ed. Norwood, NJ: Ablex Publishing, 2003.

Kuhn, Thomas S. *The Essential Tension: Selected Studies in Scientific Tradition and Change.* Chicago: University of Chicago Press, 1977.

_____. *The Structure of Scientific Revolutions.* Chicago: University of Chicago Press, 1970.

_____. *The Structure of Scientific Revolutions.* 3rd ed. Chicago: University of Chicago Press, 1996.

Kumpulainen, Sisko. "Library and Information Science Research in 1975: Content Analysis of the Journal Articles." *Libri* 41, no. 1 (1991): 59–76.

Kwon, Nahyun. "A Mixed-Methods Investigation of the Relationship Between Critical Thinking and Library Anxiety Among Undergraduate Students in their Information Search Process." *College & Research Libraries* 69, no. 2 (2008): 117–31.

Kvale, Steinar. *InterViews: An Introduction to Qualitative Research Interviewing.* Thousand Oaks, CA: Sage, 1996.

Kyker, Penny. "Selected World Wide Web Sites for Library Grants and Fund-Raising." *Library Administration & Management* 12 (Spring 1998): 64–71.

Labaree, Robert V. "Encounters with the Library: Understanding Experience Using the Life History Method." *Library Trends* 55, no. 1 (2006): 121–39.

_____. "Tips for Getting Published in Scholarly Journals: Strategies for Academic Librarians." *College & Research Libraries News* 65, no. 3 (March 2004): 137–39.

Lakner, Edward. "Optimizing Samples for Surveys of Public Libraries: Alternatives and Compromises." *Library & Information Science Research* 20, no. 4 (1998): 321–42.

Lancaster, F. Wilfrid. *If You Want to Evaluate Your Library* ... Champaign, IL: University of Illinois, Graduate School of Library and Information Science, 1988.

_____. *If You Want to Evaluate Your Library* ... 2nd ed. Champaign, IL: University of Illinois, Graduate School of Library and Information Science, 1993.

Lance, Keith Curry. "What Research Tells Us About the Importance of School Libraries." *Knowledge Quest* 31 Supplement (September-October 2002): 17–22.

Lankes, R. David. "The Digital Reference Research Agenda." *Journal of the American Society for Information Science and Technology* 55, no. 4 (Feb. 2004): 301–11.

Lankes, R. David, Scott Nicholson, and Abby Goodrum. *The Digital Reference Research Agenda, Publications in Librarianship,* No. 55. Chicago: Association of College and Research Libraries, 2003.

Lavoie, Brian. "Mining for Copyright Evidence." Paper presented at the ASIS&T 2008 Annual Meeting, Columbus, OH, October 28, 2008.

_____. "On Lemons and Bibliographic Data ... Creating Value through WorldCat Data-Mining." Paper presented at the OCLC Members Council Digital Libraries Research Interest Group meeting, Dublin, OH, May 16, 2005.

Lavoie, Brian, Lorcan Dempsey, and Lynn Silipigni Connaway. "Making Data Work Harder." *Library Journal* 131, no. 1 (2006): 40–42. http://www.libraryjournal.com/article/CA6298444.html.

Lavoie, Brian, Lynn Silipigni Connaway, and Edward T. O'Neill. "Mapping World-Cat's Digital Landscape." *Library Resources and Technical Services (LRTS)* 51, no. 2 (April 2007): 106–15.

_____. "Mining for Digital Resources: Identifying and Characterizing Digital Materials in WorldCat." Paper presented at the ACRL 12th National Conference: Currents and Convergence: Navigating the Rivers of Change, Minneapolis, MN, April 7–10, 2005.

Lavoie, Brian, and Roger C. Schonfeld. "A Systemwide View of Library Collections." Paper presented at the CNI Spring 2005 Task Force Meeting, Washington DC, April 4–5, 2005.

LeCompte, Margaret, Judith Preissle, and Renata Tesch. *Ethnography and Qualitative Design in Educational Research.* 2nd ed. New York: Academic Press, 1993.

Lee, Raymond, and Lea Esterhuizen. "Computer Software and Qualitative Analysis: Trends, Issues, and Resources." *International Journal of Social Research Methodology* 3, no. 3 (2000): 231–43.

Leedy, Paul D. *How to Read Research and Understand It.* New York: Macmillan, 1981.

———. *Practical Research: Planning and Design.* 2nd ed. New York: Macmillan, 1980.

Leedy, Paul D., and Jeanne Ellis Ormrod. *Practical Research: Planning and Design.* 8th ed. Upper Saddle River, NJ: Pearson Merrill Prentice Hall, 2005.

Leimkuhler, Ferdinand F. "Operations Research." In *Encyclopedia of Library and Information Science*, vol. 20, edited by Allen Kent, Harold Lancour, and J. E. Daily, 412–39. New York: Dekker, 1977.

Lewins, Ann, and Christina Silver. *Using Software in Qualitative Research: A Step-by-Step Guide.* Los Angeles: Sage, 2007.

Library History Round Table, American Library Association. "Statement on History in Education for Library and Information Science." http://www.ala.org/ala/mgrps/rts/lhrt/governance/lhrtpositions/historyeducation.cfm.

Library Normative Data (Sirsi). "Normative Data Project for Libraries." http://www.librarynormativedata.info.

Liebscher, Peter. "Quantity with Quality? Teaching Quantitative and Qualitative Methods in an LIS Master's Program." *Library Trends* 46, no. 4 (1998): 668–80.

Lincoln, Yvonna S. "Insights into Library Services and Users from Qualitative Research." *Library & Information Science Research* 24 (2002): 3–16.

Lincoln, Yvonna S., and Egon G. Guba. *Naturalistic Inquiry.* Newbury Park: Sage, 1985.

Line, Maurice B., and Alexander Sandison. "'Obsolescence' and Changes in the Use of Literature with Time." *Journal of Documentation* 30 (September 1974).

Lipetz, Ben-Ami. "Catalog Use in a Large Research Library." *Library Quarterly* 42, no. 1 (1972).

Littman, Justin, and Lynn Silipigni Connaway. "A Circulation Analysis of Print Books and e-Books in an Academic Research Library." *Library Resources & Technical Services* 48, no. 4 (2004): 256–62. http://www.oclc.org/research/publications/archive/2004/littman-connaway-duke.pdf.

Lochstet, Gwenn, and Donna H. Lehman. "A Correlation Method for Collecting Reference Statistics." *College & Research Libraries* 60, no. 1 (1999): 45–53.

Lofland, John, and Lyn Lofland. *Analyzing Social Settings: A Guide to Qualitative Observation and Analysis.* 2nd ed. Belmont, CA: Wadsworth, 1984.

Lofland, John, David A. Snow, Leon Anderson, and Lyn H. Lofland. *Analyzing Social Settings: A Guide to Qualitative Observation and Analysis.* 4th ed. Belmont, CA: Wadsworth/Thomson Learning, 2006.

Lopez-Lee, David. "Indiscriminate Data Aggregations in Meta-Analysis: A Cause for Concern Among Policy Makers and Social Scientists." *Evaluation Review* 26, no. 5 (2002): 520–44.

Losee, Robert M., and Karen A. Worley. *Research and Evaluation for Information Professionals.* San Diego: Academic Press, 1993.

Lucas, Thomas A. "Time Patterns in Remote OPAC Use." *College & Research Libraries* 54 (1993): 439–45.

Lundeen, Gerald W. "Research Record." *Journal of Education for Librarianship* 24 (Winter 1984): 206–7.

Lynch, Mary Jo. *Proposal Procedures: Guidelines for ALA Units.* Chicago: ALA Office for Research, 1981.

———. "Research and Librarianship: An Uneasy Connection." *Library Trends* 32 (Spring 1984): 367–83.

_____, ed. "Research Questions for the Twenty-first Century." *Library Trends* 51, no. 4 (Spring 2003): 499–86.

Mabry, Linda. "Case Study in Social Research." In *The Sage Handbook of Social Research Methods*, edited by Pertti Alasuutari, Leonard Bickman, and Julia Brannen, 214. Los Angeles: Sage, 2008.

MacKee, Monique. *A Handbook of Comparative Librarianship*. 3rd ed. London: Clive Bingley, 1983.

MacQueen, Kathleen, Eleanor McLellan-Lamal, Kelly Bartholow, and Bobby Milstein. "Team-Based Codebook Development: Structure, Process, and Agreement." In *Handbook for Team-Based Qualitative Research*, edited by Greg Guest and Kathleen MacQueen, 119–23. Lanham, MD: Altamira Press, 2008.

Maines, David R., Jeffery C. Bridger, and Jeffery T. Ulmer. "Mythic Facts and Park's Pragmatism: On Predecessor-Selection and Theorizing in Human Ecology." *Sociological Quarterly* 37 (Summer 1969): 521–49.

Maines, David R., and Shing-Ling Chen. "Information and Action: An Introduction to Carl Couch's Analysis of Information Technologies." In *Information Technologies and Social Orders*, edited by Carl J. Couch. New York: Aldine de Gruyter, 1996.

Mann, Chris, and Fiona Stewart. "Internet Interviewing." In *Handbook of Interview Research: Context & Method*, edited by Jaber F. Gubrium and James A. Holstein, 603–27. Thousand Oaks, CA: Sage, 2002.

Marchant, Maurice P., and N. M. Smith. "Research Thrust of Brigham Young University's Library School." *Journal of Education for Librarianship* 20 (Fall 1979): 129–35.

Markey, Karen. *Subject Searching in Library Catalogs: Before and After the Introduction of Online Catalogs*. Dublin, OH: OCLC, 1984.

Marshall, Catherine, and Gretchen B. Rossman. *Designing Qualitative Research*. 4th ed. Thousand Oaks, CA: Sage, 2006.

Marshall, Joanne G. *An Introduction to Research Methods for Health Sciences Librarians*. Courses for Continuing Education. Chicago: Medical Library Association, 1989.

Martyn, John, and F. Wilfrid Lancaster. *Investigative Methods in Library and Information Science: An Introduction*. Arlington, VA: Information Resources Press, 1981.

Mason, Jennifer. "Mixing Methods in a Qualitatively Driven Way." *Qualitative Research* 6 (2006): 9–25.

Matthews, Anne J. "An Overview of Issues, Proposals, and Products in Library/Information Research." *Journal of Education for Library and Information Science* 29 (Spring 1989): 251–61.

Matthews, Joseph R. *The Evaluation and Measurement of Library Services*. Westport, CT: Libraries Unlimited, 2007.

_____. *Measuring for Results: The Dimensions of Public Library Effectiveness*. Westport, CT: Libraries Unlimited, 2004.

Matthews, Joseph R., Gary S. Lawrence, and Douglas K. Ferguson. *Using Online Catalogs: A Nationwide Survey, A Report of a Study Sponsored by the Council on Library Resources*. New York: Neal-Schuman, 1983.

Maxstadt, John M. "A New Approach to Reference Statistics." *College & Research Libraries* 49 (February 1988).

Maylone, Theresa, ed. "Qualitative Research." *Library Trends* 46, no. 4 (1998): 597–768.

Mazzei, Lisa A. *Inhabited Silence in Qualitative Research: Putting Poststructural Theory to Work*. New York: Peter Lang, 2007.

Mazzei, Lisa, and Alecia Youngblood Jackson. "Introduction: The Limit of Voice." In *Voice in Qualitative Inquiry: Challenging Conventional, Interpretive, and*

Critical Conceptions in Qualitative Research, edited by Lisa Mazzei and Alecia Youngblood Jackson. London: Routledge, 2009.

McClure, Charles R. "Increasing the Usefulness of Research for Library Managers: Propositions, Issues, and Strategies." *Library Trends* 38 (Fall 1989): 280–94.

_____. "Management Data for Library Decision Making: The Role of the Researcher." In *Library Lectures*, vol. 56, edited by Robert S. Martin. Baton Rouge: Louisiana State University Libraries, 1988.

McClure, Charles R., and Ann Bishop. "The Status of Research in Library/Information Science: Guarded Optimism." *College & Research Libraries* 50 (March 1989): 127–43.

McClure, Charles R., and Peter Hernon, eds. *Library and Information Science Research: Perspectives and Strategies for Improvement*. Norwood, NJ: Ablex Publishing, 1991.

McGrath, William E. "Current Theory in Library and Information Science." *Library Trends* 50, no. 3 (2002): 309–569.

McKechnie, Lynne (E. F.), and Karen E. Pettigrew. "Surveying the Use of Theory in Library and Information Science Research: A Disciplinary Perspective." *Library Trends* 50, no. 3 (2002): 406–17.

McNall, Scott G. *The Sociological Experience*. Boston: Little, Brown and Company, 1969.

McNicol, Sarah. "Is Research an Untapped Resource in the Library and Information Profession?" *Journal of Librarianship and Information Science* 36 (September 2004): 119–26.

Mead, George H. *Mind, Self and Society*. Chicago: University of Chicago Press, 1962.

Meadows, A. J. *Communicating Research*. San Diego: Academic Press, 1998.

Meho, Lokman. "E-Mail Interviewing in Qualitative Research: A Methodological Discussion." *Journal of the American Society for Information Science and Technology* 57, no. 10 (2006): 1284–95.

Mellon, Constance Ann. "Library Anxiety: A Grounded Theory and Its Development." *College & Research Libraries* 47 (March 1986): 160–65.

_____. *Naturalistic Inquiry for Library Science: Methods and Applications for Research, Evaluation, and Teaching*. With a foreword by Robert Bogdan. New York: Greenwood Press, 1990.

Mertens, Donna M., and Pauline E. Ginsberg, eds. *The Handbook of Social Research Ethics*. Los Angeles: Sage, 2009.

Meyyappan, Narayanan, Suliman Al-Hawamdeh, and Schubert Foo. "Task Based Design of a Digital Work Environment (DWE) for an Academic Community." *Information Research* 7, no. 2 (2002), http://InformationR.net/ir/7-2/paper125.html.

Microcase, Wadsworth/Cengage Learning. "Microcase." http://microcase.com/index.html.

Miles, Matthew, and Michael Huberman. *Qualitative Data Analysis: A Sourcebook of New Methods*. Beverly Hills, CA: Sage, 1984.

_____. *Qualitative Data Analysis: A Sourcebook of New Methods*. 2nd ed. Beverly Hills, CA: Sage, 1994.

Miller, Delbert C., and Neil J. Salkind. *Handbook of Research Design & Social Measurement*. 6th ed. Thousand Oaks, CA: Sage, 2002.

Millsap, Larry, and Terry Ellen Ferl. "Research Patterns of Remote Users: An Analysis of OPAC Transaction Logs." *Information Technology and Libraries* 12 (1993): 321–43.

Minitab Inc. "Minitab Statistical and Process Management Software for Six Sigma and Quality Improvement." http://www.minitab.com.

Morgan, David L. *Focus Groups as Qualitative Research*. Newbury Park, CA: Sage, 1988.

_____. "Practical Strategies for Combining Qualitative and Quantitative Methods: Applications to Health Research." In *Emergent Methods in Social Research*, edited by Sharlene Nagy Hesse-Biber and Patricia Leavy, 165–82. Thousand Oaks, CA: Sage, 2006.

Morris, Betty J. "Getting Published: What Every Library Media Specialist Needs to Know." *Knowledge Quest* 26, no. 3 (March/April 1998): 16–17.

Morse, Janice. "Designing Funded Qualitative Research." In *Handbook of Qualitative Research*, edited by Norman Denzin and Yvonna Lincoln, 220–35. Thousand Oaks, CA: Sage, 1994.

_____. "Principles of Mixed Methods and Multimethod Research Design." In *Handbook of Mixed Methods in Social and Behavioral Research*, edited by Abbas Tashakkori and Charles Teddlie, 193–95. Thousand Oaks, CA: Sage, 2003.

Moukdad, Haidar, and Andrew Large. "Users' Perceptions of the Web as Revealed by Transaction Log Analysis." *Online Information Review* 25, no. 6 (2001): 349–59.

Mouly, George J. *Educational Research: The Art and Science of Investigation.* Boston: Allyn and Bacon, 1978.

Mudrock, Theresa. "Revising Ready Reference Sites: Listening to Users Through Server Statistics and Query Logs." *Reference and User Services Quarterly* 42 (Winter 2002): 155–63.

Muller, Robert H. "The Research Mind in Library Education and Practice." *Library Journal* 92 (March 1967): 1126–29.

Mullins, Nicholas. *Theories and Theory Groups in Contemporary American Sociology.* New York: Harper and Row, 1973.

Nachmias, David, and Chava Nachmias. *Research Methods in the Social Sciences.* 2nd ed. New York: St. Martin's Press, 1981.

Nardi, Peter M. *Interpreting Data: A Guide to Understanding Research.* Boston: Allyn and Bacon, 2006.

National Institute of Child Health and Human Development. "Quick Tips: Most Common Reasons for Disapproval."

Neal, James G. "Editorial: The Librarian Research and Publication Imperative." *Library & Information Science Research* 17 (Spring 1995): 199–200.

_____. "The Research and Development Imperative in the Academic Library: Path to the Future." *Portal: Libraries and the Academy* 6 (2006): 1–3.

Nelson, Janet L. "An Analysis of Transaction Logs to Evaluate the Educational Needs of End Users." *Medical Reference Services Quarterly* 11, no. 4 (1992): 11–21.

Neuendorf, Kimberly. *The Content Analysis Guidebook.* Thousand Oaks, CA: Sage, 2002.

Neuman, Delia. "Research in School Library Media for the Next Decade: Polishing the Diamond." *Library Trends* 51, no. 4 (Spring 2003): 503–24.

Newman, Isadore, Carolyn Ridenour, Carole Newman, and George DeMarco, Jr. "A Typology of Research Purposes and its Relationship to Mixed Methods." In *Handbook of Mixed Methods in Social and Behavioral Research*, edited by Abbas Tashakkori and Charles Teddlie, 170–71. Thousand Oaks, CA: Sage, 2003.

Newman, John. "Academic Librarians as Scholars." *College & Research Libraries News* 59, no. 1 (January 1998): 19–20.

Nicholas, David, and Maureen Ritchie. *Literature and Bibliometrics.* London: Clive Bingley, 1984.

Nicholls, William L. II, Reginald P. Baker, and Jean Martin. "The Effect of New Data Collection Technology on Survey Data Quality." In *Survey Measurement and Process Quality*, edited by Lars E. Lyberg, Paul Biemer, Martin Collins, Edith de Leeuw, Cathryn Dippo, Norbert Schwarz, and Dennis Trewin, 221–48. New York: Wiley, 1996.

Nicholson, Scott, Lynn Silipigni Connaway, and Bob Molyneux. "Capturing Untapped Descriptive Data: Creating Value for Librarians and Users." In *Information Realities Shaping the Digital Future for All: Proceedings of the ASIS&T Annual Meeting, Vol. 43, 2006*, edited by Andrew Grove. Silver Springs, MD: American Society for Information Science and Technology, 2006.

Nielsen, Brian. "What They Say They Do and What They Do: Assessing Online Catalog Use Instruction Through Transaction Log Monitoring." *Information Technology and Libraries* 5 (1986): 28–33.

Norden, David J., and Gail Herndon Lawrence. "Public Terminal Use in an Online Catalog: Some Preliminary Results." *College & Research Libraries* 42 (1981): 308–16.

Norlin, Elaina, and C. M. Winters. *Usabilty Testing for Library Websites: A Hands-on Guide*. Chicago: American Library Association, 2002.

Norman, Geoffrey R., and David L. Streiner. *PDQ Statistics*. 3rd ed. Hamilton, Ontario: B. C. Decker, 2003.

Northcutt, Norvell, and Danny McCoy. *Interactive Qualitative Analysis: A Systems Method for Qualitative Research*. Thousand Oaks, CA: Sage, 2004.

Nour, Martyvonne M. "A Quantitative Analysis of the Research Articles Published in Core Library Journals of 1980." *Library & Information Science Research* 7 (July 1985): 261–73.

Observer's Dictionary of Library Science Information and Documentation in Six Languages. Observer Scientific, 1973.

OCLC Research. "Data Mining Research Area." 2009. http://www.oclc.org/research/activities/past/orprojects/mining/default.htm.

O'Connor, Daniel O., and Soyeon Park. "Guest Editorial: Crisis in LIS Research Capacity." *Library & Information Science Research* 23, no. 2 (2001): 103–6.

O'Connor, Daniel O., and Phyllis Van Orden. "Getting into Print." *College & Research Libraries* 39 (September 1978): 389–96.

ODLIS Online Dictionary of Library and Information Science. Edited by Joan M. Reitz. http://lu.com/odlis/.

O'Neill, Edward T. "OhioLINK Collection Analysis Project: Preliminary Analysis." Paper presented at the ASIS&T 2008 Annual Meeting, Columbus, OH, October 28, 2008.

_____. "Operations Research." *Library Trends* 32 (Spring 1984): 509–20.

O'Neill, Edward T., Lynn Silipigni Connaway, and Timothy J. Dickey. "Estimating the Audience Level for Library Resources." *Journal of the American Society for Information Science and Technology* 59, no. 13 (2008): 2042–50.

Onwuegbuzie, Anthony, and Nancy Leech. "On Becoming a Pragmatic Researcher: The Importance of Combining Quantitative and Qualitative Research Methodologies." *International Journal of Social Research Methodology* 8 (2005).

Orr, R. H. "Measuring the Goodness of Library Services: A General Framework for Considering Quantitative Measures." *Journal of Documentation* 29 (September 1973): 315–32.

Osareh, Farideh. "Bibliometrics, Citation Analysis and Co-Citation Analysis: A Review of Literature I." *Libri* 46 (1996): 149–58.

Osborne, Larry N. "Research Record." *Journal of Education for Library and Information Science* 25 (Spring 1985): 316–19.

Ottensmann, John R. "Using Geographic Information Systems to Analyze Library Utilization." *Library Quarterly* 67 (1997): 24–49.

Paris, Marion. "Thoughts on the Case Study." *Journal of Education for Library and Information Science* 29 (Fall 1988): 138.

Partnership: The Canadian Journal of Library and Information Practice and Research. http://www.criticalimprov.com/index.php/perj/.

Patton, Michael Quinn. *Qualitative Evaluation and Research Methods.* 2nd ed. Newbury Park, CA: Sage, 1990.

Paul, Richard, and Linda Elder. *The Miniature Guide to Critical Thinking: Concepts and Tools.* 4th ed. Dillon Beach, CA: Critical Thinking Press, 2007.

Peischl, Thomas M. "Benchmarking: A Process for Improvement." *Library Administration & Management* 9, no. 2 (Spring 1995): 99–101.

Peritz, Bluma C. "The Methods of Library Science Research: Some Results from a Bibliometric Survey." *Library Research* 2 (Fall 1980): 251–68.

_____. "On the Objectives of Citation Analysis: Problems of Theory and Method." *Journal of the American Society for Information Science* 43, no. 6 (July 1992): 448–51.

_____. "Research in Library Science as Reflected in the Core Journals of the Profession: A Quantitative Analysis (1950–1975)." Ph.D. diss., University of California at Berkeley, 1977.

Perrault, Anna H., and Ron Blazek. "Transforming Library Services Through Action Research." *Florida Libraries* 40, no. 3 (1997): 60–61.

Perry, Suzanne. "Getting a Foundation Grant Takes More Than a Good Idea, Program Officers Say." *Chronicle of Higher Education* 25 (October 1982): 25–28.

Peters, Thomas A. *The Online Catalog: A Critical Examination of Public Use.* Jefferson, NC: McFarland, 1991.

_____. "Using Transaction Log Analysis for Library Management Information." *Library Administration & Management* 10 (Winter 1996): 20–25.

_____. "When Smart People Fail: An Analysis of the Transaction Logs of an Online Public Catalog." *Journal of Academic Librarianship* 15 (1989): 267–73.

Pettigrew, Karen E., and Lynne (E. F.) McKechnie. "The Use of Theory in Information Science Research." *Journal of the American Society for Information Science and Technology* 52 (2001): 62–73.

Phelps, Renata, Kath Fisher, and Allan Ellis. *Organizing and Managing Your Research: A Practical Guide for Postgraduates.* Los Angeles: Sage, 2007.

Pickard, Alison Jane. *Research Methods in Information.* London: Facet Publishing, 2007.

Polkinghorne, Donald. *Methodology for the Human Sciences: Systems of Inquiry.* Albany: State University of New York Press, 1983.

Pomeranz, Jeffrey. "A Conceptual Framework and Open Research Questions for Chat-based Reference." *Journal of the American Society for Information Science and Technology* 56, no. 12 (October 2005): 1288–1302.

Poole, Carolyn E. "Guest Editorial: Importance of Research and Publication by Community College Librarians." *College & Research Libraries* 61, no. 6 (2000): 486–89.

Poole, Herbert L. *Theories of the Middle Range.* Norwood, NJ: Ablex Publishing, 1985.

Powell, Ronald R. "Evaluation Research: An Overview." *Library Trends* 55 (Summer 2006): 102–20.

_____. "Impact Assessment of University Libraries." In *Encyclopedia of Library and Information Science*, vol. 55, edited by Allen Kent, 151–64. New York: Marcel Dekker, 1994.

_____. "Recent Trends in Research: A Methodological Essay." *Library & Information Science Research* 21, no. 1 (1999): 91–119.

_____. "Research Competence for Ph.D. Students in Library and Information Science." *Journal of Education for Library and Information Science* 36 (Fall 1995): 319–29.

Powell, Ronald R., Lynda M. Baker, and Joseph J. Mika. "Library and Information Science Practitioners and Research." *Library & Information Science Research* 24 (2002): 49–72.

Powell, Walter W., and Paul J. DiMaggio. *The New Institutionalism in Organizational Analysis*. Chicago: University of Chicago Press, 1991.

Prasse, Michael J., and Lynn Silipigni Connaway. "Usability Testing: Method and Research." In *Academic Library Research: Perspectives and Current Trends*, edited by Marie L. Radford and Pamela Snelson. Chicago: Association of College and Research Libraries, 2008.

Puchta, Claudia, and Jonathan Potter. *Focus Group Practice*. London: Sage, 2004.

Publication Manual of the American Psychological Association. 5th ed. Washington, DC: American Psychological Association, 2001.

Pyrczak, Fred. *Evaluating Research in Academic Journals: A Practical Guide to Realistic Evaluation*. 4th ed. Glendale, CA: Pyrczak Publishing, 2008.

"Questions and Answers." *ISR Newsletter* (Spring–Summer 1982): 6–7.

Radford, Marie L. "The Critical Incident Technique and the Qualitative Evaluation of the Connecting Libraries and Schools Project." *Library Trends* 55, no. 1 (2006): 46–64.

Rao, I. K. Ravichandra. *Quantitative Methods for Library and Information Science*. New York: John Wiley and Sons, 1983.

Reed, Sarah R., ed. "Evaluation of Library Service." *Library Trends* 22, no. 3 (1974).

Reilly, Kevin D. "The Delphi Technique: Fundamentals and Applications." In *Targets for Research in Library Education*, edited by Harold Borko. Chicago: American Library Association, 1973.

Reips, Ulf-Dietrich. "The Methodology of Internet-Based Experiments." In *The Oxford Handbook of Internet Psychology*, edited by Adam N. Joinson, Katelyn McKenna, Tom Postmes, and Ulf-Dietrich Reips, 373–90. Oxford: Oxford University Press, 2007.

Reips, Ulf-Dietrich, Thomas Blumer, and Christoph Neuhaus. "Wexstor: Ten Steps to your Experimental Design." http://wextor.org/wextor/en/.

Reis, Harry, and Shelly Gable. "Event-Sampling and Other Methods for Studying Everyday Experience." In *Handbook of Research Methods in Social and Personality Psychology*, edited by Harry T. Reis and Charles M. Judd. Cambridge: Cambridge University Press, 2000.

Research Trends' Editorial Board, "What is Research Trends?" *Research Trends*. http://info.scopus.com/researchtrends/whatis.html.

Reynolds, Rodney A., Robert Woods, and Jason Baker. *Handbook of Research on Electronic Surveys and Measurements*. Hershey, PA: IGI Global, 2006.

Rice Virtual Lab. "Rice Virtual Lab in Statistics (RVLS)." (Last update 12/3/08). http://onlinestatbook.com/rvls.html.

Riggs, Donald E. "Losing the Foundation of Understanding." *American Libraries* 25 (May 1994): 449.

Robbins, Jane B. "Affecting Librarianship in Action: The Dissemination and Communication of Research Findings." In *Applying Research to Practice*, edited by Leigh L. Estabrook. Urbana-Champaign: University of Illinois, Graduate School of Library and Information Science, 1992.

_____. "The Quality of Published Library and Information Science Research." *Library & Information Science Research* 13 (Spring 1991): 315–17.

_____. "Research in Information Service Practice." *Library & Information Science Research* 12 (April 1990): 127–28.

Robbins, Kathryn, and Ruth Holst. "Hospital Library Evaluation Using Focus Group Interviews." *Bulletin of the Medical Library Association* 78, no. 3 (July 1990): 311–13.

Robinson, A. M. *Systematic Bibliography*. London: Clive Bingley, 1979.

Robinson, Barbara M. *A Study of Reference Referral and Super Reference in California*. Sacramento: California State Library, 1986.

Roselle, Ann, and Steven Neufeld. "The Utility of Electronic Mail Follow-ups for Library Research." *Library & Information Science Research* 20, no. 2 (1998): 153–61.

Rowntree, Derek. *Statistics without Tears: A Primer for Non-Mathematicians*. 1981. Reprint, Boston: Pearson, 2004.

Rubin, Herbert J., and Irene Rubin. *Qualitative Interviewing: The Art of Hearing Data*. 2nd ed. Thousand Oaks, CA: Sage, 2005.

Runes, Dagobert D., ed. *Dictionary of Philosophy*. Totowa, NY: Littlefield, Adams and Company, 1962.

———, ed. *The Dictionary of Philosophy*. New York: Citadel Press, 2001.

Russell-Einhorn, Michele K., and Thomas Puglisi. *Institutional Review Board (IRB) Reference Book: Protecting the People Who Volunteer to Participate in Research*. [Washington, DC]: PricewaterhouseCoopers, 2001.

Ryan, Kenneth J. "Scientific Misconduct in Perspective: The Need to Improve Accountability." *Chronicle of Higher Education* B1 (1996): B1-B2.

SAS Institute, Inc. "SAS Business Analytics and Business Intelligence Software." http://www.sas.com.

Scharf, M. K., and Jean Ward. "A Library Research Application of Focus Group Interviews." In *Association of College and Research Libraries National Conference, Energies for Transition*, 191–93. Chicago: ACRL, 1986.

Schonlau, Matthias, Ronald D. Fricker, and Marc N. Elliott. *Conducting Research Surveys via E-mail and the Web*. Santa Monica, CA: Rand, 2002.

Schroeder, Carol F., and Gloria G. Roberson. *Guide to Publishing Opportunities for Librarians*, New York: Haworth Press, 1995.

Schuman, Patricia G. "From Book Idea to the Contract." In *Librarian/Author: A Practical Guide on How to Get Published*, edited by Betty-Carol Sellen. New York: Neal-Schuman Publishers, 1985.

Schutt, Russell K. *Investigating the Social World: The Process and Practice of Research*. 5th ed. Thousand Oaks, CA: Sage, 2006.

Schwartz, Morris, and Charlotte Schwartz. "Problems in Participant Observation." *American Journal of Sociology* 60 (1955): 343–56.

Schwerzel, Sharon W., Susan V. Emerson, and David L. Johnson. "Self-Evaluation of Competencies in Online Searching by End-Users After Basic Training." In *Proceedings of the Forty-fifth ASIS Annual Meeting*, edited by Anthony E. Petrarca, Celianna I. Taylor, and Robert S. Kohn, 272–75. White Plains, NY: Knowledge Industry, 1982.

Seidman, Irving. *Interviewing as Qualitative Research: A Guide for Researchers in Education and the Social Sciences*. 3rd ed. New York: Teachers College Press, 2006.

Selltiz, Claire, Lawrence S. Wrightsman, and Stuart W. Cook. *Research Methods in Social Relations*. Rev. ed. New York: Holt, Rinehart and Winston, 1959.

Shachaf, Pnina, and Debora Shaw. "Bibliometric Analysis to Identify Core Reference Sources of Virtual Reference Transactions." *Library & Information Science Research* 30 (2008): 291–97.

Shafer, Robert J., ed. *A Guide to Historical Method*. 3rd ed. Homewood, IL: Dorsey Press, 1980.

Shaughnessy, Thomas W. "Library Research in the 70's: Problems and Prospects." *California Librarian* 37 (July 1976): 44–52.

Shera, Jesse H. "Darwin, Bacon, and Research in Librarianship." *Library Trends* 3 (July 1964): 141–49.

_____. "On the Value of Library History." *Library Quarterly* 22 (July 1952): 240–51.

Sheridan, Judson D. "Perspectives from 202 Jesse Hall: The Research Continuum." *Graduate School and Research Notes* 14, no. 6 (February 1988): 1–2.

Shi, Xi. "A Theory-Guided Approach to Library Services Assessment." *College & Research Libraries* 66 (May 2005): 266–77.

Shiflett, Lee. "Sense-Making and Library History." *Journal of Education for Library and Information Science* 41, no. 3 (Summer 2000): 254–59.

Shiflett, Orvin L. "Clio's Claim: The Role of Historical Research in Library and Information Science." *Library Trends* 32 (Spring 1984): 385–406.

Sieber, Joan. *Planning Ethically Responsible Research: A Guide for Students and Internal Review Boards.* Newbury Park, CA: Sage, 1992.

Silverman, David, and Amir Marvasti. *Doing Qualitative Research: A Comprehensive Guide.* London: Sage, 2008.

Silverstein, Craig, Hannes Marais, Monika Henzinger, and Michael Moricz. "Analysis of a Very Large Web Search Engine Query Log." *SIGIR Forum* 33, no. 1 (1999): 6–12.

Simpson, Charles W. "OPAC Transaction Log Analysis: The First Decade." In *Advances in Library Automation and Networking*, edited by Joe Hewitt, 35–67. Greenwich, CT: JAI Press, 1989.

Simpson, Ian S. *Basic Statistics for Librarians.* 3rd ed. London: Library Association, 1988.

_____. *Basic Statistics for Librarians.* 3rd rev. ed. London: Library Association, 1989.

Simsova, Sylva. *A Primer of Comparative Librarianship.* London: Clive Bingley, 1982.

Smith, Charles. "Content Analysis and Narrative Analysis." In *Handbook of Research Methods in Social and Personality Psychology*, edited by Harry T. Reis and Charles M. Judd. Cambridge: Cambridge University Press, 2000.

Smith, Linda C. "Citation Analysis." *Library Trends* 30 (Summer 1981): 83–106.

Smith, Martha M. "Survival and Service: The Ethics of Research on the Uses of Information Provided by Librarians." *North Carolina Libraries* 65 (1994): 64–67.

Smith, Robert. *Cumulative Social Inquiry: Transforming Novelty into Innovation.* New York: Guilford Press, 2008.

Smith, Todd, Anthony Ruocco, and Bernard J. Jansen. "Digital Video in Education." In *Proceedings of the 30th ACM SIGCSE Technical Symposium on Computer Science Education*, edited by Daniel T. Joyce, 122–36. New York: Association of Computing Machinery, 1999.

Smithson, Janet. "Focus Groups." In *The Sage Handbook of Social Research Methods*, edited by Pertti Alasuutari, Leonard Bickman, and Julia Brannen, 358–59. Los Angeles: Sage, 2008.

Special Libraries Association. "Putting OUR Knowledge to Work: A New SLA Research Statement June 2001: The Role of Research in Special Librarianship." June 2001. http://www.sla.org/content/resources/research/rsrchstatement.cfm.

Spink, Amanda, Dietmar Wolfram, Bernard J. Jansen, and Tefko Saracevic. "Searching the Web: The Public and Their Queries." *Journal of the American Society for Information Science and Technology* 52, no. 3 (2001): 226–34.

Spink, Amanda, and Jack L. Xu. "Selected Results from a Large Study of Web Searching: The Excite Study." *Information Research* 6, no. 1 (2000).

Spirer, Herbert F., Louise Spirer, and A. J. Jaffe. *Misused Statistics.* 2nd, rev. exp. ed. New York: M. Dekker, 1998.

SPSS Inc., an IBM Company. *SPSS 16.0 Brief Guide.* Chicago: SPSS Inc., 2007.

_____. *SPSS 18.0 Integrated Student Version for Business Statistics.* Englewood Cliffs: Prentice Hall, 2010.

_____. *SPSS Base 16.0 User's Guide*. Chicago: SPSS Inc., 2007.

_____. "SPSS: Data Mining, Statistical Analysis Software, Predictive Analysis, Decision Support Systems." http://www.spss.com.

_____. "SPSS Statistics." http://www.spss.com/media/collateral/statistics/pasw-statistics-specs.pdf.

St. Clair, Gloriana. "Improving Quality: An Editor's Advice to Authors." *College & Research Libraries* 54 (May 1993): 195–97.

Statistical Solutions. "BMDP Statistical Software Package: ANOVA, Regression, Survival Analysis, Time Series, Nonparametric Analysis." http://www.statistical-solutions-software.com/products-page/bmdp-statistical-software/.

StatPac Inc. "StatPac Survey Software Online Surveys Overview." http://www.statpac.com/survey-software.htm.

Steffen, Nicolle O., Keith Curry Lance, and Rochelle Logan. "Time to Tell the Who Story: Outcome-Based Evaluation and the Counting on Results Project." *Public Libraries* 41 (July-August 2002): 222–28.

Stempel, Guido. "Content Analysis." In *Research Methods in Mass Communication*. 2nd ed., edited by Guido Stempel and Bruce Westley. Englewood Cliffs, NJ: Prentice Hall, 1989.

Stephen, Peter, and Susan Hornby. *Simple Statistics for Library and Information Professionals*. 2nd ed. London: Library Association Publications, 1997.

Stevens, Michael. "The Pragmatic Biblioblogger: Examining the Motivations and Observations of Early Adopter Librarian Bloggers." *Internet Reference Services Quarterly* 13, no. 4 (2008): 311–45.

Stevens, Rolland E., ed. *Research Methods in Librarianship: Historical and Bibliographical Methods in Library Research*. Urbana: University of Illinois, Graduate School of Library Science, 1971.

Stoerger, Sharon. "Research Ethics." http://www.web-miner.com/researchethics.htm.

Stokes, Donald E. *Pasteur's Quadrant: Basic Science and Technological Innovation*. Washington, DC: Brookings Institute Press, 1997.

Strauss, Anselm L. *Qualitative Research for Social Scientists*. New York: Cambridge University Press, 1987.

Suchman, Edward A. *Evaluative Research*. New York: Russell Sage Foundation, 1967.

Sullivan, Laura A. "Grant Funding for Libraries." *Bottom Line: Managing Library Finances* 20, no. 4 (2007): 157–160.

Sullivan, Peggy A. "Research in Librarianship: Achievements, Needs, and Prospects." *Illinois Libraries* 60 (May 1978): 510–14.

Swisher, Robert. "Focus on Research." *Top of the News* 42 (Winter 1986): 176.

Swisher, Robert, and Charles R. McClure. *Research for Decision Making: Methods for Librarians*. Chicago: American Library Association, 1984.

Systat Software. "SYSTAT: Statistical and Graphical Software." http://systat.com.

Talja, Sanna. "Analyzing Qualitative Interview Data: The Discourse Analytic Method." *Library & Information Science Research* 21, no. 4 (1999): 459–77.

Taylor, Steven J., and Robert Bogdan. *Introduction to Qualitative Research Methods*. 2nd ed. New York: John Wiley & Sons, 1984.

_____. *Introduction to Qualitative Research Methods: A Guidebook and Resource*. 3rd ed. New York: John Wiley & Sons, 1998.

Tibbo, Helen R. "Primarily History in America: How U.S. Historians Search for Primarily Materials at the Dawn of the Digital Age." *The American Archivist* 66, no. 1 (Spring/Summer 2003): 9–50.

Todd, Ross. "The Evidence-Based Manifesto for School Librarians." *School Library Journal* 4 (2008). http://www.schoollibraryjournal.com/article/CA6545434.html.

Tolle, John E. *Current Utilization of Online Catalogs: A Transaction Log Analysis.* vol. 1. Dublin, OH: OCLC Office of Research, 1983.

Tosh, John, and Sean Lang. *The Pursuit of History: Aims, Methods and New Directions in the Study of Modern History.* 4th ed. London: Pearson Longman, 2006.

Townley, Charles T. "Developing Relationships Between Academic Libraries and the State Library of Pennsylvania: A Report of the Research Recommendations." Unpublished consultant's report, report no. ED250542, August 1984.

Trahan, Eric. "Applying Meta-Analysis to Library Research and Information Science Research." *Library Quarterly* 63 (January 1993): 73–91.

Trochim, William M. K., and James P. Donnelly. *The Research Methods Knowledge Base.* 3rd ed. Mason, OH: Thomson, 2007.

Tufte, Edward. *Envisioning Information.* 1990. Reprint, Cheshire, CT: Graphics Press, 2006.

_____. *The Visual Display of Quantitative Information,* 2nd ed. (Cheshire, CT: Graphics Press, 2001).

Turner, Barry. "Some Practical Aspects of Qualitative Data Analysis: One Way of Organizing the Cognitive Processes Associated with the Generation of Grounded Theory." *Quality and Quantity* 15, no. 3 (1981): 225–47.

U. S. Department of Education Office of Libraries and Learning Technologies. *A Library and Information Science Research Agenda for the 1980's.* Los Angeles: Cuadra Associates, 1981.

University of Alberta Learning Services. "Editorial Policies: Focus and Scope." http://ejournals.library.ualberta.ca/index.php/EBLIP/about/editorial Policies#focusAndScope

_____. "Evidence Based Library and Information Practice: Home." http:// ejournals.library.ualberta.ca/index.php/EBLIP/index

The University of Illinois Graduate School of Library and Information Science. "Center for Informatics Research in Science and Scholarship (CIRSS)." http:// cirss.lis.illinois.edu/index.html.

University of Ljubljana (Slovenia) Faculty of Social Sciences. "WebSM: Web Survey Methodology." http://www.websm.org/.

Vakkari, Pertti. "Growth of Theories on Information Seeking. An Analysis of Growth of a Theoretical Research Program on Relation between Task Complexity and Information Seeking." *Information Processing & Management* 34, no. 3/4 (1998): 361–82.

_____. "Task Complexity, Problem Structure and Information Actions: Integrating Studies on Information Seeking and Retrieval." *Information Processing & Management* 35, no. 6 (1999): 819–37.

Vakkari, Pertti, and Martti Kuokkanen. "Theory Growth in Information Science: Applications of the Theory of Science to a Theory of Information Seeking." *Journal of Documentation* 53, no. 5 (1997): 49–519.

Vaughan, Liwen. *Statistical Methods for the Information Professional: A Practical, Painless Approach to Understanding, Using, and Interpreting Statistics.* ASIST Monograph Series. Medford, NJ: Information Today, 2001.

Van House, Nancy A. "Assessing the Quantity, Quality, and Impact of LIS Research." In *Library and Information Science Research: Perspectives and Strategies for Improvement,* edited by Charles R. McClure and Peter Hernon. Norwood, NJ: Ablex Publishing, 1991.

Van House, Nancy A., Beth Weil, and Charles McClure. *Measuring Academic Library Performance: A Practical Approach.* Chicago: American Library Association, 1990.

Van House, Nancy A., and others. *Output Measures for Public Libraries: A Manual of Standardized Procedures.* 2nd ed. Chicago: American Library Association, 1987.

Vaughan, Liwen. *Statistical Methods for the Information Professional: A Practical, Painless Approach to Understanding, Using, and Interpreting Statistics.* ASIST Monograph Series. Medford, NJ: Information Today, 2001.

Verny, Roger, and Connie Van Fleet. "Conducting Focus Groups." In *Library Evaluation: A Casebook and Can-Do Guide,* edited by Danny P. Wallace and Connie Van Fleet, 43–51. Englewood, CO: Libraries Unlimited, 2001.

Via, Barbara J. "Publishing in the Journal Literature of Library and Information Science: A Survey of Manuscript Review Processes and Acceptance." *College & Research Libraries* 57 (July 1996): 365–76.

Vickery, B. C. "Academic Research in Library and Information Studies." *Journal of Librarianship* 7 (July 1975): 153–60.

Vogt, Paul W. *Dictionary of Statistics and Methodology: A Nontechnical Guide for the Social Sciences.* 3rd ed. Thousand Oaks, CA: Sage, 2005.

von Ungern-Sternberg, Sara. "Teaching Bibliometrics." *Journal of Education for Library and Information Science* 39, no. 1 (1989): 76–80.

Wagner, Mary M., and Suzanne H. Mahmoodi. *A Focus Group Interview Manual.* Chicago: American Library Association, 1994.

Wallace, Danny P. "Bibliometrics and Citation Analysis." In *Principles and Applications of Information Science for Library Professionals,* edited by John N. Olsgaard, 10–26. Chicago: American Library Association, 1989.

_____. "The Use of Statistical Methods in Library and Information Science." *Journal of the American Society for Information Science* 36 (November 1985): 402–10.

Wallace, Danny P., and Connie Jean Van Fleet. *Library Evaluation: A Casebook and Can-Do Guide.* Englewood, CO: Libraries Unlimited, 2001.

Wallace, Patricia M. "How Do Patrons Search the Online Catalog When No One's Looking? Transaction Log Analysis and Implications for Bibliographic Instruction and System Design." *RQ* 33 (1993): 239–52.

Walters, Suzanne. *Focus Groups: Linkages to the Community.* Denver: US West Communications, 1988.

Wang, Chih. "A Brief Introduction to Comparative Librarianship." *International Library Review* 17 (1985): 107–15.

Ward, Jean, Kathleen A. Hansen, and Douglas M. McLeod. "The News Library's Contribution to Newsmaking." *Special Libraries* 79, no. 2 (Spring 1988): 143–47.

The Warwick Workshop. "Digital Curation and Preservation: Defining the Research Agenda." *Library Hi Tech News* 23, no. 3 (April 2006): 23.

Waters, Richard L. "Fund Raising: Grants and Other Bits of Information." *Public Library Quarterly* 17, no. 3 (1999): 51–54.

Wayne State University. "Wayne State University Policy and Procedures Regarding Scientific Misconduct, Executive Order 89–4." *Wayne State University: University Policy.* 1995. http://wayne.edu/fisops/universitypolicy.pdf

Weber, Robert Phillip. *Basic Content Analysis.* 2nd ed. London: Sage, 1990.

Weick, Karl. *Sensemaking in Organizations.* Thousand Oaks, CA: Sage, 1995.

Weiss, Carol H. *Evaluation Methods for Studying Programs and Policies.* 2nd ed. Upper Saddle River, NJ: Prentice Hall, 1998.

_____. *Evaluation Research: Methods for Assessing Program Effectiveness.* Englewood Cliffs, NJ: Prentice Hall, 1972.

Weitzman, Eben. "Software and Qualitative Research." In *Collecting and Interpreting Qualitative Materials,* 2nd ed., edited by Norman Denzin and Yvonna Lincoln, 310–39. Thousand Oaks, CA: Sage, 2003.

Westbrook, Lynn. *Identifying and Analyzing User Needs.* New York: Neal-Schuman Publishers, 2001.

_____. "Qualitative Research Methods: A Review of Major Stages, Data Analysis Techniques, and Quality Controls." *Library & Information Science Research* 16, no. 3 (1994): 241–54.

White, Emilie C. "Bibliometrics: From Curiosity to Convention." *Special Libraries* 76 (Winter 1985): 35.

White, Marilyn Domas, and Emily Marsh. "Content Analysis: A Flexible Methodology." *Library Trends* 55, no. 1 (2006): 22–45.

Whitlatch, Jo Bell. "Evaluating Reference Services in the Electronic Age." *Library Trends* 50, no. 2 (2001): 207–17.

Whyte, William. "On Making the Most of Participant Observation." *American Sociologist* 14, no. 1 (1979): 56–66.

Wicht, Heather, and Lynn Silipigni Connaway. "Using Circulation, ILL, and Collection Characteristics for the Development of Policies for Collections and ILL Services." In *Charleston Conference Proceedings, 2003*, edited by Katina P. Strauch, Rosann Bazirjian, and Vicky H. Speck, Westport, CT: Libraries Unlimited, 2004.

Widdows, Richard, Tia A. Hensler, and Marlaya H. Wyncott. "The Focus-Group Interview: A Method for Assessing Users' Evaluation of Library Service." *College & Research Libraries* 52 (July 1991): 352–59.

Wiedenbeck, Susan, Robin Lampert, and Jean Scholtz. "Using Protocol Analysis to Study the User Interface." *Bulletin of the American Society for Information Science* 15 (1989): 25–26.

Wiegand, Wayne, comp. *Libraries in the U.S. Timeline*. Published by the American Library Association and the ALA Public Information Office, December 1999; inserted in *American Libraries* 30, no. 11 (December 1999).

Wildemuth, Barbara M. *Applications of Social Research Methods to Questions in Information and Library Science*. Westport, CT: Libraries Unlimited, 2009.

Williams, James F. II, and Mark D. Winston. "Leadership Competencies and the Importance of Research Methods and Statistical Analysis in Decision Making and Research and Publication: A Study of Citation Patterns." *Library & Information Science Research* 25, no. 4 (2003): 387–402.

Williams, Robert. "Bibliography of Statistics of National Scope on Libraries in the United States, 1829–1999." http://www.libsci.sc.edu/bob/LibraryStatistics/LibraryStatisticsGuide.html.

Willis, Jerry. *Foundations of Qualitative Research: Interpretive and Critical Approaches*. With Muktha Jost and Rema Nilakanta. Thousand Oaks, CA: Sage, 2007.

Wilson, Concepcion S. "Informetrics." In *Annual Review of Information Science and Technology*, vol. 34, edited by Martha E. Williams. Medford, NJ: American Society for Information Science, 1999.

Wilson, Tom D. "Electronic Resources for Research Methods: Research Methods." *InformationR.net*. http://informationr.net/rm/RMeth6.html.

_____. "InformationR.net: The Quality Source for Research on Information Management, Information Science and Information Systems." http://informationr.net.

Winkler, Karen J. "Disillusioned with Numbers and Counting, Historians Are Telling Stories Again." *Chronicle of Higher Education* 28 (June 1984): 5–6.

Wolcott, Harry R. *Writing Up Qualitative Research*. 2nd ed. Thousand Oaks, CA: Sage, 2001.

Wolfram, Dietmar. *Applied Informetrics for Information Retrieval Research*. Westport, CT: Libraries Unlimited, 2003.

Woods, Peter. *Successful Writing for Qualitative Researchers*. 2nd ed. London: Routledge, 2006.

Wurzburger, Marilyn. "Conducting a Mail Survey: Some of the Things You Probably Didn't Learn in Any Research Methods Course." *College & Research Libraries News* 48 (December 1987): 697–700.

Wynar, Bohdan S. *Introduction to Bibliography and Reference Work.* 4th ed. Rochester, NY: Libraries Unlimited, 1967.

Wynar, Dan. *Syllabus for Research Methods in Librarianship.* Denver, CO: Graduate School of Librarianship, 1962.

Xu, Chen, Fenfei Ouyang, and Heting Chu. "The Academic Library meets Web 2.0: Applications and Implications." *Journal of Academic Librarianship* 35, no. 4 (2009): 324–31.

Xu, Jack L. "Internet Search Engines: Real World IR Issues and Challenges." Paper presented at the Conference on Information and Knowledge Management, CIKM99, Kansas City, MO, 1999.

Yin, Robert K. *Case Study Research: Design and Methods.* 4th ed. Thousand Oaks, CA: Sage, 2008.

Young, Heartsill, ed. *The ALA Glossary of Library and Information Science.* Chicago: American Library Association, 1983.

Young, Victoria L. "Focus on Focus Groups." *College & Research Libraries News* 7 (July–August 1993): 391–94.

Young Adult Library Services Organization, a division of the American Library Association. "A Research Agenda for YALSA." *Youth Services in Libraries* (Spring 1995): 267–71.

Zhang, Jin, Dietmar Wolfram, and Peiling Wang. "Analysis of Query Keywords of Sports-Related Queries Using Visualization and Clustering." *Journal of the American Society for Information Science and Technology* 60, no. 8 (2009): 1550–71.

Zhang, Yin, and Athena Salaba. "What is Next for Functional Requirements for Bibliographic Records? A Delphi Study." *Library Quarterly* 79/2 (April 2009): 233–55.

Zink, Steven D. "Monitoring User Search Success Through Transaction Log Analysis: The Wolf-PAC Example." *Reference Services Review* 19, no. 1 (1991): 49–56.

Zweizig, Douglas L. "Measuring Library Use." *Drexel Library Quarterly* 13 (July 1977): 3–15.

_____. "With Our Eye on the User: Needed Research for Information and Referral in the Public Library." *Drexel Library Quarterly* 12 (1976): 48–58.

Zweizig, Douglas, Debra Wilcox Johnson, and Jane Robbins with Michele Besant. *The Tell It! Manual: The Complete Program for Evaluating Library Performance.* Chicago: American Library Association, 1996.

Zweizig, Douglas, and Eleanor Jo Rodger. *Output Measures for Public Libraries: A Manual of Standardized Procedures.* Chicago: American Library Association, 1982.

Author Index

Subject Index

About the Authors

LYNN SILIPIGNI CONNAWAY, Ph.D., is a Senior Research Scientist at OCLC Research. She spent a semester as a Visiting Researcher at the University of Sheffield, Information Studies Department. While in the UK, she worked on several projects addressing user behaviors, including virtual research environments and digital repositories funded by the Joint Information Steering Committee (JISC). Her current research projects include studying bibliographic issues related to how people look for and get their information and mining WorldCat bibliographic and use data to facilitate library decision making. She was the co-principal investigator of an IMLS-funded project to study and evaluate the sustainability and relevance of virtual reference services (VRS), and a co-investigator on another IMLS-funded study to investigate the information-seeking behaviors of faculty, graduate students, and undergraduates. She was the Vice-President of Library Services and Research at NetLibrary, the director of the Library and Information Services Department at the University of Denver, and was on the faculty of the Library and Informational Science program at the University of Missouri, Columbia.

RONALD R. POWELL, Ph.D., is professor emeritus of the School of Library and Information Science at Wayne State University, Detroit, MI. His published works include Libraries Unlimited's *The Next Library Leadership: Attributes of Academic and Public Library Directors* and *Convergence and Collaboration of Campus Information Services*. His awards include the 2001 Scholarly Research Award from Wayne State University.

BROOKHAVEN FREE LIBRARY

MAR — 2017

TO RENEW
CALL 286-1923

CPSIA information can be obtained
at www.ICGtesting.com
Printed in the USA
BVOW04s0643170217
476439BV00002B/3/P